# AI Governance, Law, Policy and Ethics in Green Finance and ESG

Kozma Dorottya Edina
https://orcid.org/0000-0002-4948-8815
*University of Pannonia, Hungary*

Laeeq Razzak Janjua
https://orcid.org/0000-0002-1948-5859
*WSB University, Poland*

Hammouch Hind
https://orcid.org/0000-0002-5897-1649
*University Sidi Mohamed Ben Abdellah, Morocco*

Evi Purwanti
*Universitas Tanjungpura, Indonesia*

Bhupinder Singh
https://orcid.org/0009-0006-4779-2553
*North Bangkok University, Thailand*

IGI Global
Scientific Publishing
Publishing Tomorrow's Research Today

| | |
|---|---|
| Vice President of Editorial | Melissa Wagner |
| Director of Acquisitions | Mikaela Felty |
| Director of Book Development | Jocelynn Hessler |
| Production Manager | Mike Brehm |
| Cover Design | Jose Rosado |

Published in the United States of America by
IGI Global Scientific Publishing
701 East Chocolate Avenue
Hershey, PA, 17033, USA
Tel: 717-533-8845 | Fax: 717-533-7115
Website: https://www.igi-global.com E-mail: cust@igi-global.com





Library of Congress Cataloging-in-Publication Data

(CIP Data Pending)
ISBN13: 979-8-2600-1308-3
Isbn13Softcover: 979-8-2600-1309-0
EISBN13: 979-8-2600-1310-6
British Cataloguing in Publication Data
A Cataloguing in Publication record for this book is available from the British Library.

# Table of Contents

# Detailed Table of Contents

were linked to global politics and strategy, global diplomacy, and justice. Because AI has significant ramifications for politics, security, and energy, the struggle for control is comparable to the struggle for control over green transitions. This chapter enables you to examine these connections from a global political perspective, allowing you to consider critically how nations, corporations, and international institutions such as the United Nations are reacting to a new "green-tech" regime.



Ethical AI means that technology should be fair, open, accountable, and include everyone. This is to encourage technology-driven development, even though it may not fix existing inequalities. In finance, responsible AI means better ways to find fraud, identify risk, make sure rules are followed, and come up with long-term investment plans. In business, it helps with better supply chain management, border trade, and predictive modeling. But to fix problems like algorithmic bias, data privacy, silly national rules, and the rise of digital divides, countries will need to work together. If AI is going to work in the long run, it needs to be ethical in fiscal and trade systems. "The Growth of World Finance trade trends gradually and consumer capitals are most normalizing. Ethical AI, in order to ensure that we actual can driver efficiency as much as fairness within the changing faces of global finance and trade"



This chapter addresses the environmental, social, and governance (ESG) principles in order to address these global issues and promote more sustainable behaviors. The technology that has received a lot of attention and is being used in many different sectors is artificial intelligence. ESG must be included into AI if we want to reduce risks, hold it responsible and make it contribute to ethical investment and societal objectives. The concept of artificial intelligence is transforming environmental, social and governance-oriented analytics in the new digital economy. So, ESG-scoring techniques, which include a company's sustainability, social impact, and governance performance, are being supplemented by AI technologies that can manage massive volumes of organized and unstructured data.

The notion of human-centered automation of sustainable finance is a paradigm shift in which artificial intelligence and automated systems are instituted, implemented and regulated with people at the heart of the systemic nature-people-values-needs-agency-and-well-being and the pure efficiency and maximization of profits are considered peripheral to all other human considerations. In contrast to conventional automation where it frequently replaces human labour directly, this strategy focuses on augmentation: AI can be used to process data-intensive jobs such as crunching large volumes of ESG (Environmental, Social, and Governance) data, detecting greenwashing in corporate reports and green investment portfolios, and automate compliance checks of regulations such as the Sustainable Finance Disclosure Regulation or other forthcoming global standards. This model ensures that ethical considerations are used to derive the results by keeping humans in the loop by providing explainable interfaces, collaborative decision-making tools and oversight mechanisms



The algorithm incorporation of artificial intelligence into the system of Environmental, Social and Governance (ESG) may be viewed as a radical shift in the sustainable financial field, including the jurisdictional and contractual one in green investment law. AI-based applications support advanced processing of data, predictive analytics, and real-time monitoring, which are useful in improving the evaluation of ESG risks, identifying cases of greenwashing, automating compliance with new regulatory tools such as the Corporate Sustainability Reporting Directive (CSRD) and the AI Act and allocating capital to low-carbon initiatives more efficiently. Such technical abilities are offering investors the opportunity to meet high levels of risk-adjusted returns in addition to their further development towards broader sustainability targets,

*Ashwin Yadav, Amity Law School, Amity University, Gwalior, India*
*Vijay Srivastava, Amity Law School, Amity University, Gwalior, India*
*Hemant Singh, Amity Law School, Amity University, Gwalior, India*

The emerging breakthrough in technology in artificial intelligence and automation technologies present incredible opportunities to drive the truly green investment in India specifically in the spheres of renewable energy, sustainable finance and climate-resilient infrastructure. These tools will facilitate faster allocation of resources to environmentally friendly projects by reducing the risk of investments in these projects forecasting and automating the monitoring of compliance with environmental protection and commitments, which are consistent with the net-zero India by 2070 and the United Nations Sustainable Development Goals. Nonetheless, the growth of green brand digital platforms, fintech programs, and sustainability efforts increases the vulnerability to cyber form of squatting known as bad-faith domain name registration to tap into the goodwill acquired over time or overtime cyber interference. This type of activity trims down investor confidence, brand integrity, and efficient digital marketing that is a necessity to attract green funds.


*Kishore Subramanya Hebbar, Intercontinental Exchange Inc., USA*
*Shilpi Yadav, Independent Researcher, USA*
*Jaykumar Ambadas Maheshkar, USBancorp, USA*
*Pavan Kumar Asu, Gallagher, USA*
*Tarun Kumar Kaushik, Sharda University, Greater Noida, India*

A key pillar of green investment has become regulatory compliance, where financial institutions are required to fund a portfolio in a way that reflects a sustainability requirement, as well as exhibit a clearly proven impact on the environment. The purpose of disclosure is entailed in such elements as a global frameworks, namely a formal regulation such as the EU Sustainable Finance Disclosure Regulation (SFDR), such formal regulation as the Corporate Sustainability Reporting Directive (CSRD), such formal regulation as the EU Taxonomy Regulation, and such formal regulations as the international sustainability standards board (ISSB) IFRS S1 and S2, which require comprehensive disclosures on the related risk of climate issues as well as greenhouse-gas emissions, transition plans, and alignment to net-zero ways.

The application of AI in green finance has enormous potential to tackle climate change, but its effect would be determined by the strength and integrity of governance mechanisms as well as well-designed incentives. Good policy serves to set the bar but also incentives and responsible use in finance in AI applications. In the absence of such governance, exposures including algorithmic discrimination, data mining and unequal access to technology are likely to compound rather than advance social goals. Thus, AI governance has become a priority for governments, financial regulators and multilateral organisations. Policy frameworks achieve two parallel goals: on the one hand they provide boundaries to invest in technology and at the same time these very policy mechanisms direct capital towards environmentally friendly investment through incentives like tax benefits, financial grants, green debts etc.



The legal parameters for artificial intelligence and automation in investment environmental, social and governance (ESG) standards are transforming as nations, companies and investors seek to maintain innovation and accountability. AI and automation are increasingly used to evaluate sustainability data, predict climate change risks and guide responsible investment strategies. But without clear rules or ethical norms there will be great difficulties in building transparency and morale into green finance. Legally green investments are covered by a patchwork of environmental and financial laws that look to ensure funds are part of genuinely sustainable development rather than simply a matter "greenwashing." As AI systems come to oversee such functions as portfolio analysis, impact measurement and carbon emissions accounting, it becomes all the more imperative to lay down clear legal prescriptions for data accuracy, fair algorithms and disclosure obligations on investors.

The legal strategy that incorporates cutting-edge concepts like artificial intelligence and green finance with established laws like the Insolvency and Bankruptcy Code and the Real Estate (Regulation and Development) Act (RERA). It need to develop long-term solutions since real estate projects are at a standstill. Money issues, regulation infractions, or developer bankruptcies cause many projects to be delayed. Both investors and homebuyers suffer as a result. "Sustainable" funding is defined by green finance as investments that will result in environmentally responsible and beneficial initiatives. AI-based analytics may improve project management, ensure that real estate ecosystems are transparent and honest, and forecast the likelihood of current bankruptcy. A Grand Unified Theory of Law might safeguard stakeholders, expedite project completion, and improve the environmental sustainability and technical sophistication of India's real estate sector for future recovery models by ensuring that RERA and IBC operate in tandem.



The real estate sector has particular challenges when someone files for bankruptcy. The process might take a long time if it is not halted immediately, and production assets gradually lose value over time. Since the cost of bankruptcy with real estate has been declining in all regions for some time and is generally agreed, it investigate the relationship between green finance and artificial intelligence here. It is now less expensive and more environmentally friendly. Many investors are anxiously awaiting an improvement in the bankruptcy-related real estate issue, which has received a lot of attention. This is not only a haphazard observation; rather, it is supported by several case studies, including those conducted by renowned specialists as the Corporate Insolvency Resolution Process may be facilitated by AI solutions.

AI-enabled ESG systems. This is a result of the emphasis on data governance, transparency and lowering ethical risks.

# Preface

The rapid convergence of artificial intelligence (AI), green finance, and environmental, social, and governance (ESG) frameworks marks a defining moment in the evolution of global financial systems. This volume, *AI Governance, Law, Policy and Ethics in Green Finance and ESG*, brings together diverse scholarly perspectives to examine how technological innovation is reshaping financial markets, regulatory structures, and ethical considerations across jurisdictions. As AI systems increasingly influence investment decisions, compliance mechanisms, and sustainability reporting, the need for robust governance frameworks that ensure fairness, accountability, and inclusivity has never been more urgent.

Financial systems today are inherently global, interconnected, and data-driven. AI technologies are transforming how risks are assessed, fraud is detected, and capital is allocated, particularly in the context of green investments and sustainable development goals. However, these advancements also introduce complex challenges, including regulatory fragmentation, algorithmic bias, data privacy concerns, and unequal access to technological resources. This book responds to these challenges by critically exploring the legal, policy, and ethical dimensions of AI-driven green finance and ESG integration.

A central theme throughout this volume is the necessity of harmonized global governance. The contributors emphasize that while national regulations remain important, transnational cooperation is essential to address cross-border financial activities, geopolitical tensions, and emerging cyber risks. Equally important is the human dimension—ensuring that AI systems are designed and deployed in ways that prioritize human well-being, promote inclusivity, and build trust among stakeholders.

The chapters collectively highlight the transformative potential of AI in enhancing ESG analytics, improving regulatory compliance, strengthening corporate governance, and enabling sustainable investment strategies. At the same time, they underscore the importance of ethical safeguards, transparent auditing mechanisms, and adaptive legal frameworks to mitigate risks such as greenwashing, cybercrime, and systemic inequalities.

This volume is structured to provide a comprehensive and multidisciplinary understanding of the subject.

## CHAPTER OVERVIEW

The first chapter explores the need for transnational governance frameworks in AI-driven finance, focusing on equity, accountability, and regulatory harmonization across borders.

Chapter 2 examines the geopolitical dimensions of AI and green investment, highlighting their influence on global power dynamics, diplomacy, and international cooperation.

Chapter 3 Discusses the role of responsible and ethical AI in global trade and finance, emphasizing fairness, transparency, and collaborative regulation.

The fourth chatpter analyzes bias, ethics, and accountability in AI-powered ESG analytics, with a focus on improving sustainability assessments and decision-making.

Chapter 5 introduces human-centered automation in sustainable finance, prioritizing inclusivity, trust, mental well-being, and ethical system design.

The sixth chapter investigates regulatory challenges and legal risks in AI-powered ESG systems, while identifying opportunities for improving green investment law.

The seventh chapter explores the automation of sustainability practices through AI in ESG regulation and green finance law, including real-time monitoring and compliance.

Chapter 8 reviews regulatory frameworks governing AI applications in sustainable banking and investment compliance within financial services law.

Chapter 9 Provides a legal analysis of AI and automation in enhancing green investment, with a focus on emerging cyber risks such as domain misuse.

Chapter 10 examines AI-powered reporting and regulatory compliance mechanisms in green investment, emphasizing transparency and standardized disclosures.

The eleventh chapter analyzes policy frameworks and incentive structures that shape AI adoption in green finance and guide sustainable capital allocation.

The twelfth chapter discusses evolving legal frameworks governing AI and automation in ESG investment strategies, focusing on transparency and accountability.

Chapter 13 explores sustainable legal solutions for stalled real estate projects through the integration of AI, green finance, and insolvency frameworks.

Chapter 14 examines the role of AI and green finance in improving efficiency in real estate insolvency and bankruptcy resolution processes.

Chapter 15 investigates cybercrime risks in AI-enabled green platforms and the associated legal challenges in ESG investing and financial loss mitigation.

The sixteenth and final chapter analyzes corporate governance frameworks and board-level oversight of AI in sustainability strategies and risk management.

By bringing together insights from law, finance, policy, and technology, this book aims to contribute to ongoing academic discourse and inform practitioners, regulators, and policymakers. It aspires to serve as a valuable resource for understanding how AI can be responsibly leveraged to advance sustainable finance while safeguarding ethical principles and legal integrity.

Ultimately, the future of green finance will depend not only on technological innovation but also on the collective commitment to governance systems that are transparent, inclusive, and aligned with global sustainability objectives. This volume is a step toward that vision.

Chapter 1

# Global Governance of AI in Finance: Justice Beyond Boundaries

**Anurag Kumar**
http://orcid.org/0000-0003-2984-5325
*School of Finance and Commerce, Galgotias University, Greater Noida, India*

**Mohd Shamshad**
http://orcid.org/0000-0001-9859-5337
*School of Finance and Commerce, Galgotias University, Greater Noida, India*

**Deepak Chauhan**
http://orcid.org/0009-0001-7885-2006
*School of Finance and Commerce, Galgotias University, Greater Noida, India*

**Vineeta Bhati**
http://orcid.org/0009-0006-9255-4853
*School of Finance and Commerce, Galgotias University, Greater Noida, India*

## ABSTRACT

*AI is becoming more common in financial markets. It has transformed how risks are detected, how fraud is stopped, how trading across borders is done, and how laws are obeyed. But technology also brings up new problems with rules, ethics, and how things are run. Finance is global, and global systems need governance institutions that are transnational and that make sure that everyone is treated fairly, held accountable, and included in society. This chapter examines the concept of global governance of AI in finance, emphasizing equity in institutions beyond national boundaries. It looks at the problems caused by fragmented national regulation and opposing economic interests. It also stresses the need for cooperative frameworks*

DOI: 10.4018/979-8-2600-1308-3.ch001

*that protect consumers, investors, and weak economies. The chapter concludes by emphasizing the necessity of worldwide regulatory harmonization, transparent AI audit mechanisms, and equitable access to emerging financial technology.*

## 1. INTRODUCTION

People are more interested than ever in how AI influences society as instead of being universal symbols of ethics and fairness, more and more critical research looks at bias and discrimination in AI through the viewpoint of social justice and human rights. A lot of this criticism in the West might even be developing its own blind spots because of where it is. The existing structure of the global AI supply chain (data, computational power, resources, natural resources, and labor) is similar to the inequities of colonialism in the past and keeps the countries in the Global South under control. This chapter elucidates the dominant narratives from the Indian government and the United Nations Conference on Trade and Development (UNCTAD) concerning these regions in the context of the AI economy. People in the government are against these policies because they are unfair and give one group too much power. This illustrates the importance of understanding the political economy of AI in its full range of dimensions: global, national and, more specifically, from communities hit hardest in this economy. If we don't actively fight to center these conversations, the mainstream discourse about AI justice will develop alongside (and perhaps contradict) the demands from governments and communities in the Global South (Maghami, 2024).

Governmental and international organization's international AI governance initiatives have been ongoing. The UN has been having discussions on how to regulate Lethal Autonomous Weapons Systems (LAWS) under the Convention on Certain Conventional Weapons since 2014.

The voluntary efforts have struggled to keep up with all the problems that AI creates. Principles at this elevated level the kind the G20 agreed can be opaque and open to interpretation. Discuss facial recognition technology and the concept of AI fairness, one of the principles all G20 members share. The EU acts on this principle by banning these technologies, but for social stability, China doesn't prohibit ethnic-recognition technologies at all. There have been difficulties in attempting to construct on such shaky normative premises. But since UNESCO's AI Recommendation was approved in November 2021, just under a quarter of those who signed the AI Recommendation have collaborated with the organization to mobilize the policy tools proposed. The deal is not a legally binding one, and there are no consequences for the signatories who have not honored it. There is not very much to show in terms of consensus around meaningful governance activity, even from new AI-specific organizations with fewer members, as new groups such as the GPAI.

The draft convention on AI that the CoE is working on is more encouraging because consultations are already far gone and states that ratify it will need to pass it into law in their country. But the process of CoE conventions being ratified is notoriously slow and this is a problem when AI is moving so fast. Even states that did not contribute to writing CoE conventions have also opted to not ratify them in the past on the basis they felt they were not legitimate. Rather, they sought a more representative UN-led process. Private actors have also established rules for AI governance. The International Organization for Standardization (ISO) and the International Electrotechnical Commission (IEC) are two international organizations for standardization that have released standards for AI products and processes. This standards are not mandatory, although some may be (or, in combination of other standards) de jure compulsory by legislation and others are industry best practice dual referenced de facto compulsory. Industry, too, has established new global governance bodies that create rules (Roberts et al., 2024). In 2016, a group of "big tech" companies along with civil society organizations and academic bodies established the Partnership on AI (PAI) to develop principles and inform public policy. In 2023, four big tech companies founded the Frontier Model Forum in order to establish good ways to run advanced systems.

International standards bodies have made inroads in launching governance initiatives, but their primary purpose remains how best to set standards that guide organizations' growth by ensuring that the rules are the same everywhere. It also appears that these organizations are playing a larger role for AI. For instance, the EU's draft AI Act relies on standards bodies to flesh out governance concerns, which is rich with value. But such rules generally are not conducive to business, and this generates a "principal moral hazard," since companies have the least to gain from tightening protections. This misaligned incentive structure also presents challenges for privately operated governance projects such as the PAI. Access Now, a digital rights organization, quit the PAI in 2020 because it had been unable to change the way member companies thought (Erman & Furendal, 2022).

## 2. ARTIFICIAL INTELLIGENCE IN FINANCE: TRANSFORMING FINANCIAL SYSTEMS WITH AI

Artificial intelligence is changing the financial world in a big way, sparking changes that have never been seen before. AI helps banks and other financial institutions move from traditional, linear processes to dynamic, data-driven systems by using machine learning and deep learning. This change is most clear in risk management, where AI algorithms look at huge, varied datasets like market trends, social media sentiment, and alternative credit data to figure out if someone is creditworthy and find fraud with amazing accuracy. This new ability not only keeps institutions safe from financial crime, but it also makes it easier for people who have not had access to credit in the past to get it, which promotes greater financial inclusion.

AI-powered chatbots and virtual assistants help with customer service by answering questions right away, 24 hours a day, 7 days a week. This frees up human agents to deal with more complicated client needs. This makes things better for customers and cuts down on costs by a lot. AI algorithms can build and manage portfolios for wealth management and investment.

It does this by using the speed of the market itself to boost profits while lowering profit margins. But this new technology also comes with a lot of problems. Some AI models are hard to understand, there is a chance of algorithmic bias, and a small number of companies control the whole field of technology, from data collection to processing, analysis, and AI development. This need strong governance frameworks and ongoing oversight right away. So, need AI to drive future finance so that everyone can have fair markets and peace on our asset markets (Santoni de Sio et al., 2024).

## 2.2 Risk Assessment, Fraud Detection and Market Integrity

AI is a revolutionary technology that transforms everything in finance. Financial institutions gain from these changes. AI helps them manage risk, prevent fraud, or keep the markets clean more easily. Even though AI has less data than people, it is better at processing and understanding data in real time. So, when it comes to keeping your money safe, you may now take a more proactive and active approach than ever before. Risk assessment: it looks at more data points than ever before, such as transaction history and behaviors. This is different from standard credit rating (Ricaurte, 2022).

This is where machine learning algorithms identify data that didn't seem to be connected but actually worked together in a way that signaled a prospective risk, like a business going out of business. A borrower who probably won't be able to pay back a loan from someone else. More sophisticated credit risk models make it easier for lenders to lend money. Lenders making loans to every person in their country (which is impossible by definition). The notion of maximizing utility is what trading market risk is based on. AI combines news mood, economic indicators, and real-time market data from all over the world to guess when things will become bad and when they will get better. A defense system that uses machine learning (Walter, 2024). A rule-based system that finds fraud quickly becomes outdated since criminals are continuously coming up with new and more complex ways to conduct crimes. AI also employs machine learning to always gather new data and find and report anything unexpected that happens right away. For instance, it can locate an uncommon place where someone buys a lot of things and mark this as suspicious activity. If a fresh link from another terminal shows up in a usual pattern of online conduct, it might also send out an alarm wordage, but it is always different from their personal spending style (Unver, 2023).

### 2.3 Ethical Dilemmas and Algorithmic Bias

Algorithms progressively arbitrate human interactions, and these extend from hiring practices up to credit scoring (Zaidan & Ibrahim, 2024). Careful examination is required for the hazards presented by prejudiced algorithms (Gordon et al. 2022). Institutions confront an exceedingly problematic quandary. Individuals should employ AI-derived understandings, but they also should circumvent strengthening established prejudice. To allay such trepidations, we should thoroughly integrate data ethics models within AI oversight, stressing impartiality, transparency, and answerability (Erman & Furendal, 2024).

## 3. CONCEPTUALIZING GLOBAL GOVERNANCE IN AI AND FINANCE

Policymakers are worried about global AI governance, but there hasn't been any empirical or normative research on the topic. The formulation of a global AI governance framework should be grounded in empirical and normative research. The agreements that come with it should be founded on the law and what is right. It's hard and vital to figure out how to manage AI in finance all across the world (Birkstedt et al., 2023). This need a single set of rules that take into consideration the particular hazards of AI, such as algorithmic bias, system instability, and a lack of transparency. This will also help new technologies come up. It does not aim to build one global body; instead, it seeks a strategy that involves many people and levels.

The Financial Stability Board (FSB), the G7, and the G20 are some of the international bodies that are taking part. A patchwork and disorganized regulatory framework in each country doesn't function since AI operates swiftly and smoothly all around the world. Second is transparency and explainability, which implies that banks and their AI models should be able to articulate why they made a specific choice, especially if it meant refusing service to someone (Taeihagh, 2021). Third is accountability, which includes making it obvious who is to blame when an AI system goes wrong or hurts someone. It is also important for countries to work together to set common standards and best practices. Groups like the OECD and the European Union are still talking about and working on a framework, which makes this evident. The financial industry can securely and effectively harness AI's benefits if they eventually get it right. They can also keep the global financial system safe (Boppiniti, 2023). A global AI governance framework should address concerns related to data usage and algorithm development both within and outside national boundaries. Empirical and normative research can help us figure out how this framework can adapt to the rapidly evolving world of AI technology. This two-pronged strategy can assist design rules that are fair and technically sound for the government.

## 3.1 Global Governance in Finance: Principles and Dimensions

As AI enters its second decade of being safeguarded and preserved, the call for improved AI is widespread all across the world. Like riding a bike with different parts on different speeds, the last ten years of AI advancement have been recorded and published. This is a long and dull process that a lot of people don't know about. People have always told me not to believe this story. Is it going to be a lemming that goes to the top of the cliff? It's easy to see how AI could go too far because it contains built-in dangers and risks that could kill people. People all throughout the world have been worried about AI for a long time because of real hazards, moral problems, and a more cautious assessment of its benefits (Stiglitz & Rodrik, 2025). The United Nations Educational, Scientific and Cultural Organization (UNESCO) just adopted its Recommendation on the Ethics of AI November 2021 as proof of this. People have also learned that a set of non-binding ethical rules or principles would not automatically make AI and machine learning safe to move forward. With this ethical basis, AI rules become more important, and the danger of the global story of the AI race becomes clear.

Now, the competition to build AI has moved into the area of law As people all across the world are now racing to make rules for AI. The EU's proposal for an Artificial Intelligence Act (AIA) in April 2021 officially initiated this race. It takes a wide-ranging and thorough strategy to leading AI (Tallberg et al., 2023). After the National People's Congress passed three significant AI laws algorithm-generated ideas, deep blending technology, and generation AI China decided to focus on a centralized industry-based strategy. The race to AI around the world heated up even more after President Biden of the United States enacted an executive order.

The peoples present understanding of the AI regulatory global race narrative uncovers numerous errors. In these cases, it has been renamed as a "Digital Empire War Entitled to Govern Technology." This discourse is false and damaging pedantry, yet it also lends strength for a number of reasons. Instead, it should say "run towards regulating AI videos-about-a-globe." The important reason is that "digital sovereignty" is an oxymoron since it combines two conceptions that are opposite:

"sovereignty," which is based on geographical authority, and "digital," which is cyberspace without borders (Holzinger et al., 2025). The digital world is, at best, one gigantic empire. It cannot be controlled all the time unless countries or regions cooperate together in some way. Second, the loopholes in regulation are getting wider, and time is running out.

AI development is going faster than it ever has. Third, the current tale will only make the differences between national and regional AI laws bigger and deeper. This will eventually cause problems between countries and their own laws (Nitzberg & Zysman, 2022). Fourth, the rhetoric goes against the fact that AI and related technologies are used in numerous fields, cultures, and countries (Gill & Germann, 2022). This new race to construct AI is considerably different from earlier contests to make things. It is strongly related to other technologies, like 5G networks for wireless cell phone communications, the Internet of Things (IoT), neurotechnologies, and augmented and virtual reality technologies, which can no longer be completely developed (Gehl Sampath, 2021). The and most significantly, no matter what occurs in future arguments over global governance, it is very crucial to underline that the AI regulatory system has a much better future (Newell et al., 2023)

## 4. LEGAL AND REGULATORY FRAMEWORKS: NATIONAL REGULATIONS AND FRAGMENTATION IN AI GOVERNANCE

They don't have good historical examples to help them make decisions (Chen & Wang, 2023). There is a lot of study going on about different areas of AI, but we still don't know much about how to regulate AI. The guidelines for AI in finance are hard to keep up with because the sector is continually changing. Right present, the trend is toward rules that apply to all countries but not to the whole world (Pujari et al., 2024). International banking institutions have a lot of problems because the rules for examiners vary from country to country and area to region.

The EU AI Act is the first law in the EU to use a risk-based approach because AI systems can be at four different levels of risk: unacceptable, high-risk, limited-risk, and minimal-risk. There are different rules for each level. AI systems used in the financial sector for credit scoring or risk assessment are "high risk," and there are severe restrictions regarding how clear, precise, and human oversight they must be (Akinrinola et al. 2024). This law affects people outside of the country; hence it only applies to a firm if that company is situated in the country. They have to go through regular inspections at checkpoints if they sell goods or services that use AI in the EU. Countries like Japan utilize them as criteria for quality control. This strategy creates a powerful, unified market standard that could transform how things are done all around the world.

The United States, on the other hand, has embraced a decentralized, sector-specific strategy. There is not just one federal law. There are many separate laws and rules that come from different authorities (Kolade et al., 2024). The Consumer Financial Protection Bureau (CFPB) and the Federal Reserve, for example, are looking into how employing AI to make lending or credit decisions fits with rules that protect consumers, like the Equal Credit Opportunity Act. Many US initiatives are based on the National Institute of Standards and Technology's (NIST) AI Risk Management Framework, which is an example of a voluntary framework. It gives counsel, but it doesn't have to be followed. This American patchwork allows people be more creative, but it also makes the rules less clear and more confusing (Chhillar & Aguilera, 2022).

The economy could become more efficient and people's lives could get better with new uses of AI, but these uses can also have unforeseen impacts and side effects, as well as new hazards that need to be controlled. Governments all over the world need to know about the risk dimension and how it affects AI's opportunities in order to be able to effectively oversee and regulate these dangers (Bakeer et al., 2024) (Yadava, 2023). In the end, this kind of fragmentation at the national level can make it harder for global financial institutions to link in a safe and full way. It can also make it tougher for governments to cooperate together on things like cyber risk and market integrity. It is very hard to make sure that ethical standards and consumer protection are always the same around the world when there is no one norm that everyone follows. This hope that the replies will help them deal with these problems and obstacles better (Muthusubramanian et al., 2024). In this kind of place, it's not unexpected that there are still a lot of things to learn about.

## 5. TOWARD\S A MULTILATERAL APPROACH TO AI IN FINANCE: NEED FOR HARMONIZATION AND STANDARDIZATION

The governance of artificial intelligence has recently arisen as a subject of research and practice; yet, the structural and functional components of AI governance (AIG) systems remain inadequately appreciated by researchers and practitioners. This employ service system analysis and thematic analysis to provide a novel framework for examining AI governance systems at many levels, including international, national, subnational, sectoral, and organizational governance systems. We apply our analytical methodology to the empirical analysis of Canada's national AIG system. We use qualitative data from 20 leaders of Canadian AIG initiatives and subject matter experts to describe and analyze the actors, impacts, resources, networks, activities, logics, norms, and regulations that are important for the structure and operation of a national AIG system, using Canada as a case study (Szabo et al., 2022).

Because of the challenges with global governance right now, AI should only be used in finance by a lot of countries. There isn't a single right way to do things, so what works for one country could not work for another. Japanese financial firms have to follow different rules in each country, which can make it hard for them to do so and stop new ideas from coming up. A multilateral approach would enable the world agree on a set of rules and principles for how to use AI technology. This would make it easier for different regions of the world to work together and follow the same norms. The idea is not to make regulations the same in every place, but to make sure that any standards that do come up work well together and are pretty stable. Some of the most notable international groups that are already working on AI in finance are the Financial Stability Board (FSB), the G20, and the Bank for International Settlements (BIS). They achieve this by putting out reports or "best practice" guidelines that help make systems more stable and keep people all across the world safe (Kuzio et al., 2022).

What good things would arise from a project like this that involves many countries. Are there still difficulties to overcome after the international financial system is more reliable and efficient. Without a common way to measure things, it's hard to know how well we're doing at controlling AI systems around the world. Confucius noted, however, that it would be hard and not fun to deal with people directly because everyone does things their own way. Instead, systems should be built so that each portion checks on the others to make sure they are all completing their jobs as a group. So, it need to agree on some basic criteria for building these systems so that they do not get in each other's way and are easy to use at home, as long as they work right. As long as countries agree on common ethical standards (also known as due diligence and caring themes), fair practices will win.

This manner, their AI algorithms will always be fair enough. When transparency is the norm, people will be able to be held responsible for what they do. For example, regulatory arbitrage may involve businesses choosing to set up shop in places with less strict rules to avoid more scrutiny in other regions. This is something that needs to be looked at in the context of harmonization (Zhu et al., 2024). If there were a common mechanism for all countries to not only eliminate AI governance that is the least common denominator, but also to truly lo at stretching global If these governments wish to deal with the same dangers that businesses that cross borders do, they will need to make sure that AI companies can talk to each other on a frequent basis. It will still be challenging, but now it is feasible. Groups like the OECD and The Global Partnership on AI, which define international financial standards, are presently editing the first drafts of this. There is a lot of disagreement between the OECD and the Global Partnership on AI concerning their multi-stakeholder approach to international financial regulation. But from there, a fight to the death is coming. But this is the first step in building a system that is both new and strong as a whole.

Based on findings, it propose three directions for future research: (1) conduct further analysis on these topics within our dataset, (2) examine the structures and dynamics of Canada's national AIG system at both institutional and ecosystem levels, and (3) utilize our framework, data, and findings to investigate AIG systems in alternative contexts (Garcia-Segura, 2024).

## 5.1 Role of Global Institutions (IMF, World Bank, BIS, WTO, UN)

International financial institutions, including the International Monetary Fund (IMF), World Bank, Bank for International Settlements (BIS), World Trade Organization (WTO), and the United Nations (UN), are highly instrumental in how the global economy operates. Also, we will showcase the objectives and contribution of these organizations to the overall financial environment and in ensuring the establishment of economic growth across the globe (Büthe et al., 2022). The organization was established with the primary goal of enhancing the growth of the international economy, re-establishing financial stability, and facilitating trade interactions and exchange rates.? What is the primary goal of the IMF?

The World Bank is a multilateral development bank that channels roughly $25 billion annually to help poor countries develop their economies.? How does the World Bank help to develop countries. The BIS is an international monetary and financial institution that operates as a bank for central banks, the purpose of which is to support monetary and financial stability.? What is the role of the BIS in the global financial system?. The WTO is a global organization, legislating international trade issues, and also providing a platform for negotiations and disputes between the member nations.? What is the main objective of the WTO?. The UN is an intergovernmental organization established to promote international peace, stability, human rights, social and economic development, environmental protection, and also to provide humanitarian aid.? What is the significance of the UN in the global arena. Global institutions like the IMF, World Bank, BIS, WTO, and UN are the main drivers of the global economy, and all are working towards promoting sustainable development (Khan, 2024). This collaboration among nations improves the stability, the prosperity, and the equality of the world economy.

## 6. ETHICAL AND SOCIO-ECONOMIC DIMENSIONS: ALGORITHMIC FAIRNESS AND HUMAN RIGHTS IN FINANCE

The element focuses with how strict and flexible rules govern AIG actions in organizations. It is intriguing that the examined literature addressed laws, despite the exclusion of hard law from the search parameters. Even though an independent literature review is needed for legislative issues, It will quickly talk about regulations as they were mentioned in the studied literature. AI poses a lot of problems regarding fairness and human rights when it comes to money (Popa Tache & Sararu, 2024). It also has a huge impact on morals and society. AI systems, such as those employing machine learning, are taught on extensive datasets. These knowledge stores may have biases that have been around for a long time or that are ubiquitous in society. For example, say that a credit score algorithm obtains its prior loans from white individuals and that banks don't usually encounter black people when they give out these loans. This is because they have to wait in line behind generations of whites who have better ways to pass on their money. There are both hard laws (laws that must be followed) and soft governance approaches for AIG right now. These include standards, certificates, audits, and AI systems that can be explained (Farahani et al., 2022). The research examined underscored the significance of regulating AI and algorithms within the framework of legislative governance. Also, AIG's rules include harsh regulations like the EU General Data Protection Regulation and anti-discrimination laws.

Even if the model doesn't utilize any racial or ethnic attributes, one conceivable effect is that many minorities who were wrongly labeled as "undeserving" because they were perceived to be poor in general would have a greater rate of loan refusals. This is accurate since data clearly exposes bigger societal problems like residential segregation and differing income levels. These difficulties lead to unfair results that make it hard for people to receive vital financial services like a mortgage for their home or student loans to go to college. The main problem is that AI can make biases that are already there worse instead of getting rid of them. This makes me really worried about human rights when it comes to not being biased and having equal opportunities.

If someone is unfairly denied a loan because the algorithms are functioning in a black box, that individual can't buy a home or establish a business. A lot of advanced AI models which means it's hard to figure out why a given choice was made. This takes away their right to know why and their ability to appeal fairly (Kuldova, 2022). So, AI models need to be clear and easy to understand. Regulators and the general public both need to be able to understand and explain the choices that AI makes for banks and other financial firms. The goal is to build an AI that is not only smart, but also fair and open to everyone when it comes to money. To do this, it needs to carefully look for bias in AI models and make sure the findings are ethical. This review focuses on soft governance tools, such as standards, which demonstrate less institutional rigidity and increased adaptability relative to hard law.

A recent study emphasizes the imperative for industry self-governance tools, as organizational self-regulation alone insufficiently mitigates and oversees the risks associated with AI deployment. However, the standardization of real AIG implementation remains in its nascent phase. Standards are supposed to make it easier for firms to work together and lead to AIG practices that are based on the industry (Schotter et al., 2025). The IEEE and the International Organization for Standardization (ISO) are the two most major groups that make rules for AIG. Because of this, the ISO has put together a group to look into AI trustworthiness, transparency, and traceability. The IEEE has also begun the P7000 family of standards. P7001 is about making autonomous systems easier to understand and figuring out why they make decisions. Different parties, including certification bodies, can employ these kinds of standards to develop levels of transparency that can be measured (Judge et al., 2025).

## 7. CONCLUSION

AI's global governance in finance includes not only rules but also the kind of justice that is available. This justice is not limited to any one country; it is intended to safeguard those most immediately impacted by the shifting dynamics of power, technology, and wealth. Banks and other financial businesses already utilize a lot of AI in their systems. It can be used for a wide range of things, including as finding fraud, scoring credit, managing risk, and making investment plans. This could have a huge effect on the economy and the stability of the world in the future. But without a system that treats everyone equitably with this technology, it might just as easily make things worse and make biases stronger, so that it only works for a few powerful countries or firms. This does not need a bunch of different national policies; we need to work together. A governance approach that depends on everyone being accountable and engaged A responsible way to apply AI in finance would require to know the differences between strong and weak communities, powerful financial players and weak communities, and between people who make technology and people who have to use it. A fair global governance framework should make sure that algorithms are explicit, that choices are made with the input of marginalized people, and that there are no practices that cross boundaries that could be misused. But it will still need governments from all over the world to work together. To establish a foundation in human rights, it is insufficient to merely impose national self-interests; it necessitates transcending these interests to discover mechanisms that are flexible, tangible, and rooted in robust ethical principles. So, the issue with AI in finance isn't just about making things run better. It's also about how to make the world's money fair. When it comes to AI, responsible governance involves making sure that new technologies serve everyone, that money helps everyone instead of just a few, and that justice is a common moral ideal, not just something that happens in one country. After that, we can only employ AI in finance to make the world economy more fair, strong, and trustworthy.

## REFERENCES


Akinrinola, O., Okoye, C. C., Ofodile, O. C., & Ugochukwu, C. E. (2024). Navigating and reviewing ethical dilemmas in AI development: Strategies for transparency, fairness, and accountability. *GSC Advanced Research and Reviews, 18*(3), 050-058.

Bakeer, H., Alzamily, J. Y., Almadhoun, H., Abu-Nasser, B. S., & Abu-Naser, S. S. (2024). AI and Human Rights.

Birkstedt, T., Minkkinen, M., Tandon, A., & Mäntymäki, M. (2023). AI governance: Themes, knowledge gaps and future agendas. *Internet Research*, *33*(7), 133–167. DOI: 10.1108/INTR-01-2022-0042

Boppiniti, S. T. (2023). Data ethics in ai: Addressing challenges in machine learning and data governance for responsible data science. *International Scientific Journal for Research*, *5*(5), 1–29.

Büthe, T., Djeffal, C., Lütge, C., Maasen, S., & Ingersleben-Seip, N. V. (2022). Governing AI–attempting to herd cats? Introduction to the special issue on the Governance of Artificial Intelligence. *Journal of European Public Policy*, *29*(11), 1721–1752. DOI: 10.1080/13501763.2022.2126515

Chen, W., & Wang, M. (2023). Regulating the use of facial recognition technology across borders: A comparative case analysis of the European Union, the United States, and China. *Telecommunications Policy*, *47*(2), 102482. DOI: 10.1016/j.telpol.2022.102482

Chhillar, D., & Aguilera, R. V. (2022). An eye for artificial intelligence: Insights into the governance of artificial intelligence and vision for future research. *Business & Society*, *61*(5), 1197–1241. DOI: 10.1177/00076503221080959

Erman, E., & Furendal, M. (2022). The global governance of artificial intelligence: Some normative concerns. *Moral Philosophy and Politics*, *9*(2), 267–291. DOI: 10.1515/mopp-2020-0046

Erman, E., & Furendal, M. (2024). Artificial intelligence and the political legitimacy of global governance. *Political Studies*, *72*(2), 421–441. DOI: 10.1177/00323217221126665

Farahani, M. S., Esfahani, A., Moghaddam, M. N. F., & Ramezani, A. (2022). The impact of Fintech and artificial intelligence on COVID 19 and sustainable development goals. *International Journal of Innovation in Management. Economics and Social Sciences*, *2*(3), 14–31.

Garcia-Segura, L. A. (2024). The role of artificial intelligence in preventing corporate crime. *Journal of Economic Criminology*, *5*, 100091. DOI: 10.1016/j.jeconc.2024.100091

Gehl Sampath, P. (2021). Governing artificial intelligence in an age of inequality. *Global Policy*, *12*(S6), 21–31. DOI: 10.1111/1758-5899.12940

Gill, A. S., & Germann, S. (2022). Conceptual and normative approaches to AI governance for a global digital ecosystem supportive of the UN Sustainable Development Goals (SDGs). *AI and Ethics*, *2*(2), 293–301. DOI: 10.1007/s43681-021-00058-z

Gordon, G., Rieder, B., & Sileno, G. (2022). On mapping values in AI governance. *Computer Law & Security Review*, *46*, 105712. DOI: 10.1016/j.clsr.2022.105712

Holzinger, A., Zatloukal, K., & Müller, H. (2025). Is human oversight to AI systems still possible? *New Biotechnology*, *85*, 59–62. DOI: 10.1016/j.nbt.2024.12.003

Judge, B., Nitzberg, M., & Russell, S. (2025). When code isn't law: Rethinking regulation for artificial intelligence. *Policy and Society*, *44*(1), 85–97. DOI: 10.1093/polsoc/puae020

Khan, A. (2024). The intersection of artificial intelligence and international trade laws: Challenges and opportunities. *IIUMLJ*, *32*(1), 103–152. DOI: 10.31436/iiumlj.v32i1.912

Kolade, T. M., Aideyan, N. T., Oyekunle, S. M., Ogungbemi, O. S., Dapo-Oyewole, D. L., & Olaniyi, O. O. (2024). Artificial intelligence and information governance: Strengthening global security, through compliance frameworks, and data security. *Available at SSRN* 5044032. DOI: 10.9734/ajrcos/2024/v17i12528

Kuldova, T. Ø. (2022). The Compliance-Industrial Complex. In *Compliance-Industrial Complex: The Operating System of a Pre-Crime Society* (pp. 47–70). Springer Nature Switzerland. DOI: 10.1007/978-3-031-19224-1_3

Kuzio, J., Ahmadi, M., Kim, K. C., Migaud, M. R., Wang, Y. F., & Bullock, J. (2022). Building better global data governance. *Data & Policy*, *4*, e25. DOI: 10.1017/dap.2022.17

Maghami, M. (2024). New Global Governance and Overreaching Frameworks: Re-imagining the Rule of Law, AI and ESG for the Betterment of the World. *Denning LJ*, *33*(1), 177–200. DOI: 10.5750/dlj.v33i1.2353

Muthusubramanian, M., Jangoan, S., Sharma, K. K., & Krishnamoorthy, G. (2024). Demystifying explainable AI: Understanding, transparency and trust. *International Journal For Multidisciplinary Research*, *6*(2), 1–13.

Newell, P., Daley, F., Mikheeva, O., & Peša, I. (2023). Mind the gap: The global governance of just transitions. *Global Policy*, *14*(3), 425–437. DOI: 10.1111/1758-5899.13236

Nitzberg, M., & Zysman, J. (2022). Algorithms, data, and platforms: The diverse challenges of governing AI. *Journal of European Public Policy*, *29*(11), 1753–1778. DOI: 10.1080/13501763.2022.2096668

Popa Tache, C. E., & Săraru, C. S. (2024). Evaluating today's multi-dependencies in digital transformation, corporate governance and public international law triad. *Cogent Social Sciences*, *10*(1), 2370945. DOI: 10.1080/23311886.2024.2370945

Pujari, T., Goel, A., & Sharma, A. (2024). Ethical and responsible AI: Governance frameworks and policy implications for multi-agent systems. *International Journal of Smart Technologies*, *3*(1).

Ricaurte, P. (2022). Ethics for the majority world: AI and the question of violence at scale. *Media Culture & Society*, *44*(4), 726–745. DOI: 10.1177/01634437221099612

Roberts, H., Hine, E., Taddeo, M., & Floridi, L. (2024). Global AI governance: Barriers and pathways forward. *International Affairs*, *100*(3), 1275–1286. DOI: 10.1093/ia/iiae073

Santoni de Sio, F., Almeida, T., & Van Den Hoven, J. (2024). The future of work: Freedom, justice and capital in the age of artificial intelligence. *Critical Review of International Social and Political Philosophy*, *27*(5), 659–683. DOI: 10.1080/13698230.2021.2008204

Schotter, A. P., Maznevski, M., Stahl, G. K., & Doz, Y. (2025). Towards a dynamic theory of lateral collaboration across multinational enterprise structures: A collection of insights. *Journal of World Business*, *60*(4), 101647. DOI: 10.1016/j.jwb.2025.101647

Stiglitz, J. E., & Rodrik, D. (2025). Rethinking global governance: Cooperation in a world of power. In *The New Global Economic Order* (pp. 26–38). Routledge. DOI: 10.4324/9781003571384-3

Szabó, I. G., Golden, D., & Erne, R. (2022). Why do some labour alliances succeed in politicizing Europe across borders? A comparison of the Right2Water and Fair Transport European Citizens' Initiatives. *Journal of Common Market Studies*, *60*(3), 634–652. DOI: 10.1111/jcms.13279

Taeihagh, A. (2021). Governance of artificial intelligence. *Policy and Society*, *40*(2), 137–157. DOI: 10.1080/14494035.2021.1928377

Tallberg, J., Erman, E., Furendal, M., Geith, J., Klamberg, M., & Lundgren, M. (2023). The global governance of artificial intelligence: Next steps for empirical and normative research. *International Studies Review, 25*(3), viad040. DOI: 10.1093/isr/viad040

Unver, M. B. (2023, June). Rebuilding'ethics' to govern AI: How to re-set the boundaries for the legal sector? In *Proceedings of the Nineteenth International Conference on Artificial Intelligence and Law* (pp. 306-315).

Walter, Y. (2024). Managing the race to the moon: Global policy and governance in Artificial Intelligence regulation—A contemporary overview and an analysis of socioeconomic consequences. *Discover Artificial Intelligence*, *4*(1), 14. DOI: 10.1007/s44163-024-00109-4

Yadava, A. (2023). Ethical and regulatory challenges of AI adoption in the financial services sector: A global perspective. *International Journal of Science and Research Archive*, *10*(13), 10–30574.

Zaidan, E., & Ibrahim, I. A. (2024). AI governance in a complex and rapidly changing regulatory landscape: A global perspective. *Humanities & Social Sciences Communications*, *11*(1), 1121. DOI: 10.1057/s41599-024-03560-x

Zhu, Y., Yu, K., Wei, M., Pu, Y., & Wang, Z. (2024). AI-enhanced administrative prosecutorial supervision in financial big data: New concepts and functions for the digital era. *Journal of Advanced Computing Systems*, *4*(5), 10–26. DOI: 10.69987/JACS.2024.40502

# Chapter 2
# Geo Political Aspects Concerning AI and Green Investment With Reference to International Relations

**Sanchita Ray**
http://orcid.org/0009-0008-1615-5169
*Sharda University, India*

**Avinash Krishna Goswami**
http://orcid.org/0009-0006-7951-3627
*Lloyd Law College, Greater Noida, India*

**Saurabh Chandra**
http://orcid.org/0000-0003-4172-9968
*Bennett University, Greater Noida, India*

## ABSTRACT

*Green investments and artificial intelligence have never been more profitable. Global government, the economy, and the environment are all changing as a result of the two forces. Two factors the environment and technologies are altering the balance of power and the way nations engage with one another. AI geopolitics and green investment as a whole which was not just motivated by money or new technology were linked to global politics and strategy, global diplomacy, and justice. Because AI has significant ramifications for politics, security, and energy, the struggle for control is comparable to the struggle for control over green transitions. This chap-*

DOI: 10.4018/979-8-2600-1308-3.ch002

*ter enables you to examine these connections from a global political perspective, allowing you to consider critically how nations, corporations, and international institutions such as the United Nations are reacting to a new "green-tech" regime.*

## 1. INTRODUCTION

The combination of green investment with artificial intelligence represents a new trend in the global political economy. Three conventional theories of international relations realist, liberal institutionalism, and constructivism all provide distinct justifications for this shift. From a realist standpoint, AI is just the newest strategic tool like nuclear power or fossil fuels in the past and countries' competition for control over data, algorithmic tools, and technological know-how is automated. In a world where climate change poses a danger, green promises are also seen as a means for a nation to demonstrate its might and safeguard its energy supply (Yang et al., 2025). The emphasis should be on collaborating via multilateral accords such as the Paris Agreement, the UN Sustainable Development Goals (SDGs), and the G20 Green Finance initiatives, according to liberal institutionalism. According to the liberal theorists, green investment powered by artificial intelligencc improves communal security, reduces environmental conflicts, and creates reciprocal benefits. Conversely, constructivists focus on the normative and ideal aspects of objects. This indicates that they are interested in how common identity, values, and ideas influence the concept of sustainability, which is also digital and responsible (Iqbal et al., 2025).

The geopolitical stakes of artificial intelligence have increased in this new era of technical competitiveness and digital sovereignty. The leaders in AI at the moment are the US, China, and the EU, although their strategies vary. Despite being dominated by Google, Microsoft, and OpenAI, the U.S. has developed a market-led innovation system that is robust enough to leverage its private sector glitz to establish worldwide norms. Conversely, the Chinese promote their state-led strategy for AI research. "Digital silk roads" are being constructed by China as part of the Belt and Road Initiative (BRI). These highways will offer BRI nations AI-enabled infrastructure and link them. An ethical, transparent, and human-centered approach to AI is supported by the EU AI Act and other regulations (Ocelík & Kolk, 2024).

AI functions by striking a balance between the various forms of governance in these three-way relationships: ethics-efficiency, innovation-regulation, and autonomy-accountability. By combining AI development into policies for inclusive digitalization and sustainable development that are also important to peripheral, second, and third-order nation-states such as South Africa, Brazil, and India, there is a trend to spread influence beyond the center areas. Beyond technology, this battle of the future is very political and involves being prepared for trade agreements, data diplomacy, and cyber security. In the competition for supremacy in AI, nations are currently investing both cooperatively and competitively. Being green is no longer the only consideration; financial gain is also a factor. These initiatives can include sustainable infrastructure, renewable energy, or climate financing. After that, individuals began to firmly think that they were in charge for both political and financial reasons (Mnif et al., 2024).

To aid in the global transition to a low-carbon economy, nations are increasingly turning to green funding. As shown by the USA (IRA), China (wind and solar), and Europe's Green Deal, policies that promote sustainability are tied to industrial policy or technological rivalry. In this bold new world, the Global South—which encompasses portions of Africa, Latin America, and Southeast Asia—will encounter both chances and difficulties. It may also be an opportunity to create employment, exchange ideas, and develop in an environmentally friendly manner. Some inhabitants of certain nations may be placed in a dependent position, and they might see private interests from their own or another nation using their data and resources against them. There is much more to green finance politics than just the given amount of money. It may also be seen as a broader category of green fiscal strategies that are not limited to the four previously listed approaches. In this instance, other elements like justice, fairness, and accessibility provide us with more crucial information (Criekemans, 2022). However, it also increases people's reliance on digital systems operated by technologically more sophisticated businesses or nations (Kuzemko et al., 2025).. The geopolitical impact is evident: nations that dominate AI also control the information and narratives that influence international environmental policy. The objective of more inclusive global climate governance would be undermined by this inequity, which would simply strengthen hierarchies (Ibekwe, 2024).

We must shift the way nations engage with one another in order to realize this vision: from monopolies on technology to shared ecosystems of invention, and from competition to collaboration. International security may be significantly impacted by the issue of how nations strike a balance between their strategic objectives and their shared environmental responsibilities. In order to prevent further division in the international relations system, trust, transparency, and respect for one another are critical to the governance of AI and green finance (Peters & Besley, 2025). AI and green investment may be used as tools of international solidarity rather than geopolitical rivalry if policies are in place that promote open data sharing, cooperative research projects, and capacity development among poor countries.

There are both positive and negative geopolitical implications for the global order from AI and green investment. As countries prepare for this twin revolution, issues of survival, justice, and sovereignty are at stake in addition to economic advancement (Abbas et al., 2023). The interaction between artificial intelligence and green finance is a modern conundrum: the same technologies that have the potential to rescue the earth might equally endanger it. The fundamental concepts of geopolitics, such as environmental justice, digital ethics, and global inclusion, would have to be included into international relations. We shall discover in the next decades whether or not humans are intelligent and progressive enough to utilize AI and green investments as instruments for collaboration rather than as weapons for conflict. This will assist us in establishing a just, sustainable, and cooperative international order (Radanliev, 2025).

## 1.1 Contextualizing AI and Sustainable Finance in Global Politics

Green diplomacy employs sustainability and technology as “soft” power tactics in the era of artificial intelligence. These days, nations employ artificial intelligence (AI) and green technologies as diplomatic “carrots” to boost their standing and win friends worldwide (Scheffran 2023). Examples of how nations utilize technology to address environmental challenges include the US collaborations for climate innovation or AI research, China's support for the “smart” renewables sector via its Belt and Road Initiative, and the EU's use of climate diplomacy as a kind of digital transparency. These tactics provide technology codes that provide you with a competitive advantage in commerce, military might, or moral authority. Different groups of recyclers are at odds with one another on what recycling is and what the ethical and technological boundaries of global sustainability are. An argument has erupted around this tale of “green leadership” (Herranz-Surralles, 2024).

## 1.2 Relevance to Climate Diplomacy and Technological Sovereignty

However, the complex moral and governance challenges that arise with both AI development and green investment make the situation much more nuanced. When nations defend their own interests rather than cooperating to advance technology, this is known as techno-nationalism. Inconsistent rules and digital silos result from this (Allan et al., 2021). Two key terms emerge from a literal translation of these definitions: “digital colonialism,” which refers to the way large nations or corporations utilize technology to exert control over smaller ones by gathering and handling their data and digital content, sometimes posing as an established economic pathway. In the context of green investment, it is referred to as “greenwashing” or “carbon colonialism” when wealthy nations dump their carbon emissions and fabricate sustainability narratives in order to maintain control over globalized capital and production. In order to cope with high uncertainty, these elements make individuals consider moral frameworks that place a strong focus on individual accountability and transparency in digital and natural environments (Albert, 2022).

## 2. INTERNATIONAL RELATIONS, TECHNOLOGY AND SUSTAINABILITY: REALISM, LIBERAL INSTITUTIONALISM AND CONSTRUCTIVISM IN THE CONTEXT OF AI AND GREEN DIPLOMACY

Green diplomacy and AI Green diplomacy and artificial intelligence are examples of how mankind is pursuing technical progress while also adopting ecological stewardship (Ai et al., 2021). However, established theories of international relations like constructivism, liberal institutionalism, and realism serve as the foundation for how nations attempt to achieve these objectives. Divergent perspectives on how international actors handle emerging technology and sustainable governance are provided by these ideas. As two key instruments for change, IO and GD demonstrate how the international system is in conflict between power and ethics, sovereignty and interdependence, and competition and cooperation (Belaid et al., 2023).

Realists believe that there is no central authority structure to control state behavior, and that the world is anarchic. State action is often motivated by the nation's interests and the desire for power, which entails maximizing influence and security (Li et al., 2022). Given this, green technology and artificial intelligence are crucial instruments for acquiring geopolitical influence, and green diplomacy is a novel approach of doing so. AI research and use are seen as a scientific frontier as well as a means of manipulating and discouraging individuals. Similar to the Cold War rivalry between American and Soviet nuclear weapons, the US and China are engaged in a furious race over artificial intelligence where the winner is determined by data, processing capacity, and algorithmic innovation (Wang et al., 2025).

Cloud computing networks and the semiconductor supply chain are examples of AI infrastructure that provides nations control over the military and the economy. They are force multipliers in the same sense as climate technologies, green investments, and sustainability are. There is a lot of soft and hard power in nations that can produce or market renewable technology like solar panels, electric vehicles, or smart networks. According to realists, these sorts of skills enhance strategic security, national autonomy, and energy independence i.e., a state's ability to not rely on outside resources (De Goede & Westermeier, 2022). The realism approach views even pledges to combat climate change through the prism of self-interest. This is due to the fact that governments engage in green diplomacy to further their economic interests, their international reputation, or their access to markets, not because they are concerned about Mother Nature.

A different interpretation is provided by the liberal institutionalist perspective. under order to promote collective action, liberal institutionalists focus on international institutions, regulations, and interdependence. They act in this way because collaboration may sometimes occur even under anarchy. According to this viewpoint, encouraging a cooperative multilateral process among nations is the best way to advance AI governance and green diplomacy (Broeders et al., 2023). The Paris Climate Accord, the Sustainable Development Goals (SDGs) of the UN, and future ethical partnerships in AI are all products of liberal institutionalism. This is the notion that issues like digital inequality and climate change, which impact everyone, must be resolved together. This is only one of the many ways that technology promotes cooperation rather than conflict. By making climate change data more accessible and simpler to monitor and forecast, artificial intelligence is stretching the boundaries of diplomacy (Cicerone et al., 2023).

According to liberal institutionalists, there might be a "spillover effect" from technological interdependence, wherein networks for data sharing, AI research, and green investment promote stability and peace (Qobo & Mzyece, 2023). Economic globalization, which has connected nations, has been made feasible by digital connection. As a result, cooperation has become more beneficial and conflict more costly. The increasing significance of institutions such as the World Bank's Green Climate Fund, UNEP, and the OECD AI Policy Observatory demonstrates how governance systems function to align state practices by establishing guidelines and allocating funds so that AI can be used globally to support the shift to sustainability (Ma et al., 2022).

In that it offers a conceptual and normative framework for comprehending green diplomacy and artificial intelligence. International relations, according to constructivists, are based on socially created norms, values, and identities as well as institutional frameworks and material power. To put it another way, states will rank technical and environmental challenges according to their own perceptions, collective awareness, and historical experiences. According to constructivism, digital ethics and sustainability are not universal ideas but rather result from moral, political, and cultural ideals (Bednarski et al., 2025). For example, the European Union's emphasis on "human-centric technology" and "ethical AI" is consistent with its positioning as a champion of democratic governance and human rights. "Ecological civilization" refers to a style of thinking about civilization and development in the Chinese culture that blends environmental preservation with economic advancement.

There are two distinct interpretations are socially created responsible AI governance and green diplomacy (Yang et al., 2023). Through global networks, these players alter the regulations pertaining to environmental justice, renewable investment, and digital responsibility. It has expanded as nations exercise their influence via eco-leadership, ethical digital enterprises, and clean technology. For example,

Scandinavian nations have influenced the worldwide discussion on eco-innovation by leveraging their positive environmental image. The EU Green Deal has developed into a moral and financial basis for international cooperation (Meyer & Li, 2022).

A thorough examination of AI and green diplomacy is offered by constructivism, liberal institutionalism, and realism. While cautioning us against utopian ideals, realism exposes the strategic and competitive forces that shape technology. The importance of cooperative regimes and institutions in addressing global challenges is emphasized by liberal institutionalism (Kramfskyl et al., 2024). Intergovernmental relationships clarify how countries socially create sustainability and technical authority, then use paradigm shifts to translate these ideas into a policy domain. According to these theories, rather than being dictated by institutions or technical capability, all AI futures and green diplomacies are defined by a "altered disposition to rethink power, progress, collaboration – but also more than that technology use" within a digital-ecological revolution (Jahid, 2025).

International relations theory must remain a part of the politics of technology and sustainability analysis. Global diplomacy will need to find a way to strike a balance between constructivism's moral vigilance, liberalism's emphasis on collaboration, and realism's concentration on security, as artificial intelligence accelerates the transition to a greener world. How can we reconcile these viewpoints and support the advancement of AI-driven ecological justice? This shift would usher in an era when technology is not a competitor but rather a means of creating a just, sustainable, and inclusive global order (McNamara, 2024).

## 3. GEO-POLITICAL DYNAMICS OF ARTIFICIAL INTELLIGENCE DEVELOPMENT: STRATEGIC AI INVESTMENTS AND GLOBAL POWER RIVALRIES

Global power politics having access to oil, a nuclear weapon, or an industrial base were in the past, controlling data flows and being in command of the global computer infrastructure and algorithms might be considered a type of geopolitical power in the twenty-first century. AI systems are currently used in almost every aspect of society, including government, industry, education, healthcare, and military. Building tanks, battleships, and intercontinental ballistic missiles in the 20th century is analogous to the rush to harness AI's capabilities (Muller, 2023). The US, China, the EU, and India are the four main institutions whose plans best illustrate the geopolitical ramifications of AI development. Divergent views on digital sovereignty, governance, and ethical responsibility are shown by the methods, investments, and ideological frameworks that each has devised to gain control in the AI arms race.

In terms of AI innovation, America continues to dominate the globe. This is a result of a robust venture capital system, the vigor of the private sector, and excellent educational standards. According to the Strategy, America can maintain its leadership position by fostering open innovation, fostering market competition, and safeguarding intellectual property. Because it understands how crucial AI is for strategy and security, the U.S. government has been using AI more extensively in the military, intelligence, and cyber security sectors (Sullivan, 2023).

There are examples of the convergence of the military and civilian innovation pipelines include DARPA's AI Next Campaign and the National AI Initiative Act (2020). We are beginning to realize that our society requires ethical and responsible AI governance that prioritizes technical advancement while maintaining public confidence, as shown by the Biden Administration's Executive Order on Safe, Secure, and Trustworthy AI (2023). However, domestic political challenges, tech monopoly antitrust issues, and the U.S.'s dependence on international semiconductor supply chains are making it more difficult for the country to maintain its lead in AI over the long run.

AI is seen as a crucial component of strategic independence and national rebirth under China's centralized, state-driven paradigm. China should dominate the world in AI by 2030, according to the PRC government's own Next Generation Artificial Intelligence Development Plan (2017). It also discusses the appropriate applications of AI in military, education, industry, and surveillance (Collins & O'Brien, 2023). The U.S. version has less government guidance and is centered on private innovation. The government, state-owned enterprises (SOEs) with whom these businesses want to collaborate, and tech giants like as Baidu, Alibaba, Tencent, and Huawei, on the other hand, work closely together in China's AI ecosystem.

So, adding AI solutions will allow Daqing to expand rapidly, but privacy and surveillance issues will always exist. China's "AI diplomacy" goes beyond domestic improvement. As part of the Belt and Road Initiative, the nation is also using AI for its Digital Silk Road. China has done this by sending 5G networks, face recognition software, and smart infrastructure to partner nations in Asia, Africa, and Latin America (Calderaro & Blumfelde, 2022). China hopes to utilize them to combat Western control over digital norms and ethics and to establish international standards that are beneficial to its system of governance. However, nations concerned about data dependency and digital authoritarianism, as well as issues brought on by export restrictions and technology constraints imposed by the US and its allies, are opposing China's approach.

As, regarding AI, the EU is distinct from other nations worldwide. It prioritizes human rights, ethical frameworks, and regulatory leadership above the newest and greatest technology. Who is interested in EU-made AI? In order to take the lead in the global discussion, the EU aims to establish the guidelines for transparent and reliable AI (Francisco & Linner, 2023). This is because it is aware that, in terms of AI innovation, it is now lagging behind China and the United States. The first international legislation that addresses every facet of artificial intelligence is the European AI Act of 2024. The European AI Act, which took three years to pass, is the largest and most intricate collection of AI regulations to date (Buthe et al., 2022).

The initiatives like the Digital Europe Programme and Horizon Europe are funding AI research that benefits everyone, the environment, and society. Although the EU is a pioneer in regulation with an international influence, some individuals are concerned that excessive regulation might impede innovation. For instance, if foreign businesses want to sell their goods in the EU's sizable market, they must adhere to European norms (Irekponor, 2025). This "Brussels Effect" makes the EU the ethical and legal steward of a new AI order, notwithstanding its technological behind.

India is a growing power and digital democracy that utilizes technology to improve people's lives in the real world. NITI Aayog's 2018 National Strategy for Artificial Intelligence (AI for All) to increase AI's usability and accessibility for all. Large issues including healthcare, agriculture, education, and urban growth would benefit from this. India has no desire to compete with the US or China in the development of powerful artificial intelligence. Rather, it seeks to use AI for the benefit of society and to support more sustainable economic development. (Lee et al., 2023). In international AI discussions, India also aims to seem impartial and fair by discussing capacity development and ensuring that all people in the Global South have access to digital tools (Gabor & Braun, 2025). Because it collaborates with QUAD members and is a member of international organizations like the Global Partnership on AI (GPAI), it is a geopolitical show-off between partnerships that lean toward the West and digital governance autonomy. However, before India can establish itself as a leader in AI in the developing world, it must address issues with its infrastructure, privacy, and the digital divide.

A multi-polar AI order with disparate views on innovation, governance, and ethics is emerging, as seen by the AI policies of the US, China, the EU, and India. The market drives innovation in the United States, the state governs technical sovereignty in China, ethics, rights, and people govern regulation in the European Union, and inclusion and development are the foundations of artificial intelligence in India (Diodato et al., 2023). These opposing paradigms reflect grave disputes about the direction of world order and are not only about technology. Nowadays, artificial intelligence is transforming society, the economy, and how people live. The future phase of international relations will be shaped by AI's geopolitics, where power is determined by data, algorithms, and digital governing skills rather than by territory or commerce. Being the best at technology is just one aspect of the global AI competition. It also involves establishing the moral compass, values, and regulations for the digital era (Reezi et al., 2023).

## 4. GLOBAL GREEN INVESTMENT AND THE POLITICAL ECONOMY OF SUSTAINABILITY: GREEN FINANCE, CARBON MARKETS AND AI-DRIVEN INVESTMENT ANALYTICS

The global economy is shifting toward a lower carbon footprint as the climate catastrophe worsens. Green investment is becoming the most significant aspect of the global economy, not merely a characteristic. The carbon trade, improved information processing with artificial knight surfaces, and environmentally friendly financing methods are now the most crucial components of planning for a sustainable international system (Adebayo et al., 2023). Economic prosperity is closely linked to their attempts to safeguard the environment. These are not only technical or financial instruments; they are also linked to the global distribution of power, the functioning of national governments, and the advancement of technology in all contexts (Shaik et al., 2023). Governments, corporations, and international organizations will collaborate and compete for funding via a number of avenues in the growing field of green project investment. This involves generating funds to achieve the Sustainable Development Goals (SDGs) of the UN and the Paris Agreement. We must combine economic rationality, digital innovation, and political urgency for sustainable development. The phrase "green finance" refers to environmentally friendly financial methods and goods. Green bonds, sustainability-linked loans, and climate funds have all increased in the last 10 years: The financial system throughout the globe is in disarray. By 2024, more than $1.5 trillion in green bonds will have been issued globally. This indicates that an increasing number of individuals want to make financial investments in environmentally friendly ventures. The rise of green finance further demonstrates the growing significance of environmental, social, and governance (ESG) considerations in financial decision-making.

People in the public and commercial sectors are being forced to consider how to make things last as a result. Central banks and governments are adjusting their macroeconomic frameworks to account for climate change at the same time as this growth (Chu et al., 2023). For example, central banks may collaborate on climate-related financial risks via the Network for Greening the Financial System (NGFS). The emergence of green finance has revealed significant geopolitical divides. The majority of influence over green capital markets still lies with wealthier nations, while poorer regions are hampered by inadequate institutions that make participation difficult, investor reluctance, or restricted credit availability. As a result, green finance is not only a means of preserving the environment but also a worldwide struggle to determine which nations are eligible to receive sustainable income and how (Wang et al., 2025).

Because they impose a cost on greenhouse gas emissions, these carbon markets are a crucial component of the global green economy. By adopting carbon pricing, emission trading, and carbon offset certificates, these market participants want to integrate environmental costs into their operations and encourage individuals to reduce their emissions. The largest and most established carbon market in the world is the EU ETS. It serves as a template for carbon pricing elsewhere (Markelius et al., 2024). At least a few more locations have followed suit today, and over 20% of world emissions come from China, Canada, and California alone. In addition to holding companies accountable for their environmental impact, the greenhouse gas market enables us to participate in the global carbon market and begin trading carbon.

However, their political economy is difficult to comprehend. Some claim that carbon markets are harmful because they allow negative events to continue. Instead of contributing to cumulative emissions themselves, they provide wealthy nations and large corporations with the funds to purchase offsets (Hofmann & Pawlak, 2023). The carbon trade might increase global inequality, forcing poor countries to counteract this imbalance by giving rich countries cheap emission permits, similar to past examples of international dependency (Falkner et al. 2024).

A novel approach to long-term financial success is the use of AI and data analytics in green investments. In order to improve the accuracy, transparency, and utility of green finance, AI-powered systems examine further intricate data sets that quantify energy use, environmental effect, and climate (Schneider 2023). The financial impacts or opportunities of various climate change scenarios might be modeled using machine learning techniques. For instance, the chance that a green bond would fail and its yield will drop to zero, as well as the most effective strategy for making money on renewable energy companies. Real-time emission monitoring enabled by AI reduces bogus claims and allows for the verification of carbon credits. In the carbon markets, this is quite beneficial. To assist investors in identifying green prospects, they examine items like environmental performance indices, satellite imagery, and social impact data (Png, 2022).

This is the collection of tools you need to make data-driven choices and align the environmental end-point with the economic return. AI-driven ESG score models are being used as a safety net for investments by firms such as BlackRock and HSBC. An ESG rating may be used to determine the current potential impact of an investment on government, society, or the environment. AI is being used by the Climate Trace partnership to monitor emissions from companies worldwide (Aswani et al., 2022). The digital gap, algorithmic bias, and data monopolization are all being impacted by AI's expanding use in green finance. Multinational firms and wealthy countries may integrate AI infrastructure with climate data. Instead, they might be exploited to create narratives about sustainable financing that harm local residents and small companies. Green investment and AI analytics convey two signals from a political economics perspective: sustainability is essential to the economy and it alters the geopolitical landscape. When it comes to creating regulations for the global market and climate, nations and companies who possess data-driven financial systems and green technology are at a competitive advantage. For instance, by investing in battery research, renewable energy, and AI-powered climate monitoring, the European Union's Green Deal blends industrial policy with environmental objectives to safeguard technical sovereignty (Yoshimatsu, 2023).

As shown by its leadership in the production of solar panels and the use of AI to manage energy, it has once again decided to concentrate on a particular sector of the economy that is at the nexus of development and sustainability: the goal is to connect ecological modernization with expansion in the global economy (Zuniga et al., 2024). The US has connected climate investment to industrial regeneration and strategic rivalry, both as a strategy to oppose the statist Chinese power grab and as a way to prepare for the future conflict (clean energy investments would be domestic (Bordoff & O'sullivan, 2023).

There are two concepts that are prevalent in international politics of cooperation and competition form the foundation of thc global map of green finance and AI-powered sustainability. Countries and organizations are working together more because of climate change, but power disparities are becoming greater as a result of the competition for financial and technical leadership. Making digital innovation and green capital accessible to everybody will be the challenge of the future. This entails ensuring that all nations have access to AI-enabled sustainability (Ajuwon et al., 2023).

## 5. CONCLUSION AND FUTURE CORRIDORS: TOWARD EQUITABLE AND COOPERATIVE GEO-POLITICAL FRAMEWORKS

These tensions are lessened by international organizations. Meanwhile, efforts have been made to integrate AI and green finance into global governance via the United Nations, the World Bank Group, the International Monetary Fund, and new multilateral organizations like BRICS. Examples of initiatives to ensure that new technologies are utilized in ways that promote sustainable development include the IMF's climate financing programs and the UN's AI for Good project. However, it may sometimes be challenging to maintain consistency and implement them due to institutional fragmentation and conflicting mandates. For example, most poor nations see these as obstacles to entering the IT industry, despite the EU's desire for AI to be utilized in very ethical ways. Mandatory worldwide carbon markets aim to democratize green investment in a similar way, but the north benefits from the disparity between corporate and financial power in the north and the technical and financial capability in the south. The international system has two challenges: balancing efficiency and equality and coordinating innovation and regulation.

Investing in AI and "green technology" combined has the potential to alter the laws of global competitiveness and collaboration. A more open and data-driven approach to climate and sustainability governance may be made possible by the rise of "AI-supported green diplomacy". Following natural catastrophes, adaptive governance, resource optimization, and decision-making may all be aided by predictive analytics and machine learning. Similar to this, regional initiatives like the African Union's AI policy and global plans like the UN's Digital Cooperation Roadmap may assist poor nations in making a substantial contribution to the global digital-green transformation. By promoting global collaboration in AI ethics, sharing digital infrastructure, and transferring green technologies, the North-South divide may result in more equitable geopolitics.

## REFERENCES


Abbas, J., Wang, L., Belgacem, S. B., Pawar, P. S., Najam, H., & Abbas, J. (2023). Investment in renewable energy and electricity output: Role of green finance, environmental tax, and geopolitical risk: Empirical evidence from China. *Energy*, *269*, 126683. DOI: 10.1016/j.energy.2023.126683

Adebayo, Y., Basha, S. S., & Ghaffar, A. (2023). AI-Driven Forecasting Models for Green Tech Stocks: Linking Carbon Capture Innovation to Stock Market Trends in 2025.

Ai, Y. H., Peng, D. Y., & Xiong, H. H. (2021). Impact of environmental regulation intensity on green technology innovation: From the perspective of political and business connections. *Sustainability (Basel)*, *13*(9), 4862. DOI: 10.3390/su13094862

Ajuwon, A., Adewuyi, A., Oladuji, T. J., & Akintobi, A. O. (2023). A Model for Strategic Investment in African Infrastructure: Using AI for Due Diligence and Portfolio Optimization. *International Journal of Advanced Multidisciplinary Research and Studies*, *3*(6), 1811–1826. DOI: 10.62225/2583049X.2023.3.6.4402

Albert, M. J. (2022). The global politics of the renewable energy transition and the non-substitutability hypothesis: Towards a 'great transformation'? *Review of International Political Economy*, *29*(5), 1766–1781. DOI: 10.1080/09692290.2021.1980418

Allan, B., Lewis, J. I., & Oatley, T. (2021). Green industrial policy and the global transformation of climate politics. *Global Environmental Politics*, *21*(4), 1–19. DOI: 10.1162/glep_a_00640

Aswani, R. S., Sajith, S., & Bhat, M. Y. (2022). Realigning India's Vietnam policy through cooperative sustainable development: A geostrategic counterbalancing to China in Indo-Pacific. *East Asia (Piscataway, N.J.)*, *39*(2), 97–115. DOI: 10.1007/s12140-021-09371-0 PMID: 34276182

Bednarski, L., Roscoe, S., Blome, C., & Schleper, M. C. (2025). Geopolitical disruptions in global supply chains: A state-of-the-art literature review. *Production Planning and Control*, *36*(4), 536–562.

Belaid, F., Al-Sarihi, A., & Al-Mestneer, R. (2023). Balancing climate mitigation and energy security goals amid converging global energy crises: The role of green investments. *Renewable Energy*, *205*, 534–542. DOI: 10.1016/j.renene.2023.01.083

Bordoff, J., & O'sullivan, M. L. (2023). The age of energy insecurity: How the fight for resources is upending geopolitics. *Foreign Affairs*, *102*, 104.

Broeders, D., Cristiano, F., & Kaminska, M. (2023). In search of digital sovereignty and strategic autonomy: Normative power Europe to the test of its geopolitical ambitions. *Journal of Common Market Studies, 61*(5), 1261–1280. DOI: 10.1111/jcms.13462

Buthe, T., Djeffal, C., Lütge, C., Maasen, S., & Ingersleben-Seip, N. V. (2022). Governing AI–attempting to herd cats? Introduction to the special issue on the Governance of Artificial Intelligence. *Journal of European Public Policy, 29*(11), 1721–1752. DOI: 10.1080/13501763.2022.2126515

Calderaro, A., & Blumfelde, S. (2022). Artificial intelligence and EU security: The false promise of digital sovereignty. *European Security, 31*(3), 415–434. DOI: 10.1080/09662839.2022.2101885

Chu, L. K., Doğan, B., Abakah, E. J. A., Ghosh, S., & Albeni, M. (2023). Impact of economic policy uncertainty, geopolitical risk, and economic complexity on carbon emissions and ecological footprint: An investigation of the E7 countries. *Environmental Science and Pollution Research International, 30*(12), 34406–34427. DOI: 10.1007/s11356-022-24682-2 PMID: 36512279

Cicerone, G., Faggian, A., Montresor, S., & Rentocchini, F. (2023). Regional artificial intelligence and the geography of environmental technologies: Does local AI knowledge help regional green-tech specialization? *Regional Studies, 57*(2), 330–343. DOI: 10.1080/00343404.2022.2092610

Collins, N., & O'Brien, D. (2023). Neo-mercantilism in action: China and small states. *International Politics, 60*(3), 635–658. DOI: 10.1057/s41311-022-00419-3 PMID: 40478077

Criekemans, D. (2022). Geotechnical ensembles': how new technologies change geopolitical factors and contexts in economy, energy and security. *Geopolitics and International Relations*, 61.

De Goede, M., & Westermeier, C. (2022). Infrastructural geopolitics. *International Studies Quarterly, 66*(3), sqac033. DOI: 10.1093/isq/sqac033

Diodato, D., Huergo, E., Moncada-Paternò-Castello, P., Rentocchini, F., & Timmermans, B. (2023). Introduction to the special issue on "the twin (digital and green) transition: Handling the economic and social challenges". *Industry and Innovation, 30*(7), 755–765. DOI: 10.1080/13662716.2023.2254272

Falkner, G., Heidebrecht, S., Obendiek, A., & Seidl, T. (2024). Digital sovereignty-Rhetoric and reality. *Journal of European Public Policy, 31*(8), 2099–2120. DOI: 10.1080/13501763.2024.2358984

Francisco, M., & Linner, B. O. (2023). AI and the governance of sustainable development. An idea analysis of the European Union, the United Nations, and the World Economic Forum. *Environmental Science & Policy, 150*, 103590. DOI: 10.1016/j.envsci.2023.103590

Gabor, D., & Braun, B. (2025). Green macrofinancial regimes. *Review of International Political Economy, 32*(3), 542–568. DOI: 10.1080/09692290.2025.2453504

Herranz-Surralles, A. (2024). The EU energy transition in a geopoliticizing world. *Geopolitics, 29*(5), 1882–1912. DOI: 10.1080/14650045.2023.2283489 PMID: 39318503

Hofmann, S. C., & Pawlak, P. (2023). Governing cyberspace: Policy boundary politics across organizations. *Review of International Political Economy, 30*(6), 2122–2149. DOI: 10.1080/09692290.2023.2249002

Ibekwe, K. I., Etukudoh, E. A., Nwokediegwu, Z. Q. S., Umoh, A. A., Adefemi, A., & Ilojianya, V. I. (2024). Energy security in the global context: A comprehensive review of geopolitical dynamics and policies. *Engineering Science & Technology Journal, 5*(1), 152–168. DOI: 10.51594/estj.v5i1.741

Iqbal, A., Zhang, W., & Jahangir, S. (2025). Building a Sustainable Future: The Nexus Between Artificial Intelligence, Renewable Energy, Green Human Capital, Geopolitical Risk, and Carbon Emissions Through the Moderating Role of Institutional Quality. *Sustainability (Basel), 17*(3), 990. DOI: 10.3390/su17030990

Irekponor, O. (2025). Designing resilient AI architectures for predictive energy finance systems amid data sovereignty, adversarial threats, and policy volatility. *International Journal of Research Publication and Reviews, 6*(6), 73–100. DOI: 10.55248/gengpi.6.0625.2125

Jahid, M. S. R. (2025). AI-driven optimization and risk modeling in strategic economic zone development for mid-sized economies: A review approach. *International Journal of Scientific Interdisciplinary Research, 6*(1), 185–218. DOI: 10.63125/31wna449

Kuzemko, C., Blondeel, M., Bradshaw, M., Bridge, G., Faigen, E., & Fletcher, L. (2025). Rethinking energy geopolitics: Towards a geopolitical economy of global energy transformation. *Geopolitics, 30*(2), 531–565. DOI: 10.1080/14650045.2024.2351075

Lee, C. C., Zhang, J., Yu, C. H., & Fang, L. (2023). How does geopolitical risk affect corporate innovation? Evidence from China's listed companies. *Emerging Markets Finance & Trade, 59*(7), 2217–2233. DOI: 10.1080/1540496X.2023.2170698

Li, J., Van Assche, A., Li, L., & Qian, G. (2022). Foreign direct investment along the Belt and Road: A political economy perspective. *Journal of International Business Studies*, *53*(5), 902–919. DOI: 10.1057/s41267-021-00435-0

Ma, W., Nasriddinov, F., Haseeb, M., Ray, S., Kamal, M., Khalid, N., & Ur Rehman, M. (2022). Revisiting the impact of energy consumption, foreign direct investment, and geopolitical risk on CO2 emissions: Comparing developed and developing countries. *Frontiers in Environmental Science*, *10*, 985384. DOI: 10.3389/fenvs.2022.985384

Markelius, A., Wright, C., Kuiper, J., Delille, N., & Kuo, Y. T. (2024). The mechanisms of AI hype and its planetary and social costs. *AI and Ethics*, *4*(3), 727–742. DOI: 10.1007/s43681-024-00461-2

McNamara, K. R. (2024). Transforming Europe? The EU's industrial policy and geopolitical turn. *Journal of European Public Policy*, *31*(9), 2371–2396. DOI: 10.1080/13501763.2023.2230247

Meyer, K. E., & Li, C. (2022). The MNE and its subsidiaries at times of global disruptions: An international relations perspective. *Global Strategy Journal*, *12*(3), 555–577. DOI: 10.1002/gsj.1436

Mnif, E., Jarboui, A., & Mouakhar, K. (2024). Strategic insights into carbon markets, digital finance and geopolitical risks for advancing green sustainability investments. *Management of Environmental Quality*, *35*(7), 1622–1649. DOI: 10.1108/MEQ-10-2023-0369

Muller, M. (2023). The 'new geopolitics' of mineral supply chains: A window of opportunity for African countries. *The South African Journal of International Affairs*, *30*(2), 177–203. DOI: 10.1080/10220461.2023.2226108

Ocelík, V., & Kolk, A. (2024). Sustainability in a digital world: Geopolitics, values and international business policy. In *Handbook of International Business Policy* (pp. 327–345). Edward Elgar Publishing. DOI: 10.4337/9781035308682.00027

Peters, M. A., & Besley, T. (2025). The geopolitics of postdigital educational development: From territories to networks to rival World Systems. In *The Geopolitics of Postdigital Educational Development* (pp. 41–50). Springer Nature Switzerland. DOI: 10.1007/978-3-031-99378-7_3

Png, M. T. (2022, June). At the tensions of south and north: Critical roles of global south stakeholders in AI governance. In *Proceedings of the 2022 ACM Conference on Fairness, Accountability, and Transparency* (pp. 1434-1445). DOI: 10.1145/3531146.3533200

Qobo, M., & Mzyece, M. (2023). Geopolitics, technology wars and global supply chains: Implications for Africa. *The South African Journal of International Affairs*, *30*(1), 29–46. DOI: 10.1080/10220461.2023.2191988

Radanliev, P. (2025). Cyber diplomacy: Defining the opportunities for cybersecurity and risks from Artificial Intelligence, IoT, Blockchains, and Quantum Computing. *Journal of Cyber Security Technology*, *9*(1), 28–78. DOI: 10.1080/23742917.2024.2312671

Scheffran, J. (2023). Limits to the Anthropocene: Geopolitical conflict or cooperative governance? *Frontiers in Political Science*, *5*, 1190610. DOI: 10.3389/fpos.2023.1190610

Schneider, E. (2023). Germany's Industrial strategy 2030, EU competition policy and the Crisis of New Constitutionalism.(Geo-) political economy of a contested paradigm shift. *New Political Economy*, *28*(2), 241–258. DOI: 10.1080/13563467.2022.2091535

Shaik, M., Jamil, S. A., Hawaldar, I. T., Sahabuddin, M., Rabbani, M. R., & Atif, M. (2023). Impact of geo-political risk on stocks, oil, and gold returns during GFC, COVID-19, and Russian–Ukraine War. *Cogent Economics & Finance*, *11*(1), 2190213. DOI: 10.1080/23322039.2023.2190213

Sullivan, J. (2023). The sources of American power: A foreign policy for a changed world. *Foreign Affairs*, *102*, 8.

Wang, Q., Sun, T., & Li, R. (2025). Does Artificial Intelligence (AI) enhance green economy efficiency? The role of green finance, trade openness, and R&D investment. *Humanities & Social Sciences Communications*, *12*(1), 1–22. DOI: 10.1057/s41599-024-04319-0

Wang, Q., Sun, T., & Li, R. (2025). Does artificial intelligence promote green innovation? An assessment based on direct, indirect, spillover, and heterogeneity effects. *Energy & Environment*, *36*(2), 1005–1037. DOI: 10.1177/0958305X231220520

Yang, X., Chen, H., Li, B., Jia, D., & Ahmad, M. (2025). The relationship between artificial intelligence, geopolitical risk, and green growth: Exploring the moderating role of green finance and energy technology. *Technological Forecasting and Social Change*, *217*, 124135. DOI: 10.1016/j.techfore.2025.124135

Yang, Y., Xia, S., & Qian, X. (2023). Geopolitics of the energy transition. *Journal of Geographical Sciences*, *33*(4), 683–704. DOI: 10.1007/s11442-023-2101-2

Yoshimatsu, H. (2023). Japan's strategic response to China's geo-economic presence: Quality infrastructure as a diplomatic tool. *The Pacific Review*, *36*(1), 148–176. DOI: 10.1080/09512748.2021.1947356

Zuniga, N., Burton, S. D., Blancato, F., & Carr, M. (2024). The geopolitics of technology standards: Historical context for US, EU and Chinese approaches. *International Affairs*, *100*(4), 1635–1652. DOI: 10.1093/ia/iiae124

# Chapter 3
# The Role of Responsible AI in Global Trade and Finance

**Rajeev Mathew**
http://orcid.org/0009-0005-8764-1701
*Jaipuria School of Business, Ghaziabad, India*

## ABSTRACT

*Ethical AI means that technology should be fair, open, accountable, and include everyone. This is to encourage technology-driven development, even though it may not fix existing inequalities. In finance, responsible AI means better ways to find fraud, identify risk, make sure rules are followed, and come up with long-term investment plans. In business, it helps with better supply chain management, border trade, and predictive modeling. But to fix problems like algorithmic bias, data privacy, silly national rules, and the rise of digital divides, countries will need to work together. If AI is going to work in the long run, it needs to be ethical in fiscal and trade systems. "The Growth of World Finance trade trends gradually and consumer capitals are most normalizing. Ethical AI, in order to ensure that we actual can driver efficiency as much as fairness within the changing faces of global finance and trade"*

## 1. INTRODUCTION

AI techniques and algorithms have advanced quickly, changing many businesses in the global economy. For example, AI is used in finance and trade to find fraud, predict markets, optimize supply chains, and help people make decisions. As AI systems become more important in making important decisions in international markets, questions of responsibility, transparency, fairness, and accountability have

DOI: 10.4018/979-8-2600-1308-3.ch003

become more important. Responsible AI aims to guarantee that the ethical, legal, and social ramifications of AI technology deployment align with its transformative potential and do not conflict with overarching global priorities, including economic stability, financial inclusion, and sustainable development.

Global finance is more than just an interconnected network. It is an ecosystem of investments that cross borders, as well as legal and digital systems that make it easier for money to move around the world. AI has sped up and improved financial processes. AI tools have made it possible to do predictive analysis and compliance help, as well as real-time monitoring. But AI systems like this could be bad for everyone: if they aren't carefully planned and guided, they could make existing inequalities worse, reinforce bias, and make people less trusting of international financial institutions. Algorithmic credit scoring and lending could also unintentionally discriminate against groups that are already at a disadvantage. (8) The logic is that the AI might only lend to certain demographic groups because of biased data, which would be illegal racial discrimination. Trading that isn't clear and is done by AI can also cause problems in the market. Responsible AI gives us a way to deal with these risks by making sure that financial technologies are used in a way that is clear, fair, and accountable.

Responsible AI is just as important for changing international trade. Because there are so many people involved in modern supply chains, each of them has to deal with different rules and economies. AI is also used to make trade logistics easier, predict changes in demand, find mistakes, and make it easier for goods to cross borders. In these areas, responsible AI will make sure that everyone benefits from trade fairly, that workers' rights are protected, that the environment is protected, and that everyone has equal access to the benefits of trade. Responsible AI is also very important for keeping customer data safe, encouraging fair competition, and stopping market manipulation on digital trading platforms and in e-commerce. By adding AI systems to global trade rules set by groups like the World Trade Organization (WTO), responsible AI can also make international trade more reliable and strong.

## 1.1 Background and Importance

It is also important for responsible AI in finance and trade to be the same all over the world. That's because having more than one regulatory system can make things confusing and slow. For instance, different countries have different laws about data protection, A.I. ethics, and money, which makes it hard to set universal standards. Along with the problems listed above, it is especially hard for complex financial models that use proprietary models to be clear and easy to understand. This information-dark environment makes it hard to hold people responsible, especially in areas with a lot of rules, like cross-border lending, anti-money laundering (AML) laws, and international taxation. But these are problems that global governance needs to work on together. The IMF, OECD, WTO, and UN are examples of intergovernmental organizations that would be the focus of these efforts to encourage cooperation and create a consistent framework for responsible AI.

## 1.2 Study Scope and Methodology

The problems with Responsible AI International Finance and Trade face a big problem in global governance and technical progress. Now is a good time to think about how we can make sure that A.I.-powered technologies are used safely, since more and more governments and enterprises are starting to employ them. Ethics in AI Ensure that technology prioritizes users and integrates principles such as equity, responsibility, and inclusivity into intelligent products and services. In this age of technology, becoming responsible AI is both a source of new ideas and a way to protect against systemic risk in finance and commerce, which are both important parts of the global socio-economic system that technology and responsible AI will be a bigger part of in the future. In this chapter, it critically examine the role of AI4R in global trade and finance, aiming to comprehend how AI4R could reshape existing realities while also presenting ethical dilemmas for government. The magazine's goal is to help people learn how AI can help global commerce and financial systems, come up with use cases, lower risks, and set norms for fair and long-term economic growth.

# 2. RESPONSIBLE AI AND THE PRINCIPLES OF RESPONSIBLE AI INCLUDE FAIRNESS, OPENNESS, RESPONSIBILITY, AND ETHICS

The problems with Responsible AI International Finance and Trade face a big problem in global governance and technical progress. Now is a good time to think about how we can make sure that A.I.-powered technologies are used safely, since more and more governments and enterprises are starting to employ them. Ethics in AI Ensure that technology prioritizes users and integrates principles such as equity, responsibility, and inclusivity into intelligent products and services. In this age of technology, becoming responsible AI is both a source of new ideas and a way to protect against systemic risk in finance and commerce, which are both important parts of the global socio-economic system that technology and responsible AI will be a bigger part of in the future. In this essay, it critically examine the role of AI4R in global trade and finance, aiming to comprehend how it could reshape existing realities while also presenting ethical dilemmas for government. The magazine's goal is to help people learn how AI can help global commerce and financial systems, come up with use cases, lower risks, and set norms for fair and long-term economic growth.

Fairness is one of the most important and also controversial ideas for responsible AI because it has to do with bias, discrimination, and treating everyone the same. Algorithms are only as good as the data they learn from. The author said, "When the data is biased in a historical or systemic way, those biases can carry over into the choices we make based on that data." In finance, for example, credit-scoring algorithms that were trained on biased data may often leave out poor communities, which keeps financial inequality going.

AI systems in international trade could give richer countries or bigger companies an edge over smaller businesses in developing countries. Fair AI intuition says we need to keep an eye on and deal with these kinds of bias, maybe by using tools like algorithmic auditing, machine learning models that are aware of fairness, and data sources that are different from each other. Fairness means more than just technical fixes. It also means procedural justice, the right of those affected to get help, and making decisions that are culturally and socially appropriate. So, justice is more than just fighting discrimination; it also means making systems that support and include people, as well as qualify and affirm them.

Another principle of responsible AI is transparency, which means that all relevant stakeholders should be able to understand, interpret, and explain AI systems. Deep learning and other "black-box" AI models make decisions that are very accurate but completely unclear; it's hard to see how they got to those decisions. In high-stakes areas like finance, health, and trade, where all the stakeholders need to be clear about how decisions are being made, this kind of opacity is not only bad, but it also becomes impossible. Transparency encompasses disclosing the constraints of AI models, elucidating the rationale behind algorithmic outputs, and acknowledging the data utilized in training systems (Fritz-Morgenthal et al., 2022).

For example, in the financial services industry, customers who are turned down for a loan should know why, and regulators should be able to check AI systems to make sure they follow laws against discrimination and protect consumers. In international trade as well, transparency is important to make sure that tools for optimizing the supply chain and predictive analytics that are often used to figure out tariffs or clear customs are not misused and follow international law. Responsible AI builds trust between users, institutions, and regulators, promotes openness, and encourages people to follow the rules.

It's really vital to fairly and openly assign blame for systems that are hurting us or acting in ways we didn't expect. One of the biggest problems with AI governance is the responsibility gap. that is accountable for the results of algorithmic decisions: coders, implementers, regulators, or the individuals that utilize the final product?

In the digital-everywhere world of banking and business, where models can span borders and involve a lot of people, things are much more complicated. The story of responsible AI, on the other hand, shows that responsibility needs to be built into every step of the AI lifecycle, from design and training to deployment and monitoring.

This includes making audit trails, giving people the chance to look into things on their own, and setting up the legal and regulatory systems that will make sure that those who are proven guilty are penalized. Companies that use AI also have a duty to keep asking questions, measuring its effects, and giving humans a chance to criticize AI's conclusions. Accountability changes AI from being "free" tools that we don't have to watch to something that has to follow the same moral and legal rules as well-meaning decision-makers do.

When it comes to being fair, honest, and responsible, ethics is our guiding light. Following the regulations and the legislation is not enough to be responsible with AI ethics. It also entails thinking about the bigger issues of what is right and wrong and how we might all benefit from each other's good fortune. When we talk about it in an ethical sense, we mean that you treat people with respect, safeguard their rights, want to include everyone, and make sure that technology advances in a way that benefits everyone. In finance, that could mean putting long-term sustainability ahead of short-term earnings. Investing with AI in methods that make sure their investments are responsible according to the leaders' ESG (environmental, social, and governance) viewpoints could also be helpful. And that means making sure that AI-powered supply chain systems don't take advantage of people, hurt the environment, or give huge businesses an unfair advantage over small ones. To make AI that is responsible, the process of producing and governing AI needs to incorporate not only the manufacturers, but also the voices of vulnerable groups, ethicists, and civil society. By following ethical AI guidelines, everyone can make sure that the benefits of AI are not only making things work better, but also protecting basic human rights and supporting social justice (Ridzuan et al., 2024).

There are four important ideas that guide responsible AI are honesty, openness, responsibility, and decency. They affect how the application and deployment will be used for the greater good in the future. But it's hard to follow regulations like that when they often overlap and even go against each other. Being more open, for instance, can mean giving up some privacy in order to be less productive. We need to move past these kinds of problems in a more equitable and context-aware way, given how complicated these kinds of socio-technical systems are. These ideas show how to deal with risks and advantages with A.I. in important areas like international trade and banking, where the stakes are quite high. Responsible AI is more than just a technique to look ahead to new things. It's about technology that is fair, trustworthy, accountable, and values-based. It's about progress that lasts forever and includes everyone.

## 2.1 Global Rules and Frameworks for Responsible AI

Principles and standards for responsible AI have become one of the best ways to make sure that AI is used in a fair, legal, and socially responsible way in different countries or industries around the world. AI is now a part of many fields, including government, business, health care, and finance. Because of these things, it's really necessary for everyone to find a polite approach to build and use AI. A lot of nations, international organizations, and multilateral institutions have come up with ideas and plans to help make AI more fair, accountable, open, inclusive, and long-lasting.

The OECD AI Principles are the most important set of rules. Last year, both the G20 and the OECD agreed to them. They emphasize transparency, strength, accountability, and values that are centered on people. They show us how to make sure that AI supports democratic values in both business and government. The A.I. Act is also one of the first big moves that the E.U. and other governments across the world have taken to develop a list of laws for A.I. It does this in part by putting AI systems into groups according on how likely it is that they will become harmful, such unacceptable, high, moderate, and low. It creates additional rules for high-risk uses, like biometric surveillance, credit scoring, and medical devices. Pro-innovation enforcement was the only way for an EU enterprise or person to protect their basic rights.

The UNESCO Recommendation on the Ethics of Artificial Intelligence (2021) is another important step forward. The 193 member states have agreed on the first set of global rules for AI ethics. It lays out a set of values (human rights, sustainability, diversity, peace) and specific suggestions for how to handle data, the environment, gender equality, and other issues (Ozturk, 2024). This model shows that we need to think about how AI will affect things in the future across technical, legal, social, cultural, and environmental areas.

The United Nations Secretary-General's Roadmap for Digital Cooperation (2020) says that there needs to be more international cooperation around trustworthy AI. This fits with its goal of pushing for multilateralism in order to build global agreement. And organizations like the World Economic Forum (WEF) have been very important by giving people the tools they need to use AI responsibly, whether in finance or in supply chains, through things like "AI Governance Frameworks." The IEEE's "Ethically Aligned Design" project was seen as very promising by the Ethical Society (Buckley et al., 2021).

The US, Canada, China, Japan, and Singapore have all made their own AI strategies and principles. These are different from each other in terms of what they want to focus on. But they all depend on the basic ideas of openness, accountability, and putting people first in design. The Canadian Directive on Automated Decision-Making says that federal agencies can't use AI to make decisions unless they first do an algorithmic impact assessment. The draft Model AI Governance Framework from Singapore, on the other hand, focuses on things like fairness, explainability, and human oversight when it comes to AI systems used in business. China has also made ethical rules that stress privacy, control, and fairness. This again shows that everyone sees responsible AI as a strategic asset.

The fragmentation and lack of unity are still big problems for work like this. It's hard to enforce a consistent set of rules and practices because different areas have different ideas about what is fair and who is responsible for what. The EU, for example, likes a narrow, rights-based model, while the US likes a broad, sectoral, innovation-friendly model. Developing countries may have trouble enforcing ethical standards because they don't have enough resources (Challoumis, 2024). These differences could lead to regulatory silos that make it harder for countries to work together to govern AI, especially in global trade and finance, where trust and compatibility are very important. To close these gaps, we need to make international frameworks more similar, encourage countries to learn from each other's standards, and help developing countries build their capacity so that everyone can take part in the AI-powered global economy (Khan, 2024).

## 3. RESPONSIBLE AI IN GLOBAL FINANCE

Responsible AI in international finance is changing the way the world's financial systems work by making them more efficient, helping with risk management, finding fraud, making sure rules are followed, and improving customer service. At the same time, it raises moral, legal, and governance questions about how to use it in a responsible way. Making decisions in real time and looking at huge amounts of data are two big parts of the financial services industry. That's why it was one of the first to use AI.

Watson has been the main character in the AI model for a few years now. It is also the engine behind credit scoring, algorithmic trading, risk analytics, anti-money laundering (AML) monitoring, and cross-border payment solutions, among other things. If these goals aren't built into these technologies and how they're used, AI might make differences worse, keep biases going, or make markets less competitive (Rizinski et al., 2022). For example, if biased data is used to train machine learning for credit scoring, it could unintentionally leave out those with low incomes or people from minority groups. This kind of exclusion is bad for the ethics of credit scoring. In the same way, a high-frequency, algorithmic trading system that is open could make markets unstable without meaning to.

Fraud detection and risk management are two of the most important uses of responsible AI in global finance. As cybercrime and financial fraud get more complicated, organizations are using AI more and more to look through hundreds of millions of transactions in real time for anything that seems strange or suspect. Responsible AI also makes these products better by making sure that, among other things, fraud detection algorithms are fair, clear, and protect people's privacy. (Owolabi et al., 2024). For instance, responsible AI can be used in cross-border finance to find strange transaction patterns that are linked to money laundering or aiding terrorists but don't break any international laws. It protects people and businesses and makes the global financial network more reliable.

Responsible A.I. also changes how people follow regulations in other places. The Basel III capital adequacy regulations and anti-bribery and corruption laws are just two examples of the many restrictions that the international financial industry must follow. AI helps banks follow these rigorous requirements by automating the process of assessing and reporting compliance. Responsible AI also means that the Compliance Tools are clear and can be checked by regulators to make sure the algorithmic outputs are correct (Rane et al., 2023). For example, it states, "AI-driven compliance systems can automatically flag risky transactions, police sanctions lists, and make sure that international investments meet environmental, social, and governance (ESG) standards." Responsible AI that includes explainability and accountability may not only make it easier for governments to regulate, but it also gives decentralized organizations around the world more faith in the technology.

Millions of people, especially in developing countries, don't have bank accounts or don't have enough money to open one because of structural barriers. AI-powered mobile banking, microcredit systems, and digital wallets can help close this gap by giving people in those underserved communities products that better meet their financial needs. Responsible AI, on the other hand, says that these tools can't lead to predatory lending, that consumer data must be protected, and that they must be designed to work in a variety of social and economic settings (El Hajj & Hammoud, 2023). International microfinance programs' responsible AI systems can use other types of data, like mobile phone use or utility payments, to check someone's creditworthiness. They must do this in a way that is fair, unbiased, and respects human dignity. Responsible AI also helps with global financial inclusion, which is another important goal of the UN's SDGs.

AI makes responsible investing products. This is happening now and will become more essential in responsible finance. Investors are using AI technologies more and more to look at ESG performance, find green investment opportunities, and figure out long-term climate risks (Radanliey et al., 2024). AI's role in global banking isn't so much about technology as it is about putting ethics at the center of all the world's financial systems. Responsible AI helps establish trust and resilience in global finance by fostering justice in lending and trading, openness in algorithmic decision-making, and accountability in following the rules. It also aligns with ethical aims for sustainability (Addy et al., 2024). This is especially true in global financial markets, where dangers and opportunities are everywhere and the way regulations and laws are enforced and administered must be the same. In the end, ethical AI makes the global financial system fairer, greener, and stronger. It also encourages innovation and lowers the risk of the world economy.

## 3.1 Evaluating Risks and Finding Fraud

AI can quickly go through a lot of data on financial transactions to find outliers and make very accurate predictions about when financial crimes might happen. These kinds of systems help make decisions more fair, open, and accountable by following responsible AI principles. The ethical AI models lower the chance of false positives in fraud detection, which can unfairly punish customers or transactions that are otherwise legitimate. AI helps banks and regulators figure out if someone is creditworthy, keep an eye on systemic risks, and predict how the market will change. They shouldn't discriminate against people or small economies that are weak or vulnerable, but that's what's happening. Also, responsible AI helps meet international goals, like those of the Financial Action Task Force (FATF), to make sure that fraud detection systems respect privacy rights and are set up in a way that is accountable. Ethical AI in risk management and fraud detection builds trust and balances consumer protection, which makes the global financial ecosystem more stable (Rawas, 2024).

## 3.2 Following the Rules, Following the law and Cross-Border Governance

Responsible AI is changing International Finance in five important ways. Financial institutions must adhere to numerous cross-border financial regulations, such as Regulations like Basel III, Anti-Money Laundering (AML), and sanctions laws that apply in more than one country (Begum et al., 2022). AI-powered compliance tools make this process easier by looking at transactions, finding high-risk behaviors, and automating reporting requirements. But accountable AI means making these tools clear, understandable, and open to inspection so that regulators and other interested parties can trust the results of algorithms.

Responsible AI is very important for cross-border finance because it helps to balance the different regulatory needs and make it easier to deal with the local quirks that often get in the way of trade and investment flows around the world. Accountability and fairness are built into compliance systems, which means that responsible AI can protect consumers from regulatory arbitrage and help keep the global economy stable (Ahmadi, 2024). This ultimately leads to a governance model where innovation is based on legal and moral standards, which builds trust in the financial systems that are becoming more and more connected.

## 4. RESPONSIBLE AI IN GLOBAL TRADE: IMPROVING THE SUPPLY CHAIN, LOGISTICS, AND AI IN CROSS-BORDER TRANSACTIONS AND DIGITAL TRADE

The responsible AI is changing global trade by making the supply chain better, making logistics easier, and encouraging safe digital trade ecosystems. Antara The murky side of trade India's newer trade partners like African countries, Latin America and parts of central China are bound to have flimsy or no rules to monitor the extraction of raw materials and prevent their misuse. Using AI for these tasks has made them more efficient by allowing for predictive analytics, smart automation, real-time monitoring, and even fraud detection (Addy et al., 2024).

The value of AI in international trade is huge. However, responsible AI makes sure that AI technology is used in a fair, open, and accountable way. It also encourages ethical use of AI to protect vulnerable stakeholders from being taken advantage of and to avoid the risks of algorithmic bias, data misusc, and unequal access. Responsible AI is about finding the right balance between new ideas, including everyone, and rules. This is to make sure that any improvements in trade efficiency go along with global efforts to protect the environment and promote fair economic growth.

The most immediate effect of responsible AI on international trade may be better supply chain management and logistics (Chang & Ke, 2024). There are even more layers to supply chains around the world today. For example, raw material suppliers work with their manufacturers, and manufacturers work with their distributors and retailers in different countries and economies. You might not even want to save fuel or make saving fuel your top priority. You might want to think about things like traffic congestion in that part of town and how what you're doing affects the environment in terms of your carbon footprint and how that relates to Australia's greenhouse gas commitments (Jain, 2023).

Responsible AI will make logistics more open, which will also make it easier to hold people accountable. This is because stakeholders will be able to check where goods come from, how they are made, and how they are delivered. This will help stop problems like fake goods and forced labor. These ways of holding companies accountable make customers feel better about doing business with them and help them meet international standards like the UN Guiding Principles on Business and Human Rights.

Responsible AI will also change cross-border transactions, which are important for international trade but can be hard to do because of rules, changes in currency value, and the risk of fraud. AI can also make customs better by automating paperwork, making sure that tariffs and trade deals are followed, and making it easier to find fraud. AI systems that have been trained on past trade data may be able to find problems with cross-border transactions, which could mean money laundering or breaking sanctions (Herrmann, 2023). To meet these needs, AI must be responsible, which means it must follow ethical and social norms and not discriminate. It must also protect sensitive financial and business data. "The explainability of AI models ensures that regulators can audit automated decisions, which will decrease the black box that most digital trade systems. This accountability is all the more important as cross-border digital trade grows, and includes small and medium-sized enterprises (SMEs) from developing countries, who may not have the capacity to challenge such opaque or biased systems. By making AI-led transactional systems open and inclusive, responsible AI democratises access to global markets and ensures that the nexus of trust between trading partners is strengthened (Zhu et al., 2024).

AI is driving digital trade ecosystems like e-commerce platforms, digital payment systems, and blockchain-based trade documents more and more. Responsible AI means that these systems will protect consumer rights, stop anti-competitive behavior, and support fair competition in the market. For example, e-commerce companies use AI to personalize recommendations, keep track of inventory, and find fake sellers. If left to their own devices, these algorithms could favor established companies, leaving out small and medium-sized businesses and skewing fair competition.

Responsible AI builds fairness into these systems and gives all businesses, especially smaller ones, the same chance to be seen and get customers. AI in digital trade could also help protect intellectual property, automate dispute resolution, and secure smart contracts. However, it also needs legal liability and ethical safeguards for its responsible use (Khan, 2024). This is especially important because digital trade has become the backbone of global commerce, with billions of dollars in goods and services crossing the internet every day. By following responsible AI principles, digital trade systems can also help speed up inclusivity, spreading the benefits to new markets and underserved groups of people instead of just a few big players.

## 4.1 Using Predictive Analytics to Make Trade Predictions

The other side of responsible AI in global trade is about sustainability and resilience. Climate change, geopolitical instability, and pandemics have made global supply chains more vulnerable. Ethical AI lets us build stronger systems that can predict problems and suggest ways to adapt. For example, AI can predict how bad weather will affect shipping routes or how ports will get clogged. A framework that also upholds ethics will shape future predictions that are responsible, taking workers' well-being into account and making sure that risks are fairly distributed and vulnerable economies recover fairly. In this way, responsible AI could help not only efficiency but also the robustness and sustainability of the global trading network (Delecraz et al., 2022).

Even though responsible AI has the potential to change the game, putting it into practice in global trade is still hard. The region's fragmented regulatory framework, the lack of universal standards and universal data privacy challenges, and the difference in technical capacity between developed and emerging markets all make it hard to roll out AI fairly and universally. For example, as advanced economies use advanced AI to speed up logistics, developing economies may have trouble accessing or regulating such technology, which could make the digital divide even bigger. To meet these challenges, global governance frameworks on AI need to be harmonized, capacity building initiatives are needed, and international cooperation in organizations like the WTO and the WEF are necessary. Responsible AI can have its benefits in global trade distributed equitably only with governance of the AI mechanisms in place (Jain et al., 2024).

## 5. RISKS, CHALLENGES, AND GOVERNANCE: THE NEED FOR REGULATORY FRAGMENTATION AND HARMONIZATION

The growth of responsibility in international finance and trade, as well as in business in general, creates big chances and big risks, as well as big problems with governance. The most important of these is the need for regulatory fragmentation and harmonization. At the moment, there is no uniform international regulation of AI because different solutions are becoming popular in different parts of the world, such as the European Union, the United States, China, and other economies that are growing. The European Union's proposed Artificial Intelligence Act focuses on high-risk thresholds, human-in-the-loop provisions, and transparency. The United States, on the other hand, has so far favored sectoral, market-led regulation. China is moving to regulate A.I. through state-centric, security-focused measures.

This difference makes things harder for multinational companies, makes it harder for businesses to work together across borders, and makes it more expensive for banks and trade partners to follow the rules when using AI (Werder et al., 2022). Regulatory arbitrage, or the movement of businesses to places with lower standards, could also happen if the rules are not clear. This would hurt ethical norms and the rights of consumers. The lack of consistent data governance laws in trade, especially when it comes to digital privacy, digital taxation, and data flow across borders, makes it harder to use AI-enabled systems in logistics and e-commerce.

AI governance must be global in scope, grounded in a collective understanding of fairness, accountability, transparency, and ethics, while also being attuned to the nuances of each domestic market. The OECD, G20, WTO, and UNCTAD have all started working on harmonization, but none of them have a treaty or a way to monitor and enforce it. A unified global governance could lower the cost of implementation, provide a public benefit, foster trust in the digital financial system, and promote responsible AI for sustainable development, rather than exacerbating societal disparities. To make sure that countries in the global South aren't left out of setting the AI trade and finance agenda, we need to work together with other countries, build conversations that include both developed and developing economies, and use public-private partnerships (Nakao et al., 2023).

## 6. CONCLUSION

The challenge of responsible AI in international finance and global trade is changing quickly. This brings up a lot of ethical, regulatory, and governance issues, but it also holds a lot of promise for change. Fair, open, accountable, and ethical AI was shown to help manage risk, find fraud more easily, lower compliance costs, make cross-border trade logistics easier, and encourage long-term financial and trade practices. But there are problems with policy silos, ethical dilemmas, data privacy issues, and unequal access to responsible AI tools that make it hard to use and apply on a large scale.

We live in a world of finance and trade that is becoming more digital and connected. Let's also get to work on the important task of building systems that work for everyone. So, in the future, there should be more work done in the area of international cooperation with multilateral groups like the OECD, WTO, IMF, and UNCTAD to create interoperable standards that protect people while still allowing for new ideas. AI can also be used in green trade and sustainable finance projects to help meet the UN's Sustainable Development Goals and promote growth that includes everyone.

For AI and people who watch over it to be useful, they need to be able to explain things in a way that makes sense. This is very important for building trust between people in each country and between people from different countries. Policy should be based on how countries are growing so that there aren't any global digital divides or power imbalances when it comes to governing AI-powered trade and finance. AI can be the foundation of strong, open, and fair global economic systems if governments, businesses, and international organizations work together to create flexible governance systems that can keep up with technological progress. The future of AI in finance and trade is not just about getting more done, but also about creating a fair, responsible, and trusted global digital economy.

## REFERENCES


Addy, W. A., Ajayi-Nifise, A. O., Bello, B. G., Tula, S. T., Odeyem, O., & Falaiye, T. (2024). Algorithmic trading and AI: A review of strategies and market impact. *World Journal of Advanced Engineering Technology and Sciences*, *11*(1), 258–267. DOI: 10.30574/wjaets.2024.11.1.0054

Addy, W. A., Ajayi-Nifise, A. O., Bello, B. G., Tula, S. T., Odeyemi, O., & Falaiye, T. (2024). Machine learning in financial markets: A critical review of algorithmic trading and risk management. *International Journal of Science and Research Archive*, *11*(1), 1853–1862. DOI: 10.30574/ijsra.2024.11.1.0292

Ahmadi, S. (2024). A thorough examination of the integration of big data and AI in the financial sector and its implications for current and future opportunities. *International Journal of Current Science Research and Review*, *7*(01), 66–74. DOI: 10.47191/ijcsrr/V7-i1-07

Begum, A., Munira, M. S. K., & Juthi, S. (2022). Systematic Review Of Blockchain Technology In Trade Finance And Banking Security. *American Journal of Scholarly Research and Innovation*, *1*(01), 25–52. DOI: 10.63125/vs65vx40

Buckley, R. P., Zetzsche, D. A., Arner, D. W., & Tang, B. W. (2021). Regulating artificial intelligence in finance: Putting the human in the loop. *The Sydney Law Review*, *43*(1), 43–81.

Challoumis, C. (2024, November). The landscape of AI in Finance. In *XVII International Scientific Conference* (pp. 109-144).

Chang, Y. L., & Ke, J. (2024). Socially responsible artificial intelligence empowered people analytics: A novel framework towards sustainability. *Human Resource Development Review*, *23*(1), 88–120. DOI: 10.1177/15344843231200930

Delecraz, S., Eltarr, L., Becuwe, M., Bouxin, H., Boutin, N., & Oullier, O. (2022). Responsible Artificial Intelligence in Human Resources Technology: An innovative inclusive and fair by design matching algorithm for job recruitment purposes. *Journal of Responsible Technology*, *11*, 100041. DOI: 10.1016/j.jrt.2022.100041

El Hajj, M., & Hammoud, J. (2023). Unveiling the influence of artificial intelligence and machine learning on financial markets: A comprehensive analysis of AI applications in trading, risk management, and financial operations. *Journal of Risk and Financial Management*, *16*(10), 434. DOI: 10.3390/jrfm16100434

Fritz-Morgenthal, S., Hein, B., & Papenbrock, J. (2022). Financial risk management and explainable, trustworthy, responsible AI. *Frontiers in Artificial Intelligence*, *5*, 779799. DOI: 10.3389/frai.2022.779799 PMID: 35295866

Herrmann, H. (2023). The future of responsible artificial intelligence: A path forward through responsible innovation. *Heliyon*, *9*(3), e14379. DOI: 10.1016/j.heliyon.2023.e14379 PMID: 36967876

Jain, R. (2023). The function of artificial intelligence in banking and finance. *Journal of Management and Science*, *13*(3), 1–4. DOI: 10.26524/jms.13.27

Jain, V., Balakrishnan, A., Beeram, D., Najana, M., & Chintale, P. (2024). Utilizing artificial intelligence to improve regulatory compliance within the financial sector. *International Journal of Computer Trends and Technology*, *72*(5), 124–140. DOI: 10.14445/22312803/IJCTT-V72I5P116

Khan, A. (2024). The intersection of artificial intelligence and international trade laws: Challenges and opportunities. *IIUMLJ*, *32*(1), 103–152. DOI: 10.31436/iiumlj.v32i1.912

Khan, A. K. (2024). AI in Finance: Disruptive Technologies and Emerging Opportunities. Journal of Artificial Intelligence General Science (JAIGS) ISSN: 3006-4023, 3(1), 155-170.

Nakao, Y., Strappelli, L., Stumpf, S., Naseer, A., Regoli, D., & Gamba, G. D. (2023). Towards responsible AI: A design space exploration of human-centered artificial intelligence user interfaces to investigate fairness. *International Journal of Human-Computer Interaction*, *39*(9), 1762–1788. DOI: 10.1080/10447318.2022.2067936

Owolabi, O. S., Uche, P. C., Adeniken, N. T., Ihejirika, C., Islam, R. B., Chhetri, B. J. T., & Jung, B. (2024). Ethical implications of artificial intelligence (AI) adoption in financial decision-making. *Computer and Information Science*, *17*(1), 1–49. DOI: 10.5539/cis.v17n1p49

Ozturk, O. (2024). The influence of AI on global commerce: Prospects and obstacles. *Economies*, *12*(11), 298. DOI: 10.3390/economies12110298

Rane, N., Choudhary, S., & Rane, J. (2023). Blockchain and Artificial Intelligence (AI) integration for revolutionizing security and transparency in finance. Available at *SSRN* 4644253. DOI: 10.2139/ssrn.4644253

Rawas, S. (2024). AI: The future of humanity. *Discover Artificial Intelligence*, *4*(1), 25. DOI: 10.1007/s44163-024-00118-3

Ridzuan, N. N., Masri, M., Anshari, M., Fitriyani, N. L., & Syafrudin, M. (2024). AI in the financial sector: The line between innovation, regulation and ethical responsibility. *Information (Basel), 15*(8), 432. DOI: 10.3390/info15080432

Rizinski, M., Peshov, H., Mishev, K., Chitkushev, L. T., Vodenska, I., & Trajanov, D. (2022). Ethically responsible machine learning in fintech. *IEEE Access : Practical Innovations, Open Solutions, 10*, 97531–97554. DOI: 10.1109/ACCESS.2022.3202889

Werder, K., Ramesh, B., & Zhang, R. (2022). Establishing data provenance for responsible artificial intelligence systems. [TMIS]. *ACM Transactions on Management Information Systems, 13*(2), 1–23. DOI: 10.1145/3503488

Zhu, Y., Yu, K., Wei, M., Pu, Y., & Wang, Z. (2024). AI-enhanced administrative prosecutorial supervision in financial big data: New concepts and functions for the digital era. *Journal of Advanced Computing Systems, 4*(5), 10–26. DOI: 10.69987/JACS.2024.40502

# Chapter 4
# Bias, Ethics and Accountability in AI-Driven ESG Analytics

**Aparna Marwah**
http://orcid.org/0000-0001-6758-4424
*Institute of Management and Research, Bharati Vidyapeeth, New Delhi, India*

**Daljeet Singh Bawa**
*Institute of Management and Research, Bharati Vidyapeeth, New Delhi, India*

**Taruna Gulati**
*Department of Computer Science Engineering, Guru Tegh Bahadur 4th Centenary Engineering College, Guru Gobind Singh Indraprastha University, New Delhi, India*

## ABSTRACT

*This chapter addresses the environmental, social, and governance (ESG) principles in order to address these global issues and promote more sustainable behaviors. The technology that has received a lot of attention and is being used in many different sectors is artificial intelligence. ESG must be included into AI if we want to reduce risks, hold it responsible and make it contribute to ethical investment and societal objectives. The concept of artificial intelligence is transforming environmental, social and governance-oriented analytics in the new digital economy. So, ESG-scoring techniques, which include a company's sustainability, social impact, and governance performance, are being supplemented by AI technologies that can manage massive volumes of organized and unstructured data.*

DOI: 10.4018/979-8-2600-1308-3.ch004

# 1. INTRODUCTION

The difficult issues AI has with bias, ethics, and transparency in ESG analytics have an impact on the legitimacy, openness, and equity of sustainable evaluations. The dependability of the AI systems that provide these rankings determines how much faith can be placed in ethical business practices and sustainable financing. This is due to the fact that ESG evaluations are used to guide trillions of dollars' worth of investments. However, prejudice is likely the largest issue with AI-driven ESG assessments (Elhady & Shohieb, 2025). It originates from a variety of various sources, including data selection, computational decisions, and tags. But it also originates from the human judgment that is subjectively used while creating an ESG report. ESG data is widely dispersed and unreliable. ESG information may be found in a variety of places, including regulatory filings, social media, media sentiment, and business disclosures. This implies that the context in which it is utilized also affects it. These AI models, which are trained on historical patterns, have the potential to strengthen or even exacerbate institutional or societal prejudices if the data demonstrates them, such as the underrepresentation of enterprises in developing nations or the gender bias in corporate leadership reports.

Firms that adhere to Eurocentric reporting requirements may get too much credit from a model trained on mostly Western corporate data, whereas firms in developing economies that use local sustainable practices may receive less credit. It is not the first Chinese data collection. Bad ESG ratings may result from sentiment analysis algorithms that examine social and governance risks misinterpreting data items that are culturally or linguistically particular or that are not in english (Chang & Ke, 2024). In this sense, bias in AI-powered ESG analytics is a profoundly systemic issue that highlights the unfairness of global information ecosystems rather than only being a technological one.

## 1.1. Evolution of ESG (Environmental, Social, and Governance) Metrics

Making algorithms transparent and responsible for their activities is one of the ethical concerns in AI-driven ESG analytics, along with avoiding bias. Robots that resolve financial and environmental conflicts must also adhere to ethical AI standards of justice, responsibility, non-harm, and legal rights. There are several ethical concerns since many of the AI models that underpin ESG score, such as deep learning and proprietary algorithms, don't clearly state their solutions. Trust is weakened and it becomes more difficult for third parties to verify ESG ratings when investors, regulators, or companies are unable to understand how they are calculated. AI designs also prioritize the commercial materiality above social or environmental well-being, ethical concerns arise. This perspective turns sustainability into a metric for profit and therefore, ethical AI in ESG must ensure that algorithmic evaluations are grounded in the larger sustainable development objectives (SDGs) rather than only in a single company's interests. To achieve this, it must include human-centered ideals into AI models that support democratic government, environmental stewardship and social justice.

## 1.2. Role of Artificial Intelligence and Data Analytics in ESG Evaluation

There are various parties, including data producers, algorithm developers, rating agencies, and business users, should share this obligation. However, when the AI systems are so dispersed, that becomes more difficult. It is much more difficult to hold someone responsible when errors or biases occur since many ESG rating organizations depend on data from outside sources and machine learning algorithms from outside suppliers. The only way to prevent this is to have strong governance systems. So, viewing AI through an ESG lens empowers investors and organizations to manage impacts and guide sustainable AI development. Despite its significance, this area remains underexplored. To address this gap, we introduce the ESG-AI framework for investors, developed from insights. The programming officer is represented by the "dimensions of fairness" and the "mechanisms of reflecting algorithmic auditing, impact assessment, and ethical review should be institutionalized to make sure that ESG analytics follow principles of justice and transparency." As, the proposed AI Act from the European Union already establishes legal guidelines for AI responsibility. These consist of risk assessment, disclosures of transparency, and human supervision of high-risk applications of AI, such as sustainability or financial services analytics.

## 1.3. Significance of Addressing Bias, Ethics, and Accountability: Understanding AI-Driven ESG Analytics

The absence of uniformity in AI techniques and ESG reporting also leads to the ethical conundrum. Because they use different data sources, techniques, or algorithmic weightings, the many ESG rating agencies often assign disparate ratings to the same issuer. These AI models' outputs are predicated on the system's inconsistency and unreliability. This discrepancy fails the ESG-investor accountability and ethical fairness tests. Future sustainability developments, such as a company's pledge to decarbonize or develop new socially responsible practices, are difficult to predict due to AI's strong dependence on previous data. Instead of pushing companies to alter their business practices, algorithmic ESG analytics will therefore continue to depend on a last-ditch effort to maintain the status quo. Therefore, these models of continuous learning with sustainability indicators that look forward the future while being frank about the models' limitations and assumptions will need to be the focus of ethical governance.

## 2. THE DATA PIPELINE: FROM ESG DATA SOURCES TO AI MODELS

Explainable AI (XAI) has the potential to address these issues by facilitating more transparency and understanding of ESG statistics. Also, unlike explainable AI (XAI) frameworks, black box models do not provide human-interpretable explanations for algorithmic results. XAI may be used in ESG applications to identify bias in data inputs, identify the elements that most affected a firm's environmental or social rating, and explain why a company obtained a certain grade. By establishing trust, it puts a lot of pressure on data scientists and AI engineers to work with investments. However, moral integrity can only be partially replaced by explainability. In the event that the underlying data or design goal does not conform to sustainability standards, a model may be understandable but also display prejudice or immoral traits.

Explainability has to be positioned under an all-encompassing framework of ethical governance and algorithmic responsibility. This methodical approach provides a framework for evaluating the substantial effects of AI, closely examining business pledges to ethical AI, and reducing the dangers involved. By discussing how it was developed and what it is composed of, we demonstrate how it may be utilized to advance digital sustainability, assist individuals in making ethical investments in AI, and assist them in making better judgments. This research shows how effective the framework is in guiding AI innovation toward ESG principles, which is advantageous for businesses and society as a whole (Bahangulu & Owusu-Berko, 2025).

### 2.1 Machine Learning and Natural Language Processing in ESG Ratings

These concepts are related is shown by the discussion of bias, ethics and responsibility in AI-augmented ESG analytics. The first safeguards our moral position against prejudice, the second ensures that accountability procedures are equitable and do not give preference to those in positions of power, and the third provides the framework necessary to identify and assess bias. When these factors are combined, responsible AI becomes a long-term governance operational plan. An organization's performance in corporate governance, environmental sustainability, and social responsibility may be evaluated using the Environmental, Social, and Governance

(ESG) framework. Aside from financial indicators (which are normally looked at by new recruits), these types of broad characteristics may be utilized to assess how well a firm is performing and what kind of image it is creating throughout the globe (Jo, 2025).

The fast expanding area of artificial intelligence may have an influence on company development comparable to that of electricity and the internet. Businesses might use it to create products and services, access new markets, conserve energy, and provide value for consumers. One method to consider how these three affinities should cooperate is to use a multi-tiered approach. For instance, algorithmic audits may assist identify systemic problems, data governance can help ensure quality and representativity, ethical review boards can help ensure that we adhere to our shared values, and regulatory monitoring can help ensure that we are legally accountable. By ensuring that a range of opinions and values are taken into consideration when creating and using algorithms, cooperation between many stakeholders including the investors, regulators, companies, AI developers, and civil society can also contribute to the democratic nature of ESG analytics.

### 2.2 Predictive Modelling for Sustainability and Corporate Governance

The businesses and legislators worldwide are beginning to recognize that ethical and responsible AI methods must be a part of ESG analytics. Also the fairness, transparency, human-centered methods, and risk management are at the core of the EU AI Act, the UNESCO Recommendation on the Ethics of Artificial Intelligence, and the OECD AI Principles. Sustainable finance and responsible AI have also been discussed often by SEBI and NITI Aayog in India. So, following of these guidelines will be challenging, however, since they must be applied in various data and jurisdictional contexts (Fernandes et al., 2024). It is particularly the difficult for developing nations to develop their capacity for AI governance, which hinders their ability to participate in international ESG analytics networks that are mostly managed by Western businesses. It must address these inequities in order to make the AI-ESG canvas more equitable globally.

## 3. NATURE OF BIAS IN ESG ALGORITHMS

The investors, companies and regulators now see sustainable performance in Environmental, Social, and Governance (ESG) analytics differently because to artificial intelligence and machine learning (ML). They may get real-time risk assessments and sustainability information by using AI-powered ESG systems that can analyze vast volumes of complex data in real time, such as business disclosures, satellite photos, and social media sentiment. Data-driven, formulaic-algorithmic, human, and systemic forms are all included in ESG algorithms; inclusion is not one-sided and takes place within the institutional and social framework of ESG governance.

The source of bias in ESG algorithms is data bias, or the biases present in the corpus used to train AI models. A range of sources, including news stories, business reports, NGO databases, and third-party sustainability indicators, may provide information on each ESG criteria. These sources vary in terms of quality, completeness and representativeness. As the large international corporation, for example, is probably able to provide comprehensive sustainability statistics and has solid disclosure standards (Pria et al., 2024). The smaller companies or those in developing nations may not be able to the provide such thorough information.

AI models trained on these imbalanced datasets often reward better-reporting enterprises over those that are really more sustainable. So, the biased ESG data from corporate reports may be the result of selective disclosure and green-washing. The algorithms that are trained on biased data will unavoidably partially replicate corporate narratives and giving preference to businesses who have mastered sustainability reporting over those that behave in a really favorable manner in real life. ESG analytics data skew often reflects knowledge asymmetries seen in international marketplaces (Rane et al., 2024).

## 3.1 Measuring and Auditing Bias in ESG AI Systems

The biases in the corpora used to train the AI systems are the reason why ESG algorithms might be prejudiced. Each of these ESG criteria may be found in a variety of sources, such as news stories, corporate reports, databases maintained by non-governmental organizations, and third-party sustainability indices. These data varies in terms of representativeness, quality, and extent. A major international firm, for instance, is likely to have high disclosure requirements and be able to provide you with comprehensive information about its sustainability. The smaller or more recent businesses in developing areas may be not have as much comprehensive data.

As a result, AI models trained on this imbalanced information often give preference to businesses that report better than those that are more sustainable. Also, selective disclosure and greenwashing may skew company ESG data in reports. The algorithms that are trained on biased data will unavoidably replicate corporate narratives may giving preference to companies who excel in sustainability reporting over those that carry out positive actions in real life (Islam & Faria, 2025). Therefore, information asymmetries that are visible in international marketplaces are often shown by the data skew in ESG analytics.

The subjective assessments and presumptions that analysts, programmers, and rating agencies make on ESG are shown by those related to human and cognitive biases. Although artificial intelligence systems are frequently seen as objective instruments, they are really human-made and represent the beliefs and values of their designers. A study team led by an ESG advisor determines which frameworks such as GRI, SASB, and TCFD to use, which indicators are most crucial, and how to translate qualitative evaluations into quantitative data. So, everything from classifying data and creating features to analyzing models is methodically skewed by these arbitrary decisions. Western analysts could concentrate on corporate governance frameworks such as the independence of board members, but Asian analysts might concentrate on the standards of stakeholder harmony and relationship-based trust. These epistemic biases affect how AI models are taught and how ESG standards are applied to across cultural and legal divides. Because of the social and economic context as well as the developer's background, AI systems that seem neutral are often biased (Khaddam & Alzghoul, 2025).

## 4. ETHICAL DIMENSIONS OF AI-DRIVEN ESG ANALYTICS

The systemic and the structural bias is a much greater issue in ESG analytics than algorithmic or human prejudice. The structural bias is supported by the worldwide imbalance of data infrastructure, regulatory requirements, and ESG reporting standards. The majority of AI-powered ESG frameworks are developed in developed economies with established data access and regulatory frameworks in North America and Europe. As, these algorithms may not be appropriate for the unique development requirements or cultural backgrounds of the Global South since they are predicated on Western conceptions of sustainability (Domingo, 2025).

The environmental metrics that focus on carbon footprint could not adequately capture the social sustainability context of rural livelihoods or informal employment in underdeveloped countries. The kind of epistemic injustice known as structural prejudice occurs when some knowledge systems and value systems are given preference in the global conversation on sustainability while others are marginalized. The fact that large ESG rating agencies and AI analytics firms have significant influence on sustainability narratives and investment trends further exacerbates this bias.

### 4.1. Principles of Responsible and Ethical AI

The data, computational, human and structural biases are cross-collateralized, creating a feedback cycle that exacerbates ESG analytics distortions. The algorithmic bias guides human interpretation, data bias informs algorithmic design and the structural bias provides institutional support for these tendencies. As, money will likely continue to flow to businesses that meet a biased concept of sustainability, for instance, if biased AI algorithms provide ESG ratings that influence investment choices. In addition to causing poor markets and pricing, this unhealthy cycle also hinders the effectiveness of ESG principles. A loop of prejudice might be created by discriminatory ESG algorithms if the undervalued enterprises are consistently found in underdeveloped locations, sectors with more subtle societal repercussions, or a place that isn't used to sustainable measures.

ESG algorithms have a variety of biases, including as financial, social, and moral ones. Inaccurate ESG ratings may result in poor capital allocation and risk management. By making lenders even more skeptical of how successfully ESG ratings assist companies in strengthening their corporate governance, they may erode societal trust. Because they provide preference to some actors and narratives over others, these biases contradict the ESG's commitment to justice, fairness, and sustainability (Mitra & Maity, 2025). Due to the widespread automation of these biases, AI systems have made unjust choices the norm. This makes locating and repairing them challenging. In addition to being a technical need, worries about bias in ESG algorithms are also a moral and governance requirement.

## 4.2. Ethical Implications of Automated ESG Scoring and Rating Systems

The measuring of a company's sustainability performance has also become simpler with the increasing usage of AI in ESG analytics. However, it raises a number of ethical concerns around accountability, transparency, and justice. In order to provide automated scores and grades, the AI for ESG uses algorithms to analyze vast volumes of environmental, social, and commercial data. So, even if these systems are fair and scalable, discrimination is more likely to occur if they are badly designed and operated. The difficulty of comprehending how algorithms make judgments is a significant ethical concern. This is among the factors that make it difficult for regulators, investors, and the general public to comprehend how firms are assessed. As a result, consumers struggle to make wise selections and don't believe the ratings (Safeei et al., 2025). Such ambiguity may not only conceal systemic (system-level) biases but also result in unethical outcomes, such as over-reporting sustainability ratings by top-line stating or green-washing corporations.

## 5. ACCOUNTABILITY AND GOVERNANCE FRAMEWORKS

AI and ESG Governance There are several ethical concerns with accountability and governance frameworks when using AI for environmental, social, and governance (ESG) analytics. These illustrations demonstrate how automated decision-making systems may preserve justice, accountability, and trust. There is more to being responsible than just abiding by the law. It also entails being aware of the obligations and the risks associated with algorithmic ESG review.

Therefore, the metaphor only goes so far in describing our relationship with AIs, even though AI systems are becoming more important in directing our investment flows (for instance, when businesses jeopardize their sustainability policies or reputations) and because the absence of clear accountability mechanisms is an ethical risk (where moral disengagement is possible and decisions are unclear). Openness, fairness, inclusiveness, and explainability are ethical issues that must be included into governance frameworks that enable ESG-related analytics at any level of development and service delivery (Homavazir et al., 2025). In order to share responsibilities with algorithm creators, sound ethical governance requires a cooperative structure among stakeholders, including data sources, businesses, ESG rating organizations, and regulators. This sacrifice becomes more tangible and difficult to overlook when everyone stands to lose something. The aim is to ensure that individuals cannot "get around it" by disbanding groups or by making the technology too demanding.

The other ethical issue with ESG governance is an unfair allocation of access and authority. Large banks and western rating agencies are the sources of the vast collection of AI-driven ESG models. These models often include culturally biased or one-dimensional sustainability norms that may not be applicable elsewhere in the globe (Alshi, 2025). There are concerns about epistemic unfairness would arise from this focus as it ignores other ethical viewpoints, particularly those from poor nations, when creating global sustainability standards. For the ethical decision-making to avoid monopolization, fair governance must be pluralistic and participative, including opinions from all sectors. In order for stakeholders to understand how ESG ratings are determined and contest inaccurate or unjust classifications, government systems must also let the public to see how AI operates in accordance with the ethical concept of transparency.

The ESG frameworks for monitoring non-financial risks and obligations are causing investors, who are often stockholders and have significant influence over how businesses utilize AI, to become more concerned. However, the majority of ESG ratings still don't probe AI sufficiently, thus they lack a clear method for identifying and addressing more surface-level RAI. RAI and ESG share many of the same goals and approaches (Thiruma Valavan, 2023). AI poses significant issues that need an

ESG framework to address. Among them include energy consumption, prejudice and discrimination, loss of employment, privacy issues and a lack of openness. Companies may consider initiatives that do not adhere to RAI regulations yet have ethical issues, reputational hazards, or regulatory issues that conflict with their ESG objectives since there is no RAI supervision. It is not intended to be a stand-alone item, but rather a component of the ESG framework. This is how it can contribute to and view responsible AI from an ESG perspective.

The accountability tools have moral value because they embody the answerability principle, which is the moral duty to defend deeds and right wrongs. ESG is susceptible to moral hazard and is likely to be exploited if there is no good governance counterpart (Iyer et al., 2025). This need regulations that standardize algorithmic audits and ethical review boards in engineering in order to lower these hazards. As, among other things, it must use social and environmental indices to monitor AI's contribution to society (Suri & Sadriwala, 2025). The ethical credibility for AI-enabled ESG governance has to go beyond simple compliance and promote a morally responsible culture that demands accountability, equality, and transparency in all machine-driven choices that affect sustainability throughout the world.

## 6. AI EXPLAINABILITY AND TRUST IN ESG ANALYTICS: TECHNIQUES FOR ENHANCING EXPLAINABILITY AND INTERPRETABILITY

The aspects of monitoring and reporting on sustainability and corporate responsibility may be facilitated by the use of AI and machine learning in ESG analysis. In order to get more and better information, banks, governments, and companies may now search through vast volumes of data, including supply chains, human rights reports, and carbon declarations. People are interested in knowing more about how sustainability ratings and classifications are produced using AI and machine learning algorithms used in ESG analytics. This is due to the fact that ESG analytics play a significant role in influencing public opinion, deciding which legislation to enact, and deciding which investments to make. Explainable AI (XAI), a broader area that includes AI explainability, is crucial for fostering justice, accountability, and confidence in ESG evaluation frameworks (Naqvi & Momin, 2025). Therefore, the most crucial concern is not whether AI can provide ESG ratings with accuracy, but rather whether or not humans can comprehend, verify, and have faith in the models' decision-making processes.

In artificial intelligence, explainability refers to a system's ability to articulate how and why it arrived at a certain decision or forecast. To discuss how an AI model ranks a company's sustainability based on factors like emissions figures, gender diversity, and corporate governance standards, it may be referred to as ESG analytics. Because it's difficult to understand how they make decisions, there exist neural networks and other deep learning and traditional machine learning models (Ozkan, 2024). This is particularly problematic in the context of ESG, where stakeholders need lucid, ethical assessments that impact a company's financial viability and public perception. If ESG ratings are difficult for consumers to grasp or don't align with the opinions of human experts or grading systems, they may be disregarded. Being candid does not build trust. The first, confidence in AI, stems from the second: without transparent decision-making procedures, investors, regulators, and society as a whole will not be able to accept that AI-driven ESG analytics are impartial, fair and morally fulfilling.

## 7. BIAS, ETHICS AND ACCOUNTABILITY: BALANCING INNOVATION WITH REGULATION AND SOCIAL RESPONSIBILITY

Laws and moral norms will finally ensure that justice, accountability, and transparency are maintained, even if they may not be able to catch up with AI-based ESG analytics fast enough. To counterbalance technology that prevents prejudice, injustice, or moral anarchy, we need technology that promotes equality and social inclusion. How to keep ahead of the competition in the digital era without violating the law or acting unethically is one of the main challenges. This is the issue that arises when responsibility, ethics, and prejudice are combined in AI systems, particularly in ESG analytics (Irfan et al., 2025).

Because it helps identify risks to global sustainability, where to invest, and how companies are behaving, artificial intelligence (AI) is crucial to sustainable finance. The AI bias is more than just a flaw in the system; it's a social and moral problem that dictates who gains from novel concepts and who must bear their repercussions. In te ESG analytics or any other context, biased algorithms have the potential to exacerbate already-existing disparities by misrepresenting qualitative data such as that pertaining to cultural diversity and community welfare, misweighing social factors or distorting businesses based on developing economies. While ostensibly impartial, the AI models trained on historical data that represent socioeconomic gaps at the local or nation-state level may unintentionally replicate these injustices. So, ESG algorithms that prioritize financial indicators over ethical ones can also exhibit bias. Sustainability becomes a commodity as a result. It is more than just technological solutions, like rebalancing data sets or using fairness measurements are needed to address this prejudice; a deep ethic of concern for the moral and ethical principles hidden in algorithms is also necessary (Salim, 2025). The ethical AI needs to be aware of whose viewpoints, information, and priorities it incorporates and whose it does not fully understand.

Ethics will thus serve as the cornerstone of responsible innovation as they need to provide guidelines for the application of AI. In addition to data quality, accountability, autonomy, fairness, and transparency are ethical concerns related to AI in ESG. When AIs really comprehend human culture and profit-making is no longer sufficient, they will take control. Beyond only optimizing profits, sustainability analytics must take into account all societal effects, such as advancing environmental health and social justice. This implies that principles like beneficence, non-maleficence not harming others and justice ensuring that things are fair should permeate every stage of the AI life cycle, from data collection to deployment. Algorithmic transparency, or the capacity for those impacted by AI processes to comprehend them, and explainability and the ability for humans to verify the reasoning behind choices, are also necessary for ethical governance (AR & BRAHMBHATT, 2025). The insufficient safeguards might allow market forces to seize control of AI advancements in order to benefit from the legitimacy that comes with "sustainability" without being held accountable for their actions. Therefore, the foundation of ethical AI is not neutrality toward technology but rather moral intent: creating systems that benefit everyone and represent human ideals.

The concept of accountability transforms moral values into enforceable regulations, allowing individuals and institutions to be held accountable for AI choices. The accountability in the context of ESG analytics refers to the duty of data sources, model developers, ratings sellers, and investors to ensure that assessments of social effect are impartial and accurate. However, accountability is distributed in the majority of AI applications. For instance, it might be difficult to assign blame when it comes to data and algorithms (Hussain, 2025). This must be audit algorithms, do effect analyses, and take ethics into account in order to hold them responsible.

The combining of the innovation with regulation does not halt technological advancement; rather, it directs it toward societally beneficial objectives (Huang & Yao, 2025). The excessive regulation might hinder innovation and restrict AI's capacity to address sustainability-related issues. However, a lack of control may result in prejudice, abuse, and moral failings. The adaptive regulation and the governance structure that can evolve with new technologies, is the aim. This is what the European legislation attempts to achieve, however it is not always effective. It must be adopt a co-regulatory strategy that combines volunteer ethical norms with legal requirements (Behera et al., 2024). Also, the regulatory sandboxes would allow innovators to test AI-enabled solutions under the supervision of a system that strikes a balance between experimentation and responsibility. There are number of different individuals would be able to join together to define standards for ethical AI in ESG applications with the aid of multi-stakeholder governance, which includes regulators, AI developers and users, investors or purchasers of AI goods and services, and civil society. People may be brought together by this type of knowledge which also enables creativity based on what it means to be human (UGWUODO et al., 2024). It may guard against technological determinism, which occurs when computers make moral and social decisions without human input.

Therefore, social responsibility provides us with the moral direction we need in order to strike a balance between innovation and control. It would serve as a reminder to businesses and AI developers that technological advancements should not just help one firm but also benefit everyone. The second aspect of the Responsible Use of AI for ESG Analytics Social responsibility in the context of ESG analytics refers to ensuring that AI systems support rather than undermine public confidence in sustainability reporting. Then there are AI systems that affect emerging economies and local communities. They don't need to be pampered, yet they are the ones who most require representation. "Learn." Being transparent about data, granting fair access to technology, and upholding people's privacy and dignity are all components of socially responsible AI governance (Nauman, 2025). Additionally, because we are living in a data-driven sustainability era, companies and organizations need to answer for their actions and compliance with the law.

## 8. COMPARATIVE ANALYSIS: GLOBAL PRACTICES AND STANDARDS

The dynamic ecosystem with a range of regulatory ideologies, ethical perspectives and institutional skills is shown by a comparative study of international best practices and standards in AI ESG analytics. The AI is used in the sustainability reporting, investment decision-making and corporate accountability in a variety of ways. Each has taken a different approach to addressing prejudice which ensuring that AI is used honestly and transparently, and maintaining ethical governance in specific AI application domains (Alshahmy & Sahiner, 2024). The aspects of philosophical conflicts about governance models based on innovation and rights, these variances demonstrate that individuals throughout the globe have varied preferences. The understanding of these distinctions is crucial to developing uniform worldwide rules that encourage ethical AI development while preserving the environment and society.

Governments in the EU are collaborating on AI-enabled ESG. The origins of regulatory philosophy are not limited to these sources. It is the world's most comprehensive AI legislation and has been in force since 2024. It divides AI systems into four categories according to their level of hazard. Minimal Levels Unacceptable, Limited, and High Level. Sector research claims that ESG data analytics is a kind of “high-risk” activity that may quickly result in automated judgments that might affect society and the economy (Chakrabarti et al., 2025). The regulation specifies that algorithms must be able to be understood by both computers and humans, and they must also be reviewed for prejudice and danger. The SFDR and CSRD concentrate on the ethical use of AI for sharing non-financial data and rating sustainability performance. The EU's strategy is unique since it integrates AI governance with environmental objectives. This supports the ethical and legal connection between new ideas or technology and preserving the environment and acting in the best interests of society (Abdellatif, 2025).

In the US, we think businesses should have self-control rather than aggressive legislation. Although the US lacks legislation similar to the EU AI Act, many agencies, including the FTC and SEC, have released recommendations for AI and ESG experts that support transparency, equity, and consumer protection. The optional manual on how to create and use AI in an ethical, transparent, and trustworthy manner. The private ESG rating businesses may have their own criteria and potential conflicts of interest since there aren't many regulations governing what constitutes ESG data or ratings (Vali et al., 2024). An excellent illustration of liberal market philosophy is the US system. It is founded on laissez-faire principles that respect creativity and companies' autonomy. But it also brings up ethical concerns regarding the distribution of duties and the possibility of algorithmic bias in the absence of safeguards.

When it comes to regulations, the UK falls in between the EU's cautious approach and the US's market-driven system. The principles of safety, transparency, equity, and accountability form the foundation of its adaptable and industry-focused AI regulation system. A code of ethics for the use of AI in financial and sustainability evaluations has been developed by the FCA and the Department for Business and Trade. ESG integration and AI governance are also connected to the UK Green Finance strategy. It states that models and indicators for sustainability should be transparent (BENAISSA et al., 2025). So, in addition to providing rewards to businesses that adhere to the highest ethical standards, its pragmatic, value-based design permits flexibility without raising the cost of compliance.

There are a lot of varied approaches in the Asia-Pacific area due to variations in the economy and regulatory requirements. According to Japan's 2019 Social Principles of Human-Centric AI, society and AI should collaborate, and algorithms should consider inclusivity, safety, and justice when making judgments. Singapore's Model AI Governance Framework is the most comprehensive strategies for making AI ethical, emphasizing transparent, accountable, and open design. The foundation for the expansion of ESG analytics and sustainable finance based on human-beneficial and innovative concepts has been established by Singapore's norms. China has opted for a state-led authoritarian regulatory framework instead. ESG and AI are closely linked under national policy supervision via its Corporate Social Credit System and Generative AI Measures (Singhal et al., 2025).

## 9. CONCLUSION AND FUTURE ASPECTS

The market is obviously expanding and companies are taking considerations of it. The all countries all across the globe are enacting new AI regulations, such as the EU AI Act. The regulations are evolving. In order to influence the ethical path of AI-based ESG analytics, it is crucial to strike the correct balance between innovation and regulation. AI can identify significant sustainability issues that humans may overlook. However, if undue reliance is put on opaque algorithms that are unconstrained by morality or the law, the spirit of ESG may be broken. Instead, the best approach to go ahead is to encourage an AI that is more in accordance with the ideals of sustainable development that is open, accountable, and inclusive. The companies must ensure that their algorithms are transparent, that there are independent audits, and that they have open data policies. Global standards must be established by regulators, and the public and investors should demand more transparency and accountability from ESG rating firms. The only way AI-driven ESG analytics can fully realize its positive potential is in this manner. It has the power to alter our perspective on sustainability as a means of achieving genuine, equitable, and morally motivated global development. AI has both significant opportunities and risks. Several businesses use Responsible AI techniques in an effort to address these problems. Scholars argue that these programs usually fall short or are just meant to boost the image of its adopters a technique known as "machinewashing" or "ethical digital washing."

## REFERENCES


Abdellatif, S. H. R. (2025). The Intersection of AI Ethics and Corporate Social Responsibility: A Case of AI-Driven RegTech in the Banking Industry. *Available at SSRN* 5261863. DOI: 10.2139/ssrn.5261863

Alshahmy, S., & Sahiner, M. (2024). Enhancing the Issuance and Monitoring of Sustainable Finance Instruments through AI. In *Artificial Intelligence, Finance, and Sustainability: Economic, Ecological, and Ethical Implications* (pp. 217–241). Springer Nature Switzerland. DOI: 10.1007/978-3-031-66205-8_9

Alshi, C. S. (2025). Artificial Intelligence, ESG, And the Future of Financial Reporting. *Journal of Marketing & Social Research, 2*, 442–446.

AR, S. M., & BRAHMBHATT, S. (2025). AI-Enabled ESG Reporting: Bridging Sustainability and Accounting. *IJSAT-International Journal on Science and Technology, 16*(3).

Bahangulu, J. K., & Owusu-Berko, L. (2025). Algorithmic bias, data ethics, and governance: Ensuring fairness, transparency and compliance in AI-powered business analytics applications. *World J Adv Res Rev, 25*(2), 1746–1763. DOI: 10.30574/wjarr.2025.25.2.0571

Behera, I., Nanda, P., & Derbali, A. M. S. (2024). The societal impact of artificial intelligence in sustainable investment strategies. In *Social and Ethical Implications of AI in Finance for Sustainability* (pp. 268–285). IGI Global. DOI: 10.4018/979-8-3693-2881-1.ch012

BENAISSA, W. O., MAHJOUBI, S., & KABBAJ, S. (2025). Sustainability Meets Intelligence: A PRISMA-Guided Systematic Review of AI's Role in ESG Financial Decision-Making. *International Journal of Accounting Finance Auditing Management and Economics, 6*(5), 790–806.

Chakrabarti, M., Fabozzi, F. J., Narain, A., & Sood, A. (2025). Ethical AI in Asset Management: Frameworks for Transparency, Compliance, and Trust. *The Journal of Financial Data Science, 7*(1), 18–35. DOI: 10.3905/jfds.2025.7.1.018

Chang, Y. L., & Ke, J. (2024). Socially responsible artificial intelligence empowered people analytics: A novel framework towards sustainability. *Human Resource Development Review, 23*(1), 88–120. DOI: 10.1177/15344843231200930

Domingo, M. M. R. (2025). The Impact of Artificial Intelligence on ESG: A Conceptual Framework for Practitioners and Policymakers. *Journal of Management for Global Sustainability, 13*(1), 2. DOI: 10.13185/2244-6893.1269

Elhady, A. M., & Shohieb, S. (2025). AI-driven sustainable finance: Computational tools, ESG metrics, and global implementation. *Future Business Journal*, *11*(1), 209. DOI: 10.1186/s43093-025-00610-x

Fernandes, S., Sheeja, M. S., & Parivara, S. (2024). Potential of AI for a sustainable, inclusive, and ethically responsible future. *Fostering Multidisciplinary Research for Sustainability, 196*.

Homavazir, Z., Madan, S., Verma, S., Gambhir, V., & Homavazir, M. (2025). Governance for the Digital Age: ESG-Driven Framework for Ethical and Inclusive Innovation. *Advances in Consumer Research. Association for Consumer Research (U. S.)*, *2*(3).

Huang, C., & Yao, X. (2025). Synergies Among Responsible Artificial Intelligence (RAI), Environmental, Social and Governance (ESG), and Sustainable Development Goals (SDGs). *IEEE Computational Intelligence Magazine*, *20*(4), 20–41. DOI: 10.1109/MCI.2025.3593452

Hussain, S. (2025). Integrating Al into Corporate Social Responsibility (CSR) for. *Integrating Sustainability Principles With AI-Driven Entrepreneurial Strategies*, 41.

Irfan, M., Dias, R. T., Khemka, M., Mondal, P., & Mohan, N. (2025). Navigating Towards Sustainability: The Role of Corporate Governance and AI-Driven Behavioral Interventions. In *Behavioral Finance and AI Tools for Sustainability* (pp. 201-226). IGI Global Scientific Publishing.

Islam, Q. T., & Faria, M. H. (2025). Ethics in AI-Driven Sustainable Finance: Balancing Innovation With Integrity. In *Behavioral Finance and AI Tools for Sustainability* (pp. 129-150). IGI Global Scientific Publishing.

Iyer, S. S., Subramanian, R., Raji, B., & Arora, R. (2025). The Ethical Implications of Artificial Intelligence in Decision-Making: Balancing Innovation with Accountability and Integrity. *Journal of Economics & Management Research. SRC/JESMR-417. DOI: doi. org/ (6), 305*, 2-11.DOI: 10.47363/JESMR/2025

Jo, H. (2025). The Effect of AI on CSR and ESG Ethics. *Journal of Finance Issues*, *23*(2), 57–78. DOI: 10.58886/jfi.v23i2.9437

Khaddam, A. A., & Alzghoul, A. (2025). Artificial intelligence-driven business intelligence for strategic energy and ESG management: A systematic review of economic and policy implications. *International Journal of Energy Economics and Policy*, *15*(4), 635–650. DOI: 10.32479/ijeep.19820

Mitra, A., & Maity, A. (2025). Balancing Green and Fair: Ethical AI in Sustainable Finance. *International Journal of Business Management & Legal Affairs*, *1*(1), 55–76.

Naqvi, A., & Momin, M. (2025). The Intersection of Sustainability, Responsible Analytics, and Ethical AI. In *Insights in Banking Analytics and Regulatory Compliance Using AI* (pp. 313–332). IGI Global Scientific Publishing. DOI: 10.4018/979-8-3373-0209-6.ch015

Nauman, M. (2025). AI in Sustainable Investing: A Dual-Edged Sword. In *FinTech and Robotics Advancements for Green Finance and Investment* (pp. 383-416). IGI Global Scientific Publishing. DOI: 10.4018/979-8-3373-0355-0.ch013

Ozkan, B. (2024). The transformative impact of AI on CSR, ESG, and sustainability: Critical review and case studies. In *Responsible Firms: CSR, ESG, and Global Sustainability* (Vol. 23, pp. 203-218). Emerald Publishing Limited.

Pria, S., Al Rubaie, I., & Prasad, V. (2024). Enhancing business intelligence through AI-driven integration of sustainability metrics via ESG factors. In *Risks and Challenges of AI-Driven Finance: Bias, Ethics, and Security* (pp. 57-89). IGI Global. DOI: 10.4018/979-8-3693-2185-0.ch004

Rane, N., Choudhary, S., & Rane, J. (2024). Artificial intelligence driven approaches to strengthening Environmental, Social, and Governance (ESG) criteria in sustainable business practices: a review. *Social, and Governance (ESG) criteria in sustainable business practices: a review (May 27, 2024).*

Safeei, R., & Marzuki, M., Mustaffa4D, S. M. S. A. H., Fadzilah, N. S. M., & Tajarahim, N. A. (2025, August). Harnessing AI: Transforming Social and Environmental Accountability in Accounting Practices. In *Proceedings of the 3rd International Conference on Business, Finance, Management and Economic (BizFAME 2024)* (p. 13). Springer Nature. DOI: 10.2991/978-94-6463-827-1_3

Salim, P. S. (2025). Artificial intelligence in corporate social responsibility. *Era of Management: Adapting Strategies for a Changing Environment*, 148.

Singhal, N., Goyal, S., Khan, M., & Singhal, T. (2025). AI for Sustainable Finance: Driving Innovation and Ethical Growth. *Financial Innovation for Global Sustainability*, 529-559.

Sinha, S., & Chopra, P. (2025). Algorithmic Governance in ESG Ratings: Addressing Bias and Enhancing Transparency in AI-Driven Sustainable Finance. In *Behavioral Finance and AI Tools for Sustainability* (pp. 375-402). IGI Global Scientific Publishing.

Suri, G. K., & Sadriwala, N. (2025). Using Artificial Intelligence for Sustainable Accounting Practices: A Data-Driven Approach. In *Intelligent Systems for Sustainable Infrastructure: AI Solutions Shaping a Green Future: Leveraging AI Innovations for Eco Friendly Infrastructure and Environmental Resilience* (pp. 171–186). Springer Nature Switzerland.

Thiruma Valavan, A.Thiruma Valavan A. (2023). AI Ethics and Bias: Exploratory study on the ethical considerations and potential biases in ai and data-driven decision-making in banking, with a focus on fairness, transparency, and accountability. *World Journal of Advanced Research and Reviews, 20*(2), 197–206. DOI: 10.30574/wjarr.2023.20.2.2245

UGWUODO, E., Humphrey, O. N. U. H., & Ugwu, P. (2024). Artificial Intelligence (AI) and Environmental Accounting: Implications for the Accounting Profession and Stakeholder Value Creation. *Research Journal of Financial Sustainability Reporting, 7*(1).

Vali, J., Yadav, P., & Thota, U. (2024, October). AI for Climate Action: Enhancing Sustainable Development Through ESG Analytics. In *Proceedings of the Second International Workshop on Artificial Intelligence: Empowering Sustainable Development,* Lucknow, India (Vol. 2).

# Chapter 5
# Human-Centered Automation in Sustainable Finance:
## Promoting Inclusivity, Trust, and Mental Health Through Ethical AI


**Vandana Gaur**
http://orcid.org/0000-0002-4675-6458
*S.D.M. Government (PG) College, Doiwala, India*

**Neeta Gupta**
http://orcid.org/0000-0001-9425-7015
*D.A.V. (P.G.) College, Dehradun, India*

**Sujata Gupta**
*D.A.V. (P.G.) College, Dehradun, India*


## ABSTRACT


*The notion of human-centered automation of sustainable finance is a paradigm shift in which artificial intelligence and automated systems are instituted, implemented and regulated with people at the heart of the systemic nature-people-values-needs-agency-and-well-being and the pure efficiency and maximization of profits are considered peripheral to all other human considerations. In contrast to conventional automation where it frequently replaces human labour directly, this strategy focuses on augmentation: AI can be used to process data-intensive jobs such as crunching large volumes of ESG (Environmental, Social, and Governance) data, detecting greenwashing in corporate reports and green investment portfolios, and automate compliance checks of regulations such as the Sustainable Finance*



DOI: 10.4018/979-8-2600-1308-3.ch005

*Disclosure Regulation or other forthcoming global standards. This model ensures that ethical considerations are used to derive the results by keeping humans in the loop by providing explainable interfaces, collaborative decision-making tools and oversight mechanisms*

## 1. INTRODUCTION

Human-centered automation is appropriate in the context of sustainable finance, in which choices made have effects on planetary health, social equity, and long-term economic resilience, such as SDG 8 (decent work and economic growth), SDG 10 (reduced inequalities), SDG 13 (climate action), and SDG 17 (partnerships for the goals). The foundation here is ethical AI, instilling in it values such as fairness, transparency, accountability, privacy, and non-maleficence using a framework such as that promoted by UNESCO, EU AI Act, or the guidelines of the world health organization on responsible AI in health-related spheres (extrapolated analogously to the financial domain) (Visciola, 2025). These principles ensure that any algorithms are free of the biases that might widen the exclusion (e.g. discriminatory models of credit scoring that have an adverse impact on marginalized populations in the new markets) and, instead, promote the systems that reveal the inequities and rectify them in real time.

One of the key pillars of this strategy is the encouragement of inclusivity. There has been an access barrier issue with sustainable finance: underserved communities in rural areas, low-income households, women entrepreneurs and minority communities often have restricted access to credit, investing or investment opportunities, or insurance because of incomplete data or biasing conventional solutions. Human-centred automation is the answer to this, as it uses AI to expand financial inclusion without compromising ethics. An example is that, combining alternative data sources, such as mobile utilisation trends, utility payments or satellite images of agricultural feasibility with ethical machine learning make possible more precise, equitable credit ratings in areas without formal credit histories. Development of such tools is participated by different stakeholders such as representatives of the community, NGOs and end-users in participatory design processes with the aim of ensuring that such tools capture the real life situations and that they are not ethnically or demographically blind. Information-intensive AI-based microfinance apps or robo-advisors targeted specifically at green portfolios can be used to democratize access to sustainable investment such as impact bonds or green ETFs so that small scale investors can take part in renewable energy transitions or climate-resistant agriculture (Sargiotis, 2024).

This is also applied to the emerging markets, where AI is used to close the data gaps within ESG reporting in local companies, so that they can attract international investment. The elimination of exclusionary biases by conducting regular audits, training data diversity, and human control, make these systems complement SDG 1 (no poverty) and SDG 5 (gender equality) as the financial system begins to promote fair growth rather than imprisoning it. Empirical findings through projects in the fintech sector indicate that inclusive tools do not only increase the market reach, but also enhance both repayment rates and long-term financial resilience in case they are designed with user feedback loops.

The critical bond that glues the human aspect of automation in sustainable finance manifests as trust. In its absence, even the most advanced AI faces the threat of rejection among investors, regulators, institutions, and even the population. The process of building trust is achieved by radical transparency: explainable AI (XAI) methods allow black-box models to be interpretable and show how an algorithm balances ESG considerations or raises red flags over unethical business practices. Audit trails, third party certifications and open-source elements can be scrutinized and deployments are managed by ethical review boards which include ethicists, sustainability specialists, and civil society.

Human-AI collaboration models, including augmented advisory system where professionals make use of AI awareness, yet control ultimate evaluations in higher-stake choices such as dropping fossil fuel, maintain accountability and steer clear of overdependence. Transparency in cross-referencing unstructured news, filings, and social media data is a credible asset of AI in the greenwashing scandals era that offers verifiable sustainable indicators of data. Institutional trust is also strengthened by regulatory alignment i.e. adherence to new global standards of trustworthy AI. Research and trade publications suggest that open human-enhanced systems speed up the adoption of the sustainable products: investors are less reluctant to invest into the ESG funds when they are familiar with the automation behind it and trust it. This type of trust relationship also lowers the risks of systems - opaque automation may increase the volatility of the market or redistribute capital towards real sustainability transition, and enables building trust among stakeholders that are needed to scale impact investing (Purwanto, 2025).

The aspect of mental health and psychological well-being in this automated environment is equally very important, albeit neglected. The fast adoption of AI in the financial industry, where it is capable of trading, risk modeling, compliance, and client services, may cause a lot of stress to both the professionals and the end-users. Among the finance workers, anxiety about job loss, continuous upskilling, the ways they are monitored with AI analytics on their work performance, and overwhelming decisions due to augmented workflows are a few factors leading to anxiety, burnout, and depression. The studies point to the indirect increase in mental health issues alongside the adoption of AI, as it has been found that an increased number of people in financial services experience increased job insecurity, with polls indicating that large segments of workers are worried about the obsolescence of their position.

Human-centered design addresses it by focusing on supportive interfaces: simple dashboards that ease cognitive load, workload distribution that does not cause overload, and such functionality as AI-based wellness suggestions (e.g. telling a user that they spend excessive time on their device or should take a break). The privacy of any mental health-related data use is not compromised by the use of ethical guidelines. Everything is positive in the fact that automation can liberate humans to work on meaningful and creative tasks such as strategic sustainability analysis, stakeholder interactions, ethical considerations, and this will improve job satisfaction and fulfillment. To end-users, AI driven by ethical applications provides stress alleviating services; budgeting tools that bring behavioral data into the mix, early alarms about financial instability based on mood changes, or even non-exclusive advisory, which instills confidence instead of fear. Human-centered automation by incorporating well-being measures into sustainable financial systems (i.e. monitoring employee psychological well-being in corporate ESG reporting or user satisfaction in impact investments) fosters healthy ecosystems. This prevents vicious cycles in which the stress created by automation compromises productivity or destroys confidence in financial systems (Saha, 2025).

## 2. FOUNDATIONS AND PRINCIPLES OF ETHICAL AI IN SUSTAINABLE FINANCE

The Foundations and Principles of Ethical AI in Sustainable Finance are the baseline toward integrating the use of artificial intelligence into the systems that command the utilization of capital to all environmental safety and security, social equity and good governance. AI in this field is more than just technical performance, but it entails the sub-text of fundamental values that would make AI useful to humanity and the Earth without harm. The core values are fairness (avoiding discriminatory results of the investment decision or ESG evaluation), transparency (researching AI processes to make them auditable), accountability (making the determinations made by models clear-cut responsibilities), privacy (sensitive data is not compromised when it comes to financial or sustainability reporting) and explainability (enabling users to understand how the models reached their conclusions, e.g., eco-rating or detecting greenwashing) (Zallio et al., 2025).

These are based on such well-known global frameworks as Recommendation on the Ethics of Artificial Intelligence (2021) of UNESCO that specifically endeavours to connect AI with the UN Sustainable Development Goals (SDGs) by evaluating environmental effects and being more inclusive. These are further operationalised in the EU AI Act which defines these in terms of a risk-based approach and categorises quite a large number of financial AI applications, including creditworthiness assessment, automated portfolio optimization, or ESG analytics, as high-risk and requires stringent data governance, risk management systems, accuracy, robustness, cybersecurity, and human control to avoid opaque "black-box" decisions that would discredit trust or reinforce inequalities. The principles of sustainable finance solve specific problems: AI processes vast, typically unstructured ESG information of corporate reports, satellite photography, news, and social media to make informed decisions about impact investing, yet lacking ethical principles it may lead to increasing greenwashing (pretending to be sustainable) or misdirecting capital to actual shifts to low-carbon economies.

ESG scores would be biased against a firm in an emerging market or underserved industry due to biased training data representing historical disparities. Industry and regulatory responses such as CFA Institute and OECD AI principles emphasize these values have to be integrated early in design to balance between the innovation and responsibility. Other aspects are environmental sustainability of AI, i.e., energy-intensive models need to reduce the carbon footprint to conform to climate objectives; justice, i.e. make the benefits of AI more fairly distributed. On the whole, these foundations transform sustainable finance not as an efficiency-oriented automation but as a system of values that would contribute to the stability of the market with AI that would promote and improve the long-term welfare of society and the planet through systemic governance, regular audits, and alignment with changing standards.

## 2.1 Role of Human-centered Design in Mitigating Algorithmic Bias and Promoting Responsibility

It is an important factor that should ensure that AI in sustainable finance is not only equitable and responsible but also value-oriented, and, therefore, not subject to a flawed system. Human-centered design (HCD), also known as human-centered AI (HCAI), puts people at the forefront in the AI lifecycle, i.e. between ideation and data selection to deployment and continual monitoring, by engaging various stakeholders (users, ethicists, affected communities, sustainability experts) in the participatory process that reveals blind spots and context-specific needs. In contrast to pure technical fixes, HCD does not only see bias as a data or algorithmic problem, but as a complex challenge that is based on systemic, statistical, and human aspects, such as prejudices in the history of financial data in the society (Nkwo et al., 2025).

Algorithms in sustainable finance may also create an unfair downtick of ESG ratings of companies in developing nations because training data is not complete or western-focused, resulting in lower access to green capital and worsening global inequalities (the opposite of SDGs 10 and 13). HCD reduces it with active measures: rich and representative data sets enhanced with non-computational data (e.g. local communities or satellite derived agricultural data); bias audits at all levels, via such tools as fairness metrics and debiasing methods (pre processing to balance data, in-processing during model training, post processing to produce fair outputs); human in the loop mechanisms, such as AI advice reviewed by professional judgment in a high-stakes setting, such as divestment decision making or impact bond rating. NIST, EY, and others models embrace HCD as they base decisions on the societal situational context, perform frequent impact evaluations, and encourage the development of multidisciplinary teams to question assumptions.

This enforces accountability through creating accountability trails, ethical review boards, and feedback loops that can support a continuous improvement- users can mark unfair results, which will cause the model to be retrained. Practically, HCD generates trust: explainable interfaces demonstrate the weighting of ESG factors, which increases transparency, eliminating the lack of trust in sustainable products. It, too, is the antidote to excessive automation by retaining human judgment in making subtle ethical decisions, including balancing trade-offs among environmental benefits and social harms. With a dcsign that prioritizcs human nccds (in particular, marginalized voices) over technology, HCD can make AI a source of equity rather than bias, and a sustainable finance can promote an inclusive transition on the condition of prioritizing moral and regulatory considerations such as the high-risk criteria of transparency and non-discrimination as part of the EU AI Act (Ozmen Garibay et al., 2023).

## 3. PROMOTING FINANCIAL INCLUSIVITY THROUGH HUMAN-CENTERED AUTOMATION

Human-Centered Automation as a Promotional Strategy to Financial Inclusivity can be viewed as a pillar in the ongoing transformation of sustainable finance, as it allows breaking the historical barriers to accessing financial services, especially by disadvantaged and marginalized communities. Low-income people, rural population, women, ethnic minorities and small businesses in the emerging markets have been ossified out of traditional financial systems because of impoverished credit records, remote locations, high-transactions costs, and discriminated assessment models based on past history. Human-centered automation enables the solution to these inequities by creating AI that augments but does not substitute human knowledge, by using alternative data methods, like mobile money transactions, the payment of utilities, social media patterns, satellite imagery of crop yields, behavioral analytics, to form more precise and context-sensitive portraits of credit scoring, micro-lending, insurance, and investment opportunities (Martini et al, 2024).

This can be applied in sustainable finance to allow small-scale investors and communities to invest in and benefit in transitions in line with SDGs 1 (no poverty), 5 (gender equality), 8 (decent work), 10 (reduced inequalities), and 13 (climate action). As an illustration, generative AI and machine learning applications offer hyper-personalized financial advice in the local language, overcoming the barriers of literacy and trust and providing real-time coaching, coaching nudges, and customized products to save money and increase the repayments rate. The programs in the countries such as India, Colombia and Africa show that GenAI copilots in the microfinance organization can accelerate onboarding, visibly clarify the repayment projects and reach rural locations, making sustainable products friendly and comprehendible. These systems reduce exclusionary biases, like penalizing informal economies or underrepresented demographics, and increase the legitimacy of the systems to the extent that these systems are transparent and allow user responses. In addition to increasing market coverage amongst the providers, this strategy enhances further economic resilience because access to long-term sustainable means of finance is inclusive, and development within an inclusive framework is equitable, poverty traps are minimized, and community-led environmental initiatives are supported (Mhlanga, 2022). Human-centered automation reinvents finance as an instrument of social justice and planetary health, transforming technical innovation into a driver of bridging the inclusion divide in the world and improving sustainable transitions speedily without anyone falling behind.

## 3.1 Human Oversight Mechanisms to Enhance Equity and Legitimacy in Decision-making

Human Oversight Mechanisms to Improve Equity and Legitimacy in Decision-making These will be irreplaceable safety nets in sustainable finance and human-oriented automation, where artificial intelligence-based procedures should be equitable, responsible, and focused on ethical commitments instead of deepening inequalities. ESG risk assessment Fully autonomous systems already used in high-stakes decisions such as automated credit decisions, green investment portfolio allocations, or detecting fraud in impact funds can perpetuate biases in training data or fail to account for socially complicated situations (Tariq, 2026). Human oversight systems such as the so-called human-in-the-loop (HITL) or human-on-the-loop are systems that incorporate professionals, ethicists, or community representatives at key decision points: before making final decisions, checking the outputs of AI-based systems, approving recommendations of high impact (e.g., selling off high-carbon industries or providing microloans to marginalised populations), and intervening in the cases of edges where the AI is not absolutely confident. EU AI Act, OECD guidelines, and industry provisions (e.g. MUFG Responsible AI Policy or BNP Paribas AI Governance Charter) specify such oversight of high-risk applications as mandated explainability tools, audit logs, active monitoring and contact measures to enforce accountability.

In sustainable finance, it improves equity by permitting human judgment to rectify biases like an underestimation of the community-based sustainability endeavors in the emerging market and legitimacy by including a wide range of views indicating real-world impacts on marginalized stakeholders. An example is hybrid systems that integrate predictive models with advisor-in-the-loop validation that can translate complex outputs of ESG into comprehensible stories and make sure that the decisions made are consistent with the contexts of the user and ethical considerations. Monitoring is also ensured through frequent bias audits, ethical review boards and stakeholder feedback loops which lead to retraining of the model in the case of inequities. These processes establish an institutional as well as popular trust, minimize systemic risks such as misallocated sustainable capital, and encourage adherence to rules and regulations that focus on non-discrimination and human agency. Having conserved human experience in the moral considerations such as the trade-off between the benefits of the environment and the costs of society, regulation can turn AI into a working solution and not a potential source of exclusion, but a process that can be used to justify reputable results, which are both more efficient and provable to be fair and objectively just (Enyiorji, 2022).

## 3.2 Strategies for Inclusive Design: Participatory Development involving Diverse Stakeholders

This highlight the role of co-creation as the mechanism that introduces genuinely equitable AI to sustainable finance and focuses on the top-down development and instead includes a wide spectrum of voices in the development of automation tools. Human-centered methodologies Particulate design ideas apply to the underrepresented people, groups, and communities in the AI lifecycle: problem definition and data selection to prototyping, testing, and iteration. This overcomes exclusion by uncovering contextual demands, cultural specifics, and possible harms early such as the way the dominance of Western-focused datasets could put local sustainable initiatives at a disadvantage or language obstacles could impede the usage of green finance apps.

Such strategies are workshops, focus groups, co-design sessions, citizen juries in which different stakeholders can provide requirements, test prototypes, and get feedback to make sure that such tools as AI credit scorers or ESG analytics platforms are relevant and equitable. In fintech and sustainable finance, in Latin America (as exemplified by the Financial Inclusion Lab at CAF accelerating AI solutions to needy populations) and world-wide (as illustrated by the Guidelines on Participatory and Inclusive AI at Partnership on AI), collaboration with marginalized communities to create hyper-personalized, multilingual products that overcome barriers in literacy, trust, etc. are observed (Jain, 2025). Diversity in development teams is also part of inclusive design that believes in challenging assumptions, as well as accessibility features (e.g. voice interfaces to help users with low literacy). These measures will ensure empowerment, minimize algorithmic harm, and increase the uptake of sustainable products, including impact investments driven by the community, by following conceptual frameworks like IDEAS (Inclusion, Diversity, Equity, Accessibility, Safety). The outcome is more legitimate, more resilient systems that promote financial inclusion in addition to fostering SDGs based on equal innovative practices, transforming the input of the varied stakeholders into a platform that produces technology that benefits everyone and not a selected few.

## 4. BUILDING TRUST IN AI-DRIVEN SUSTAINABLE FINANCE SYSTEMS

Developing Trust in AI-based Sustainable Finance Systems is the key to the ubiquity of automation in making capital sustainable-friendly and ensuring its long-term effectiveness since mistrust may slow the adoption of green technologies and raise the risk of greenwashing, as well as lose faith in products where ESG is embedded. The development of trust is not achieved solely through technology but rather by intentional combination of transparency, explainability, human-AI collaboration, accountability measures, e.g., audit trails and ethical review boards and the feedback mechanisms among the stakeholders that, combined, mitigate the lack of transparency that tends to accompany AI model processing of large unstructured datasets of corporate reports, satellite images, social media, and other data sources.

Opaque automation could be detrimental to reputation, regulatory sanctions, misplacement of capital instead of real transitions, and systemic instability in the face of unsustainable behavior in cases where algorithms replicate biases or does not do so very well in identifying unsustainable behavior in the face of unsustainable practices in sustainable finance (where decisions impact climate action, social equity, and governance, directly affecting SDGs 13, 10, and 8). An example is that AI applications in ESG scoring or green bond verification should inspire confidence within retail investors who are skeptical of latent biases, institutional investors who need to know that they are compliant, and regulators who need to see that they are making verifiable sustainability statements (Ozturkcan, 2025). The importance of trust is supported by empirical evidence: researchers have found that transparency leads to a substantial increase in trust, which, in turn, strongly mediates the intention to adopt AI-driven financial platforms, and the effects of transparency in the context of emerging markets are mediated by the risk perception.

Nationally, 72% of people worldwide accept the use of AI, but more than half (54) remain skeptical, with trust decreasing, and worry increasing to 62, although, in emerging economies, it is higher than in advanced ones, as people view AI use as beneficial, and repeat benefits (performance) increase their trust and adoption levels. Green innovation and internal controls positively correlate with AI adoption, which leads to better ESG performance and stakeholder trust and social capital in case of crisis, especially in larger and tech-intensive companies. Human-centric methodologies - augmenting and not substituting skills - enhance layered resilience and complete disclosure, and structures focus on the pillars of governance such as transparency, reduction of bias, auditability to ensure credibility of the people and the institution. Explainable AI (XAI) and human supervision can reduce black-box risks to prevent discrimination in lending or the ESG rating, and is consistent with regulations such as the high-risk provisions of the EU AI Act. Practically, trust enhances the uptake of sustainable products faster, investors tend to commit higher to audited ESG funds with processes in place that are auditable and helps in maintaining stability in markets by alleviating volatility due to untrusted signals. Examples of using technologies together to improve traceability and verification and attract more capital to environmental initiatives include AI-improved climate risk analytics or blockchain-verified green bonds. In conclusion, strong trust technologies will turn AI into a liability of the company into a believable enabler of sustainable finance, which will create robust ecosystems where ethical automation will produce real effects, fairness, and trust among users, institutions, and society (Adedoyin et al., 2025).

## 4.1 Transparency and Explainability as Foundations for User and Institutional Trust

Transparency and Explainability as Foundations of User and Institutional Trust The viability of AI in sustainable finance is built on the premises of demystifying complex models and allowing scrutiny, as well as ensuring that the decisions made regarding ESG ratings, detection of greenwashing, optimization of portfolio, or climate risk assessment are not arbitrary or biased. AudIT trails and verifiable processes are useful to the institution, especially in meeting the requirements of the EU AI Act of high-risk systems (accuracy, robustness, human oversight) and international standards that focus on non-discrimination.

The transparency leads to higher user trust and adoption of digital financial services, which are fundamental pillars, as well as bias reduction and data protection. XAI in ESG reporting makes insights usable and verifiable, which is the counterargument related to greenwashing because it would penalize claims by taking consistent monitoring and cross-checking and enhance trust in stakeholders and respond to the investor requirements of responsibility. Among them is NLP to extract ESG report content to classify, AI to provide transparency on climate risk (e.g., Jupiter AI), or blockchain-AI hybrids (e.g., Luxembourg LGX DataHub or BIS Project Genesis) to automate green bond proceeds tracking to increase verification and market confidence (Usmani et al., 2023). There are still dilemmas, such as the lack of visibility about datasets, training bias, and complexities of algorithms, but with XAI, these issues can be resolved, which in turn will build ethical AI that will serve the wider interests of fairness and responsibility.

## 4.2 Human-AI Collaboration Models

These models are a paradigm shift where automation is seen as being replacement based and instead sustainable finance uses AI to augment human efforts, with humans in charge of ethical decision-making, contextual sensitivity, creativity, and ultimate responsibility-maintaining the agency and maximizing the results. One of them is human-in-the-loop (HITL), in which practitioners consider and authenticate AI recommendations prior to action (e.g., by approving impact investments or intervening in edge-case ESG risk analysis); another is human-on-the-loop, in which ongoing monitoring occurs; and a third is human-on-the-loop, in which AI and humans are treated as equal partners, with the former being fast/scaling and the latter being strategic/emotional in making complex decisions. AI is applied in wealth management to perform complete analysis and predictive intelligence on the ESG-related factors and help advisors customize sustainable approaches and improve customer satisfaction. In sustainable application, AI complements, not substitutes, skill in supply chain optimization, trade finance (cutting credit decision time many times and enhancing access of SMEs), or environmental accounting, which is validated by human means, to make it robust and trustworthy (Patil, 2025).

Such models alleviate biasness by involving a wide range of human supervision, compliance by means of explainable reviews, and mental health by means of workload distribution to facilitate meaningful and purpose-oriented work, such as ethical deliberations beyond routine work. These advantages are that AI can make high-quality decisions, AI can work on volume and people balance trade-offs, such as environmental benefits and social costs, AI means fewer mistakes, AI makes decisions more fair and more accountable, and human beings are still responsible in making high-stakes decisions. Frameworks are more focused on transparency, accountability, and fairness to generate worker/stakeholder trust, leading to inclusive innovation. In reality, this creates resiliency: AI finds the opportunity of green investments through machine learning of the historic ESG data, whereas humans place these opportunities within local consequences or new perils. With a focus on collaboration, sustainable finance can bypass the over-reliance traps, can be adopted more readily due to its perceived reliability, and conforms to the human-centered approach, which eventually leads to more equitable, effective shifts to low-carbon, inclusive economies where technology complements human skills and knowledge.

## 5. SAFEGUARDING MENTAL HEALTH AND WELL-BEING IN AN AUTOMATED FINANCE LANDSCAPE

This is a reflection on a crucial but often underestimated aspect of human-centered automation in sustainable finance the extensive psychological impact that fast AI adoption has on both the individuals working in the field and its consumers, as well as how to use ethical AI to promote resilience, purpose, and positive well-being outcomes. High-stakes decision-making, market volatility, regulation, and performance pressure have led to fast adoption of AI in the finance industry, which has had uses in algorithmic trading, ESG data processing, risk modeling, compliance automation and personalized sustainable investment advisory.

These tools improve efficiency and allow prioritizing strategic, high-impact work, including ethical portfolio alignment or stakeholder participation in green transitions, but also are a source of stressors: omnipresent job obsolescence threats, skill obsolescence under the onslaught of mandatory upskilling and ongoing process monitoring by AI, cognitive overload due to processing augmented information, and emotional burnout as a result of working with multilayered human-AI relationships (Winslow & Garibay, 2024). Recent research indicates that adoption of AI indirectly increases burnout and depression via job insecurity as a mediator (job insecurity is the most relevant factor), and that employees are afraid of some automation stealing their jobs and causing anxiety, work-related passion, and emotional exhaustion, with surveys showing 66 percent of workers in the U.S. report being burned out in 2025 (even higher than during the pandemic) and white-collar workers in the financial sector report high levels of AI-related anxiety about the long-term opportunities. In financial services in particular, 57 per cent of respondents in the UK in the financial services sector have experienced burnout themselves due to the increasing expectations of AI, increased workloads and uncertainty, whereas international reports show how opaque automation increases decision overload and reduces job satisfaction in banking and investment careers. To the end-users, especially susceptible populations using inclusive sustainable finance offerings, excessive dependence on automated technology may cause financial decision fatigue, feelings of being treated like a robot, or an increased stress state during turbulent ESG-linked investments, which worsens mental well-being in a state of precarity.

The human-centered design mitigates these risks by addressing supportive, emphatic interfaces: user-friendly dashboards to reduce cognitive load, AI to alert of work overloads or propose rest, clauses that clarify information so that there is no uncertainty, and redistributing work without losing meaningful human input such as ethical considerations of sustainability trade-offs. Ethical AI models, based on UNESCO, EU AI Act impacts, and workplace standards of the future require privacy considerations of any well-being-related information (e.g., preventing intrusive surveillance of stress indicators), a required informed consent to AI uses, mitigation of bias to avoid discriminatory outcomes that might make a person more anxious, and the existence of accountability mechanisms, such as ethical review boards. Things work out well: positively, automation is freeing up time to pursue other interests: finance professionals are moving on to creative sustainability strategy, community impact analysis, or client relationship-building, which add to purpose and job satisfaction when they resonate with personal values in sustainable finance (Benlalia et al., 2025).

The possibility of AI proactively supporting mental health is also there, including personalized financial wellness applications that give behavioral prompts in case of stress management, earlier identification of financial disturbance based on mood trends (with stringent privacy), and inclusive advisory that instills user confidence by means of sympathetic and multilingual engagements. By including well-being indicators into ESG reporting, i.e. monitoring employee mental health levels or user satisfaction in impact investments, sustainable finance can be in line with holistic value creation, promoting SDGs 3 (good health and well-being) and 8 (decent work).

The issues involve negotiating information privacy in wellness applications, over-medicalizing financial advice, and the environmental impact of AI itself to avoid the ironical stress of sustainability contradictions. The future looks at multidisciplinary directions: technologists, psychologists, ethicists, and leadership of finance to create resilient ecosystems in which AI will contribute to flourishing humanity. The human-centered automation of sustainable finance can not only alleviate psychological harms by focusing on mental health protections, in the form of supportive design, ethical governance and purposeful role evolution, but also produce flourishing people and institutions that can facilitate fair and robust transformations to a low-carbon economy (Desolda et al., 2025). Such a comprehensive consideration means that technology will act as a partner of humanity in the face of adversity, and that what might be viewed as a danger to a person will be turned into a benefit of improved well-being, productivity, and social contribution in an increasingly automated world.

## 6. CONCLUSION

Human-centered AI-driven automation in the synthesis process is a sustainable finance that is no longer a niche issue but a mainstream force that does good. It promotes inclusiveness through democratizing access, minimizing bias, enhances trust in terms of transparency and teamwork, and protects mental health through a human-centered flourishing in a changing technology. Things are not so easy, though: the key is to provide equal access to AI, mitigate the energy consumption of big models, and overcome regulatory fragmentation but the way to go is multidisciplinary governance: a mix of technologists, ethicists, policymakers, financiers, and civil society. Autonomation is not a threat, but an excellent facilitator of a more just, resilient and sustainable financial world when humans are burrowed into the center of it. Such a shared vision does not only offer economic gains but also regeneration of the society in which the technological expertise and capabilities are balanced with human values that will be honored over a long period of time.

## REFERENCES


Adedoyin, F., Dogan, H., Cetinkaya, D., & Jiang, N. (2025, May). Human-Centered AI in FinTech: A Conceptual Model and Strategic Research Agenda. In *2025 IEEE Conference on Artificial Intelligence (CAI)* (pp. 180-187). IEEE. DOI: 10.1109/CAI64502.2025.00036

Benlalia, Z., Al-Kateb, G., Mzili, M., & Diamanti, K. (2025). Reimagining intelligence: A comprehensive review of human-centric AI systems and their societal and healthcare integration. *Mesopotamian Journal of Artificial Intelligence in Healthcare*, *2025*, 173–186. DOI: 10.58496/MJAIH/2025/017

Desolda, G., Esposito, A., Lanzilotti, R., Piccinno, A., & Costabile, M. F. (2025). From human-centered to symbiotic artificial intelligence: A focus on medical applications. *Multimedia Tools and Applications*, *84*(27), 32109–32150. DOI: 10.1007/s11042-024-20414-5

Enyiorji, P. (2022). Human-centered responsible AI product development lifecycles merging participatory design, stakeholder alignment, and risk modeling for equitable digital financial service delivery. *International Journal of Science and Engineering Applications*, *11*(12), 452–468.

Jain, A. (2025). Designing for ethical and inclusive AI through a human-centered design lens. *Glob. Bus. Econ. J.* https://gbej. org/articles/designing-for-ethical-and-inclusive-ai-through-a-human-centered-design-lens/. *Accessed, 27.*

Martini, B., Bellisario, D., & Coletti, P. (2024). Human-centered and sustainable artificial intelligence in industry 5.0: Challenges and perspectives. *Sustainability (Basel)*, *16*(13), 5448. DOI: 10.3390/su16135448

Mhlanga, D. (2022). Human-centered artificial intelligence: The superlative approach to achieve sustainable development goals in the fourth industrial revolution. *Sustainability (Basel)*, *14*(13), 7804. DOI: 10.3390/su14137804

Nkwo, M., Ikwunne, T., Adejoro, C., & Anuyah, O. (2025). Exploring Usability of AI Systems in the Global South—Toward Responsible Human-Centered AI for Sustainable Cities and Communities. In *Usability for the World: Building Better Cities and Communities* (pp. 125–165). Springer Nature Switzerland. DOI: 10.1007/978-3-031-88326-2_5

Ozmen Garibay, O., Winslow, B., Andolina, S., Antona, M., Bodenschatz, A., Coursaris, C., Falco, G., Fiore, S. M., Garibay, I., Grieman, K., Havens, J. C., Jirotka, M., Kacorri, H., Karwowski, W., Kider, J., Konstan, J., Koon, S., Lopez-Gonzalez, M., Maifeld-Carucci, I., & Xu, W. (2023). Six human-centered artificial intelligence grand challenges. *International Journal of Human-Computer Interaction, 39*(3), 391–437. DOI: 10.1080/10447318.2022.2153320

Ozturkcan, S. (2025). Responsible robot integration for inclusive and sustainable work. *Discover Sustainability, 6*(1), 912. DOI: 10.1007/s43621-025-01928-w

Patil, M. (2025). Enterprise Strategy for Human-Centered AI. In *Handbook of Human-Centered Artificial Intelligence* (pp. 1–62). Springer Nature Singapore. DOI: 10.1007/978-981-97-8440-0_108-1

Purwanto, A. N. I. (2025). Human-Centered AI: Designing Intelligent Systems that Empower, Not Replace. *RIGGS: Journal of Artificial Intelligence and Digital Business, 4*(3), 3212–3221. DOI: 10.31004/riggs.v4i3.2450

Saha, A. (2025). Human-centred innovation in Society 5.0. *Society 5.0: A Transformation towards Human-Centered. Artificial Intelligence*, •••, 143.

Sargiotis, D. (2024). Fostering Ethical and Inclusive AI: A Human-Centric Paradigm for Social Impact. *Available at SSRN* 4879372. DOI: 10.2139/ssrn.4879372

Tariq, M. U. (2026). Bridging the Digital and Human Divide: Fostering Inclusion and Well-Being in Tech-Driven Workplaces. In *Leading Inclusive Workplaces Through Digital Transformation and Organizational Change* (pp. 139-168). IGI Global Scientific Publishing.

Usmani, U. A., Happonen, A., & Watada, J. (2023, June). Human-centered artificial intelligence: Designing for user empowerment and ethical considerations. In *2023 5th international congress on human-computer interaction, optimization and robotic applications (HORA)*. IEEE.

Visciola, M. (2025). Rethinking Human-Centered Design: From Automation to Sustainable Innovation. *Interactions (New York, N.Y.), 32*(4), 22–27. DOI: 10.1145/3733153

Winslow, B., & Garibay, O. O. (2024). Human-centered AI. In *Human-Computer Interaction in Intelligent Environments* (pp. 108–140). CRC Press. DOI: 10.1201/9781003490685-4

Zallio, M., Ike, C. B., & Chivăran, C. (2025). Designing Artificial Intelligence: Exploring Inclusion, Diversity, Equity, Accessibility, and Safety in Human-Centric Emerging Technologies. *AI, 6*(7), 143. DOI: 10.3390/ai6070143

# Chapter 6
# AI-Powered ESG and Navigating Regulatory Challenges, Ethical Risks, and Opportunities in Green Investment Law

**Anshu Dwivedi**
http://orcid.org/0009-0008-2940-6297
*Amity Law School, Amity University, Gwalior, India*

**Kunal Rohira**
*School of Legal Studies and Governance, Career Point University, Kota, India*

**Shobhitabh Srivastava**
http://orcid.org/0009-0007-1627-788X
*International University of Legal Education and Research, Goa, India*

**Vijay Srivastava**
http://orcid.org/0000-0002-3034-9903
*Amity Law School, Amity University, Gwalior, India*

## ABSTRACT

*The algorithm incorporation of artificial intelligence into the system of Environmental, Social and Governance (ESG) may be viewed as a radical shift in the sustainable financial field, including the jurisdictional and contractual one in green investment law. AI-based applications support advanced processing of data, predictive analytics, and real-time monitoring, which are useful in improving the evaluation*

DOI: 10.4018/979-8-2600-1308-3.ch006

*of ESG risks, identifying cases of greenwashing, automating compliance with new regulatory tools such as the Corporate Sustainability Reporting Directive (CSRD) and the AI Act and allocating capital to low-carbon initiatives more efficiently. Such technical abilities are offering investors the opportunity to meet high levels of risk-adjusted returns in addition to their further development towards broader sustainability targets, such as the achievement of net-zero transitions and the United Nations Sustainable Development Goals.*

## 1. INTRODUCTION

The integration of AI in ESG brings with it substantive regulatory dilemma based on fragmentary worldwide standards, high-risk AI categories that require transparency and accountability, and the heavier European requirements and the more ambiguous U.S. strategies (Nauman, 2025). Ethical risks are also notable and include algorithmic bias which can perpetuate social inequities, intensive energy and water usage which increase AI environmental footprint and the risk of promoting more advanced greenwashing in the event of poor governance. This paper explores, how negotiating these regulatory, ethical and operational nuances can then unravel formative openings in the field of green investment law, which will then facilitate profitable and principled sustainable finance policies in the face of an intensifying technological and policy transformation.

The recent pace of AI convergence with ESG issues is refining the experience of sustainable finance and green law of investment, with its unparalleled opportunities and simultaneously challenges as the world strives to reduce climate change, social inequality, and maladaptive governance. At present, AI has become an essential facilitator in the ESG process (installed in the last few years), in which big data analytics, machine learning, natural language processing, and predictive modeling are used to convert massive, unstructured data, such as disclosures of corporations, satellite images, news sentiment, and supply-chain tracking, into valuable information in a manner that cannot be identified by conventional human analytics (Samanvitha et al., 2025).

With this technological breakthrough, it can be possible to score ESG more accurately, more timely, and in a more granular way, and this will allow investors to know when a company is a genuine sustainability leader, be able to predict financial risks due to climate, and allow the company to allocate capital to green areas of endeavor, including renewable energy infrastructure, sustainable agriculture, and circular-economy projects (Domingo, 2025). Such as, now, AI-powered systems handle emissions tracking, point out potentially fraudulent instances of greenwashing under the pretext of sustainability by detecting irregularities in sustainability reporting, and assist in predictive analytics of the flow of both physical and transition risks in line with requirements including the Task Force on Climate-Related Financial Disclosures and the International Sustainability Standards Board (ISSB). In turn, those developments positively affect decision-making in green investment law where such tools as green bonds, sustainability-linked loans, EU- Taxonomy-aligned investments are intended to request strong, verifiable data to be able to qualify to share incentives and to escape such regulatory penalties.

## 1.1 Definition and Evolution of AI in ESG Frameworks

The prospects presented by AI are especially overwhelming in consideration of the growing sustainability demand in the globe. Bringing together financial institutions, major economies aim to close their information asymmetries and complete the decarbonization of their portfolios, as well as to create alpha as a consequence of ESG integration: with major economies like China, the EU, and the United States all making commitments to significant emission reduction by 2030 and to net-zero targets by 2050, AI can facilitate this process (Mitra & Maity, 2025). According to the empirical studies conducted in 2025, the adoption of AI is associated with increased overall ESG performance in approaches to environmental protection for better use of resources and reduction of emissions social responsibility as e.g. more equitable monitoring of supply chains and governance as better compliance and transparency.

AI in green finance is used to make smarter capital mobilization, both by finding high-impact thematic investments in clean technologies, and by lowering the cost of manually-compiled ESG reporting, which has often become a barrier to smaller issuers and asset managers. Generative-AI technologies make the process of preparing required disclosures in a regulated environment like the CSRD, which has two materiality tests and must include the value-chain information, smoother, hence helping companies prove their commitment to sustainable development-related targets, as well as help them draw responsible capital (Pancholi & Shukla, 2025).

## 1.2 Role of AI in transforming sustainable and green finance

However, such advantages are also accompanied by a complicated number of regulatory issues that should be carefully navigated. Both the regulatory landscape of AI in sustainable finance is in a fragment state and in rapid development. By prioritizing some artificial intelligence systems in financial services as being of high-risk, the EU AI Act adopted in 2024, with phased implementation beginning in 2025. subjects requirements for risk management, data governance, transparency, and human oversight, especially the use of these systems in ESG assessments affecting investment decisions or credit scoring (Alam et al., 2025). This overlaps the CSRD and the Corporate Sustainability Due Diligence Directive (CSDDD) imposes cumulative compliance burdens, resulting in inflates expenses and legal liabilities against non-compliance.

American landscape can be characterized by continued uncertainty in litigation of the mandated publication of climate disclosures in SEC, whereas jurisdictions like China pave the way to mandatory ESG reporting depending on green finance provisions but decay in overall AI-related protection. These divergences create compliance blind spots particularly to multinational investors since the AI innovation rate is often outpacing policy formulation which creates ambiguity as to whether the auditability, explainability, and responsibility can be traced in instances where AI production is used to support green investment assertions. In a quest to avail asset-backed solutions that aid the sustainability of sustainable finance markets across the globe, regulators are grappling with the need to promote or at minimum safeguard the integrity of such markets (Rane et al., 2024).

## 1.3 Intersection with Global Sustainability goals

No less urgent is the risk of ethics that is associated with implementing AI in terms of ESG. One of these is algorithmic bias, meaning that, given historical inequities, AI models may discriminate against underrepresented regions, sectors or population groups when rating sustainability, which undermines principles of social equity as defined by the S pillar; or lead to green capital ascending others that are genuinely threatened by climate change, which is not the purpose behind the green pillar (Chen, 2024). The large energy and water requirements of AI to train and infer it can create an environmental impact of its own, contradicting the ESG the company is promising in its own right data centers that operate large models are becoming under CSRD-type regimes reviewed to ensure their Scope 2 and Scope 3 emissions. Other risks include privacy breach of data processing of sensitive non-financial data, labor displacement in the ESG analytics functions and the irony that AI could make greenwashing more sophisticated one by creating polished and unsubstantiated sustainability stories.

Such regulatory-legal and ethical barriers highlight why responsible governance systems must be established to utilize the potential of AI in a way that does not undermine sustainability goals (Singh et al., 2024). The new best practices focus on explainable AI (XAI) approaches to improve traceability, adoption of global standards, like the ones issued by the OECD on trustworthy AI, and effective internal control tools at financial institutions. It is invited both by investors and regulators to make ethical deployment the priority deployment of biases, impact assessment, and stakeholder/inclusive design to reduce harms and seek to maximize the benefits to society. Such a balanced strategy can be used in the green law with regard to green investment to create new practices like AI-assisted green-bond checks, and climate-sensitive portfolio construction, bringing between profitability and planetary limits in the end.

## 2. OPPORTUNITIES OF AI IN ESG AND GREEN INVESTMENT STRATEGIES

The introduction of artificial intelligence to Environmental, Social and Governance (ESG) systems and green investment practices has provided transformational opportunities as a fundamental change to how investors seek, evaluate and extract sustainable opportunities by 2026. By operating on large, unstructured data, such as satellite images, supply-chain data, social media sentiment, company announcements, and real-time environmental indicators, which are hard to work with traditionally, AI performs well at processing a large volume of data and does it more effectively. This allows higher predictive analytics of climate-related risks, including physical impact forecasting of extreme weather or transition risks due to policy changes towards net-zero, thus allowing investors to make risk-adjusted portfolio decisions in advance and have higher risk-adjusted returns.

To take an example, machine-learned models are now capable of providing significantly better risk forecasting in ESG analysis by combining unstructured data sources, which transform ambiguous sustainability pronouncements into a numerical finding and justify more serious thematic investments into renewables, clean technologies and circular economy projects (Irfan et al., 2025). One of these opportunities is the automation of ESG reporting and compliance, which greatly saves the number of people working manually, saves money, and improves accuracy and timeliness. Generative AI and natural-language-processing (NLP) tools are used to automate facilitating the creation of disclosures in frameworks like the European Union Corporate Sustainability report Directive (CSRD) and the International Sustainability Standards Board (ISSB) standards, automate the process of determining what is deemed to be material and what is not, the map of the value-chain, and the tracking of emissions across the Scopes 1-3. It is also reported in the industry that the utilization of AI has reduced the time spent on the processing significantly and has increased reporting accuracy considerably to newly allocate resources to strategic decision-making. The current enhancement is especially useful when dealing with the asset managers who control complex portfolios and where AI-driven platforms constantly check the compliance and report any deviations in real-time.

Another critical responsibility that AI has to play is ensuring that greenwashing is identified, prevented and becomes one of the perennial issues that undermine community trust in sustainable finance. By using anomaly detection, analyzing textual inconsistency, and cross-checking with some external source (like satellite-confirmed deforestation or fellow community members) AI detects deceptive statements, e.g. empty environmental claims with no content, with a very high level of accuracy. Tools based on the use of large language models (LLMs), as well as BERT-based classifiers, scan thousands of sustainability reports and executive statements, reveal discrepancies and create more credible ESG scores. This keeps reputational and financial risks away of the investors and focuses the capital toward projects that are truly sustainable better than letting it leak into the market, creating market integrity (Jebadurai & David, 2026).

## 3. REGULATORY CHALLENGES IN AI-DRIVEN ESG AND SUSTAINABLE FINANCE

Within the green investment strategy, AI streamlines the process of capital allocation by providing more complex screening of green bonds, sustainability-linked loans, and EU Taxonomy-aligned investment. Predictive models predict the output of the low-carbon technologies, and agentic AI predicts the multi-step workflow, e.g., the scenario analysis of thc dccarbonisation pathways or the optimization of the improvement of the supply-chain efficiency. The influx of AI-centric energy production has also made countercyclically more opportunity in a sustainable infrastructure renewables, nuclear, and power-privy grids, as the hyperscalers are increasingly getting clean power, via power purchase agreements, making green energy a more economical mainstream game than an ESG allocation.

AI enables tracking in real-time and dynamically scoring ESG, changing the paradigm to not periodic but proactive and ongoing evaluations. Such is more consistent with world aims, such as the United Nations Sustainable Development Goals (SDGs) and the targets of the Paris Agreement, but will allow investors to tap into new themes, like AI-enabled smart agriculture, carbon capture in hard-to-abate industries, and equitable social progress with data-driven equity analysis. Closing information gaps and reducing the biases involved in human judgment make AI democratise access to better ESG insights regardless of the scale investors and small market size, respectively (Joseph et al., 2025).

The fast application of AI tools coincides with a dynamic (and in many cases disjointed) international regulatory framework tailored to the needs to promote transparency, accountability, and fairness of financial and sustainability choices. The main conflict is the speed of innovation versus protection against the risks of bias, lack of transparency, and abuse in applications of high stakes. Major schemes are EU AI Act that subjects to risk-related requirements, CSRD and Corporate Sustainability Due Diligence Directive (CSDDD) that requires more detailed disclosure of ESR requirements, and divergent United States Securities and Exchange Commission (SEC) climate regulations during litigation and political changes. This poses a threat to multinational investors in the face of compliance fragmentation: Europe bases its strict, prescriptive strategy on more rigorous and conservative strategies in other regions, including Asia or emerging markets, which poses jurisdictional arbitrage risks and increases operational risks in global operations.

The main issues will be making sure that AI outputs utilized in ESG scoring, investment screening, or green labeling of finance are auditable and verifiable. Regulators require decisions based on explainability regarding decisions that affect capital allocation or ratings, but most of the advanced models are black boxes, which would be difficult to demonstrate either in the application of double-materiality of compliance or alignment with the Taxonomy. This challenge is further compounded by the data quality problems, since AI uses large, even partial or distorted datasets, which may produce faulty ESG ratings, which can be considered misleading by regulators due to the anti-greenwashing regulations. There are implementation loopholes, and ad hoc controls allow discrepancies, and the vast scale of compulsory reporting by the CSRD puts pressure on resources, especially those of smaller companies.

The rate of AI development is much higher than is policy adaptation, and it creates uncertainty. Other newer techniques, including agentic AI and geospatial intelligence, are being developed faster than guidelines emerge, meaning that a firm cannot be sure of what classifications await or what responsibilities lie in the future (Sundharesalingam et al., 2023). The possibility of this regulatory lag is that it will result in stified adoption or incentive circumvention, and over-regulation might become a bottleneck to ESG development by adding to compliance overheads.

## 3.1 High-risk AI classifications in financial and sustainability applications

Financial services and sustainability applications Ai systems are often described as high-risk when they are involved in making major areas of decisions, including creditworthiness, risk profiling, or ESG assessments with consequences on investment outcomes. A list of high-risk uses presented in Annex III can contain AI as a credit score, assess risk in insurance and lending, and schemes that determine access to any essential services, such as ESG tools that support portfolio construction, green-bond validity, or sustainability ratings, but which create risks to fundamental rights and safety, or discrimination in any aspect of sustainability.

## 3.2 Navigating regulatory uncertainty and the pace of AI innovation vs. policy development

The degree to which AI has already surpassed the regulatory development pace is a source of constant for AI-driven sustainable finance. Companies need to look ahead and manage their requirements and potential inclusion of additional items to high-risk lists or explainability requirements before they over-invest in non-scaling compliance with premature commitments. Such a regulatory lag creates an incentive to delay adoption, and investors can be too frightened of ex post facto punishment, which is why laggards are afraid of being under competitive disadvantage. Different strategies (the precautionary model of the EU compared to innovation-friendly experiments of the U.S.) present challenges on a global scale and require multinational actors to be flexible and modular in their AI designs and perpetually scan their horizons. Examples of best practices include co-operating with regulators, pilot projects within sandbox circumstances, and voluntary standards. To navigate this terrain, the regulation must be perceived as scaffolding in which can be found trustworthy innovation and which allows sustainable finance to scale in such a manner that it will be able to meet the fast-changing technological and environmental needs in a responsible way (Vodenska ct al., 2025).

# 4. ETHICAL RISKS ASSOCIATED WITH AI IN ESG PRACTICES

Artificial intelligence integration into Environmental, Social, and Governance (ESG) systems, which provide powerful tools of data-based sustainability, also brings about the deepest ethical risks and strips the very concept of ESG of its protective qualities that the academic rhetoric reveals. Algorithms partiality is the central issue of this problem, according to which the AI models that have been trained on older or incomplete datasets replicate or increase the inequities that were present, especially in a social aspect of ESG. As an example, preferential training information can fall against underrepresented territories, population groups, or industries in ESG rating, such as the under-appraisal of the social effects of a developing market or bias in credit ratings related to sustainable lending, which will lead to unequal distribution of capital and increase inequality instead of mitigating it. As points out by empirical reports of 2025, unless such a change is conducted according to strict bias audits and against, AI may entrench itself as systemic exclusions, where the tools that are meant to lead to major sustainability are inclusive become tools of discrimination.

This problem is aggravated by AI systems which undermine transparency and accountability in ESG decision-making. Complex neural network designs often produce an output like ESG rating, greenwashing, or materiality, without necessarily providing clear guidance on the basis behind its logic, thus making it challenging or impossible to establish fairness and challenge false conclusions by investors, regulators or stakeholders (Pothula et al., 2025). Such obscurity increases risks in high-stakes processes e.g. portfolio screening or compliance reporting as part of the Corporate Sustainability Reporting Directive (CSRD) where ambivalent decision-making may result in misleading on alignment to net-zero goals or social due diligence, which breed mistrust and liability.

Another, ironical ethical issue is the environmental footprint of AI itself, which is directly opposite to the environmental pillar of ESG that it is portended to serve. The high-energy demands of the explosive growth of generative AI and very large models demand large quantities of computational resources and therefore a significant amount of energy which is both a significant contributor to the greenhouse effect through the use of non-renewable energy and water resources are used to cool data-centers (Ghaemi Asl, 2025). The assessments show that AI-driven data centers are playing a significant role in pressures on the world electricity demand, and that the public opinion about AI has shifted largely negative in regard to the carbon intensity since 2022, enhancing the worries about sustainability hypocrisy. Therefore, to the extent AI applications in the fields of emissions monitoring or climate risk assessment are based on energy-intensive infrastructures, they face the risk of greenwashing in their relation; the tool thus cancels the politics thus negating the definition in the field of sustainable finance.

Other risks involve invasion of privacy of data and exploitation of sensitive information. AI on ESG often works with unstructured data in large volumes, including personal or owned non-financial information on supply chains, employee records or impacts on the community, generating GDPR-like issues in cross-border activities. Several of the previously mentioned issues of unauthorized access or weak defenses may reveal vulnerabilities, and the social responsibility by labor is jeopardized by losing jobs in the analytical position to AI-controlled ESG analytics without sufficient provision to the displaced worker. The possibility of AI being used to enact more advanced calculus of greenwashing represents a systematic ethical risk: incorrectly or poorly managed systems can be used to generate the illusion of sophisticated sustainability reporting: false-narratives (such as unrealistically high ESG scores based on fabricated inputs or cherry-picking data points) that allow companies to overclaim their competence and solvency, and lead unwary investors to make misinformed investment choices (Tariq, 2025). This market corrosion also this prevents capital acquisition in truly effective green projects which postpones climate action.

## 5. BALANCING RISKS AND GOVERNANCE IN AI-ESG INTEGRATION

These ethical risks have a nexus all the bias can result in opaque and privacy-invasive outputs that support the execution of greenwashing, and the high energy requirement can compromise environmental arguments. The unregulated implementation of AI would cause reputational damage, regulatory fines, investor backlash, and more widespread societal damage as AI becomes even more deeply integrated into ESG processes in 2026, creating a dire need to approach changes with ethical rigor and prevent AI displacing sustainability as the real aim in artificial sustainability, creating a strong necessity to undertake ethical scrutiny of AI to avoid adverse outcomes. All these issues should be met with active directives like reducing bias, explainable techniques, and life-cycle impact analyses in order to match the potential of AI with the moral responsibility of ESG (Alshahmy & Sahiner, 2024).

To ensure the transformation potential is utilized and ethical, regulatory and sustainability goals are preserved in AI-ESG integration, it is crucial to balance the high risks with good governance in the moveable environment. Sustainable frameworks offer systemic channels to reduce evil but make AI an honest facilitator instead of a position of weakness in green finance. The key pillars of this equilibrium are a set of international standards, such as the OECD AI Principles, that focus on inclusive growth, human values, transparency, robustness, and accountability. They are not binding but popular guidelines attentive to fairness, privacy, and societal well-being, which are directly connected to ESG purposes of encouraging reliable systems accountable of leadership to democratic principles and degrading prejudice or discrimination in the processes of sustainability ratings.

In addition to this, the EU AI Act establishes regulatory requirements on high-risk AI use in the financial and other environmental sustainability sectors, such as risk-management systems, quality datasets, technical documentation, explainable output (through XAI methods), human supervision, conformity checking, and post-market vigilance. To areas of ESG tools that impact investment choices, credit scoring, or sustainability ratings, these conditions impose traceability and auditability, thus diminishing the element of secrecy and favoritism and tackling environmental effects by documenting resource use.

Ormerging investor-driven initiatives, like the responsible AI models developed by organizations like Parnassus Investments (2025) provide useful suggestions to ethical technologies governance, including bias audit, impact evaluation, and design involving stakeholders. These playbooks help financial institutions create internal compliance frameworks, e.g. AI ethics committees or oversight boards to review deployments using ESG criteria (Bansal et al., 2025).

The best practice in governance is the use of explainable AI (XAI) practices (rule extraction, visualizing importance of features or counterfactual explanations) to enable black box models to be understandable so that stakeholders can challenge and understand ESG outputs. Frequent bias analysis of varied data, and data-governance measures to provide privacy thwart the continuation of inequalities.

In order to address AI environmental footprint, a multiplicity of governance frameworks is steaming to require life-cycle assessments, quantify energy, water and emissions, emphasise efficient models, replaceable power infrastructure and considering planetarity. Internal procedures must include multi-level risk management: the impact assessment that should be carried out before deployment, active supervision of the drift or anomalies, the procedures of ethical concerns escalation. Interoperability through regulatory sandboxes, industry consortia and voluntary standards can enhance innovation as it creates a resilient compliance.

Governance, in green investment situations, makes AI-assisted disclosures reliable and verifiable e.g. audit-ready data on emissions or verifications in green bonds and results in increased transparency, and minimized environmental deception. When integrated within the companies, these mechanisms can enable them to evolve ahead of regulatory change, transform possible ethics traps into competitive plus that generate value in the long term. To balance effectively, it is necessary to see governance as a compliance issue but rather as the infrastructure of developing AI-ESG synergies that are sustainable. Organising themselves around strong, open, and participatory structures puts institutions in a position to mobilise capital in ways that are both responsible and net-zero transitions, social equity, and healthy governance, and in doing so, causes AI work in the direction of reinforcing, not harming the integrity of green finance in a period of increasing technological and environmental transformation (Patnaik & Patnaik, 2026).

## 6. Opportunities and Strategies for Navigating Green Investment Law

The possible opportunities and approaches to green investment law adaption via AI integration provides an effective way-out entry in order to achieve better compliance, efficiency, and impact in the sustainable finance by February 2026. Law frameworks Green investment law, including EU Green Bond Standard (EU GBS), ICMA Green Bond Principles, alignment with the EU Taxonomy, and those in development as law (several national taxonomies) such as China, Canada, and Vietnam requires strict verification, even distribution of proceeds, and its environmental impact to be eligible for incentives, evade penalties, and make it appealing to capital investors. To tackle these imperatives, AI aims to automate the complexities of the processes, lower the costs, and enhance accuracy in the face of an increase in the issuances: sustainable bond market is set to grow in this direction.

The first proactive measure is to use AI to conduct gap analysis and future-proof portfolios against the changing of regulators. Machine learning models read changing standards, such as 85 per cent (or higher) compliance with the EU GBs means qualifying as premium labeling, and simulate compliance conditions, which give issuers a chance to structure framework changes sooner and investors the opportunity to filter opportunities accurately. This controls risks associated with jurisdictional fragmentation, with the prescriptive rules of EU contradicting the more relaxed ICMA-based ones or new bonds that focus on biodiversity.

AI is also useful in carrying out active regulatory realignment through the real-time adaptation of policies through natural language processing of regulatory text, consultation, and enforcement activities (Sundharesalingam et al., 2025). Tools signal future alterations, e.g. possible extensions of transition bonds, natural resources-based instruments under the supervision of ICMA, and enable companies to respond promptly to strategies and earn bonuses, e.g., tax advantages or priority access to financing in green programmes.

The improvement of the congruity with incentives is core: AI is used to optimise the choice and structure of projects to reap the greatest benefits in terms of green bond premiums or sustainability-linked reward incentives (financing). Predictive analytics predict impact measures (e.g., benefits to emissions reduction, biodiversity improvements), which makes sure the proceeds fund high-additional activity, in addition to profitable returns based on enhanced risk pricing. The mentioned benefits arise multiplied through stakeholder engagement means- AI generated insights encourage cooperation with the regulators through sandboxes and pilots proving responsible innovation. AI platforms like Clarity 3:00 algorithm can automate the evaluation of EU Taxonomy alignment of green bonds, faster evaluation and more credible in scale below USD3 trillion outstanding assessments.

## 6.1 Leveraging AI for better alignment with green bond standards and incentives

AI is transforming compliance with green bond criteria and incentives by offering automated, scalable tools of verification and optimisation techniques that have been put into strict requirements such as EU Green Bond Standard, enabling EU issuances of green bonds), ICMA Green Bond Principles, and regional taxonomies. When the value of green bonds outstanding will exceed USD trillion and yearly issuance is expected to persist in momentum due to AI-driven energy needs, AI will improve proceeds monitoring, measuring impacts, and determining eligibility (Homavazir et al., 2025).

AI blockchain is used as a hybrid to provide audit addresses on how funds are allocated, and continually reviewing whether the proceeds are funding certified individuals and employing green sources as e.g., renewables, green buildings and are experiencing anomalies suggesting misallocation or greenwashing. Social networks like Clarity Schedule report provide automated scoring based on EU Taxonomy requirements, like making extensive contribution to environmental aims and not causing extensive harm, indicating the percentage of alignment and providing recommendations on actions to refine the score in order to maximise qualification.

Predictive models are used to predict the outcomes of projects in terms of performance and impact, including CO 2 avoidance or energy efficiency improvements, allowing issuers to construct the optimum bond, which has premium prices on EU GBS labeled instruments but does not gain tax benefits, or appears in sustainability indices (Al-Sabahi et al., 2025). This underscores an increase in investor demand in credible and high-impact assets in a market where almost 30 per cent of climate-congruent bonds failed to match rigorous taxonomy standards in the past. To investors, AI-based screening will pinpoint more focused opportunities that have better alignment and allow them to cut down on due diligence expenditures and increase risk-adjusted returns through more effective diversification into a transition and nature-based bond that is about to come to fruition in 2026. Issuers also enjoy efficient external reviews and second party opinions and can speed up time-to-market and enhance credibility.

## 6.2 Enhancing stakeholder trust through transparent, AI-supported disclosures

In a green investment environment, involving investors, regulators, or the general population, verify the validity of any green investments made by companies, the disclosure of those initiatives, employees, board, and/or executive team will be crucial in ensuring trustworthiness on the part of the investors, authorities, or the populace accordingly. AI converts the narrative-weighted disclosures in reports to structured and machine-readable, real-time formats (e.g., XBRL-tagged) allowing automatic analysis and reducing the fog surrounding these disclosures.

The use of explainable AI (XAI) visualization of feature importance features and rule extraction, ensures that ESG outputs are understandable so that stakeholders can comprehend the models how to generate ratings, materiality, or data on emissions (Almuqwishi, 2025). This will cover the issue of black boxes, explaining all the arguments behind making decisions to claim green bonds or portfolio alignments, which creates a sense of credibility and decreases doubts. AI can be used to identify anomalies in most types of reports as claims will be cross-verified with external sources (satellite records, records of the supply chain) to indicate inconsistencies and cover double-materiality. Generative tools facilitate the preparation process but do not sacrifice accuracy, reducing the time to process and permitting the delivery of timely and detailed disclosures and therefore meeting the expectations of investors to quantify the risks or opportunities.

The trust of stakeholders increases since AI allows managing annual snapshots through constant control, promoting preemptive participation, e.g., dashboards that report on progress towards net-zero routes or social effects. Research associates good and transparent AI-ESG heroin with improved reputation, better access to capital and competitive benefits through stakeholder legitimacy (Sulaiman et al., 2024). A firm's commitment to genuine performance(s) through its focus on audit-ready, traceable products, as well as, ethical governance (bias audit, privacy protection) will, in contrast to greenwashing perception, both counter the perception and align the disclose with global standards. It is an inductive executive that facilitated investor attraction, topics sustainable green investments, and established sustainable finance integrity through this type of trust.

## 7. CONCLUSION AND FUTURE OUTLOOK

AI, ESG and green investment law signify a renaissance of sustainable finance in which technological innovation is able to bypass regulatory challenges, avoid ethical traps, and find immense opportunities in which profitable and effective green strategies can be made. Using state-of-the-art risk analytics and greenwashing technology, enabled by AI, will enable stakeholders to switch capital along with global biodiversity, fairer development amid the dynamism of 2026, which will be characterized by increasing issues of sustainable bond issues. Ahead of the curve, the integration will go further, as predictive sustainability analytics, agentic AI in autonomous processes, standardised ESG measures will become the norm and regulatory gaps will be bridged with joint global conventions and ethical lapses will be filled with XAI and responsible governance. The two-faceted nature of AI as a solution to climate problems and a source of energy needs will promote digital infrastructure innovation based on sustainable infrastructure and renewable energy and adaptive investments. Suggestions are still obvious, clear, investors would need to focus on explainable, audited AI tools; regulators would benefit sandboxes and harmonization as corporations would need to integrate ethical guidelines on credible deployment. One way to make AI-enabled ESG trigger sustainable, inclusive development is by balancing innovation and responsibility to make the law of green investment develops as a catalyst of planetary and economic sustainability.

## REFERENCES


Al-Sabahi, K., Al Mabsali, Y. K., Almaqtari, F. A., & Al-Rashdi, S. A. S. (2025). Transforming Sustainable Finance: The Impact of Artificial Intelligence. In *AI Integration for Business Sustainability: For a Resilient Future* (pp. 73–100). Springer Nature Singapore. DOI: 10.1007/978-981-96-3464-4_4

Alam, M., Ansari, Z. A., & Jafar, S. H. (2025). The technological landscape of AI and sustainable finance: An exploration. In *Green Horizons: Role of AI in Sustainable Finance* (pp. 37–53). Springer Nature Singapore. DOI: 10.1007/978-981-96-6495-5_3

Almuqwishi, M. A. (2025). Navigating Governance in a Globalised World: Ethical, Regulatory, and Strategic Dimensions. [IJRTBT]. *International Journal on Recent Trends in Business and Tourism*, *9*(3), 1–16. DOI: 10.31674/ijrtbt.2025.v09i03.001

Alshahmy, S., & Sahiner, M. (2024). Enhancing the Issuance and Monitoring of Sustainable Finance Instruments through AI. In *Artificial Intelligence, Finance, and Sustainability: Economic, Ecological, and Ethical Implications* (pp. 217–241). Springer Nature Switzerland. DOI: 10.1007/978-3-031-66205-8_9

Bansal, N., Taneja, S., & Özen, E. (2025). AI-Powered Sustainability: Transforming Finance Sector for a Better Tomorrow. In *Achieving Sustainability with AI Technologies* (pp. 27-46). IGI Global Scientific Publishing.

Chen, Y. (2024). A Panoramic Overview of the Opportunities and Challenges Artificial Intelligence Brings to ESG Investing. *Artificial Intelligence, Finance, and Sustainability: Economic, Ecological, and Ethical Implications*, 19-32.

Domingo, M. M. R. (2025). The Impact of Artificial Intelligence on ESG: A Conceptual Framework for Practitioners and Policymakers. *Journal of Management for Global Sustainability*, *13*(1), 2. DOI: 10.13185/2244-6893.1269

Ghaemi Asl, M. (2025). A novel AI-driven approach to greenwashing: Breakthroughs in the future fit between domain-specific Islamic enterprises with varying developmental progress and ESG landscapes. *Future Business Journal*, *11*(1), 93. DOI: 10.1186/s43093-025-00497-8

Homavazir, Z., Madan, S., Verma, S., Gambhir, V., & Homavazir, M. (2025). Governance for the Digital Age: ESG-Driven Framework for Ethical and Inclusive Innovation. *Advances in Consumer Research. Association for Consumer Research (U. S.)*, *2*(3).

Irfan, M., Dias, R. T., Khemka, M., Mondal, P., & Mohan, N. (2025). Navigating Towards Sustainability: The Role of Corporate Governance and AI-Driven Behavioral Interventions. In *Behavioral Finance and AI Tools for Sustainability* (pp. 201-226). IGI Global Scientific Publishing.

Jebadurai, D. J., & David, S. (2026). AI-Driven ESG Investing: Transforming Sustainable Finance in the Digital Age. In *Building AI-Driven Decision Making Competencies for Sustainability* (pp. 29-70). IGI Global Scientific Publishing.

Joseph, O. O., Kevin-Alerechi, E., Olumide, O. J., Sunday, D., Fagbohun, O., & Olanrewaju, S. (2025). Reimagining Green Financing with AI: A Technological Approach to Sustainability. *J Artif Intell Mach Learn & Data Sci, 3*(1), 2346–2352. DOI: 10.51219/AIMLD/Omotoso-Oluwayomi-Joseph/509

Mitra, A., & Maity, A. (2025). Balancing Green and Fair: Ethical AI in Sustainable Finance. *International Journal of Business Management & Legal Affairs, 1*(1), 55–76.

Nauman, M. (2025). AI in Sustainable Investing: A Dual-Edged Sword. In *FinTech and Robotics Advancements for Green Finance and Investment* (pp. 383-416). IGI Global Scientific Publishing. DOI: 10.4018/979-8-3373-0355-0.ch013

Pancholi, K., & Shukla, P. (2025). Harnessing AI for sustainability: innovations, policies, and investment paradigms. In *Diversity, AI, and Sustainability for Financial Growth* (pp. 97-124). IGI Global Scientific Publishing. DOI: 10.4018/979-8-3693-6011-8.ch005

Patnaik, D., & Patnaik, B. (2026). Smart Sustainability: Harnessing AI for Investment Monitoring. In *E-Financial Strategies for Sustainable Development* (pp. 19-44). Apple Academic Press.

Pothula, S. S. K., More, P., & Khan, P. A. (2025). AI-Infused Applications in Sustainable Finance and Challenges. In *Green Horizons: Role of AI in Sustainable Finance* (pp. 197–213). Springer Nature Singapore. DOI: 10.1007/978-981-96-6495-5_11

Rane, N., Choudhary, S., & Rane, J. (2024). Artificial intelligence driven approaches to strengthening Environmental, Social, and Governance (ESG) criteria in sustainable business practices: a review. *Social, and Governance (ESG) criteria in sustainable business practices: a review (May 27, 2024).*

Samanvitha, C., Dharmendra, H., Nethravathi, N., & Velmurugan, P. R. (2025). Artificial intelligence for sustainable futures: navigating social and environmental responsibility. In *Advancements in Intelligent Process Automation* (pp. 129–154). IGI Global.

Singh, S., Yadav, S., Singh, A., Krishna, Y. J., & Singh, A. (2024). Harnessing Technology for a Sustainable Future in Finance: The Role of Artificial Intelligence in Promoting Environmental Responsibility. In *Anticipating Future Business Trends: Navigating Artificial Intelligence Innovations* (Vol. 2, pp. 367–378). Springer Nature Switzerland. DOI: 10.1007/978-3-031-63402-4_30

Sulaiman, A. D. B., Sentosa, I., Osman, M. Z., Roslan, H., & Juhar, K. N. N. A. (2024, December). Environment, Social, Governance (ESG) Investment in Artificial Intelligent (AI) to Improve Power Grid focusing Peninsular Malaysia using System Dynamic. In *2024 8th International Symposium on Innovative Approaches in Smart Technologies (ISAS)* (pp. 1-6). IEEE.

Sundharesalingam, P., Somasundaram, R., Sushmitha, S. S. S., & Rithanya, R. (2025). AI Enhanced FinTech Strategies for Driving. In Proceedings of the 15th International Conference on Soft Computing and Pattern Recognition (SoCPaR 2023).: Real world applications (Vol. 4, p. 221). Springer Nature.

Sundharesalingam, P., Somasundaram, R., Sushmitha, S. S. S., Rithanya, R., & Archana, M. (2023, December). AI Enhanced FinTech Strategies for Driving ESG Investments in Sustainable Finance. In *International Conference on Soft Computing and Pattern Recognition* (pp. 221-228). Cham: Springer Nature Switzerland.

Tariq, M. U. (2025). The Challenge of Artificial Intelligence in Environmental Sustainability: Opportunities, Risks, and Policy Implications. In *Nexus of Environmental Quality and Technology Innovation* (pp. 267–292). IGI Global Scientific Publishing. DOI: 10.4018/979-8-3373-1822-6.ch012

Vodenska, I., Trajanov, R., Lazarev, G., Chitkushev, L., & Trajanov, D. (2025). Navigating Global ESG Investment Regulations Using AI. In *Sustainable Investing* (pp. 153–194). Problems And Solutions.

# Chapter 7
# Automating Sustainability and the Role of Artificial Intelligence in ESG Regulation and Green Finance Law

**Abhishek Baplawat**
http://orcid.org/0000-0001-8603-4874
*Faculty of Law, Manipal University Jaipur, India*

**Aakash Gupta**
http://orcid.org/0009-0008-3920-9991
*Amity Law School, Amity University, Gwalior, India*

**Ishu Gupta**
http://orcid.org/0009-0003-5277-5676
*Amity Law School, Amity University, Gwalior, India*

**Gopalam Sultania**
http://orcid.org/0000-0002-2115-1962
*Amity Law School, Amity University, Jaipur, India*

## ABSTRACT

*Artificial intelligence is particularly causing a rapid revitalization in automation of sustainability practices, especially in the aspects of environmental, social and governance (ESG) regulation and green-finance law. Using machine learning and natural language processing and predictive analytics, AI helps to conduct the efficient aggregation of data of unstructured origins, real-time monitoring*

DOI: 10.4018/979-8-2600-1308-3.ch007

*of emissions, and compliance gaps analysis in accordance with the frameworks like the Corporate Sustainability Reporting Directive of the European Union, the International Sustainability Standards Board standards, and national green taxonomies, minimizing the risk of manual error and preventing greenwashing. Sustainable investment screening, climate-risk prediction, validation of green bonds and alignment of portfolios with net-zero targets, thereby going in the direction of low-carbon transitions, AI enhances green finance performance in the area.*

## 1. INTRODUCTION

AI implementation significantly improves overall ESG performance of a corporation in terms of all pillars, fosters green innovation and helps to adhere to the requirements of regulators in constructs of changing mandates. However, there are certain problems, such as algorithmic bias, lack of data quality, and the fact that AI systems have a significant environmental footprint and limitations to transparency and responsibility. With AI-specific metrics becoming common parts of the ESG reporting, and AI-driven developments developing via the EU AI Act, AI is becoming a two way catalyst either propelling real sustainability or compelling sound governance in order to ensure that the results of AI use are fair and verifiable towards meeting the goals of global climate.

Automation of sustainability and artificial intelligence is an unprecedented paradigm change in how organisations deal with the environmental, social and governance (ESG) imperatives and meet the requirements of the law of green-finance. Companies are faced with increasing pressure to generate verifiable, timely and correct sustainability disclosures as global regulatory regimes increase, whether through European Union regulations like the Corporate Sustainability Reporting Directive (CSRD), Regulatory, SFDR or the newer and emerging in China, the proposals of the U.S. Securities and Exchange Commission, or the emerging markets themselves. Once-conducted traditional manual means to ESG data collection, aggregation and reporting are becoming ever less sustainable because of the volume, velocity and diversity of the information needed, ranging over Scope 1-3 emissions, supply-chain traceability, social-impact metrics and governance transparency.

It is scaled by using AI technologies such as machine-learning algorithms, natural-language processing (NLP), predictive analytics and large-language models. As a case in point, NLP tools can analyse unstructured data on annual reports, news feeds, social media, regulatory filings and satellite images to identify and categorise ESG-relevant data, normalise heterogeneous data and identify inconsistencies or anomalies in real time. A multi-framework alignment (e.g., GRI, TCFD, ESRS) is automated by such platforms as Hitachi RitaONE or agents-in-the-middle emerging artificial intelligence solutions, forming matching gaps against changing regulations and producing custom reports, which decreases the weeks to hours reporting cycle and improves accuracy and reduces human error. This trend of adoption is expected to grow, with more than 50 percent of companies using AI-based analytics to comply in 2025, with tools that allow real-time monitoring and risk modelling using predictive analytics, foreseeing climate-related financial risks, biodiversity harm or social-governance malpractices before they materialise.

AI is a central aspect of the green-finance law in operationalising the aspects of sustainable investment and capital allocation. The green-finance solutions are green bonds, sustainability-linked loans, carbon-credit markets and blended finance, which are based on strong verification and impact measurement to avoid misallocation and to make sure that these solutions are aligned with the objectives of the Paris Agreement. AI functions allege through huge datasets to select feasible green projects, dual-environmental returns to optimise portfolios and analyse predictive scenarios given divergent climate paths. As an example, multimodal AI can combine satellite data and IoT sensors, financial indicators with each other to monitor the usage of green bonds funds, account of carbon, and improve due diligence on sustainable lending. Chinese listed firms studies, as well as global studies confirm that artificial intelligence tools are associated with better ESG scores, and especially in terms of better green innovation, resource efficiency and internal controls. The use of big data at scales that have never been seen eliminates latent sustainability zones, alleviates transition risks and diverts trillions of dollars to low-carbon technologies, renewable energy and circular economic projects using AI.

## 1.1 Automation in environmental and corporate sustainability

This automation is not only compliance based, but it generates strategic value. Artificial intelligence enables proactive sustainability management: predictive modelling makes the trend of regulatory changes, measures net-zero paths and supports impact investing, through the measurement of performance against other companies. AI is being applied in energy production to optimise cleaner production by allocating resources and making future emissions predictions, and compliments green-finance incentives to rapidly decarbonise energy generation. Fintech solutions expanded by APIs and AI instantiate ESG reasoning in fundamental processes of business - loan scoring on environmental metrics and creating dynamic, real-time portfolios and real-time reporting to stakeholders (Joseph et al., 2025).

Even with these developments, considerable issues have dampened the outlook of AI in ESG regulation and green-finance. Quality of data has been one of the fundamental obstacles: incomplete, inconsistent or biased data may spread errors, and this contributes to poor ESG study or accidental promotion of greenwashing.

There is a risk of algorithmic bias, based on lack of balanced training data, which could further disadvantage low-represented regions, sectors or populations to sustainability assessments, which could in turn bend capital flows. The very nature of AI also generates an ironic paradox; training large models consumes vast resources of energy and water, and it is projected that AI may contribute up to 15 per cent of the total global greenhouse-gasses by 2040 if not mitigated, which highlights the need to develop energy efficient models, and to operate data centres based on renewable power sources.

## 1.2 Emergence of AI as a key enabler for scalable sustainability efforts

Ethical and governance issues also make integration more complex as these models cannot be explained, and therefore become auditably hard to trust by stakeholders, which is a major issue in regulated forms of ESG where transparency is required. Functioning by detecting greenwashing through AI-based use of NLP through cross-referencing claims in verifiable metrics, the method has potential prospects although the use case must be supported by large-scale, high-quality labelled data implementation and human supervision. Regulatory actions, including the risk-based groupings and the transparency of high-risk systems of the EU AI Act, and voluntary disclosure in CSRD reports, are indicators of increased attention to the role of AI in sustainability (Alam et al., 2025). Excess use of automation can undermine human responsibility, and psychosocial risks arising due to AI based decisions require balanced governance models which focus on fairness, mitigation of bias and ethical use.

## 1.3 Intersection with ESG frameworks and green finance objectives

The emergence of scalable net-zero transitions made by AI, improved measurement of impact in new carbon markets and equitable green growth is possible when the AI is addressed proactively. The stakeholders such as regulators, corporations, investors and technologists may need to cooperate on responsible AI use through the development of explanable models, creation of bias-free ESG datasets, testing AI assurance protocols and integrating sustainability impact into AI governance. Responsibly used, AI will not only serve the purpose of compliesment but an inspiration in order to get financial systems and planet Earth in line with one another and with social equity in our age of urgent climate action. After all, AI automation of sustainability has the promise of establishing a break between the noble worldwide targets and the practical results, should moral guardrails be adhered to that guarantee technological development contributes to real, verifiable environmental and social development.

## 2. ESG AND GREEN FINANCE LAW WITH CORE COMPONENTS OF ENVIRONMENTAL, SOCIAL AND GOVERNANCE (ESG) CRITERIA

The Environmental, Social, and Governance (ESG) standards are the core building blocks of modern sustainable business measurement in which non-financial risks and opportunities have been incorporated in the company strategy, investment choice, and regulatory adherence as the domain of green finance law. The pillar of the environment evaluates how a company affects the natural environment, both directly and indirectly, and includes such major elements as emission of greenhouse gases, including Scope 1,2 and 3, energy consumption, energy efficiency, the use of renewable resources, waste production and waste management, the elimination of pollution, the use of water, the preservation of biodiversity and mitigation of climate changes. These indicators assess the extent to which businesses cause or avoid planetary degradation and frameworks like the EU Taxonomy categorise economic activities as green depending on the capacity to meet objectives like those related to climate-change mitigation, adaptation, sustainable water utilisation, transition to a circular economy, pollution avoidance, and biodiversity conservation (Krishna, 2025). Practically, this involves organisations having to measure carbon footprints, using low-emission technology, and reporting transition plans to net-zero targets, which are usually under the mandatory regimes, including the Corporate Sustainability Reporting Directive (CSRD) that requires reporting on the detailed environmental-impact reports beginning on the 2024-2025 financial years on large EU organisations.

The social pillar examines the relationships between organisations and people or communities, which are based on human rights, labour practices, employee well-being, diversity and inclusion, health and safety, supply-chain ethics, community involvement, data privacy, customer responsibility and product safety. The major ones are proxies like the rate of accident at the work place, level of training and development of employees, equitable pay, gender and minority representation, non-use of child labour or forced labour, and providing support to local socio-economic growth. This dimension deals with social effects along the value chain, ethical treatment of the stakeholders, or the workers in the worldwide supply chains, to end-users, and encourages fair use, which will lead to high social stability in the long run. Such regulations like the CSRD and new due-diligence regulations focus on so-called double materiality of financial impacts of social issues and outward societal impacts of these issues, making social accountability a part of corporate governance (Pavlidis, 2025).

The governance pillar analyses the structures, policies and processes which drive ethical leadership and accountability, board independence, board diversity, executive compensation consistency with the sustainability objectives, anti-corruption, shareholder right, accounting integrity, risk-management systems, decision-making transparency and intellectual property safeguards. Proper governance encourages proper risk management of ESG risks, the avoidance of conflicts of interest, and the ethical behavior, and measures often include board composition, remuneration ratios, stakeholder-engagement policies, and compliance with codes, including those of the International Sustainability Standards Board (ISSB). Resilient governance supports plausible sustainability assertions in terms of green-finance; mitigating the risks of greenwashing and creating trust with the investors (Mitra & Maity, 2025).

All these pillars are connected, which serves as the basis of ESG control and green-finance legislation, developing out of voluntary norms to compulsory information on combating climate changes in the global situation of urgency. The most important frameworks are the CSRD which requires detailed ESG reporting by thousands of companies using European Sustainability Reporting Standards (ESRS) and includes assurance requirements; the ISSB, which sets a global basclinc such as IFRS S1 on general sustainability and IFRS S2 on climate-related disclosures; the EU Taxonomy which defines sustainable activities to direct capital flows; the Sustainable Finance Disclosure Regulation (SFDR) which requires financial products to categorize the levels of sustainability; and parallel initiatives in other jurisdictions such as China which has green- Initiatives like the Omnibus package by the EU have made the burden lighter by 2025 2026 but without undermining the overall disclosure integrity e.g. scaled-down CSRD scope and timeline postponed some due-diligence and others.

In this regulatory framework, ESG integration in green finance is automated and improved by artificial intelligence (AI). Machine-learning and natural-language-processing applications can quantify and standardize ESG information in unstructured sources of work (reports, filings and satellite imagery) to provide real-time scores of emissions, anticipate risks on a climate course, generate automated assessments of compliance gaps with current CSRD, ISSB, or Taxonomy guidelines. AI helps screen green investments and verify bond proceeds, optimize portfolios to be net zero and identify greenwashing, circumventing claims that cannot be verified by any metrics. According to the 2011-2023 data, especially using Chinese companies, empirical findings show that the adoption of AI elevates the overall ESG performance across the pillars based on the pillar of green innovation, better internal controls, and resource efficiency (Das et al., 2025). The regulatory velocity occurs, using AI-controlled systems to adjust compliance rules, like the new Amendments of the IFRS Frameworks S2 GHG, and minimising compliance expenses, because of compliance architecture that parallels systematic transcription of data between frameworks (Elhady & Shohieb, 2025).

However, there exist difficulties. Weak man-in-the-middle algorithms can give biased results, poor data quality might produce incorrect results, and the energy-intensive aspect of AI might jeopardize environmental interests when powered by non-renewable energy (Al-Sabahi et al., 2025). The ethical issues about explainability, accountability, and the so-called digital ESG divide in favour of technologically advanced firms imply responsible deployment within the framework of laws like the EU AI Act, according to which high-risk systems are categorized to make them transparent. The regulatory business is now urging AI controls in ESG reporting, forcing human controls and bias reduction initiatives.

ESG standards Environment and stewardship, Social responsibility, and Governance integrity ensure the systemic analytical prism of sustainable finance law, which ensures capital flows into robust economies. With AI enhancement, these standards can scale verifiable advances to workforce world aims, including Arden Vienna treaty and the UN long run goal of climate markets, and make quality of compliance a competitive resource instead of an expense. With the increase in strict regulation and maturity in technology in 2026, the harmonised application of ESG presents equitable shifts, so long as ethical safeguards allow technology to be applied with authentic sustainability and not hypocritical figures. Such convergence helps to reposition ESG as a collection of fixed standards to a living system that can put finance back on track to the planet and societal health (Juned & Usmani, 2025).

## 3. ROLE OF ARTIFICIAL INTELLIGENCE IN SUSTAINABILITY AUTOMATION

AI is a pillar of the automaticity of sustainability efforts, with the ability to afford scalable, efficient, and outcome-focused solutions to supporting urgent environmental issues under pressure due to the increasing global regulation, including the CSRD, the ISSB standards, and the net-zero efforts (Domingo, 2025). AI-powered technologies, including machine learning and predictive analytics as well as agentic AI and generative models, automate resource-intensive procedures, which were previously performed manually, and allows organisations to track, optimize, and address the effects of sustainability in real time. As an example, AI uses large volumes of data collected by IoT sensors, satellite and supply-chain data, and operational systems to automate emissions monitoring (Scopes 1-3), energy-consumption optimization, waste minimization and in addition to that, circular-economy efforts. Specifically, agentic AI autonomously handles multifaceted workflows, like the validation of emissions information, climate simulations, adaptive control of energy sources in line with real-time data, e.g., weather predictions and grid carbon intensity, resulting in a transition between simple automation and the production of intelligent and quantifiable results e.g., lowering carbon footprints, increasing resilience, etc..

Artificial intelligence in industrial and manufacturing domains have complemented Industry 5.0 tenets through a combination with IoT to predictive maintenance and optimisation of resources and waste minimisation by artificial intelligence (AI)-based design and logistics. Companies use AI to predict energy trends, minimize inefficiencies, and assist sustainable supply chains, and factual statistics show that they translate into substantial improvements in productivity and reduction of emissions (Singhal et al., 2025). AI-driven drones in agriculture and monitoring of water systems and renewable-energy utilisation can also work to achieve goals within the UN Sustainable Development Goals (SDGs) of climate action (SDG \03) and clean water (SDG 06). AI can fast-track the transformation of non-structured information into valuable insights, allowing the creation of novel insights of early acts in order to take action: e.g. climate risks early-warning systems or autonomous adherence to changing frameworks.

Through prediction, industry forecasts suggest that the usage of AI in sustainability will be past the hype stage and more than 70 per cent of organisations will have implemented AI-enabled reporting and operational systems. This is an automation first strategy, which redesigns workflows and releases human teams to strategic oversight, creativity and complex judgment, at the same time improving efficiency and competitiveness. However, the dual interpretation of AI is twofold: its high-energy form requires sustainable implementation, e.g., of data centres using renewable energy sources, to prevent nullifying their environmental benefits. The AI frameworks, such as the EU AI Act, focus on IT transparency, the reduction of bias, and the human-in-the-loop to check AI responsible use. The end result is AI moves sustainability out of reactive compliance and into transformative action to invest in low-carbon innovation, resilience, and effects of technological advancements on global ecology in the effort to support equitable, measurable global climate outcomes.

## 4. AI APPLICATIONS IN ESG DATA MANAGEMENT AND REPORTING

AI applications will have transformed ESG data management and reporting to accommodate the growing data volume, regulatory complexities and relevance of accuracy within the frames of CSRD, ISSB, EU Taxonomy and SFDR. Older methods of manual operation have a hard time handling unorganized materials such as annuals, supplier files, news, social media, and IoT feeds, which creates discrepancies, latency, and green-, washing opportunities (Sarin & Sharma, 2025). AI is used to automate collection, integration, standardisation, and validation, especially with natural language processing (NLP), machine learning, and agentic systems to turn fragmented data into ready wisdom, which is reliable and just present as part of the audit.

The major applications comprise automated data aggregation AI consumes different streams of enterprise systems, outside parties, and public disclosures, filters anomalies, fills data issues, and normalises across jurisdictions. Persefoni, Watershed, Clarity AI, Pulsora and Microsoft Sustainability Manager are some of the platforms that use AI to monitor Scope 1-3 emissions, comply with various standards (e.g., ESRS, TCFD, GRI), and perform gap analysis in real-time. Generative AI writes its own stories, condenses the mood of stakeholders, and writes disclosures, making the preparation process take only hours to complete (some reports show a reduction of up to 90% effort and 4.5 months cut per year).

In machine learning, data-quality improvement, inconsistencies (e.g., seller emissions) are identified, anomaly identification warns about a risk, and traceability through evidence linking is provided. The AI is agentic in groups: it requests sources and remedies with rules and continually changes reports in response to rule changes (e.g. IFRS S2 GHG amendments). Some of the tools, such as ChatFin, serve as AI auditors of supply-chain claims, and Sweep and EcoActive platforms as cross-referential claims to be used in green-washing detection and in regard to double-materiality analysis.

The AI integration into sustainability reporting is growing three times over recent years, and more than 63 per cent of companies are already using or intend to use AI. Empirical research by Chinese companies on AI and better ESG pillars is associated with increased innovation and efficiency. To ensure it, AI aids audit trails and human controls, which are promoted by regulators and NGOs, including Ceres, which use AI to scale a disclosure analysis. Obstacles encompass it poses a risk of bias in training data and it requires explainability, which can be addressed by right AI governance. Altogether, these applications transform ESG into a strategic asset and allow maintaining a consistent monitoring process, predictive insight and improving the credibility in investment and stakeholder messages.

## 5. AI-DRIVEN ENHANCEMENTS IN ESG PERFORMANCE MEASUREMENT

AI-led improvements have significantly increased ESG performance measurement by the year 2026, ceasing to be a static score to a dynamic, predictive and granular measurement that is directly correlated to the better corporate performance in terms of environmental, social and governance pillars (Waykar & Yambal, 2025). Machine-learning models use historical data and real-time data to measure ESG metrics at a deeper level - e.g. the behavior of emissions in a climate scenario, relative to peers, and material risks or opportunities. Analyzes of Chinese listed companies (2011-2023) have shown that AI adoption has a large positive effect on overall ESG, and mechanisms like green innovation, supply-chain efficiency and internal controls contribute to improvement of all pillars.

AI is used to provide satellite-based, IoT, and operational data in environmental measurement to provide more accurate Scope 3 tracking, carbon-footprint, and biodiversity impacts and accept interventional processes involved in decarbonisation proactively. Predictive analytics predict the risks in transition, possible lack of water or change in energy, thus enabling net-neutral alignment and scenario planning along the Paris agreed pathways. NLP on sentiment of news and social media can enhance social performance of indicators of labour-rights or community-impact, and the governance metrics can be enhanced by automated detection of risk in board diversity, anti-corruption and executive pay alignment. AI can find concealed patterns e.g., the connection between sustainability investments and financial returns, which leads to improved investor-level analytics.

This can be improved further in the domain of impact assessment: AI determines the use of green-bonds, optimizes portfolios to produce two returns, and assists in due-diligence in sustainable finance. Moderation Digital maturity is associated with higher benefits with advanced companies finding greater value in the prescriptive recommendations of AI.

## 6. AI IN GREEN FINANCE AND SUSTAINABLE INVESTMENT DECISION-MAKING

AI has become an invaluable tool in the green finance and sustainable investment decision-making process through multiple methods as it allows investors and institutions to work with complex ESG data sets, project climate risk, and distribute capital into verifiable low-carbon transitions in a relative rigor and size never before seen. Machine-learning algorithms, natural language processing, multi-modal AI filters and sifts through huge, unstructured data, satellite surveillance, internet of things sensor data, regulatory submissions, news feeds, and supply-chain data to filter and pick out green investments that can meet international frameworks like the EU Taxonomy, SFDR and the targets of the Paris agreement (Alam, 2025). An example is the supervised and unsupervised commodities assess ESG-related factors at granulars, long-term sustainability performance ultimately, latent risks such as transitions exposures or biodiversity risks, and heavy-impact clean-yet-renewable projects, cyclical-economy ventures, and clean-tech.

The systems that are automated using AI verify green-bonds by comparing the proceeds usage to the reported metrics, identifying greenwashing by sentiment analysis and validation of claims with verifiable data, and facilitating carbon-credit trading by optimizing market dynamics and guaranteeing additionality and permanence. In portfolio management, AI predictive analytics optimally allocate between dual financial-environmental returns, rebalancing dynamically to current climate metrics of the conditions under the IPCC scenario, and delivering hedging benefits as it has been demonstrated by findings that AI-enhanced assets, as well as green-finance instruments, within the range of risk alongside net-zero transitioning between 2018 and 2024.

Climate-technology investment was also again recovering with a tailwind of AI: driven in part with capital to clean data centres, clean-power infrastructure, and efficiency technology; clean-energy transactions had increased by 31 $ billion to US 14.4 billion in 2025. Within the context of ESG incorporation, more than 90 per cent of the finance teams intend to utilise AI by 2026 so that they can employ profitable green strategy through generative AI in reporting and risk modelling. Green FinTech In Green FinTech, AI promotes sustainable lending through ESG metrics credit-score input, automated objectives of blended finance, and due diligence in private markets by measuring results per SDGs (Wang et al., 2025). The textual, visual, and quantitative data can be processed as a whole to create a more comprehensive analysis that is transforming the way asset managers like Franklin Templeton analyze sustainable fixed-income investments. The empirical study released in 2025 substantiates the statement that AI triggers better decision-making, better risk management, and higher ESG scores under the action of green innovation and resource use efficiency. However, there are still issues: algorithmic biases can favor analyses with a higher concentration of data, thereby ignoring emerging markets; AI energy cost (estimated cash outlay in Asia/US projected 23 per cent CAGR in data centres power consumption by 2030) presents a contradiction of its own unless minimized by using renewables; and excessive reliance makes greenwashing harder to manage, until it can be effectively humanized.

## 7. REGULATORY PERSPECTIVES: AI'S INTEGRATION INTO ESG AND GREEN FINANCE LAW

Regulatory In regulatory terms at the beginning of 2026, the incorporation of AI into ESG regulation and green finance legislation proceeds faster whenever utilizing risk-based frameworks (including the EU AI Act) that categorizes otherwise high-risk AI systems in sustainability contexts, such as ESG scoring, climate-risk modelling, automated reporting, etc.), as systems subject to premium disclosure, bias auditing, human oversight, and conformity auditing (Khaddam & Alzghoul, 2025). The regulators are considering AI as both an enabler of compliance by supporting real-time gap analysis, multi-framework mapping (ESRS, TCFD, ISSB), and automated PAI as well as a source of new risks on which the governance is needed, and the supervisory actions of ESMA 20232024 CSA on sustainability have focused on how asset managers include AI-driven sustainability risks in their SFDR disclosures.

The Making entity-level disclosure easier, product-level disclosure slight, definition of sustainable investment was scrapped, and three categories (Sustainable, Transition, ESG basics) are introduced with thresholds and exclusions to enhance comparability and prevent greenwashing include the CSRD, Stop -the -Clock stipulating directive to be transposed by end-2025) that postpones two more obligations to alleviate burd The new Q&As and fourth annual PAI report of the ESAs emphasize enhancing voluntary disclosures and suggest that the AI accuracy should be subjected to supervision in such metrics as water usage or energy consumption. Legal barriers in the realm of CSRD and the AI Act focus on the issues of accountability, who holds liability against AI-generated errors in the assessment of double materiality and the concept of explainability of AI to audit, data privacy in cross border cross border ESG processing and not introducing biases in new markets. Sustainability Omnibus (2025) of the EU streamlines redundant requirements of CSRD, Taxonomy and CSDDD, granting a clear preference of digital tools and AI in offering automated reporting to avoid costs under regulatory pace. Around the world, similar patterns appear: ISSB standards are helpful in base climate disclosures (IFRS S1S2), but the US regulatory agencies and the Chinese green-finance regulations are more and more heard as AI administers their ESG compliance.

The regulators require AI-specific policies in corporate reports - covering training-data quality, model validation and third-party assurance - in line with larger human-rights due diligence, (CSDDD), that now focuses on AI supply chain environmental footprints and labour concerns. Supervisory readiness deals with sustainable finance governance, regulatory responsibility, and ethical application of AI with the intention of avoiding misuse in a sustainable economy (Teixeira, 2025). The obstacles are harmonisation across borders, the so-called digital divide which puts smaller companies at a disadvantage, and even the emissions of AI which are counterproductive to the objectives of green-finance. Policy guidelines include adaptive compliance designs (AI platforms that map changing rules), pilot programmes concerning AI assurance systems and cooperation between ESAs, the EC or industry on standards regarding systems of high risk. With the AWS cramped-up enforcement of SFDR 2.0, and the AI Act, AI will no longer be considered as a tool, with the enforcement provided in 2026, but as a controlled actor, by encouraging sustainable transitions where transparency, fairness, and human oversight are ensured by sound frameworks to regulate AI.

## 8. CHALLENGES AND LIMITATIONS OF AI IN ESG REGULATION AND GREEN FINANCE

Despite the potential transformative nature of artificial intelligence (AI) when it comes to governing environmental sustainability and green finance, the issue faces serious difficulties and restrictions that can undermine its performance and credibility by the year 2026. The primary ones include data quality and standardisation problems: ESG data sets are still scattered, inconsistent, often incomplete, and take different formats depending on their jurisdiction, rating agencies, and source of the data. According to a survey by Deloitte, 57 percent of executives name data quality as their largest ESG risk and 88 percent of them put it among the three largest threats, thus, drastically limiting the ability of AI to generate credible results. Poor inputs will lead to poor tracking of emissions, poor evaluation of risks, and poor compliance studies under frameworks of CSRD, SFDR, or ISSB standards (Irfan et al., 2026).

Algorithms bias is yet another fatal threat as AI applications trained on unequal or geographically focused data have the potential to reproduce unbalance, leaving new markets, underrepresented sectors, or specific target populations behind in sustainability testing and investment decisions. This further strengthens what is often termed as the digital ESG divide, in which technologically savvy businesses are gaining benefits but the rest lags behind, which may alter the green financial flows in a unfair way. Neither ESG scoring nor investment screening can be biased as it will unwillingly reinforce unsustainable practices or green projects may be left out.

The footprint of AI in itself is an ironic and growing contradiction. The preparation and functioning of large models require huge amounts of energy and water; in Microsoft 2025 reports carbon emissions increased by a factor of 23.4 per cent, and energy consumption of AI growth increased by 168 per cent. It is predicted that data centres powered by AI can place a burden on power networks and the environment, including having an impact on water availability, especially in water-deficit areas, because the growth of renewable power may not keep up with a rise in power demand. These innovations present headwinds to net-zero ambitions because unchallenged proliferation of AI has the potential to negate accomplishments in sustainability and trigger regulatory imperatives based on new ESG reporting necessities that now include AI-specific effects including lifecycle emissions.

Weaknesses in ethical and governance exist: a lack of cybersecurity measures, ESG processing with data privacy issues, and the lack of a sufficient human control can increase the risks of sustainable finance (Nauman, 2025). Without mitigation strategies, e.g. bias reduction, renewable-powered infrastructure, explainable AI, and standardised datasets, the potential of AI in ESG and green finance are limited and may endanger instead of support genuine sustainability transitions as per the remedial urgent climate imperatives.

## 9. LEGAL AND GOVERNANCE IMPLICATIONS OF AI IN SUSTAINABILITY

The integration of AI into sustainability operations companies into accountability, liability, regulation The adoption of AI into sustainability operations presupposes far-thinking legal and governance consequences, transforming accountability, liability, regulation in law of ESG and green finance. The integration of AI into sustainability operations companies into accountability, liability, regulation. The adoption of AI into sustainability operations presupposes far-thinking legal and governance consequences by 2026, transforming accountability, liability, regulation in law of ESG and green finance. The EU AI Act based on ESG is effectively phases-phased in on a period in 20252026, which classifies many of the ESG-applicable AI systems as high-risk, such as those used in emissions modelling, risk scoring, or automated reporting, which consequently forces transparency, bias audits, data governance, human oversight, and conformity checks. This rule overlaps with the CSRD, SFDR, and Taxonomy conditions and, as such, will force companies to report AI practices, data quality of training and validations in the contexts of their sustainability reports.

The liability issue towers over: it is important to know who bears the responsibility of AI-generated mistakes concerning both materiality and licensed disclosures, or incorrect green investment solutions. Companies can face civil or regulatory fines based on misleading outputs under the CSRD assurance rules and nascent due-diligence directives (CSDDD), the debate between developers, deployers or users (Raza et al., 2025). Audit trails are undermined by the opaqueness of so-called black box models, which makes it difficult to verify by a third party and increases the risk of litigation due to greenwashing or misrepresentation.

Governance models also need to change by adding AI-relevant policies: boards now manage ethical AI usage, bias reduction, and sustainability goal alignment through the addition of such aspects into riskmanagement and internal regulations. Proposed standards will require governance disclosure in AI that includes explainability, fairness or supply-chain inquiry, including the ecological and labour consequences of AI under CSDDD. Regulators like ESMA lay stress on that AI must also be given greater attention during supervision over metrics and PAI calculations, whereas global peers like ISSB models and Chinese plans recommend similar disclosure.

The final decision in high-stake decisions will still be controlled by human beings, and this will avert the loss of accountability in automated ESG processes. Additional complexity arises because algorithmic discrimination, data sovereignty, and privacy are ethical issues in cross-border processing, and regulations are fragmented, creating more costs on compliance. The architecture of regulatory evolution policy and pilot assurances are included in response to policies (Abbas & Folorunso, 2025). Stakeholders come up with ethical guidelines when using AI to focus on interpretability and fairness that enhance trust.

## 10. CONCLUSION AND FUTURE OUTLOOK

When artificial intelligence meets the automation of the sustainability process, the regulation of ESG, and the establishment of the law of green finance, this can be considered a turning point in solving the problems of global climate, and social needs. AI has encompassed some amazing features: automation of aggregation of data, tracking of real-time emissions, predictive risk modeling, validating green investments, and facilitating compliance in complicated regimes, including CSRD, SFDR2.0, the EU Taxonomy, and ISSB standards. Empirically, the adoption of AI with enhanced ESG is associated with green innovation, efficient deployment of capital toward net-zero transitions, and a 90-percent-or-lower reduction in reporting burdens and stable portfolios is seen; through reinforcing portfolios.

Still, this development is offset by the persistent obstacles (such as inconsistencies in data, biases in algorithms, large energy and water footprint of AI, lack of explainability, greenwashing issues, and ethical issues), which require mitigation through close attention. The use of AI is treated as a regulated body of laws, including the high-risk criteria of the EU AI Act, the disclosure developments, and others, where AI is seen as an entity that maintains some transparency, human involvement, and responsibility to avoid abuse and harmonize the nature of the benefits brought to people.

AI will be an enabling platform to transformative sustainable finance. New developments reveal the increased involvement of AI into the elements of ESG operations, such as generative and agentic compliance adaptive systems, geospatial physical risk assessment, and multimodal measurement of overall impacts. The energy demands of the AI boom will likely spur clean energy investments (renewables, nuclear, and efficiency technologies) hence creating tailwinds behind green infrastructure, and capital will flow towards green digital infrastructure. Social impacts of AI (e.g. labour, data governance), biodiversity and shareholder entitlement will elevate to more important ESG concerns and resilience will emerge as a primary generator of returns in the face of climate adaptation concerns.

AI has the potential to support net-zero-scope, scalable pathways, increase carbon markets, and assist fair development in case it is proactively mitigated by standardised ESG data, AI-operated on renewable energy, interpretable neural networks, bias audit, and an international regulatory base. The ethical frameworks, assurance piloteer, as well as cross output of sectors need to assume priority among stakeholders (regulators, firms and investors) in bridging the gap between ambition and execution. Responsibly used AI will be way beyond compliance to spark actual sustainability by matching financial systems to planetary constraints, building social equity and providing quantifiable development towards the Paris Agreement and SDG targets. In a worldwide, rapidly growing urgentness, AI serves as an inventor and exponder of anarchy- impacted issues and therefore requires measured governance of technological growth where technological development is not explicitly its aim but instead the emblem of the genuine, inclusive enhanced environment and society development. This trend will lead to green finance and world sustainability with more resilience and what is fair.

## REFERENCES


Abbas, R. O., & Folorunso, E. O. (2025). The Green Future of Finance: Blockchain and AI as Catalysts. In *Energy-Efficient Deep Learning Approaches in IoT, Fog, and Green Blockchain Revolution* (pp. 233-264). IGI Global Scientific Publishing.

Al-Sabahi, K., Al Mabsali, Y. K., Almaqtari, F. A., & Al-Rashdi, S. A. S. (2025). Transforming Sustainable Finance: The Impact of Artificial Intelligence. In *AI Integration for Business Sustainability: For a Resilient Future* (pp. 73–100). Springer Nature Singapore. DOI: 10.1007/978-981-96-3464-4_4

Alam, M., Ansari, Z. A., & Jafar, S. H. (2025). The technological landscape of AI and sustainable finance: An exploration. In *Green Horizons: Role of AI in Sustainable Finance* (pp. 37–53). Springer Nature Singapore. DOI: 10.1007/978-981-96-6495-5_3

Alam, M. N. (2025). Can Green AI Get-up-and-go Sustainable Transformation in the Fintech Division? *Journal of Excellence in Management Sciences*, *4*(2), 1–19.

Das, P., Themmadath, V. V., Jeyalakshmi, S., Lateef, K., & Agnihotri, A. (2025). AI in Sustainable Finance: Identifying Green Investments through Machine Learning. *Advances in Consumer Research. Association for Consumer Research (U. S.)*, *2*(3).

Domingo, M. M. R. (2025). The Impact of Artificial Intelligence on ESG: A Conceptual Framework for Practitioners and Policymakers. *Journal of Management for Global Sustainability*, *13*(1), 2. DOI: 10.13185/2244-6893.1269

Elhady, A. M., & Shohieb, S. (2025). AI-driven sustainable finance: Computational tools, ESG metrics, and global implementation. *Future Business Journal*, *11*(1), 209. DOI: 10.1186/s43093-025-00610-x

Irfan, M., Bhute, N. S., Yadav, A. K., & Dias, R. (2026). Sustainable Investment Portfolios with Al: Bridging Green Finance and Technological Innovation. In *Legal and Regulatory Considerations of Leveraging Sustainable Finance* (pp. 235-256). IGI Global Scientific Publishing.

Joseph, O. O., Kevin-Alerechi, E., Olumide, O. J., Sunday, D., Fagbohun, O., & Olanrewaju, S. (2025). Reimagining Green Financing with AI: A Technological Approach to Sustainability. *J Artif Intell Mach Learn & Data Sci*, *3*(1), 2346–2352. DOI: 10.51219/AIMLD/Omotoso-Oluwayomi-Joseph/509

Juned, M., & Usmani, F. (2025). Technological Confluence: An In-Depth Analysis of the Nexus Between Blockchain, Artificial Intelligence, and Emerging Technologies in Facilitating Green Financial Solutions. *Financial Innovation for Global Sustainability*, 579-597.

Khaddam, A. A., & Alzghoul, A. (2025). Artificial intelligence-driven business intelligence for strategic energy and ESG management: A systematic review of economic and policy implications. *International Journal of Energy Economics and Policy*, *15*(4), 635–650. DOI: 10.32479/ijeep.19820

Krishna, N. (2025). AI-Integrated ESG Scoring System: Leveraging Real-Time Green Data Intelligence for Sustainable Finance: A Study on the Role of Artificial Intelligence in Dynamic ESG Evaluation. *Available at SSRN* 5764202. DOI: 10.2139/ssrn.5764202

Mitra, A., & Maity, A. (2025). Balancing Green and Fair: Ethical AI in Sustainable Finance. *International Journal of Business Management & Legal Affairs*, *1*(1), 55–76.

Nauman, M. (2025). AI in Sustainable Investing: A Dual-Edged Sword. In *FinTech and Robotics Advancements for Green Finance and Investment* (pp. 383-416). IGI Global Scientific Publishing. DOI: 10.4018/979-8-3373-0355-0.ch013

Pavlidis, G. (2025). Empowering sustainable finance with artificial intelligence: a framework for responsible implementation. In *A Research Agenda for Financial Law and Regulation* (pp. 23–38). Edward Elgar Publishing. DOI: 10.4337/9781803929996.00009

Raza, A., Shakeel, M., Khan, M. I., Atif, F., & Parveen, R. (2025). Identifying the recent trends, voids, and opportunities of sustainable finance via artificial intelligence, big data and analytics. *Multidisciplinary Reviews*, *8*(7), 2025234–2025234. DOI: 10.31893/multirev.2025234

Sarin, A. B., & Sharma, S. (2025). The Synergy of Artificial Intelligence and Green Finance for Sustainable Investment. In *Adaptive Strategies for Green Economy and Sustainability Policies* (pp. 83–100). IGI Global Scientific Publishing.

Singhal, N., Goyal, S., Khan, M., & Singhal, T. (2025). AI for Sustainable Finance: Driving Innovation and Ethical Growth. *Financial Innovation for Global Sustainability*, 529-559.

Teixeira, N. (2025). The evolution of sustainable investment: The role of decentralized finance and green bonds in the efficiency and transparency of green finance. *FinTech and Sustainable Innovation*, *1*, A1–A1. DOI: 10.47852/bonviewFSI52024817

Wang, Q., Qi, Y., & Li, R. (2025). Artificial intelligence and corporate sustainability: Shaping the future of ESG in the age of industry 5.0. *Sustainable Development*.

Waykar, Y. A., & Yambal, S. (2025). AI and the Evolution of Green Finance: Transforming Banking for a Greener World. In *Convergence of AI, Education, and Business for Sustainability* (pp. 285-306). IGI Global Scientific Publishing.

# Chapter 8
# Financial Services Law and Green AI:
## Regulatory Frameworks for AI Applications in Sustainable Banking and Investment Compliance

**Pradip Kumar Kashyap**
http://orcid.org/0009-0007-8156-2767
*CLC, CGC University, Mohali, India*

**Saurabh Chandra**
http://orcid.org/0000-0003-4172-9968
*Bennett University, Greater Noida, India*

**Santosh Kumar**
http://orcid.org/0009-0002-3115-6772
*Sharda University, India*

**Urmila Yadav**
*Sharda University, India*

## ABSTRACT

*There are significant changes occur when financial services, artificial intelligence and environmental sustainability are combined. We should no longer consider it a textbook concept. Everyone has come together as a result of the national discussions regarding the potential of AI in light of social and environmental issues. Only by discussing these issues in public will we be able to put yesterday's thoughts behind*

DOI: 10.4018/979-8-2600-1308-3.ch008

*us and look to the future together. AI is increasingly being used by banks and other financial institutions to assess assets for sustainability and ESG concerns as well as to adhere to new green finance regulations. Following that, national organizations in many nations began providing situation-specific input about the use of AI in sustainable banking. Like instructions on green investing methods or ESG score systems, technical reasons must be made available.*

## 1. INTRODUCTION

Maintain the accuracy of your data, "validate" green activities using automated technologies, and make financial consulting a priority when making sustainability-related choices for yourself. These are the integration issues that arise during an ESG assessment. According to these guidelines, financial choices made by AI and other unseeable algorithms must be transparent and simple to comprehend. Businesses must constantly monitor the effectiveness of AI models and ensure that there is no bias in order to adhere to these guidelines. Companies must constantly create attractive records to demonstrate to authorities that they really have, in addition to always adhering to the regulations. Thc basic idea that guides regulations for both environmental sustainability and financial stability. In order to answer these questions, several national economic laws and even international standards have produced numerous comprehensive guidelines that address each step of the procedure.

Strict guidelines for high-risk AI systems that handle money are outlined in the EU's AI Act. In 2006, the Reserve Bank of India (RBI) developed the FREE-AI architecture. It is predicated on seven fundamental principles that dictate the ethical use of AI. A set of guidelines for AI applications in green finance is becoming more widely accepted. According to these guidelines, AI apps must be equitable and fair to all demographic groups, provide a clear explanation for their sustainability decisions, and have the capability to do a real-time risk assessment to determine if financial risks are being impacted by climate change.

The nexus of financial services law is now one of the most significant and challenging areas of contemporary finance due to artificial intelligence. Because banks and other financial institutions utilize AI to manage their operations in a manner that complies with environmental regulations and safeguards natural resources, this is particularly crucial. Businesses and investment managers now see environmental hazards differently as a result of the advent of "Green AI" into the financial services industry. As a result, opinions on Environmental, Social, and Corporate (ESG) criteria have evolved among portfolio managers. These kinds of changes have made it more crucial than ever to have a robust set of regulations that hold companies accountable for their effects on human health and interests as well as the health of animals, while still allowing science and technology to advance (Alshahmy & Sahiner, 2024).

Conventional financial regulatory frameworks, which were initially created for human decision-making, are rapidly evolving into AI-powered systems that can process vast amounts of data to assess sustainability in real time; automatically verify green bonds, improve ESG investment portfolios, and set new standards while upholding current ones, even if one point is missed. Standards Even when these changes are taking place without any issues, such as individuals becoming weary, there must always be accountability and openness.

The laws governing AI governance in finance vary across the numerous "countries of origin" in the globe. For example, the European Union intends to use financial AI using a "risk-based" approach. The AI Act was created in this manner. The FREE-AI framework, sometimes referred to as The Principles, was originally used in India. Additionally, five recommendations were added, and it doesn't seem that this traffic bottleneck will be getting any better very soon! Most of the national regulatory authorities met with delegates from around Asia earlier this year. They developed particular guidelines there for the use of what are now widely used, excellent financial applications in sustainable protection. One delegate said that "such Guidelines can be expected to produce public-interest outcomes."

## 1.1 Financial Services Law and Green AI

All of these guidelines demand more transparency in the algorithms' development, particularly in the creation of ESG ratings and recommendations for environmentally friendly investments. Additionally, they want rigorous documentation of how an AI handles its lifetime, how it handles biases it may have acquired from humans or its surroundings, and integrated mechanisms for monitoring it that not only prevent greenwashing but also ensure that all groups are treated equally. Mandates for environmental sustainability and AI governance are merging due to regulatory requirements for real-time monitoring systems that will identify financial hazards associated with climate change. Additionally, the development of rules in each nation or globally is much slower than the pace of AI innovation in sustainable finance. Institutions must use proactive compliance methods to remain ahead of the competition, keep costs low, and prepare for new regulations since this may create holes in governance and consumer protection (Gupta et al., 2023).

It goes beyond just abiding by the regulations. Unfair lending practices may result if artificial intelligence is erroneously used to green financing rather than environmental impact assessments and treatment. On the other hand, not enough effort is being made to include environmental impact evaluations into green financing. The public no longer has faith in the government. We need robust legal frameworks in order to fully realize AI's promise of long-term economic development and actual climate benefits.

## 2. REGULATORY DEVELOPMENTS IN SUSTAINABLE BANKING AND GREEN FINANCE

The past several years have seen significant changes for banks and financial institutions engaged in green financing or sustainable development. major modifications have fundamentally altered how major financial institutions in nations all over the globe assess environmental risks, distribute money, and display their sustainability criteria. However, when it comes to geographical rules, the European Union has been the most inventive. These consist of the Corporate Sustainability Reporting Directive (CSRD), the EU Taxonomy Regulation, and the Sustainable Finance Disclosure Regulation (SFDR). According to these figures, over 50,000 businesses will collaborate to create disclosure papers with uniform labels by 2028. This is a component of a significant proposed rule that would mandate that banks include risks related to energy and climate policy into their core business plan.

These regulations are now so engrained that thcy hardly vary from the practices of financial organizations. Examples of the 10 common cross-sector templates for reporting physical climate risks and transitions will be provided. Numerous crucial metrics, like the Banking Book Taxonomy Alignment Ratio and the Green Asset Ratio, were absent from these designs. Minimum requirements for disclosing climate risk have also been established by the US Securities and Exchange Commission. This is not just for mutual funds to put in extra effort to avoid being labeled as greenwashed or to identify themselves as sustainability investors. Furthermore, by 2023, the global financial regulatory framework also had regulations that resembled those that applied to a particular nation, such as snugly fitting gloves that were tossed at random locations on a playground for kids.

Eventually, hundreds of local circumstances caused these rules to get jumbled, distorting the overall structure. The regulatory approach taken by the Reserve Bank of India is equally significant. It published ground-breaking standards for climate risk disclosure in February 2024, which will be applicable to all scheduled commercial banks going forward. According to the guidelines, comprehensive reports must include quantitative information about climate-related financial risks, such as whether they are eliminated when a transaction is financed through off-balance-sheet mechanisms, governance structures (including but not limited to the number of members involved), and risk management strategies that are currently in use or planned for the future. The Reserve Bank's oversight strategy, according to the authorities, incorporates both hardware and software.

This indicates that in order to increase staff understanding of climate risk problems, the bank provides several training and seminar opportunities. Even while it has only a passing connection to the dangers that we often consider to be transportation or physical, it also emphasizes the need of sensible risk management. There cannot be any loose shafts between banks in order for them to move smoothly in a single motion. Due to the fact that many routes are blocked and people are living in very frigid temperatures, all forward impetus has instead come from tight bit and spur action. China has advanced significantly in the field of green finance as well. By the conclusion of Q3 2024, the total amount of outstanding Green Credit had reached CNY 35.75 trillion. This represented 13.9% of total outstanding credit and a 19% increase over 2023. However, there are several issues with the Green Bond market (Ridzuan et al., 2024).

As it became evident that there is no environmental rescuer for global capitalism, issuance volumes fell 18% from the year before. However, if Change 4 is successful, how can you locate land that is too different or unsuitable for farming? Another increasingly significant tool for central banks worldwide to develop and oversee climate risk regulation is the Network for Greening the Financial System (NGFS). National banks have received comprehensive guidance from the NGFS on how to report financial data relating to climate change. In addition to strengthening internal capabilities and external communication tactics, this guidance urges banks to include climate risks into their administrative systems. This is so that more individuals in the financial markets are aware of the issues and that people are aware of the hazards associated with climate change. The International Sustainability Standards Board's (ISSB) broad adoption of climate-related disclosures is another example of convergence. In more than 25 countries, these rules are now legally required for over 40% of the global market value. There are still issues, however, since there are over 50 distinct taxonomies and categories for sustainable activities worldwide (Gupta, 2025).

The most reliable site for online gambling is Sunbet Casino. With a quick EFT service and an easy-to-use deposit and withdrawal mechanism, it is a model betting site for the whole industry. Like a secret camera peering down into your stomach, online betting may be a lot of fun and perhaps even rewarding in your spare time. When it came time for us to get our money back from four separate online casinos, what did all of this mean? A winning run often results from preparation and hard effort rather than luck. Because they draw in responsible clients, I believe that high-tech online gambling services, particularly those provided on websites that are safe and secure from issues like unexpected malfunctions or end-of-life events, may boost winning streaks in sports betting. Nights may be very hot or cold, as many who follow this site on a monthly basis are aware. The need of protecting gains increases with the popularity of online gambling. At Casino Online Sunbet, customers may make crucial decisions with a single click, despite the fact that the variety of bets and languages might make it challenging to place a wager swiftly (Singh, 2022).

## 2.1 Harmonizing Financial Regulation and Green AI Innovation

Maintain the accuracy of your data, "validate" green activities using automated technologies, and make financial consulting a priority when making sustainability-related choices for yourself. These are the integration issues that arise during an ESG assessment. According to these guidelines, financial choices made by AI and other unseeable algorithms must be transparent and simple to comprehend. Businesses must constantly monitor the effectiveness of AI models and ensure that there is no bias in order to adhere to these guidelines. Companies must constantly create attractive records to demonstrate to authorities that they really have, in addition to always adhering to the regulations. The basic idea that guides regulations for both environmental sustainability and financial stability.

In order to answer these questions, several national economic laws and even international standards have produced numerous comprehensive guidelines that address each step of the procedure. Strict guidelines for high-risk AI systems that handle money are outlined in the EU's AI Act. In 2006, the Reserve Bank of India (RBI) developed the FREE-AI architecture. It is predicated on seven fundamental principles that dictate the ethical use of AI. A set of guidelines for AI applications in green finance is becoming more widely accepted. According to these guidelines, AI apps must be equitable and fair to all demographic groups, provide a clear explanation for their sustainability decisions, and have the capability to do a real-time risk assessment to determine if financial risks are being impacted by climate change (Mirishli, 2025).

The nexus of financial services law is now one of the most significant and challenging areas of contemporary finance due to artificial intelligence. Because banks and other financial institutions utilize AI to manage their operations in a manner that complies with environmental regulations and safeguards natural resources, this is particularly crucial. Businesses and investment managers now see environmental hazards differently as a result of the advent of "Green AI" into the financial services industry. As a result, opinions on Environmental, Social, and Corporate (ESG) criteria have evolved among portfolio managers (Paleti, 2022). These kinds of changes have made it more crucial than ever to have a robust set of regulations that hold companies accountable for their effects on human health and interests as well as the health of animals, while still allowing science and technology to advance.

In this manner, they are able to develop models that are suitable for both rapidly evolving technology and steady financing, both of which are critical for preserving customer reputation and confidence. Developing monitoring systems that can detect and prevent AI-driven market manipulations in green finance markets, reclaimed landscapes, etc., and ensuring that explorable AI (XAI) standard operating procedures satisfy privacy and transparency requirements are some of the major issues in this field. How our accounting rules will evolve is still up in the air. The Network for Greening the Financial System (NGFS) and other collaborative organizations are increasingly discussing the establishment of global AI governance frameworks based on various Chinese and Western ideas for the responsible use of AI in sustainable finance. However, there is still significant work to be done to determine the amount of carbon emissions that computational AI generates and to ensure that green AI windfalls are really beneficial for the environment rather than just increasing the efficiency of destructive behaviors (Hassanein & Tharwat, 2024).

## 3. LEGAL FRAMEWORKS FOR ARTIFICIAL INTELLIGENCE IN FINANCIAL SERVICES

Globally, artificial intelligence is transforming the financial industry. Risk assessment, asset management, banking, insurance, and fraud detection are a few of its novel concepts. However, the meaning of ease and customisation will be altered by these new technologies. Because of its top-notch academic research, the UK has established the finest regulations for AI development and use in fields like banking. The nation is creating a friendly and open environment that promotes the responsible use of AI technology across all industries. We need even more stringent regulations to ensure that AI technology benefits people and harms them as little as possible. While still fulfilling its international commitments, these mechanisms will enable the UK to advance swiftly (Elias et al., 2024). Both new and existing enterprises' competitive and inventive edge will be safeguarded by these tactics. They will deal with issues like algorithm transparency, data privacy, and accountability (for instance, in autonomous vehicles); monitoring applications that are approved by physicians but are trademarked in China and wind up spying on people rather than helping them recover; or worse, making their disease worse. The capacity of new and established firms to be innovative and competitive will be safeguarded by stable technology. The need of these frameworks demonstrates the worldwide significance of the institutional and cultural shifts taking place in China.

These frameworks will foster innovative scientific and technological concepts, enabling China to emerge as a global leader in innovation. It is almost difficult to overestimate this geopolitical opportunity, which China has to seize quickly. New methods of doing business and new sources of significant savings will be the outcomes. Suppliers will discover new ways to conduct business, save money, and connect with their consumers thanks to these innovative ideas. However, since they use algorithms that are difficult to decipher and see through, certain AI systems operate like a "black box." This raises questions regarding their impartiality and explainability, particularly in sensitive fields like insurance underwriting or credit approval (Alam et al., 2025).

## 3.1 Crucial Guidelines for the Legal Framework of AI

The legal framework for artificial intelligence in the financial services sector is not universally applicable. Different nations' policies, market dynamics, technology advancements, and the actual requirements of financial institutions all need their unique models. Both national and international laws and regulations are subject to the following common rules: Being transparent and unambiguous: The ease of understanding of AI-based choices that impact consumers is becoming more important to regulators (Joseph et al., 2025). Banks and other financial institutions must monitor their decision-making process and provide detailed explanations to those impacted, particularly when they deny credit or financial services.

Accountability: AI information Financial firms cannot hold third-party contractors they collaborate with or enter into contracts with accountable for the choices made by their AI systems. Despite the fact that these sorts of improvcmcnts are expensive, the US experience has shown that they may contribute to the development of user confidence and trust (see below).

Fairness and Nondiscrimination: AI systems are not allowed to treat individuals differently based on their gender, race, or socioeconomic status. Regulators will keep a careful eye out for algorithmic bias in pricing models and credit scoring, for example. To ensure that no one's rights are infringed upon without a means of regaining them, they will also demand more comprehensive audits and effect analyses (Bhattacharya & Sachdev, 2024).

## 3.2 Regulatory Strategies Worldwide

The process of developing guidelines for the use of AI in the financial services sector is continuing unabated. In order to resolve insurance or credit disputes, the Act also incorporates high-risk case-based experimental criteria. They're known as "class-based transcating for sequence executing instructions." This aligns with other EU financial regulations, including PSD2 and MiFID II. Additionally, there are several laws and regulations in the US that prohibit improper use of AI (Kumari et al., 2024). The Securities and Exchange Commission (SEC) and the Consumer Financial Protection Bureau (CFPB) both provide guidance on this. Although India's strategy is still in its early phases, the Securities and Exchange Board of India and the Reserve Bank have already included suggestions for certain industries.

It's becoming more obvious that comprehensive rules pertaining to artificial intelligence will ultimately become the standard as lessons learned from other data protection domains are applied to this emerging field. Global organizations like the FSB and IOSCO are now discussing how to standardize cross-border regulations in order to reduce risk. AI Forum for the Private and Public Sectors A Public-Private Forum on AI has been established by the Bank of England to support the financial services industry. Guidance will come from a common understanding of standards and best practices. There isn't much progress in the ongoing hunt for regulatory sandboxes, ethical AI usage, and best practices. However, there are still many issues that need attention. Laws cannot keep up with the rapid advancements in AI. The lack of transparency in machine learning models, striking a balance between risk and innovation, and regulatory arbitrage—which occurs when various nations approach the same issues in different ways—are other issues that regulators must deal with (Pavlidis, 2025). Because fintech businesses compete with foreign banks for clients rather than merely one another, they are challenging to monitor and control. For the future, a dynamic, principle-based regulatory framework is crucial. It should evolve with technology, but it should always adhere to fundamental principles like accountability, transparency, and justice. To establish the ethical and legal bounds of AI in financial services, regulators, corporations, educational institutions, and civil society organizations must collaborate. This is crucial to ensure that everyone can profit from the digital transformation and to guard against falling prey to any negative outcomes (Shajar et al., 2024).

## 4. ESG COMPLIANCE: AI-DRIVEN RISK ASSESSMENT AND REPORTING

Once a business's voluntary objective, environmental, social, and governance (ESG) compliance is now required by law in many nations, impacting almost all organizations. Technical questions are also brought up by this trend in ICT compliance, such as how to size numerous prediction models using a single measure and procedure, how it will impact public traffickers who depend on this system for information, and how it will impact individuals who gather or examine market data over time in all industries. When these systems were originally implemented, they created gaps from previous inspections, which might put a business at danger.

AI is revolutionizing ESG compliance by enabling real-time data collection from a wide range of sources, including social media, operational systems, and financial records. Not only that, but machine learning algorithms can also analyze large amounts of structured and unstructured data to forecast potential compliance breaches and identify early indicators of ESG concerns. The ability of AI systems to "look" at information from any website or other source in order to generate intelligence profiles is another example (Yadava, 2023). These comprehensive profiles assist businesses with all aspects of decision-making around emerging and prospective ESG issues. Combining various monitoring techniques into a single system will save money and human lives.

AI improves ESG reporting in a number of ways, including by making it more accurate, readable, and less expensive to comply with regulations. Standardized tales that adhere to many frameworks' requirements simultaneously may be produced via an automated reporting system. For instance, it may adhere to the Global Round-Table for International Companies (G3RC), the International Integrated Reporting Council (IIRC), and the Corporate Reporting ESG regulations of emerging jurisdictions such as the planned CSRD from the European Union. AI-enabled counsel will ensure consistent reporting practices, log out data inaccuracies, and establish a trail of records that compliance authorities and stakeholders may review. You are not allowed to enter here. Dancing alone is one thing for Georgia, but dancing as if there were two people is quite another. On the global arena, gamers could have greater freedom to express themselves thanks to EAI (Environmental, Social, and Governance Artificial Intelligence). AI should be used to predict future changes in numbers by analyzing historical data. And we should strive to write them down before they happen (Buckley et al., 2021).

AI may be used by businesses to create a model of potential ESG risks and opportunities that takes historical occurrences and policy changes into account. We ought to take advantage of the opportunity. This property makes it particularly suitable for dealing with financial concerns associated to climate change since AI models can forecast how asset values or company operations would vary in various climatic scenarios. Issues including inaccurate data, prejudice in algorithms, regulatory acceptability, and the need for human supervision in complex ethical circumstances become increasingly significant as ESG compliance AI technology grows in popularity. In order to comprehend the insights that AI provides us when we make ESG decisions, businesses must retain human expertise. Additionally, they must ensure that AI systems are transparent, verifiable, and compliant with current legal requirements. Sustainable management practices will greatly benefit from EAI-driven ESG compliance systems as stakeholder expectations and human standards continue to evolve (Elias et al., 2024).

## 5. AI GOVERNANCE, TRANSPARENCY AND EXPLAINABILITY IN BANKING

The banking sector is undergoing significant change due to artificial intelligence (AI). Although AI can speed up decision-making, improve customer satisfaction, and detect fraud early, there are still some problems in the banking industry. This provides Argentina and other nations with excellent models of integrity, transparency, and accountability (Augoye et al., 2025). In the banking industry, AI governance refers to the regulations that are in place to ensure that AI operates in a responsible, secure, and lawful manner. Explainability and openness are two crucial factors in ensuring the legitimacy of this emerging subject. The "black box" issue, which occurs when many AI models employed for tasks like risk assessments don't provide enough details about what they're doing or why, may be avoided by following these steps (Anghel & Lupu, 2024).

CMC Markets has developed a comprehensive strategy for regulating AI in banking, including everything from ideation and development to implementation and ongoing monitoring. The latest recommendations from global financial regulators and central banks make it abundantly evident that this kind of governance requires much more than just immediately appointing risk managers and ethical officers. Rather, teams of data scientists, compliance officials, attorneys, and company executives should supervise AI systems in accordance with governance frameworks. These teams monitor AI models, do frequent risk and impact analyses, and ensure that those responsible for AI are aware of their responsibilities. Banks can identify and steer clear of any operational, reputational, or regulatory issues that AI technology may bring about by using these techniques (Oyewole et al., 2024).

Additionally, by offering audits and supervisory evaluations, explanations aid in ensuring that regulations are fulfilled. AI systems used for critical financial tasks must have codified decision frameworks, according to regulatory bodies. They also enable banks to establish protocols for situations requiring clerical involvement and human judgment. For example, rigorous guidelines are necessary for generative AI tools as they have the potential to transform data into a "hallucination" or other error. By providing explicit justifications for every decision taken, XAI can clarify which data sources influenced the result and how any potential biases were addressed. In addition to adhering to the regulations established by the Indian Reserve Bank and the European Banking Authority, this transparency fosters consumer confidence and enables the equitable resolution of conflicts (Macchiavello & Siri, 2022).

## 6. CHALLENGES IN IMPLEMENTING SUSTAINABLE AI REGULATORY COMPLIANCE

Maintaining regulatory compliance with AI is a difficult task. The majority of these issues are caused by organizational, geopolitical, and technological causes. They consume the resources that businesses must spend in order to complete tasks, in addition to making the task seem unattainable. Data issues that impact the whole organization are the first issue. AI requires a lot of high-quality data, and when pieces are lost in the ocean or only a portion of the picture is understandable (perhaps due to a mistake made too quickly), regulatory compliance efforts are stalled by unfixable errors and blind spots that appear in environmental and social impact readings without supporting evidence (Mei et al., 2024). Modern AI tools must be compatible with older systems since the majority of enterprises today lack a foundation that facilitates data flow across various systems. This implies that, despite their initial sweetness and niceness, these tools will soon become burdened by tasks that require managing new data, incurring additional expenses, or postponing other crucial actions due to unresolved issues that must be resolved in order to prevent further compliance gaps or bottlenecks over time (Sadati et al., 2024).

Regulation is also made more difficult by the rapid development of AI technology and the environmental damage they cause. Although they are yet mostly undeveloped, the energy consumption, carbon emissions, and water consumption that may be connected to the training and implementation of AI models should be examined in consistent, robust methods. Because of this, disclosures are inconsistent, and it becomes difficult to assign responsibility across the supply chain. However, when considering the whole lifespan of their product, sustainability teams must contend with estimations and proxies rather than precise standards (Challa, 2022). This makes it challenging to comply with new regulations, such as national greenhouse gas emissions inventories or monitoring financial risks associated with climate change.

Businesses working in the policy sector must contend with a highly fragmented global regulatory framework as well as several AI and sustainability criteria. Jurisdiction often establishes a wide range of laws and regulations in these areas. Businesses that operate in many nations must put up AI governance frameworks that are tailored to each nation's requirements (Owolabi et al., 2024). Due to the need for conformance testing and reporting, as well as the possibility of competing duties that make it difficult to implement business plans, this may be very costly. Rules also change all the time. For instance, when ESG disclosure regulations are modified or risk-based classification of AI applications is introduced. Only a flexible and adaptive compliance infrastructure that doesn't need a complete system replacement can keep up with changes this rapidly. However, many businesses don't include that sort of flexibility because they lack adequate personnel who are knowledgeable on regulatory intelligence and change management (Raihan, 2024).

Algorithm interpretability and openness have become major barriers to artificial intelligence's long-term compliance. Therefore, organizations will need explainable AI (XAI), which is a way to break open black box machine learning systems and give people understandable reasons, if regulators begin to look for real-world evidence of how AI decisions affect society, such as how they affect job prospects or whether human rights abuses are occurring in supply chains for what the EU calls "organic food" under its guidelines for environmentally friendly farming. But often, XAI-enhanced systems need a trade-off between interpretability and performance. Moreover, explainability modules are not included in a number of contemporary AI frameworks, forcing development teams to create retrofit solutions that could not fully meet the strict auditing and disclosure requirements now in place (Kazachenok et al., 2023). This conflict between more sophisticated AI capabilities and open, morally good decision-making demonstrates the need for a new kind of governance procedure that is both legally sound and technically sound. Data scientists, sustainability specialists, and attorneys from various specialties should be included in this process.

However, establishing long-lasting AI compliance systems is more difficult due to a lack of resources. Monitoring AI's effects on society and the environment requires specialized equipment, highly qualified personnel, and a significant investment in technological platforms. It's possible that smaller businesses lack the resources or personnel necessary to use comprehensive AI auditing, scenario modeling, and regulatory report tools. This further widens the disparity between the most and least resourced businesses (EI Khoury et al., 2025). According to university instructors, these disparities in capacity might result in unequal compliance areas where only well-funded companies are able to abide by regulations that aid the whole industry in moving toward justice and fairness. Holding just rich corporations responsible for all of humanity's agreements may result in unfair competition and, some would argue, acts that damage their brands. Due to well-publicized environmental issues, the manufacturer of a certain well-known vehicle from the late 20th century had a poor image. Lastly, organizational inertia and cultural opposition must be overcome in order to achieve sustainable AI governance.

We must shift our attention from regulatory compliance—which is only completing paperwork—to value creation and long-term, ethical risk management if we are to include sustainability-driven management concepts into the AI development lifecycle (Papagiannopoulos et al., 2024). In order for this shift to occur, teams must be rewarded for ensuring that AI projects satisfy the requirements from the start of their operation to the conclusion and beyond, senior management must support it, and focused training programs must be established to enhance digital and regulatory literacy. Even tech-savvy companies may not be able to fulfill their intricate and ever-evolving obligations by offering AI that improves the world without this type of all-encompassing help. When taken as a whole, these issues need government regulatory bodies to address infrastructural deficiencies and other issues that have accumulated during decades of seclusion. When they do, the institutions themselves are elevated and facilitate staff growth on all levels by strengthening comprehension and tying together disparate (reinforcing) facets of work (Pattnaik et al., 2024).

## 7. CONCLUSION AND FUTURE TRENDS

It is more crucial than ever to have strict laws and regulations in place to maximize the benefits of AI and minimize its hazards as it transforms many businesses and society at large. AI legal frameworks must strike a compromise between promoting innovation and emphasizing responsibility, equity, and moral principles. This holds true for everything, including fulfilling ESG criteria and the banking industry. This integrated, cross-sectoral strategy originated in Europe in 1957, when several models appeared internationally in certain respects. This method is reflected in China's policy framework. AI regulation Area-specific warnings from countries like the US and India (and really everywhere) are part of the disorganized patchwork of regulations that extend beyond the European Union's comprehensive AI Act. The government wants to improve data governance and management, clarify AI-driven decision-making, and empower people by facilitating the measurement of AI's social and environmental impacts. To remain adaptable in a world that is changing due to new laws and technology, businesses must simultaneously invest in flexible governance structures, a knowledge base that comprises individuals from many professions, and instruments for ongoing monitoring.

Future regulations and governance of AI will be influenced by a number of factors. Regulators are beginning to recognize that cross-border AI applications pose a systemic danger and need uniform norms to address. International collaboration and regulatory convergence in this field are probably going to accelerate as a result. Collaboration on definitions, risk categories, and reporting criteria will be facilitated via the International Organization for Standardization, the Financial Stability Board, and international forums. Second, explainable and reliable AI is moving from being a specialized field of study to a mainstream practice. Standardized audit standards, platforms that can rapidly monitor AI processes in live systems, and advancements in model interpretation have made this shift feasible. Third, there will be industry-specific AI regulations. These will be ambitious regulations that include local hazards as well as how people live, work, and relate to one another. There will be certain exceptions for social obligations, but these regulations will be applicable to highly specialized industries like national security and healthcare. Fourth, integrating AI with new technologies will lead to both new opportunities for innovation and new governance challenges. These include edge computing, which ensures that the data you save doesn't interfere with your daily life, digital twins, which can demonstrate how a change will impact things before it occurs, and blockchain, which creates records that cannot be altered.

The governance of AI should be more heavily influenced by social and ethical considerations. driven by consumer demands for manufacturing transparency, stakeholder lobbying, and the understanding that AI's long-term viability depends on its compatibility with human values and the global sustainable development objectives. Organizations and regulators will need to communicate more, exchange best practices, and adopt a bottom-up strategy that learns from each policy creation cycle as AI governance evolves. Stakeholders can provide a strong basis for the next period of AI development that balances scientific advancement with the maintenance of social welfare by implementing flexible, open, and moral frameworks.

## REFERENCES


Alam, M., Ansari, Z. A., & Jafar, S. H. (2025). The technological landscape of AI and sustainable finance: An exploration. In *Green Horizons: Role of AI in Sustainable Finance* (pp. 37–53). Springer Nature Singapore. DOI: 10.1007/978-981-96-6495-5_3

Alshahmy, S., & Sahiner, M. (2024). Enhancing the Issuance and Monitoring of Sustainable Finance Instruments through AI. In *Artificial Intelligence, Finance, and Sustainability: Economic, Ecological, and Ethical Implications* (pp. 217–241). Springer Nature Switzerland. DOI: 10.1007/978-3-031-66205-8_9

Anghel, B. I., & Lupu, R. (2024). Understanding regulatory changes: Deep learning in sustainable finance and banking. *Journal of Risk and Financial Management, 17*(7), 295. DOI: 10.3390/jrfm17070295

Augoye, O., Adewoyin, A., Adediwin, O., & Audu, A. J. (2025). The role of artificial intelligence in energy financing: A review of sustainable infrastructure investment strategies. *International Journal of Multidisciplinary Research and Growth Evaluation, 6*(2), 277–283. DOI: 10.54660/.IJMRGE.2025.6.2.277-283

Bhattacharya, S., & Sachdev, B. K. (2024). Regulatory challenges and opportunities for future Fintech and green finance. *Blockchain's Transformative Potential of Financial Technology for Sustainable Futures*, 103-122.

Buckley, R. P., Zetzsche, D. A., Arner, D. W., & Tang, B. W. (2021). Regulating artificial intelligence in finance: Putting the human in the loop. *The Sydney Law Review, 43*(1), 43–81.

Challa, K. (2022). Generative AI-Powered Solutions for Sustainable Financial Ecosystems: A Neural Network Approach to Driving Social and Environmental Impact. *Mathematical Statistician and Engineering*, 2326-9865.

El Khoury, R., Alshater, M. M., & Joshipura, M. (2025). RegTech advancements-a comprehensive review of its evolution, challenges, and implications for financial regulation and compliance. *Journal of Financial Reporting and Accounting, 23*(4), 1450–1485. DOI: 10.1108/JFRA-05-2024-0286

Elias, O., Awotunde, O. J., Oladepo, O. I., Azuikpe, P. F., Samson, O. A., Oladele, O. R., & Ogunruku, O. O. (2024). The evolution of green fintech: Leveraging AI and IoT for sustainable financial services and smart contract implementation. *World Journal of Advanced Research and Reviews, 23*(1), 2710–2723. DOI: 10.30574/wjarr.2024.23.1.2272

Elias, O., Esebre, S. D., Abijo, I., Timothy, A. M., Babayemi, T. D., Makinde, E. O., & Fatoki, I. E. (2024). Harnessing artificial intelligence to optimize financial technologies for achieving sustainable development goals. *World J. Adv. Res. Rev, 23*(2), 616–625. DOI: 10.30574/wjarr.2024.23.2.2385

Gupta, A., Dwivedi, D. N., & Shah, J. (2023). Artificial Intelligence Applications in Banking and Financial Services. *SpringerNature. DOI, 10*, 978–981.

Gupta, D. S. (2025). Sustainable Digital Banking: Exploring The Role of Fintech in Promoting Green Finance and Sustainable Development Goals. *Journal of Information Systems Engineering & Management, 10*(3).

Hassanein, A., & Tharwat, H. (2024). Artificial intelligence (AI) and green finance. In *The Palgrave Handbook of Green Finance for Sustainable Development* (pp. 859–889). Springer International Publishing. DOI: 10.1007/978-3-031-65756-6_32

Joseph, O. O., Kevin-Alerechi, E., Olumide, O. J., Sunday, D., Fagbohun, O., & Olanrewaju, S. (2025). Reimagining Green Financing with AI: A Technological Approach to Sustainability. *J Artif Intell Mach Learn & Data Sci, 3*(1), 2346–2352. DOI: 10.51219/AIMLD/Omotoso-Oluwayomi-Joseph/509

Kazachenok, O. P., Stankevich, G. V., Chubaeva, N. N., & Tyurina, Y. G. (2023). Economic and legal approaches to the humanization of FinTech in the economy of artificial intelligence through the integration of blockchain into ESG Finance. *Humanities & Social Sciences Communications, 10*(1), 1–9. DOI: 10.1057/s41599-023-01652-8

Kumari, B., Kaur, J., & Swami, S. (2024). Adoption of artificial intelligence in financial services: A policy framework. *Journal of Science and Technology Policy Management, 15*(2), 396–417. DOI: 10.1108/JSTPM-03-2022-0062

Macchiavello, E., & Siri, M. (2022). Sustainable finance and fintech: Can technology contribute to achieving environmental goals? A preliminary assessment of 'green fintech'and 'sustainable digital finance'. *European Company and Financial Law Review, 19*(1), 128–174. DOI: 10.1515/ecfr-2022-0005

Mei, H., Bodog, S. A., & Badulescu, D. (2024). Artificial intelligence adoption in sustainable banking services: The critical role of technological literacy. *Sustainability (Basel), 16*(20), 8934. DOI: 10.3390/su16208934

Mirishli, S. (2025). Regulating Ai In Financial Services: Legal Frameworks And Compliance Challenges. *arXiv preprint arXiv:2503.14541*.

Owolabi, O. S., Uche, P. C., Adeniken, N. T., Ihejirika, C., Islam, R. B., & Chhetri, B. J. T. (2024). Ethical implication of artificial intelligence (AI) adoption in financial decision making. *Computer and Information Science, 17*(1), 1–49. DOI: 10.5539/cis.v17n1p49

Oyewole, A. T., Adeoye, O. B., Addy, W. A., Okoye, C. C., Ofodile, O. C., & Ugochukwu, C. E.Adedoyin Tolulope OyewoleOmotayo Bukola AdeoyeWilhelmina Afua AddyChinwe Chinazo OkoyeOnyeka Chrisanctus OfodileChinonye Esther Ugochukwu. (2024). Promoting sustainability in finance with AI: A review of current practices and future potential. *World Journal of Advanced Research and Reviews, 21*(3), 590–607. DOI: 10.30574/wjarr.2024.21.3.0691

Paleti, S. (2022). The Role of Artificial Intelligence in Strengthening Risk Compliance and Driving Financial Innovation in Banking. *Available at SSRN* 5250770. DOI: 10.21275/SR22123165037

Papagiannopoulos, I., Ntanos, C., Pelekis, S., Tzortzis, A. M., Koutalidis, H., Karakolis, E., . . . Askounis, D. (2024, July). Enhancing green financing through AI analytics and cross-domain data sharing. In *2024 15th International Conference on Information, Intelligence, Systems & Applications (IISA)* (pp. 1-11). IEEE. DOI: 10.1109/IISA62523.2024.10786617

Pattnaik, D., Ray, S., & Raman, R. (2024). Applications of artificial intelligence and machine learning in the financial services industry: A bibliometric review. *Heliyon, 10*(1), e23492. DOI: 10.1016/j.heliyon.2023.e23492

Pavlidis, G. (2025). Empowering sustainable finance with artificial intelligence: a framework for responsible implementation. In *A Research Agenda for Financial Law and Regulation* (pp. 23–38). Edward Elgar Publishing. DOI: 10.4337/9781803929996.00009

Raihan, A. (2024). Financial technology optimization using artificial intelligence (AI) to accomplish sustainable development goals (SDGs). In *Proceedings of the International Conference on on Digital Finance, Green Innovation, and Sustainable Development.*

Ridzuan, N. N., Masri, M., Anshari, M., Fitriyani, N. L., & Syafrudin, M. (2024). AI in the financial sector: The line between innovation, regulation and ethical responsibility. *Information (Basel), 15*(8), 432. DOI: 10.3390/info15080432

Sadati, A., Gramlich, D., & Walker, T. (2024). Artificial Intelligence, Finance, and Sustainability: An Overview. *Artificial Intelligence, Finance, and Sustainability: Economic, Ecological, and Ethical Implications*, 3-16.

Shajar, S. N., Kashif, M., George, J., & Nasir, S. (2024). The future of green finance: Artificial intelligence-enabled solutions for a more sustainable world. In *Harnessing blockchain-digital twin fusion for sustainable investments* (pp. 316–328). IGI Global Scientific Publishing. DOI: 10.4018/979-8-3693-1878-2.ch013

Singh, V. K. (2022). Regulatory and legal framework for promoting green digital finance. In *Green digital finance and sustainable development goals* (pp. 3–27). Springer Nature Singapore. DOI: 10.1007/978-981-19-2662-4_1

Yadava, A. (2023). Ethical and regulatory challenges of AI adoption in the financial services sector: A global perspective. *International Journal of Science and Research Archive*, *10*(13), 10–30574.

# Chapter 9
# Enhancing Green Investment Through AI and Automation:
## A Critical Legal Study of Regulatory Frameworks Effectiveness in Tackling Cybersquatting in India

**Ashwin Yadav**
*Amity Law School, Amity University, Gwalior, India*

**Vijay Srivastava**
http://orcid.org/0000-0002-3034-9903
*Amity Law School, Amity University, Gwalior, India*

**Hemant Singh**
http://orcid.org/0000-0002-1258-5187
*Amity Law School, Amity University, Gwalior, India*

## ABSTRACT

*The emerging breakthrough in technology in artificial intelligence and automation technologies present incredible opportunities to drive the truly green investment in India specifically in the spheres of renewable energy, sustainable finance and climate-resilient infrastructure. These tools will facilitate faster allocation of resources to environmentally friendly projects by reducing the risk of investments in these projects forecasting and automating the monitoring of compliance with environmental protection and commitments, which are consistent with the net-zero India*

DOI: 10.4018/979-8-2600-1308-3.ch009

*by 2070 and the United Nations Sustainable Development Goals. Nonetheless, the growth of green brand digital platforms, fintech programs, and sustainability efforts increases the vulnerability to cyber form of squatting known as bad-faith domain name registration to tap into the goodwill acquired over time or overtime cyber interference. This type of activity trims down investor confidence, brand integrity, and efficient digital marketing that is a necessity to attract green funds.*

## 1. INTRODUCTION

The current Indian statutes lack any anti-cybersquatting specific law like the one found in the U.S. in the Anti-cybersquatting Consumer Protection Act (ACPA), but offer possible solutions through infringement lawsuits, passing-off lawsuits and arbitration manners, the present regulatory frameworks comprise the Trade Marks Act, 1999, the Information Technology Act, 2000, and the .IN Dispute Resolution Policy (INDRP). This should be seen as a legal analysis that determines how effective the frameworks are in stopping cybersquatting as part of green ecosystems that can be fuelled by AI, focussing on the lack of proactive protection, quick-notice action, and responsiveness to new online risks. It states that the existing mechanisms provided partial security, but the reactive character restricts the deterrence in the rapidly changing on-line environment, and its reforms are necessary to incorporate AI-powered monitoring and reinforce domain control to ensure the preservation of sustainable flows of investments.

The concept of artificial intelligence, automation and green investment is a critical paradigm shift in India in realizing sustainable economic growth (Mondal et al., 2025). Being the third-largest producer of greenhouse emissions in the world and a leader in the number of renewable-energy capacity additions, India is faced with dual challenge of increasing clean-technology investment and overcoming climate vulnerability. Investment in green, which includes solar, wind, hydrogen, energy storage, electric mobility and circular-economy initiatives, has been in a spurt, both through mechanisms like green bonds, sovereign green bonds, and through the National Action Plan on Climate Change (NAPCC), and India updated Nationally Determined Contributions. AI and automation are categories of force multipliers: machine-learning systems improve predictive analytics of anticipating renewable-energy yields, smart grids in terms of energy efficiency, greenwashing via automating ESG reporting, and sustainable-finance portfolio management. An example is that AI-based platforms allow assessing high-risk scenarios in real time, detecting fraud in green initiatives, and ensuring accuracy in committing funds to high-impact opportunities, which reduces the transaction costs and increases confidence in investors. Application in Supply-Chain Traceability of Green manufacturing and regulatory-compliance monitoring is also supported by automation and is part of the IndiaAI Mission and the BRS Compulsoriness of Sustainability Reporting requirements at the SEBI.

## 1.1 Conceptual Framework of AI and Automation in Green Investments

The digitalization transformation only increases the vulnerability to cyber-attacks, especially to cybersquatting, which is the unscrupulous registration of the domain names similar or identical to registered trademarks to obtain goodwill, business disruption, or phishing and fraud. Cybersquatters of well-known brands in the green-investment industry disrupt potential investors, damage reputations, and diminish the trust that is essential to crowdsourcing and generating venture-capital financings, populist-venture-capitals, and public-privax relationships. These cases may postpone project funding, augment due diligence expenses and discourage foreign-directed investment in Indian green corridors, which are optinative in scope (Meghwal., 2024).

The legal framework of cybersquatting of India is still detached and in fragmented form. In contrast to jurisdictions that have tailor-made laws including the United States Anti-cybersquatting Consumer Protection Act, India uses a patchwork of provisions. The Trade Marks Act, 1999, especially in Section 29 on infringement and passing off remedies, considers the domain names to be a protectable intellectual property as spelled out in landmark cases like Satyam Infoway Ltd. v. Sifynet Solutions where the Supreme Court expressed the separate case between domain names and business goodwill. Registering bad faith and consumer confusion proves are granted damages, transfers of domain, and injunctions. To supplement it, the Information Technology Act, 2000, touches upon the corresponding cyber harms but is not directly designed to deal with domain squatting. In the case of .in domains, the .IN Dispute Resolution Policy administered by the National Internet Exchange of India, and basing on the Uniform Domain Name Dispute Resolution Policy, applies an expedited method centered on arbitration, in which the complainant would be required to establish similarity in their trademarks, no legitimate interest of its registration by a registerer, and bad-faith registration or use of the domain name or name element. Winning cases lead to domain cancellation or assignment, which is a low cost alternative to legal action.

These tools notwithstanding, there exist serious limitations. The lack of a specific anti-cybersquatting legislation makes enforcing one a reactive, lengthy, and expensive process, especially to new green businesses with less powerful legal organizations. Speedy compensation in a borderless digital environment is hampered by judicial slowness, the scarcity of evidence of bad faith, and its narrow extraterritorial scope.

Additionally, due to the explosive development of AI, as seen in the influx of new domain registration of minimum of .ai domains and the introduction of AI-based domain surveillance, the threat space changes quicker than traditional frameworks. Automation is used by the cybersquatters to bulk-register, and the honest green investors face even greater challenges with typosquatting or malicious websites posing as sustainable websites.

### 1.2 India's Green Finance Landscape and Net-Zero Commitments

This chapter intends to give a critical analysis of the effectiveness of the regulatory frameworks in India to address cybersquatting in the setting of AI-enhanced green investment. It examines the statutory law, court precedent, INDRP resolutions and International analogies on whether laws are imperfect in terms of deterring, response time factors, and the lack of integration of technical protections. The analysis highlights the problematic nature of cybersquatting in promoting digital branding which is critical to getting green finance mobilized and could put the process of transitioning India to a low-carbon economy in stasis. This study recommends a robust techno-legal ecosystem by suggesting reforms such as AI-assisted proactive monitoring, new statutes on explicit penalties against cybersquatting, and compatibility with the emerging guidance of the AI governance (Akinbeye, 2023). This would protect intellectual property in the green sector, and, in addition, build investor confidence, pioneer the green sector more rapidly in deploying sustainable capital, and strengthen India in leadership in climate-oriented innovation as the world transitions to sustainability.

## 2. AI-DRIVEN INNOVATIONS IN GREEN INVESTMENTS AND ROLE OF AI IN ESG ANALYTICS AND PREDICTIVE MODELING

Artificial intelligence is radically transforming the scenery of green investment by empowering the allocation of capital to sustainable projects in a more precise, more efficient, and scalable way, and especially in the areas of renewable energy, adapting to climate change, and the construction of low-carbon infrastructures (Chhabra Roy & Prabhakaran, 2023). Within the context of the ambitious goals of India, including a target of 500 GW of the non-fossil fuel capacity within 2030 and a target of net-zero emissions in 2070, AI will be an essential catalyst to fund the necessary trillions of dollars. The latest AI applications in the field of innovations feature the innovative predictive modelling that can predict the renewable energy output, evaluate the risks of the climate to the project itself, and use artificial intelligence to optimise the returns eventually adjusted to risk. Based on satellite imagery, meteorological patterns, past performances, and market trends, machine-learning algorithms make predictions about the amount of energy that will be generated by solar and wind farms more accurately than previous approaches, minimising uncertainty and drawing institutional investors who have traditionally exhibited a low level of tolerance towards intermittency risk.

The pillars of AI effect are in relation to ESG analytics that AI converts fragmented and usually unreliable information to actionable data. Inconsistencies, greenwashing, and little disclosure are typical traits of traditional ESG assessment, which is especially acute in the emerging markets like India. AI helps in these gaps with the use of natural language processing (NLP) that allows the research of unstructured data obtained via corporate reports, news pieces, social media, and regulatory filings. They are used to retrieve sentiment and materiality words on the environmental, social and governance aspects. Predictive modelling, in turn, adds a notch to this process through predicting upcoming performance of ESG and possible risks, including regulatory changes, supply-chain disruption caused by climatic events, or reputational losses, and, by doing that, enables investors to expect the value loss or gain of sustainable assets. In one instance, AI initiatives incorporate geospatial information to forecast physical climate threats e.g. flood effects on infrastructure), transition risks and policy alterations favouring renewables and thus facilitate the rebalancing of a portfolio dynamically.

AI implementation boosting net ESG by achieving greater green innovation, supply-chain efficiency, as well as transparency, eventually leading to superior risk-adjusted returns, exposure to stranded assets in the fossil-fuel-contingent industry. In sustainable finance, AI-driven solutions are used to automate greenwashing by complying with frameworks including SEBI BRSR and global standards (TCFD, ISSB) by identifying anomalies by means of anomaly detection, and verifying claims with sources of verifiable information. Through this process, the increase in the investor confidence, faster capital flows to green bonds, ETFs, and impact funds and alignment of the investment with NAPCC in India and the SDGs are achieved. Through democratizing the ownership of advanced analytics, historically limited to large asset managers only, AI can also give retail and SME investors the chance to become involved in green transitions and thus increase the funds of sustainable development.

## 2.1 Automation in Carbon Tracking and Sustainable Supply Chains

The use of AI as a driver of automation is essentially transforming carbon tracking and sustainable supply chains making them become transparent, real-time and data-driven systems which can no longer be ignored in process decarbonisation. Automation in the Indian context- where manufacturing, logistics and agriculture are major contributors of Scope 3 emissions- helps to measure, report, and reduce the greenhouse gases in global value chains more precisely (Kaur, 2024). The ingestion of data by AI algorithms comes not only in the form of IoT sensors, freight invoices, supplier disclosures, and satellite photographs but also a variety of other output sources with subsequent use of standardized emissions factors (commonly those stipulated by the GHG Protocol) to compute carbon footprints at low human-level involvement. Such a strategy solves long-term issues of data silos, inaccuracies, and under-reporting, especially in regard to Scope 3 emissions, usually comprising 7090 percent of corporate totals.

The automation in supply chains allows predictive analytics, identifying hotspots (e.g. high-emitting suppliers, inefficient routes, or processes consuming a lot of waste) and proposes optimisations such as route rerouting, load consolidation or modal changes (such as rail over road). Machine-learning models are constantly being updated on new operational information to enhance their accuracy as the process proceeds and allow scenario modelling of low-carbon alternatives. As an example, logistics AI can cut fuel use by 1020 percent with dynamic routes and predictive maintenance and emit directly by mitigating disruption with increased resilience. Start-ups and businesses in India use the tools to meet new regulations in GHG reporting and CDP disclosures as things are invented and automated to create audit-ready report formats since each report covers different scopes and incorporation of net-zero roadmap.

Moreover, automation advances supplier involvement by assessing sustainability sustainability at the product scale thereby motivating a cleaner option by clear grading (Ajakaye & Lawal, 2023). This promotes coordinated decarbonisation, with AI seeing consortium sharing of cutbacks at levels within the chain of supply. Altogether, such developments not only reduce the total emissions with 1030% of reductions in the areas of focus, but also boost the efficiency of operations, reduce the costs and improve the readiness to the regulations will help to make Indian industries competitive actors in the global sustainable markets.

## 2.2 Blockchain-AI Hybrids in Renewable Energy Funding

The integration of blockchain and AI also forms strong hybrid systems that mitigate the main obstacles in the field of finance into renewable energy by improving the transparency, efficiency, and accessibility of green finance. The immutable ledgers of provenance, ownership and transactions offered through blockchain are complemented by intelligent analytics and risk assessment provided by AI, and allow predictive capabilities and the development of a tokenised asset, smart contract and decentralised funding frameworks to support solar, wind, and storage projects.

In renewable energy, blockchain tokenises physical scripts, including solar installations or green bonds, which are keenly eligible into stakes so that retail and institutional investors can buy the assets by way of a framework that certifies impact (e.g. tokenised renewable energy certificates or RECs). this is negated by Ai which analyzes the data of projects to forecast the performance, cash flows, and risks-optimizing pricing, identifying fraud, and aligning the investors with high-impact opportunities. Smart contracts allow compliance to be automated with the verification of emissions and the allocation of revenue based on smart contract ruled milestones e.g., energy generation milestones monitored by AI (Sujay, 2025).

This would combine these extensive funding divides by decreasing the number of intermediaries, cutting organization expenses, and alleviating information asymmetry, which is essential to enlarge the size of renewables in capital-poor areas like India. Peer-to-peer trading of energy on the blockchain or making cross-border investments in green investments with complete origin traceability, and AI predicting yields and eco-social responsibility are the examples of how this will be implemented. New models in the combination of AI, blockchain, and green finance enjoy lower risks in portfolios, and open liquid markets of climate resource. In India, these types of hybrids are correlated with like efforts as green bonds and the IndiaAI Mission, thus rapidly rolling out renewables and helping to achieve net-zeroes by creating new technologically-enabled funding platforms.

## 3. CYBERSQUATTING THREATS IN DIGITAL GREEN PLATFORMS

Cybersquatting on the emerging green economy in India has escalated with the proliferation of digital green spaces online portals to green bonds, renewable energy crowdfunding, applications to ESG investments, carbon credit markets and sustainability-tracking tools. They are major entry-level mobilisation of capital targets on solar farms, wind, electric-vehicle infrastructure and climate-finance projects, and they tend to be much reliant on high-quality digital branding to draw domestic and other investors. Cybersquatter capitalize on this addiction by registering domain names that resemble existing legitimate green organizations, whether as misspellings of established suggestive links, like the name tataSolar.in (that should be tatasolar.in), or as generic terms, such as greenindiafund.com, to implicate themselves as official sustainability websites. These actions redirect traffic, collect user information, or support phishing attacks on investors looking to get approved ESG opportunities (Mondal et al., 2025).

The challenge of cybersquatting in the context of India is in the fact that green-investment inflows are expected to take hundreds of billions of dollars to enable the country to achieve 2030 renewable-energy goals through digital channels, which requires that platforms remain uncompromised by cybersquatting erosion of trust. False websites may post spurious information regarding project feasibility, carbon credits or returns resulting in poor allocation of funds or losses by investors. Further, as investor onboarding and live ESG dashboards are automated with AI-enhanced platforms, squatters use automated systems to run campaigns registering large quantities of domains, which only increases the intensity and pace of attacks. Not only does it disrupt fair business activities, that is, inducing down-time, customer-support overhead and legal expenses, but it also undermines the overall use of digital green-finance instruments that should be encouraged as part of SEBI-regulated activity and the National Green Hydrogen Mission. The lack of strong preventive systems worsens the situation because the existing laws do not formulate reactive solutions that can discourage highly combined players who exploit the fact that the internet has no borders.

## 3.1 Defining Cybersquatting in AI-Enabled Sustainability Domains

Cybersquatting in sustainability-related AI-powered domains is the misappropriation of domain names that are registered and worked in bad faith and the major purpose are to make goodwill, disrupt operations, or bring harm to users in the sustainability sector. In contrast to older cybersquatting with commercial brands, in this type, domains with AI-related extensions (such as .ai) or sustainability keywords such as aigreenenergy, sustainableaiindia, or esgaiplatform are squatted, usually pretending to be some real organization in the renewable technology, carbon analytics, or smart sustainability solutions.

Squatters also take advantage of the hype in AI-enable areas such as predictive ESG modelling, automated off-the-balance sheet carbon tracking, and AI-trained renewable forecasting. Indicatively, by registering names that are similar to AI start-ups within the green technology (such as different formative names of some of the other venture brands associated with the IndiaAI Mission) one can set up phishing pages implying that the specific company is offering an innovative sustainability tool and expecting to receive investment information or credentials. Lack of legitimate interest, the intention of offering the domain to a higher price to someone instead of selling it to the genuine buyer, or directing the traffic to rival or scam websites are all forms of bad faith. This form itself involves the evolution of AI, with squatters finding valuable domain combinations in so short a time with generative tools.

These types of practices in India are included in wider IP infringement, still they do not contain special anti-cybersquatting laws, they use the Trade Marks Act, 1999, and INDRP. Nevertheless, the contribution of AI compound threat as a more personalised scam or deep-major fusion empowerment to squattled sites tricksters that a claim is AI-verified being green. This not only violates the trademarks but also continues with the greenwashing of equating false platforms with the legitimate sustainability activity (Ahmad & Kumar, 2023).

## 3.2 Vulnerabilities in Green Investment Portals and Smart Grids

The high susceptibility to cybersquatting is shown by green investment portals and smart grids, being digital-first and highly dependent on online trust as a prerequisite to mobilise capital and to be an efficient way to operate. Green portals, where investments in renewables, green bonds or impact funds are made, are based on the domains that are recognisable to acquire the users, conduct KYC, and display the deal flows.

With the use of the IoT, AI analytics, and real-time monitoring to support the integration of renewables, smart grids are further at risk. Their user-facing frontends (such as energy and utility monitoring apps aimed at consumers, utility portals) are mostly generic technology, but expos humanity to squatting. The fake websites can erudce grid operator, give false information on the availability of energy, and accept credentials used to phish, which can cause more extensive interference in the case of insider threats. Weaknesses are related to a disjointed management of domain with green technology start-ups and SMEs focusing on speedy launching rather than planning a long-term trademark-domain approach (Mathur, 2022).

Also, due to the interconnectedness and decentralisation, exposure is spread further: squatted domains can well be used to throb a social-engineering torndo at engineers or investors to steal valuable information about grid performance or investment channels. Cybersquatting leads to worse risks in the context of India, where scheme-specific smart-grid experiments are being implemented, like the Revamped Distribution Sector Scheme, as cybersquatting is important in shrinking public confidence in digital energy transitions. These systems are vulnerable to domain-based attacks, which percolate into the physical infrastructure availability and investment security as a result of limited proactive security measures and reactive legal redress.

### 3.3 Impact on Investor Confidence and ESG Compliance

Cybersquatting has a devastating consequence since it negatively impacts investor confidence in sustainable finance and makes compliance with ESG easier in the Indian green ecosystem. Duplicates in digital channels where due diligence and portfolio tracking takes place and ruling out impacts are verifiable leads investors to turn to squatted domains masquerading as legitimate green funds or ESG sites and the squatted domains divert potential investment or put the user at risk of committing fraud. It creates mistrust, where the perception of risk is increased in an already immature market by phishing or deceptive sites in the guise of legitimate sustainability projects. Such risks in sustainable finance, where trust is the key that parties make and keep in net-zero commitments, may cause capital flight, increased risk premises, or hesitation to use digital green tools, hold-up mobilisation of funds needed to achieve India 2070 net-zero objectives.

In regard to ESG compliance, cybersquatting contributes to making the problems harder by supporting greenwashing proxies. Spo fake websites may provide fake or misleading ESG reports or information, staining participation parties in legitimate entities, and make it extremely difficult to verify them in risk management frameworks likc BRSR in SEBI or global standards. The business is under increased scrutiny, to prove it was not associated with squatted domains, which compuluies the compliance responsibilities and the cost of keeping online presence monitored. It becomes a drain on the resources as reputational losses spread due to investor complaints or regulatory enquiries (Perera, 2023). More global are decreased market integrity: repeat incidences are indicative of poor digital governance, queuing institutional investors and FDI in green industries. Cybersquatting is also making it harder to trust the integrity of transparent, AI-enhanced compliance tools in India, as ESG integration is changing due to regulatory imperatives, and adoption of predictive analytics to assess risk may be decelerated.

## 4. GAPS IN CLIMATE FINANCE TAXONOMY AND CYBER RISK INTEGRATION

Such initiative is the development of taxonomy to climate aligned activities in India as the Draft Framework presented by the Department of Economic Affairs in May 2025 defines the future of India towards a net-zero target by 2070. The draft anticipates values including an important role to be played by environment goals, the do-no-significant-harm (DNSH) approach and consistency with the sovereign national aspirations, including Viksit Bharat by 2047. It separates the activities into climate-friendly ones, such as renewable energy development and energy efficiency;

and transitional ones, such as hard-to-abate sectors such as steel and cement; and adaptation needs in agriculture and infrastructure. However, there are still significant loopholes to the inclusion of cyber risks such as cybersquatting, in this framework effectively affecting its effectiveness in securing digital green platforms and sustainable flows of finance.

The main weakness of the taxonomy is the narrow scope of the matter that it focuses on especially on the environmental requirements and transitional requirements without clearly stating how digital or cyber resilience can be used as a material risk to climate finance. With artificial intelligence taking over the driving seat of green investment platforms, ESG analytics portals, and smart-grid interfaces, which rely on safe web-based branding and data resolution, cybercrime, including cybersquatting, has a direct negative impact on investor confidence, channeling funds, and perpetrating fraud that appears to be a green business opportunity (Dharshini, 2025). Although the draft taxonomy identifies the struggles in transparency of data, as well as the need to have uniform measures, it does not include cyber risk as a cross-cutting component in DNSH evaluations or eligibility requirements. Examples include the classification of carbon tracking or tokenised renewable assets digital platforms as climate-supportive, but without domain squatting or phishing vulnerabilities, this type of vulnerability is not factored into risk thresholds, which may end up misclassifying as green investments prone to cyber exploitation.

What makes this deficiency even worse is the divisiveness of sustainable finance ecosystem in India. Even though the mandatory ESG reporting in SEBI Business Responsibility and Sustainability Report (BRSR) includes regulations of financial risks related to climate, and the regulations on climate-related financial risks mandated by RBI concerns themselves, there is still no consolidated demand that brings cyber risk management into the taxonomy-consistent reporting. The resultant effect is that financial institutions might declare projects green without assessing vulnerabilities with regard to digital aspects and exposing themselves to reputational losses, operational losses, and financial losses due to cyber-attacks through this means. The barrier to micro, small and medium enterprises (MSMEs) which are necessary to scale up green projects enhance because of the limited capacity to provide cyber defences notwithstanding the variance of the high level framework of taxonomy offers does not provide specific support to the MSMEs with the simplification of disclosure templates to include cyber safeguards.

Another essential lack is the lack of proactive mechanisms of cyber risk monitoring in the implementation of the taxonomy. International best practice will focus on the importance of standards to be used across the board: interoperability, data registries; however, in India, the draft is silent on AI-enabled frameworks to be used in real-time threat detection at the green finance ecosystem, as well as a system that connects two definitions of cyber maturity and taxonomy maintenance. This reactive stance is opposed to emergent threats in which AI automates mass cybersquatting that targets sustainability keywords and destabilising platforms critical to framework mobilisation to meet climate goals of approximately USDbillion estimated cost per annum (Madhusudan, 2024).

The existence of such gaps undermines the taxonomy in terms of building investor confidence and scale finance. The lack of integration of cyber risks would tend to keep the greenwashing alive via insecure digital pathways, delaying the deployment of capitals in renewables and adaptation, and reducing the resiliency to synergistic threats by itself that are inherent to the green transition.

## 5. COMPARATIVE ANALYSIS WITH EU GREEN DEAL AND U.S. SEC RULES

An analysis of nascent climate finance structure in India against the EU Green Deal, with its Taxonomy Regulation, and on the US Securities and Exchange Commission (SEC) regulations has shown significant differences in maturity, scale, and inclusion of cyber risks, thus showing opportunities and requirements to strengthen Indian adaptations to green investments and susccptibility to cybersquatting.

Through a Regulation called (EU) 2020/852, the EU Taxonomy provides a detailed, science-based system of classification of environmentally sound activities in six objectives, including climate mitigation, adaptation, water, circular economy, pollution prevention, and biodiversity. It places demands of high contribution, DNSH, as well as minimum social safeguards, accentuating these with a comprehensive set of technical screening requirements and compelled disclosures in the Corporate Sustainability Reporting Directive (CSRD), and the Sustainable Finance Disclosure Regulation (SFDR). The CSRD is becoming increasingly entrenched with the principle of the two-materiality where data on cybersecurity incidents and risks that are required to be disclosed by the NIS2 Directive and the Digital Operational Resilience Act (DORA) should be material to the sustainability performance or financial health of an entity (Glonina, 2024). This is a holistic strategy that safeguards digital green platforms, that is, by embedding cyber resilience in governance and risk management, it eliminates greenwashing and enhances investor confidence in the sustainable finance market of the EU.

By comparison, the Draft Climate Finance Taxonomy (2025) has been clocking higher levels of abstraction due to the need to focus on mitigation, adaptation, and transition, though the principle being principles aren't established yet, and the sectorial annexes and granularity of the activities have no mandatory disclosure requirements like the EU assembly. Although it gives attention to the prevention of greenwashing, as well as hard to abate transitions, it does not explicitly tie greenwashing to cyber security, as the EU ties cyber security responsibility to sustainability reporting. As a result, the Indian green portals and ESG tools are still more susceptible to cyber-squatting since none of the taxonomy criteria measures digital security to check eligibility or DNSH analysis.

Like other global disclosure framework regulators, the United States SEC model, specifically its 2024 climate disclosure proposals since rescaved as part of defensive post-2025 in response to court action challenges), included emphasis on material risks related to climate in disclosures which included physical risks and transition risks, in terms of a governance strategy, although not with a thorough taxonomy but with standardized reporting. Cyber disclosures continue to thrive despite the setbacks of climate rules and have at least partially facilitated integrity of ESG by requiring transparency on digital threats that may affect sustainable investments.

The Indian framework is weak in respect of enforcement and integration: India lacks obligatory standard disclosures as that of the EU CSRD or SEC Item 1.05, but it has voluntary or industry based guidelines, with no specific cyber disclosure equivalent to the U.S. rules. This reactive position is in contrast to the proactive aspect of cyber considerations engrained in sustainability at the EU and a preoccupation of incident reporting at the U.S., which leave gaps that enable cybersquatting and undermine trust in green platforms.

Among the main lessons to apply to India are the introduction of EU-type technical requirements, and interoperability to promote the greater taxonomy resilience, and the introduction of U.S.-type compulsory cyber-incident and governance disclosures to protect digital-green ecosystems (Rajeswari, 2024). Sustainable finance Harmonization with international standards may increase inflows of foreign direct investment and reduce fragmentation and vulnerability to cyber threats. Integrating cyber materiality into the taxonomy and integrating reporting would help India to be more aligned to the mature frameworks, facilitate more credible mobilization of green capital, and mitigate any kinds of digital shocks.

## 6. RECOMMENDATIONS: UNIFIED CYBER-ESG FRAMEWORK AND POLICY REFORMS

The creation of a Cyberulous Cyber-ESG structure is strongly needed to protect AI-guided green investments in India against cyber squatting and other cyber attackers and promote flow through sustainable money. This framework needs to incorporate cybersecurity as a pillar of core governance into current ESG framework and extend the Draft Climate Finance Taxonomy of May 2025 by making cyber risk a material element in taxonomy eligibility, DNSH requirements and transitional activity reviews. In particular, those tasks, which involve digital platforms, including green investment portals, ESG analytics tools, carbon -tracking systems, and smart grid interfaces, need to have at least minimum cyber resiliency. These criteria encompass dynamic domain observation, AI-threat, and safeguarded branding procedures, to be climate-supportive or transition-compliant.

Under the BRSR enhancements, regulatory bodies need to integrate to create mandatory Cyber -ESG disclosure templates such as the Department of Economic Affairs (DEA), the Securities and Exchange Board of India (SEBI), and the CERT-In. The templates would weak variables of companies and financial institutions such as cyber maturity scores, incident response plans, domain protection strategies, and exposure to risk of cybersquatting in their annual sustainability reports (Pokrovskaya, 2024). It must be a policy change so much geared towards enacting specialized anti-cybersquatting laws that overcome current loopholes in Trade-Marks Act 1999 and in Information technology Act 2000. Following the example of the U.S. Anti-Cybersquatting Consumer Protection Act (ACPA), the proposed law may have statutory damages, in-rem liability over anonymous squatters, and bad-faith-based requirements specific to green and AI theatrics, including intent to pay-off sustainability keywords, interfere with the funding of renewable projects, or use fraudulent portals to facilitate greenwashing.

It is important to strengthen the Internet Domain name Registration Policy (INDRP) under the NIXI. Reforms proposed ought to include shorter arbitration rates (e.g. 30-45 days judgment) and less evidentiary threshold to new green start-ups, issue SME subsidies in case of litigation, and set proactive monitoring agreement with registrars to notify suspicious bulk registration of sustainability-related domains. The other pillar is the integration of AI and automation in the enforcement mechanisms. The policy shall require AI-based domain watch services on taxonomy compliant entities, which make possible real-time notification of cybersquatting attempts and automatic pre-emptive domain registration. Hybrids of blockchain-AI in the field of tokenised green assets should have immutable domain-verification layers to avoid impersonation. The IndiaAI Mission capacity-building program might be used to fund training of regulators, judges and green business about areas of interactions between Cyber-ESG, and SEBI may make incentives such as preferential treatment of green-bonds labelling to any organization with certified cyber resilience (Adi, 2025).

These reforms are supported by comparative lessons of the world models. CSRD and Taxonomy Regulation The CSRD and Taxonomy Regulation of the EU in-creased implementations of cybersecurity disclosures through double materiality and connection to NIS2/DORA, and identify digital risks as a part of sustainability disclosure. The U.S. SEC regulations on cybersecurity and cybersecurity although the climate reporting remains unclear include the disclosure of any incidents in time and regulation by the board of the principles, which indirectly enhances ESG integrity. Mandatory cyber-incident reporting should also be harmonised by India in the form of SEC Item 1.05 which is associated with ESG systems to ensure transparency and mitigating security risks.

The implementation roadmap will include the following phases a short-term voluntary pilot of CyberESG practices in the renewable and green-finances sectors; a middle-term (20282030) binding amendment to the taxonomy and the introduction of statutory anti-cybersquatting measures; and alignment of regulator networking with global standards in order to draw-in FDI (Chhabra Roy & Prabhakaran, 2025). Such reforms would ensure that the erosion of investor confidence due to cyber-squatting is not only reduced but also that India would set an example of a robust digital-green financial system that can transfer the necessary USD250billion+/yr of climate investments safely to net-zero 2070 targets but also generates innovation of sustainable technologies.

## 7. CONCLUSION

The intersection of artificial intelligence, automation, and green investment in India holds the potential of an enormous scale to hasten the process of the low-carbon, resilient Indian economy, in compliance with 2030 NDCs, net-zero by 2070, and global sustainability requirements. Fostering transparency, capital mobilization, and efficient use of resources helps precision of risk assessment, detection of fraud, and scalability AI-driven innovations, involving predictive ESG analytics, autonomous carbon tracking, and blockchain hybrids, including renewable funding are seen to enhance profit-maximizing efficiency, transparency, and the mobilisation of capital to launch solar, wind, hydrogen, and circular-economy projects based on their respective needs. Nonetheless, the digital transformation makes green platforms vulnerable to increased risks of cybersquatting, which can openly affect brand integrity, redirect investor traffic, and promote fraud, and even destroy trust as a fundamental building block of sustainable finance ecosystems.

The regulatory environment of India is supported by the Trade-Marks Act of 1999, the INDRP, the IT Act of 2000, and the provisions of foundational protections in terms of infringement remedies, passing-off and arbitration. However, this model is still weak, reactive, and incomplete to adapt to changing cyber strategies enhanced by AI tools. The classification of climate-supportive and transitional activities is progressed at the point of inconsistency with the Draft Climate Finance Taxonomy (2025) that satisfies a list of still missing a cyber-risk incorporation, the digital-green activity criteria and disclosure requirements, and digital-green activity resilience requirements.

Relative comparison notes the following shortcomings: the Taxonomy of the EU Green Deal combined with CSRD integrates cybersecurity with materiality costs and references to standards like NIS2 and DORA to require cybersecurity margin to sustainability oversight; U.S. SEC regulations, although retrospectively encroaching on climate factors in the 2025 policy, have a strong disclosure of cybersecurity protection reflected indirectly on sustainability standards; strengthening disclosure of cybersecurity is an imposition of U.S. SEC regulators on ESG integrity. The framework of India thus trails behind mandated and standardised Cyber-ESG integration which poses the risk of investor scepticism, slow circulation of capital and loss of global green market competitiveness.

These imperatives mean that a coherent Cyber-ESG model with policy changes to include clear cyber requirements in taxonomy design, anti-cybersquatting laws with statutory remedy, to support stronger INDRP processes, proactive defences based on AI, and to harmonise disclosures are all required. These steps will discourage malpractices, regain trust in the digital space, and defend intellectual property that is important in green branding and funding. Finally, making the techno-legal ecosystem resistant to cybersquatting is a defensive measure without being merely that; it is substitutionary thus make AI and automation facilitators of sustainable development in India and not its drivers. It will allow India to unlock the trillions in legitimately green investments, strengthen leadership in joyfully aligned innovation, and create a just and secure economic shift to a net-zero future as digital and environmental convergence are bound to increase rapidly.

## REFERENCES


Adi, A. (2025). Do Foreign AI Identity Laws Conflict With India's Personality Rights Framework? Evaluating The Guernsey, No Fakes, Elvis, And Eu AI Act Models. *Evaluating The Guernsey, No Fakes, Elvis, And Eu AI Act Models (October 12, 2025).*

Ahmad, A., & Kumar, N. (2023). A Critical Analysis of the Regulatory Framework Relating to Cybersquatting in India. *Prayagraj L. Rev.*, *2*, 1.

Ajakaye, O. G., & Lawal, A. (2023). International Trademark and Copyright Law: Harmonization, Disparities, and Global Implications for Developing Countries. *International Journal of Scientific Research in Computer Science. Engineering and Information Technology*, *9*(5), 807–837.

Akinbeye, S. (2023). An Examination of High-tech Crimes in the Digital Era. *Available at SSRN* 5269130.

Chhabra Roy, N., & Prabhakaran, S. (2023). Sustainable response system building against insider-led cyber frauds in banking sector: A machine learning approach. *Journal of Financial Crime*, *30*(1), 48–85. DOI: 10.1108/JFC-12-2021-0274

Chhabra Roy, N., & Prabhakaran, S. (2025). Cyber fraud (CF) in banking: A dual-layer, blockchain-enabled approach for prevention and managerial response. *Managerial Finance*, *51*(5), 765–796. DOI: 10.1108/MF-09-2024-0716

Dharshini, A. (2025). From Cybersquatting to Meta Tagging-The Expanding Scope of Trademark Infringement in the Digital Sphere. *LawFoyer Int'l J. Doctrinal Legal Rsch.*, *3*, 633.

Glonina, V. (2024). Back to the Future with Blockchain Domain Names: Toward a Global Policy to Fight Cybersquatting in Web 3.0. *Trademark Rep.*, *114*, 587.

Kaur, J. (2024). Towards a sustainable Triad: Uniting energy management systems, smart cities, and green healthcare for a greener future. In *Emerging Materials, Technologies, and Solutions for Energy Harvesting* (pp. 258-285). IGI Global Scientific Publishing.

Madhusudan, V. V. (2024). A Critical Analysis of Information Technology Act, 2000 with Reference to Cyber Offence and Cyber Security. *Issue 2 Int'l JL Mgmt. &. Human.*, *7*, 2529.

Mathur, H. (2022). Cybersquatting and the Related Laws. *Issue 5 Indian JL & Legal Rsch.*, *4*, 1.

Meghwal, T. (2024). Emerging Challenges in Regulating Artificial Intelligence Under Cyber Security Laws in India. *Available at SSRN* 5030258.

Mondal, A., Paikaray, J., & Chatterjee, P. S. (2025, February). Intelligent Legal and Technical Strategies to Mitigate Cybersquatting: Bridging Global Frameworks and Indian Contexts. In *2025 International Conference on Emerging Systems and Intelligent Computing (ESIC)* (pp. 913-918). IEEE. DOI: 10.1109/ESIC64052.2025.10962791

Mondal, A., Paikaray, J., & Chatterjee, P. S. (2025, February). Intelligent Legal and Technical Strategies to Mitigate Cybersquatting: Bridging Global Frameworks and Indian Contexts. In *2025 International Conference on Emerging Systems and Intelligent Computing (ESIC)* (pp. 913-918). IEEE. DOI: 10.1109/ESIC64052.2025.10962791

Perera, M. L. A. (2023). Unraveling the Digital Deception: A Comparative Study of the Legal Response to Cybersquatting in Sri Lanka. *Sri Lanka J. Legal Stud.*, *1*, 61.

Pokrovskaya, A. (2024). Protection of trademark rights on e-commerce platforms: An updated outlook. *Journal of Comprehensive Business Administration Research*, *1*(2), 65–73. DOI: 10.47852/bonviewJCBAR42022153

Rajeswari, A. (2024). Cyberspace and Intellectual Property: Evaluating Legal Frameworks through the Lens of Space Transition Theory. *Issue 2 Int'l JL Mgmt. &. Human.*, *7*, 3938.

Sujay, M. (2025). Safeguarding Intellectual Property in the Metaverse Economy through Digital Fashion and Virtual Products. *Mind to Market: The Journey of Intellectual Property*, 163.

# Chapter 10
# Regulatory Compliance and AI-Powered Reporting in Green Investment

**Kishore Subramanya Hebbar**
http://orcid.org/0009-0007-4203-8698
*Intercontinental Exchange Inc., USA*

**Shilpi Yadav**
*Independent Researcher, USA*

**Jaykumar Ambadas Maheshkar**
http://orcid.org/0009-0009-4905-7001
*USBancorp, USA*

**Pavan Kumar Asu**
http://orcid.org/0009-0006-6196-2942
*Gallagher, USA*

**Tarun Kumar Kaushik**
http://orcid.org/0000-0002-3279-8307
*Sharda University, Greater Noida, India*

## ABSTRACT

*A key pillar of green investment has become regulatory compliance, where financial institutions are required to fund a portfolio in a way that reflects a sustainability requirement, as well as exhibit a clearly proven impact on the environment. The purpose of disclosure is entailed in such elements as a global frameworks, namely*

DOI: 10.4018/979-8-2600-1308-3.ch010

*a formal regulation such as the EU Sustainable Finance Disclosure Regulation (SFDR), such formal regulation as the Corporate Sustainability Reporting Directive (CSRD), such formal regulation as the EU Taxonomy Regulation, and such formal regulations as the international sustainability standards board (ISSB) IFRS S1 and S2, which require comprehensive disclosures on the related risk of climate issues as well as greenhouse-gas emissions, transition plans, and alignment to net-zero ways.*

## 1. INTRODUCTION

The stricter global regulation requires disclosures that are credible and scalable, with verifiable, auditable disclosures able to combat greenwashing and open trillions of aligned capital, regulatory compliance and AI-powered reporting on green investment has become the key to credible, scalable sustainable finance. The new standards of the International Sustainability Standards Board (ISSB) IFRS S1 (general sustainability-related financial information) and IFRS S2 (climate-specific) effective since January 2024 are driving compulsory implementations across the globe (Ogunyemi, 2023). More than 30 jurisdictions are aligning or supporting these standards, with specific amendments to Scope 3 emissions in IFRS S2 published in December 2025 relieving financial institutions (e.g. derivatives, facilitated emissions), and amendments effective in 2027 and early application allowed. The EU has a double materiality level in order to comply with Corporate Sustainability Reporting Directive (CSRD) and European Sustainability Reporting Standards (ESRS), and is also going to implement SFDR reforms that pertain to product labeling and anti-greenwashing provisions, applicable since September 2026 under the Empowering Consumers for the Green Transition Directive. The BRSR Core framework of SEBI requires fair assurance on 49 material ESG KPIs of listed entities in a rollout with value chain reporting moving to voluntary and mandatory evaluation / assessment (Joseph et al., 2025). This development makes sustainability information a material, financial information just like standard data, climate risks are included in prudential regulation, type of investment, and cross-border flows.

The core compliance needs focus on alignment of taxonomy, transparency of emissions and planning transition. Jurisdictionally such as the EU Taxonomy sustainable activities are categorized and the draft Climate Finance Taxonomy and BIS updates in India lead to credible labeling (Mitra & Maity, 2025). The following disclosures are included: Scope 1-3 GHG emissions, physical/transition risks, nature-related dependencies (through TNFD), value chain impacts with third-party limited-to-reasonable assurance going towards full audit equivalence. The implementation of greenwashing is increased by the prohibition of unsubstantiating claims (e.g., generic labels of ecofriendliness without certification) and the obligation to substantiate the future performance claims. This, in green investment, means strictly classifying products, i.e., by SFDR Article 8/9 funds or India's green bond frameworks, where erroneous claims result in punishment, reputation and capital exodus. There are fragmented burdens on multinational investors, but attempts to achieve interoperability (e.g., G20 alignment, ISSB capacity-building) lessen duplication, although difficulties are still present in new markets with missing information and capacity issues (Nauman, 2025).

The rules put a heavy steam of liability on the asset managers, banks, and insurers to prevent greenwashing, provide proper labelling of the sustainable products and have a strictly observed reporting standard. Compliance is becoming an efficient, scalable, and auditable process as AI-powered reporting tools are making life out of a manual, error-prone, activity. To compute real-time carbon footprint and ESG scores, machine-learning algorithms aggregate data of various types, such as enterprise systems, supply-chain databases, satellite-based images and internet of things sensors, and third-party ESG databases. Natural-language-processing tools are relevant to unstructured documents, including annual reports, supplier contracts, and regulatory filings, whereas predictive analytics predict compliance risks and the effect a scenario has in each climate pathway. The effectiveness of traceability and immutability of green claims are also enhanced by blockchain and distributed-ledger technologies and can be used to verify carbon credits, green bonds, and sustainable supply chains. However, there are still issues: bias in algorithms, mismatches in data-quality and the unreliability of ESG metrics and explainable AI are required to meet regulatory oversight. Extravagant adoption, therefore, involves well-constructed governance, third party audit, and ongoing validation of the model. By exercised responsibly, AI-enabled reporting can not only guarantee compliance but also help build investor confidence, open access to sustainable capital, and hasten the move to a low-carbon economy and therefore make the idea of green investment a compliant, credible and high impact asset category.

The solution to these demands is AI as the transformative enabler, which will automatize ESG data management to ensure that it is efficient and accurate. By 2026, AI-based platforms consume unstructured information in supplier records, satellite images, Internet of Things devices and transaction records, cleaning and consolidating them to real-time mapping to different frameworks (IFRS S1/S2, ESRS, BRSR, GRI, TCFD). Machine learning has a granular Scope 3 traceability of emissions, anticipates climate scenarios, and highlights anomalies in reporting to the identification of greenwashing using pattern recognition. Generative AI writes and compliant narratives, standardizes templates, and prepares audit trails to reduce the amount of manual work by 45 to 90 percent and save several months of labor each year. Such tools as Persefoni, Sweep, or even the emerging platforms in India combine digital ledgers that facilitate tamper-proof checking, and aid in blockchain-enhanced impact monitoring in tokenized green assets. Predictive analytics can predict transition risks so that it can adjust its portfolio in advance to renewables, circular models, and nature-positive investments.

Artificial intelligence technology will increase reporting to audit-ready levels, anomaly detection provides uniformity, amassing evidence to give a green light, and adaptable modules to deal with regulatory pace (e.g., SFDR 2.0, CSRD updates). Real-time boards increase board monitoring and transparency to the stakeholders and explainable AI reduces bias and delivers ethical results to the law of data privacy such as India DPDPA. To green investors, this comprises high-quality due diligence, screening of portfolios according to taxonomies, and belief in the impact claims-triggering capital relocation to viable low-carbon projects (Bansal et al., 2025).

Some of the obstacles are the footprint of AI (data centres consume more energy, and consume more water), risk to ethics (model bias, data privacy risks), and regulatory questions (e.g. ESMA/SEC guidelines concerning AI governance). The lack of data quality and high switching costs on SMEs still exist, yet the chances are more than the obstacles with the use of human-in-the-loop supervision and the use of AI in the long term (Akram et al., 2025).

The vision of the roadmap is completely interoperable, AI-managed ecosystems, harmonized taxonomies, agentic AI to predictive insights as well as quantum-enhanced modeling (Pavlidis, 2025). Automated assurance of essential markets, savings of over 40 percent of costs, and trillions raised through credible reporting will be the hallmarks of Finance 5.0, with compliance becoming regenerative effect, green investments going along with net-zero, biodiversity, and fair objectives. With strict regulation and intelligent automation this convergence is placing green investment as a force of planet- and goal-oriented vigilance (Irfan et al., 2026).

## 2. EVOLVING GLOBAL AND NATIONAL REGULATORY LANDSCAPE FOR GREEN INVESTMENT

The changing global and national regulatory environment of green investment can be seen as a mature but disjointed attempt to make credible, interoperable, and mandatory sustainability disclosures that form the basis of credible capital allocation to low-carbon and resilient projects. On an international level, the emerging global standard is the International Sustainability Standards Board (ISSB) IFRS S1 (general sustainability-related financial disclosures) and IFRS S2 climate-specific with specific amendments finalized in December 2025, which offers critical reliefs on Scope 3 GHG emissions, especially by including the Category 15 of the controls, namely, financed emissions, to financial institutions, to loans and investments (not to derivatives, investment banking or insurance underwriting (Leitner-Hanetseder & Lehner, 2023).

Momentum towards adoption as in the UK, draft Sustainability Reporting Standards anchored on ISSB were consulted until September 2025 indicating the ultimate alignment. In Canada, voluntary or phased methods are the order of the day (CSDS 1/2) and the US has no federal requirements since the repeal of the SEC rule on climate reporting, but state-level initiatives (e.g., California SB 253/261 climate reporting as of 2026) continue to be undertaken despite legal challenges. This convergence is meant to minimize fragmentation, increase the capital market efficiency, and assist the decision making of the investor by considering sustainability data as a material financial information (Singh et al., 2024).

The scenery is ambitious and recalibrating in Europe. The Corporate Sustainability Reporting Directive (CSRD) and the European Sustainability Reporting Standards (ESRS) impose the additional materiality of large corporations, and first reports will be issued by the year 2024 and published in 2025. The scope of the 2025 Omnibus simplification package, completed in late 2025, however, is narrowed, the number of mandatory datapoints drops by approximately 61 percent (1,100 to 430), voluntary disclosures are eliminated, and phase-ins are introduced with assistance of quick-fix amendments and a stop-the-clock directive delaying wave-two/three reporting. ESRFG revised ESRS drafts (July 2025) and final technical advice (December 2025) will be adopted in early 2026, with application from financial year 2027 (reports in 2028), and are intended to reduce compliance costs and to be interoperable with the IFRS S1/S2.

## 3. CORE COMPLIANCE REQUIREMENTS IN GREEN AND SUSTAINABLE FINANCE

The foundations of credible and investor trusted flows of capital in the global capital markets as of January 2026 can be seen as core compliance requirements in green and sustainable finance, which shift voluntary commitments to enforceable and auditable requirements, and which bring environmental risks into financial decision making and labelling of products. Internationally, the IFRS S1 (general sustainability-related financial disclosures) and IFRS S2 (climate-specific) of the IFRS are the standard basis, and specific reliefs on Scope 3 GHG emissions are introduced in December 2025, with specific relaxations on financed emissions reporting of financial institutions (including in relation to loans, and investments (not including derivatives and certain underwriting are in exemption). These standards entail entities to report material sustainability-related risks and opportunities on short-, medium-, and long-term cash flows, access to financing, or capital costs, such as governance, strategy, risk management, and measures/targets such as absolute and intensity-based GHG emissions (Scopes 1, 2, and frequently 3), climate scenario analysis, and transition plans.

In the EU, large companies are subject to double materiality, i.e., financial and impact, and Corporate Sustainability Reporting Directive (CSRD) and European Sustainability Reporting Standards (ESRS) impose requirements of double materiality, simplified data-points by roughly 61% by 2025, which are staged in through amendments, whilst Sustainable Finance Disclosure Regulation (SFDR) reforms (SFDR 2.0 proposals) tighten product classifications, prohibit unsubstantiated claims to the environment and increases substantiation (Alabi, 2025). The EU Taxonomy is the technical screening of environmentally sustainable activities, which is increasingly being incorporated into CSRD reporting and product labelling. The effectiveness of greenwashing prevention enhances with the enforcement by the generic labeling of misleading labels, which is banned by the Empowering Consumers for the Green Transition Directive (since September 2026) unless certified or proven.

SEBI Business Responsibility and Sustainability Reporting (BRSR) Core framework establishes reasonable assurance of 49 top ESG KPIs to listed entities in a gradual implementation of top 500 by FY202526 and top 1000 by FY202627. Such KPIs include absolute and intensity based GHG emission (Scopes 1-3), share of renewable energy, water withdrawal/intensity, waste management, energy use, gender diversity and value chain disclosures. It is in accordance with ISSB on financial materiality and includes GRI inspired impact-based elements and India-related overlays in National Guidelines on Responsible Business Conduct. Reserve Bank of India (RBI) incorporates climate risks in prudential regulation through its Responsible and Green Finance Framework, which includes scenarios of the NGFS, differentiating risk weights (e.g., less weight on renewables and more on carbon-intensive exposures), and priority sectoral lending facilities to green projects (like EVs, affordable housing, and circular economy facilities).

The cross-cutting requirements are taxonomy alignment to have a credible definition of green activities, third-party assurance at limited to reasonable (e.g., under ISSA 5000 to sustainability information applicable 20262027 periods), and incorporation of sustainability risks in the investment classifications, risk management, and products. In the case of green investment, it translates to stringent validation of claims in bonds, loans, funds, and portfolios i.e. use-of-proceeds tracking of green bonds, KPI-related conditions on sustainability-linked instruments, and transition pathways in hard-to-abate sectors (Alshahmy & Sahiner, 2024). Fragmentation creates compliance costs to multinationals, whereas interoperability G20 alignment, ISSB endorsements helps to reduce duplication. Failure to comply could result in a penalty, a damaged reputation, capital limitations and losing investors, whereas compliance leads to trust, response of reduction of greenium, and directing capital into demonstrable low-carbon changes. These condition green finance to go beyond marketing and to robust financial prudence such that disclosures are decision-useful, comparable and verifiable and thus portfolios are de-risked and mobilized towards net-zero and resilience objectives.

## 4. ROLE OF AI IN AUTOMATING ESG AND SUSTAINABILITY DATA MANAGEMENT

The mission of AI in automation of ESG and sustainability data management in 2026 has become a strategic requirement that will streamline fragmented and manual processes into efficient and scaleable, audit-ready systems that will support increasing regulatory demands and enable actionable insights in green investment decisions. AI systems have now been programmed to accept, and process large volumes of unstructured data of various kinds as invoices by suppliers, satellite photos, IoT sensors, transaction histories, and public filings, to comply with several frameworks such as IFRS S1/S2, ESRS, BRSR Core, GRI, and TCFD, cleaning, standardizing and aggregating these data automatically. Machine learning algorithms determine emissions at high granularity, especially the Scope 3 value chain traceability, using the right factors, reconciled discrepancies, and the estimation of missing data using predictive modeling, saving 45 to 90% work manually and eradicating long-term gaps in the supplier-level reporting.

Within the trends, agentic AI, which is autonomous, multi-step reasoning systems, will become a game-changer system that will be an always-on assistant that validates the data quality, suspicious activities (e.g., energy use outliers or emissions spikes), and potential evidence of greenwashing through pattern recognition in comparison with benchmarks and immutable audit trails relating to each metric and its source evidence (Waykar & Yambal, 2025). Generative AI generates regulatory compliant narratives and standardizes templates of disclosure across jurisdictions as well as generating prospective components such as scenario analysis or transition risks and dynamic variables such as policy changes or AI-driven energy needs. Provider platform such as Schneider Electric, TCS (e.g. with Tata Motors on value chain understanding) and newer tools combine real time monitoring, and they can provide continuous reporting, which is now used to support use of materiality, joining monetary and impact views.

In the case of a green investment, AI can improve due diligence through automating portfolio screening to align with taxonomy, forecasting climate/physical risks at the asset level, and making allocations more optimized towards renewables, nature-positive or circular opportunities (Thomas et al., 2025). India AI has been used to help BRSR Core compliance of the largest listed organisations to automate calculation of KPIs (e.g. renewable energy share, water intensity) and generate assurance documentation, and RBI guidelines are soliciting AI use in climate risk modelling to support credit and supervisory efforts. Around the world, AI can save compliance expenses by up to 40% and more, and extend SME-friendly cloud-based solutions, which makes advanced reporting more democratic.

Moral and practical management is essential: explainable AI avoids bias, would be transparent in accordance to data privacy regulations (e.g., DPDPA in India) and can take care of its own environmental footprint (data center energy/water consumption). Regulators (ESMA, SEC) are still performing strategic judgment by reviewing the use of AI in disclosures. AI makes ESG management less about compliance burden and more about competitive advantage by connecting data silos and accelerating validation as well as offering predictive insights and allowing investors to allocate capital more confidently in the impact of which can be verified and moving the industry towards regenerative low-carbon finance.

## 5. AI-POWERED TOOLS FOR ACCURATE AND AUDIT-READY REPORTING

By January 2026, AI-driven tools will be essential in green investment to provide accurate and audit-ready reporting, to fill this gap, despite the increasing regulatory requirements and the realities of generating credible, verifiable disclosures of sustainability. These applications use generative AI, machine learning, anomaly detection, and guided processes to convert disjointed ESG data into compliant, evidence-based outputs resistant to third-party audit and investor inquiry. Such solutions as Persefoni, Sweep, Workiva (with Persefoni to directly integrate carbon flows into sustainability reporting), Pulsora, and new solutions such as ChatFin, Presgo and open-sourced AI Playbook to Sustainability Reporting by Google are examples of this migration, as they automate processes that previously took months of human effort to complete and integrate audit trails, data lineage, and explainability to satisfy standards such as IFRS S1/S2, CSRD/ESRS, BRSR Core in India, and SFDR reforms (Hassanein & Tharwat, 2024).

Central to them, these solutions are used to automatically ingest and validate data in a wide variety of often unstructured sources such as supplier documents, IoT feeds, satellite imagery, transaction logs, and public filings with the help of AI to clean, standardize, and reconcile these many types with a high degree of precision. An example is that generative AI will perceive the procurement activity to map emissions factors, identify anomalies within the energy consumption or emission peaks and inconsistencies that may signal both greenwashing or error. He 2026 trends Project agentic AI systems will be utilized as autonomous assistants that conduct multi-step verification, predictive modeling of missing Scope 3 data, and retain unalterable audit trails, which are used to trace the origin of each metric. Such a feature is essential in cases of CSRD and ISSB assessment of materiality twice, when the financial and impact perspectives should be strictly recorded. Manual workloads are minimized 4590 percent, and the average duration of one report saves 4.5 months per year as observed in sites such as ESGpedia and the gen AI solutions of Optisol, which means that sustainability staff can spend time on strategic analysis and not data wrangling.

Generative AI is the best at composing disclosures, stories, and standardized templates based on several frameworks at a time. The users provide internal documents (impact reports, prior disclosures, policies), choose the specific areas of interest, and encourage the AI to create the draft answers that include the words of the question, regulatory language, and company-specific details. The capabilities of the AI deployed by Gravity Climate, such as the ability to produce unified drafts of CSRD, TCFD, CDP, and SB 253/261, and C3 AI ESG drafts reports and summarizes changes in stakeholder sentiment using generative capabilities (Khaddam & Alzghoul, 2025). The AI Playbook of Google includes timely templates of validation, substantiation of claims, and accessibility and makes AI a framework of accuracy and uniformity rather than a shortcut. These drafts are already affiliated with evidence, version control and change logs, making internal reviews and external assurance of ISAE 3000/3410 or ISSA 5000 standards advance to reasonable assurance.

The features built to increase audit-readiness, such as full data lineage (e.g., Persefoni carbon ledger or Sweep Footprints Ledger), automatic gap analysis, evidence collection, and auditor-portable documentation, improve the process of audit readiness. Anomaly detection signals early outliers, predictive intelligence projects threats ahead of time, and adaptive modules can accommodate the changes of regulation, e.g. SFDR 2.0 simplifications, or the phasing of the India BRSR value chain, without reconfiguring, replicated manually. This allows alignment of taxonomy of green bonds/loans, screen avatars in real-time in the portfolio and real-world impact claims in sustainability-linked instruments, in green investment contexts. Indian entities regulated by BRSR Core (top 500 with reasonable assurance on 49 KPIs as of FY202526) under the SEBI can use AI to automate calculations of Scope 1-3 emissions, renewable energy share, and water intensity, preparing files ready to comply that will save on compliance costs and build credibility.

In the case of explainable AI, real-time dashboards allow boards and investors direct visibility, whereas mitigating bias in outputs and their traceability are guaranteed by the privacy laws such as DPDPA. Tamper-free authentication of tokenized green assets is added to some platforms with integration with blockchain or digital ledgers. Some challenges are how to handle the energy footprint of AI by deploying it in a sustainable manner, how to ensure the human-in-the-loop of ethical judgments, how to handle regulatory oversight (e.g., ESMA/SEC on AI governance). However, these tools transform periodical reporting to constant intelligence, which allows the quality management of risks and seizing opportunities in green portfolios.

According to estimates by 2030, AI-managed platforms will dominate, with obligatory AI-aided assurance in the key markets, cost savings greater than 40 percent, and trillions of dollars gathered by increasing trust in disclosure. With green investment, precise, audit-compliant reporting driven by AI can not only be used to make sure people comply but can also transform finance into a regenerative force, directing capital in a assured low-carbon shift, nature-friendly results, and fair resilience in a world constrained with climate (Alam et al., 2025).

## 6. ENHANCING TRANSPARENCY, ASSURANCE, AND INVESTOR CONFIDENCE

Improving transparency, assurance and investor trust in green investment with AI-powered instruments is a vital development of sustainable finance by January 2026 where verifiable disclosures have become the currency of trust with increasingly restrictive regulation and greater interest in greenwashing. The AI allows performing the double materiality evaluations, i.e., materiality of financial dimension (risks/opportunities to the enterprise) and materiality of impact (impacts on the environment and society), as large datasets are processed to pinpoint material problems. As an example, machine learning models combine financial reports, ESG, and satellite-based data on the environment and stakeholder information to create holistic assessments based on IFRS S1/S2, CSRD/ESRS, TNFD on nature-related disclosures, and BLR Core framework. These tools expose interdependencies, including the impact of biodiversity loss on the supply chain resilience or the effect of transition risks on asset values, which boards can act on to have a strategic oversight.

AI-driven real-time dashboards bring dynamic visibility of stakeholders, providing graphics that visualize the performance of ESG, and the trends of emissions and alignment to the taxonomies in easy-to-understand formats. The portfolio level views available to investors will aggregate data on issuers allowing the screening of green mandates, peer benchmarking, and tracking controversies in real-time. This is the end of inertial annual reports and there is the continuous interactive reporting where proactive participation and lessening information asymmetry is encouraged. In India, where BRSR Core of SEBI requires reasonable assurance on 49 ESG KPIs on leading 500 listed entities by FY202526 (and expanding to leading 1,000 by FY202627) AI platforms enable calculations of KPIs (e.g., Scope 1 emissions, renewable energy proportion, water intensity) and produce stakeholder-friendly visualizations, which increase governance and signify the organization's dedication to the 2070 net-zero journey in India.

AI-enhanced audit trails and data lineage support the third-party verification with increased strength. Tools assemble evidence packs with trackable sources, version histories and anomaly flags that facilitate limited-to-reasonable assurance processes according to standards such as ISAE 3000, ISSA 5000 or ISO 14064 of GHG verification (Pandow et al., 2024). AI-assisted sampling, risk-based attention to high-material areas, and automated consistency checks across disclosures help to increase the efficiency of auditors and at the same time enhance independence. In jurisdictions implementing the IFRS S1/S2 (more than 40 by mid-2025, subject to Scope 3 relaxations found in the December 2025 amendments), AI can be used to facilitate an assurance process, by making the disclosures auditable, with explainable outputs that reduce the concerns. This generates credibility, which we have observed in the increase in assurance use in the international market, where third party validation increases the reliability of reports and dependence by the investors.

AI confidence to investors is skyrocketing because the information it provides is verifiable, comparable and timely and de-risks green allocations. Improved due diligence software filters investments based on taxonomy criteria, forecasts consequences, and measures investments based on SDGs or NDCs, which makes it possible to make evidence-based assertions in green bonds, sustainability-linked loans, and impact funds (Challa, 2022). The low risk of greenwashing (complexity of detecting anomalies and substantiating) mitigates the fines and penalties under laws such as the EU Green Claims Directive or FCA anti-greenwashing regulations. Some studies have reported that 90 percent of institutional investors perceive that transparency with AI additions is important in accuracy and reducing errors, and surveys suggest institutional investors of all types enjoy AI-enhanced transparency, finding it more trustworthy.

This is based on ethical AI governance, which guarantees the interpretability of outputs, skewed evaluations through bias audits, and valid judgments through human oversight about high-stakes decisions. Providing inclusive green financing, AI in emerging markets such as India is making access more democratic through reduced costs on SMEs through cloud platforms. Altogether, such improvements make reporting more of value driver and less of a compliance exercise because trillions can flow in on plausible, regenerative investments that bring profitability and planetary resilience, protection of biodiversity, and just transitions closer to each other.

## 7. ADDRESSING CHALLENGES AND RISKS IN AI-DRIVEN COMPLIANCE

To overcome obstacles and threats of AI-assisted compliance in green investment, it is necessary to take action to gain the advantages and reduce the disadvantages in the next period of January 2026, characterized by blistering technological integration and changes in the regulatory environment. One of the main issues is the environmental impact of AI: training and inference of large models require enormous amounts of electricity and water, and data centers are expected to reach over 1,000 TWh / year in the future (20262028), which would overload grids and contradict the net-zero objectives. There is an overall disregard of environmental impact in responsible AI strategies because sustainability leaders commonly focus on ethics, bias, and security, with only 13% considering it major, despite AI leading to major spikes in U.S. electricity demand. The suggested measures to mitigate AI can include sustainable AI deployment, utilizing power-saving compute, energy-efficient inference, model optimization, and carbon-conscious scheduling, as well as quantifying and reporting AI emissions in ESG reports.

The risks of algorithmic bias include carrying forward inequalities in ESG ratings, including biased risk ratings in unrepresentative industries or discriminatory credit/lending based on sustainability performance (Anumolu, 2025). Misledged models on unfinished data or on historical-biased data can only increase disparities, mistrusting the model and creating litigation. Ethical governance requires a wide range of training data, frequent bias audits, fairness measures, and human-in-the-loop verification, and explainable AI in ensuring decisions that can be traced and challenged according to new regulations by ESMA, SEC, and data privacy guidelines in India, DPDPA.

The privacy and security risks of using AI are that sensitive ESG data was fed by the AI, supplier data, emissions data, or personal metrics, which may reveal the breach or misuse in third-party platforms. The regulations such as the GDPR, CCPA, PIPL, and the DPDPA require privacy-by-design, anonymization, and consent. Issues like opaque black-box processing and low-cost and uncontrolled AI tools creating unreliable reports or hallusions are challenges. The regulators are examining AI disclosure as a means of governing the company, and failure to do so can lead to penalties.

There are still regulatory and interoperability barriers: the existence of different AI regulations across jurisdictions complicates compliance, and inadequate data quality (variable sources of ESG) results in inaccurate results. The costs of transition impose costs on the SMEs and excessive dependence on AI without controls can result in new forms of greenwash in the case of false assertions by robotic drafts.

These can only be tackled through multi-layered solutions: strong AI governance systems and policies on bias, privacy and sustainability; capacity construction to work on teams; cooperation with regulators to set standards; and hybrid human-AI systems that do not obviate judgment. RBI/SEBI promote the ethical use of AI in climate risk tools in India, although it is a requirement to control (Soetan & Deloitte, 2023). Promoting responsible deployment, which is transparent, auditable, and low-impact, the AI-driven compliance becomes the source of risk instead of the contributor to credible and scalable green finance because technology can support planetary and societal interests without unwanted negative effects.

## 8. CONCLUSION

Regulatory compliance and AI-driven reporting in green investment makes the conclusion as of January 2026, in which strict, compulsory disclosures are shared with intelligent automation, a more believable, more efficient, and meaningful ecosystem. The process of converting voluntary ESG commitments to enforced standards, anchored by IFRS S1 /S2 (with Scope 3 reliefs of December 2025 to financial institutions) and CSRD/ESRS simplifications to fewer datapoints, by an order of magnitude, have taken sustainability data to material financial information. This move requires issuers and investors to address climate risks, transition plans, emissions (Scopes 1-3), and taxonomy-compliant activities with equal seriousness as the more traditional metrics, reducing the extent of greenwashing by mandating substantiation, anti-misleading labelling, and moving to frameworks that ISSA 5000 and ISAE 3000 are the most appropriate, such as limited and reasonable ones.

AI becomes the inevitable catalyst, in the process of autopiloting the ingestion of unstructured data, computing granular emissions, writing up conforming narratives, finding abnormalities, and creating audit evidence trails. Generative AI-based platforms with agentic systems and real-time dashboards minimize compliance load by 4590 and close the gap between data in Scope 3 value chains and can forecast transition risks and impact proactively. This in green investment means accurate screening of the portfolio, verifiable taxonomy alignment in the bonds/loans/funds and assured redirection of the capital towards renewables, circular models and nature-positive projects. In the case of India, where sustainable debt amounts over USD 55.9 billion (an increase of 186 percent since 2021) and the BRSR KPI is recommended to align with the national 2070 net-zero goals, AI provides support in the automation of BRSR KPI and green lending prioritization.

However, the fact of such convergence is not tension free: the energy/water intensity of data centers in AI, which is estimated to cause grid pressure during peak demand, gives reason to view the sustainable deployment of AI as necessary, whereas concerns about bias, privacy under DPDPA, and regulatory disintegration require governing the use of AI through ethics, accountability, and human judgment (Singhal et al., 2025). Such obstacles as the barriers to SME costs and interoperability have not passed, but the prospects prevail: access to AI is becoming more democratic, greenium premiums will decrease due to trust, and trillions will be redirected towards verifiable results.

Finally, AI-based regulatory compliance is the solution that transforms green investment into a wise based regenerative finance. Sustainability is no longer peripheral but forms the main part of risk management, value creation and resilience. This paradigm promotes investor confidence, de-risks investment portfolios to physical/transition shocks, and expedites fair transitioning because such disclosures are decision useful, comparable, and verifiable. This combined strategy makes finance a planetary custodian in a world where climate pressures are growing increasingly vicious, since profitability and purpose are aligned, capital mobilized on a massive scale to go net-zero, enhance biodiversity and grow inclusively. The way ahead requires sustained cooperation between regulators, technologists, issuers and investors to both tighten standards, massify ethical AI, and seal execute loop-holes and by mid-century and more the green investment would bolster the change with measurable and sustained effect on global SDGs and national climate commitments (Ahuja et al., 2025).

## 9. FUTURE ROADMAP: SCALING AI FOR REGENERATIVE GREEN INVESTMENT

The future roadmap: scaling AI to regenerative green investment by 2030 provides an ambitious but realistic pathway in which artificial intelligence will become not a compliance facilitator but an active organizer of a regenerative financial system that would actively repair the planetary health, not mentioning a much higher-quality risk-adjusted returns. Predictions suggest that by 2030 sustainable finance will have more than 40 trillion assets under management, and AI will be the digital foundation of sustainable finance and processing real-time, unstructured data, whether satellite deforestation surveillance or IoT-enabled supply chain, to provide more transparency, predictive accuracy, and optimization of impact than ever before. Bringing together harmonized international taxonomies, based on the IFRS S1/S2 interoperability (implemented in more than 40 jurisdictions by 2026, and still evolving), BRSR Core development in India towards complete value-chain assurance, and alignments with the EU CSRD/SFDR will provide a consistent base, which will decrease fragmentation and allow easier cross-border green capital flows.

Agents artificial intelligence (AI) The agents will take over by 20282030 as autonomous and multi-step logical systems, which will control the end-to-end processes: pre-screening corporate transition plans against credibility, smart grids and renewable forecasting, simulating infrastructure robustness in climate conditions, and portfolios dynamically rebalanced around high-impact themes such as climate adaptation, biodiversity credits and enablers of the circular economy (Onyeka, 2025). Quantum-enhanced modelling will help fast-track complex programs to predict AI-driven energy needs (data centers will take up 20 per cent of total world energy by 202830) against clean supply chains, investments in green data centres, nuclear/renewable hybrids, and energy-saving breakthroughs to minimise the environmental impact of AI itself.

These milestones are mandatory AI-assured market leadership by 2028, cut compliance costs by more than 40 percent and make adoption available to SMEs with cloud solutions; universal interoperability with blockchain-confirmed impact tracking on tokenized green assets; and trillions mobilized with credible and outcome-linked instruments. RBI/SEBI in India will further enhance AI in climate risk controls and green deposits, and priority sector lending, aiming at investing up to 253-355 billion annually by 2035, with applications such as ESGRisk.ai and new gen AI tools automated BRSR/ESG analytics of listed companies and NBFCs.

Capacity-building will continue to play a fundamental role: to maintain judgment on hard ethical dilemmas regulators, investors, and issuers will invest in AI literacy, ethical governance (bias audits, privacy-by-design under DPDPA) and hybrid human-AI solutions. New technologies such as agentic systems and convergence of IoT/blockchain will support real-time, auditable reporting, which replaces periodic snapshots with continuous intelligence that identifies greenwashing before it happens and measures regenerative effects - e.g. carbon sequestration, ecosystem restoration and equity benefits to society (Elias et al., 2024).

This roadmap is the reflection of Finance 5.0: human-centric, ethical, and regenerative in which AI is the planetary steward. It can solve the risks of AI (energy intensity, bias) due to sustainable practices and governance that can make technology amplify purpose without causing unintentional harm. The success will be determined by the daring cooperation, the harmonization of the G20 and the scale of blended finance, as well as by such ambitious targets as net-positive portfolios, nature-positive finance integration, and fair transitions in new markets. By 2030, AI scaled regenerative green investment will not only reduce the risks of climate change but paradoxically recreate the resilience by directing the capital to a low-carbon, inclusive future, combining profit and planetary regeneration.

## REFERENCES


Ahuja, A., Wairagade, A., & Gupta, N. (2025). AIREA: An AI-Driven Optimization Framework for Intelligent Automation in Large-Scale Enterprise Systems. *Available at SSRN* 5160312.

Akram, R., Shi, X., Khalid, F., & Srivastava, M. (2025). Artificial intelligence (AI) adoption and green investment: Driving corporate environmental responsibility. *Business Strategy and the Environment*, *34*(7), 9188–9202. DOI: 10.1002/bse.70069

Alabi, A. T. (2025). Assessing the Transformative Potential of Green Fintech Solutions in Mitigating Financed Emissions. In *FinTech and Robotics Advancements for Green Finance and Investment* (pp. 223–250). IGI Global Scientific Publishing. DOI: 10.4018/979-8-3373-0355-0.ch008

Alam, M., Ansari, Z. A., & Jafar, S. H. (2025). The technological landscape of AI and sustainable finance: An exploration. In *Green Horizons: Role of AI in Sustainable Finance* (pp. 37–53). Springer Nature Singapore. DOI: 10.1007/978-981-96-6495-5_3

Alshahmy, S., & Sahiner, M. (2024). Enhancing the Issuance and Monitoring of Sustainable Finance Instruments through AI. In *Artificial Intelligence, Finance, and Sustainability: Economic, Ecological, and Ethical Implications* (pp. 217–241). Springer Nature Switzerland. DOI: 10.1007/978-3-031-66205-8_9

Anumolu, V. R. (2025). Financial Innovation for Sustainability: Leveraging AI, XR, and Data for Impactful Investments. In *Exploring the Impact of Extended Reality (XR) Technologies on Promoting Environmental Sustainability* (pp. 133–157). Springer Nature Switzerland. DOI: 10.1007/978-3-031-88013-1_7

Bansal, N., Taneja, S., & Özen, E. (2025). AI-Powered Sustainability: Transforming Finance Sector for a Better Tomorrow. In *Achieving Sustainability with AI Technologies* (pp. 27-46). IGI Global Scientific Publishing.

Challa, K. (2022). Generative AI-Powered Solutions for Sustainable Financial Ecosystems: A Neural Network Approach to Driving Social and Environmental Impact. *Mathematical Statistician and Engineering*, 2326-9865.

Elias, O., Awotunde, O. J., Oladepo, O. I., Azuikpe, P. F., Samson, O. A., Oladele, O. R., & Ogunruku, O. O. (2024). The evolution of green fintech: Leveraging AI and IoT for sustainable financial services and smart contract implementation. *World Journal of Advanced Research and Reviews*, *23*(1), 2710–2723. DOI: 10.30574/wjarr.2024.23.1.2272

Hassanein, A., & Tharwat, H. (2024). Artificial intelligence (AI) and green finance. In *The Palgrave Handbook of Green Finance for Sustainable Development* (pp. 859–889). Springer International Publishing. DOI: 10.1007/978-3-031-65756-6_32

Irfan, M., Bhute, N. S., Yadav, A. K., & Dias, R. (2026). Sustainable Investment Portfolios with AI: Bridging Green Finance and Technological Innovation. In *Legal and Regulatory Considerations of Leveraging Sustainable Finance* (pp. 235-256). IGI Global Scientific Publishing.

Joseph, O. O., Kevin-Alerechi, E., Olumide, O. J., Sunday, D., Fagbohun, O., & Olanrewaju, S. (2025). Reimagining Green Financing with AI: A Technological Approach to Sustainability. *J Artif Intell Mach Learn & Data Sci*, *3*(1), 2346–2352. DOI: 10.51219/AIMLD/Omotoso-Oluwayomi-Joseph/509

Khaddam, A. A., & Alzghoul, A. (2025). Artificial intelligence-driven business intelligence for strategic energy and ESG management: A systematic review of economic and policy implications. *International Journal of Energy Economics and Policy*, *15*(4), 635–650. DOI: 10.32479/ijeep.19820

Leitner-Hanetseder, S., & Lehner, O. M. (2023). AI-powered information and big data: Current regulations and ways forward in IFRS reporting. *Journal of Applied Accounting Research*, *24*(2), 282–298. DOI: 10.1108/JAAR-01-2022-0022

Mitra, A., & Maity, A. (2025). Balancing Green and Fair: Ethical AI in Sustainable Finance. *International Journal of Business Management & Legal Affairs*, *1*(1), 55–76.

Nauman, M. (2025). AI in Sustainable Investing: A Dual-Edged Sword. In *FinTech and Robotics Advancements for Green Finance and Investment* (pp. 383-416). IGI Global Scientific Publishing. DOI: 10.4018/979-8-3373-0355-0.ch013

Ogunyemi, F. (2023). AI-Powered Carbon Accounting: Transforming ESG Reporting Standards for a Sustainable Global Economy. *International Journal of Multidisciplinary Research in Science, Engineering and Technology*, *6*(4).

Onyeka, E. J. (2025). Automating Financial Decision-Making in Renewable Energy: Leveraging AI and Credit Risk Models for Sustainable Investment. *Asian Journal of Economics. Business and Accounting*, *25*(4), 492–500.

Pandow, B. A., Ganai, K. A., & Hussain, G. (2024, February). A Review on AI-powered Advancements in Climate Finance and its Impact. In *2024 11th International Conference on Computing for Sustainable Global Development (INDIACom)* (pp. 1409-1413). IEEE. DOI: 10.23919/INDIACom61295.2024.10498959

Pavlidis, G. (2025). Empowering sustainable finance with artificial intelligence: a framework for responsible implementation. In *A Research Agenda for Financial Law and Regulation* (pp. 23–38). Edward Elgar Publishing. DOI: 10.4337/9781803929996.00009

Singh, S., Yadav, S., Singh, A., Krishna, Y. J., & Singh, A. (2024). Harnessing Technology for a Sustainable Future in Finance: The Role of Artificial Intelligence in Promoting Environmental Responsibility. In *Anticipating Future Business Trends: Navigating Artificial Intelligence Innovations* (Vol. 2, pp. 367–378). Springer Nature Switzerland. DOI: 10.1007/978-3-031-63402-4_30

Singhal, N., Goyal, S., Khan, M., & Singhal, T. (2025). AI for Sustainable Finance: Driving Innovation and Ethical Growth. *Financial Innovation for Global Sustainability*, 529-559.

Soetan, O., & Deloitte, L. L. P. (2023). Sustainable automation pipelines powered by lightweight AI optimizing industrial efficiency while preserving transparency, compliance, and equity in decision processes. *Int J Comput Appl Technol Res*, *12*(12), 218–233.

Thomas, M., Maheswari, G. S., & Kavitha, M. (2025). AI applications in sustainable financial management. *Revista Espanola de Derecho Canonico*, *7*(1), 58–71.

Waykar, Y. A., & Yambal, S. (2025). AI and the Evolution of Green Finance: Transforming Banking for a Greener World. In *Convergence of AI, Education, and Business for Sustainability* (pp. 285-306). IGI Global Scientific Publishing.

# Chapter 11
# Policy Landscape and Incentives on AI-Powered Green Finance

**Santosh Kumar**
http://orcid.org/0009-0002-3115-6772
*Sharda University, India*

**Neha Gupta**
http://orcid.org/0009-0005-1987-0377
*Christ University, Bengaluru, India*

**Swarnima Gorani**
http://orcid.org/0009-0004-2052-6891
*Sharda University, India*

## ABSTRACT

*The application of AI in green finance has enormous potential to tackle climate change, but its effect would be determined by the strength and integrity of governance mechanisms as well as well-designed incentives. Good policy serves to set the bar but also incentives and responsible use in finance in AI applications. In the absence of such governance, exposures including algorithmic discrimination, data mining and unequal access to technology are likely to compound rather than advance social goals. Thus, AI governance has become a priority for governments, financial regulators and multilateral organisations. Policy frameworks achieve two parallel goals: on the one hand they provide boundaries to invest in technology and at the same time these very policy mechanisms direct capital towards environmentally friendly investment through incentives like tax benefits, financial grants, green debts etc.*

DOI: 10.4018/979-8-2600-1308-3.ch011

## 1. INTRODUCTION

The combination of AI and environmental finance has become vital in humanity's fight against ecological threats and climate breakdown. Moving toward sustainable economies requires new ways of sourcing capital, investing and governance adapted to climate. In financial systems, digital technologies facilitate such modal shifts in how resources are extracted, uncertainties appraised and futures shaped. Learning machines, big data analysis/processing and predictive computational methods focus them there (on activities with positive environmentally beneficial effects.). This technology integration works behind the scenes to assist governmental and financial leaders in taking clear-headed, accountable steps toward global sustainability goals." The fusion of machine learning and finance produces a dynamic information-and evidence-based system, directly promoting SDG 7 (Clean and Renewable Energy), SDG 9 (Technological Infrastructure and Innovation) and SDG 13 (Climate Action-urgent). The trend mirrors more widespread technology adoption across industries (Lee et al., 2025).

Environmental financing at its core seeks to direct investment into projects that have lower environmental footprints. This includes the growth of renewable energy, improvements in operational efficiencies and circular economic models. Traditionally whether investments qualify for a green label was determined by subjective judgment and the absence of comprehensive data – which greatly diluted the precision of selection. Computational intelligence has transformed this landscape, from algorithm design to language understanding in machines and predictive analysis tools. It is now possible for these systems to analyze enormous sources of information quickly, determining environmental consequences as well as economic feasibility. For example, satellites can track land-use change; computers can generate scenario projections of renewable generation; and document analysis can uncover fraudulent environmental claims. Such technological advancements pro- mote the operation of financial systems with more transparency, accountability and empirical foundation.

Progress in global policy has sped up since the Paris climate accord of 2015. That deal set a key goal: to rebalance the flow of money with paths that have smaller emissions and more climate adaption. Nations across the planet have married in policy innovation. Examples include India's domestic green bonds programme, China's standardised green investment catalogues and the EU's broad disclosure requirements for sustainability reporting in addition to its activity classification system. Multilateral organizations—the World Bank, OECD and UNEP Finance Initiative, for example—have also illustrated how new computational tools can allow for increasingly complex sustainable finance processes. Execution differs greatly depending on the stage of economic development. As far as progress in integrating AI-green finances, richer countries tend to have more established systems than do poorer ones, which encounter barriers such as uncertainty over regulations, tech limitations, and a lack of operational capability (Okeke et al., 2024).

The solution is the transformative power of machine learning to sustainable investment management, in its planning, monitoring, verification and governance stages. "Automating the tracking of emissions and quantifying how well climate intervention works will secure ESG data integrity. The examination process, including the Treasury's use of AI, increases the understanding of geographic and systemic climate risk exposures in markets that regulatory authorities have. This lack of integration results in blind spots for climate risk assessment frameworks. Meanwhile, central banking authorities investigate AI-supported climate scenario analysis for financial stability consideration. This shows how technological progressions are not only speeding up sustainable finance decisions but bolstering the resilience of the financial system to environmental fluctuations.

## 1.1 The Role of AI in The Advancement of Sustainable Finance

These technical changes give rise to ethical, legal and governance issues that require policy focus. The deployment of machine learning in financial markets presents new facets of transparency and accountability, with respect to responsibilities for informational custodianship and the understandability of algorithms. Environmental finance is an area where social welfare and environmental sustainability have to be emphasized with the introduction of fair, available and sustainable technology. This leaves policymakers walking a fine line: fostering innovation while maintaining protective standards. This balance includes the need to ensure that new technologies do not conflict with principles such as the protection of information, fair access or environmental responsibility.

The lack of global shared standards on governing AI in sustainable finance yields non-integrated solutions and incentives for regulatory arbitrage: the weakest links in governance are sought after as safe havens to conduct financial and technological operations that appear too risky due to current regulations. The cross-border harmonization and coordination of information governance systems are the key to unified development of AI-green finance and international cooperation (Joseph et al., 2025).

Reward designs have a great impact on the speed of technological adoption. There are many tools that nations and financial organizations use to help channel capital into environmental technologies: green debt markets, sustainability-linked lending agreements, emissions pricing schemes and tax-incentivized backing of clean innovation. These mechanisms are improved by employing AI capabilities to identify the most promising opportunities and optimize financial allocations, based on environmental data analysis. Advanced systems can help identify renewable energy firms with the most compelling growth paths and financial fortitude, thereby facilitating more strategic capital allocation. Public-private cooperation is indispensable to generate such innovative environments, where technological know-how and financial capital give rise to new initiatives. Decisions must allow for transparency and flexibility, with access a key tenet of sustainable development goals protected through governance.

Another vital policy dimension is data infrastructure and system interoperability. Technology-based sustainable finance relies on data accuracy, normalisation and sharing across all timescales. Disconnected databases, inconsistent reporting protocols and siloed data are problems in many countries. Policy needs to therefore drive forward data-sharing standards, digital innovation hubs and regulatory sandbox for emerging AI applications. These measures help responsible tech development, allowing financial institutions to explore new approaches without creating market confusion. Regulatory sandboxes, such as the UK's innovation framework, are an example of how governments can enable experimentation in controlled 'regulatory testing zones' with mock data that complies to regulatory standards. These models exemplify the flexible regulation of new technologies while preserving systemic stability (Singh, 2022).

## 2. AI-BASED GREEN FINANCE

AI-driven environmental finance can help significantly shrink the trillion-dollar infrastructure gap in sustainable development by speeding up capital flow into climate solutions. The delicate task of balancing these calls requires inclusive governance systems. In developing economies-- notably in Asia and Africa-- the relatively poor state of infrastructure (such as roads, ports or electrification), a lack of relevant skills in such emerging economies, as well as financial constraints restrict participation. International collaboration and development financing are essential for the universal engagement in this new terrain. This line is about differentiated climate responsibility—recognizing that countries are differently resourced and capable of acting on climate.

Machine learning supports internal control and oversight of financial operations through automated tracking and analysis of transactions, enhancing disclosure and lessening susceptibility to fraud. Blockchain networks with AI improve transaction recording and impact verification to guide finance to the verified projects. This nexus furthers aims such as transparency in ESG disclosure, thwarting greenwashing and promoting ethical corporate conduct; together serving to guide commerce towards sustainability. We need policy makers to create clear certification, verification and data protection standards that ensure the integrity of these approaches, enhancing public trust in the system (Ramzani et al., 2024).

Current sustainability and innovation efforts appear to represent a shift from traditional top-down regulation towards more flexible and future-oriented forms of regulation. Policy-making maps are not static rulebooks, but rather dynamic co-evolutionary structures. These include adaptable testing sites, principles-based technological guidance and outcome-centric incentives instead of only seeing compliance indicators. This shift is especially pertinent in this age of rapid generative methodologies, complex autonomous agents and analytic climate analysis systems transforming financial transactions.

## 2.1 Global Policy Architecture

AI environmental finance regulation includes climate agreements, financial regulations, technology governance mechanisms and sustainability standards. Some foundational principles are also laid out in the 2015 Paris accord, which seeks to spur financial flows toward low-carbon, climate-resilient development. While it does not explicitly refer to AI, it sets the course for technology-based environmental finance. Global efforts UNEP Finance Initiative, Climate Risk Task Force, Network for Financial System Greening are striving to integrate data analytics, machine learning risk assessment capabilities and transparency standards into sustainable finance. These initiatives produce metastandards for AI use in environmental realms, focusing on ethics, transparency, and responsibility (Saeedi & Ashraf, 2024).

The OECD AI principles in 2019 focus on human-centered values, explainability and responsibility which are essential to the financial sector's governance of AI. The EU's AI framework provides a tiered risk-based approach to regulation, where systems are classified based on the potential level of risk produced and controls are required for higher-risk applications such as those in financial services. Whilst these international guidelines could be used as a governance base for ethical and transparent AI utilization within environmental finance, national adaptations are addressing specific economic, technical or ecological contexts.

## 2.2The Policy Responses at the Regional and National Levels

Governments around the world are increasingly incorporating machine learning and sustainability in financial planning. The European Union takes the lead with the Green Development Strategy and the mandatory release of information on sustainability (SFDR), meaning financial institutions have to communicate their environmental performance. The EU's Activity Taxonomy creates standardized "green" definitions, making possible algorithmic portfolio assessment. Responsible AI use across these levers are innovation as part of the newly launched Digital Finance Strategy.

China has pursued substantial innovation. Central bankers and securities regulators encourage green financial instrument issuance and the upgrading of monitoring and reporting to digital forms. Chinese FS associations are developing systems that use AI and distributed ledgers to guarantee data accuracy, fight false environmental claims and keep track of investment. The "New Generation Artificial Intelligence Development Plan" points out that sustainable development is one of the AIs applications. India moves through the Sovereign Green Bonds Initiative and National AI Strategy with focus on widespread technology participation. AI will drive green financing, aiding climate action plan and for digital India efforts in terms of the broader sustainability goals. This makes early groundwork for AI-incorporated sustainable finance.

The US uses market-based instruments in a piecemeal approach and lacks broad legal based statutes, but relies on regulatory bodies to manage topics and sectors. Direction of executives focuses on AI systems we can trust and hazards that we need to mitigate. These ideas are significant for the innovation of climate finance in the private sector. AI-boosted assessment and productivity cleaning up does pay Programs like the Green Investment Fund and Inflation Reduction Act help fund clean infrastructure (Hassanein & Tharwat, 2024).

Japan, South Korea and Singapore are building more sophisticated systems that put AI to good use. Japan'sConnected Society 5.0 focuses on AI-assisted sustainability, Singapore's Green Finance Strategy incorporates analytics and machine learning for robust investments. These models demonstrate how the proliferation of AI in financial services leads nations to focus on digitally transforming their economies to address environmental goals.

## 2.3 Development of Institutional Architecture and Supervisory Framework.

One main challenge is to coordinate institutions between financial authorities, technology overseers, environmental departments and central banks. The Network for Greening the Financial System brings together more than 140 authorities working on ways to integrate climate considerations into financial stability monitoring. This network is investigating the use of machine learning to refine climate hazard interpretation, the evaluation of stress footprints for portfolios and early-warning detection with respect to market vulnerabilities.

The IFRS framework and International Standards Board for Sustainability are used to facilitate harmonization of global environmental reporting. This allows standardized computation of patient data and scoring. Yet fragmentation among national frameworks means that there are inconsistencies in data and definitions of ESG, which detract from the ability of AI to deliver. Policy must support integration of data and harmonization of classification by providing shared taxonomies and a facilitating information transfer protocols (Siriman et al., 2025).

Regulators increasingly use test beds, in which forward-thinking firms can experiment with machine-learning environmental finance solutions under regulatory supervision. Examples are a testing programme in the UK, an innovation sandbox in Singapore and testing initiatives in India. Such frameworks allow concept validation under protective conditions encouraging cross-regulatory cooperation and governance that supports responsible innovation.

## 2.4 Legal and Ethical Dimensions

AI in finance deployment raises legal, ethical questions regulators need to ponder. Financial regulation in the classical sense is set up to optimize decision control, not algorithmic systems. It is still difficult to have rules adjusted for the hybrid decision-making condition between computational and human judgment. Transparency – institutions are compelled to explain the algorithmic rationale of decisions, which is a breath of fresh air! Show transparency and integrity The EU framework's first requirement is that any high-risk AI system needs to be transparent and have them in check. International principles such as the OECD guidelines and UNESCO ethics recommendations put the responsibility, equity and human supervision in full sight of implementation.

For environmental financing in particular, data veracity and green feet bear equivalent importance. To train machine-learning models, accurate diverse and representative training information is necessary. Low information quality may lead to incorrect assessment and violation of "those causing harm bear costs" principles. Threats can be reduced by mandating independent verification of environmental and ESG metrics' measures based on a set methodology. Banks or tech firms might create committees on technology ethics in governance and oversight structures (Fu et al., 2023).

The importance of privacy and security is still high, despite the a large amount of environmental and financial data being collected by AI systems. Algorithms are subject to regulation under the European laws and comparable regulations elsewhere about access to and use of sensitive information. Policy across the world has to marry these privacy protections with sharing sustainability data, so we're balancing transparency and rights.

## 2.5 The Information Architecture and Digital Infrastructure

AI-driven enviro-finance poses high-quality, compatible information accessible to this AI. Computational systems also must digest environmental, governance and sustainability metrics, satellite data plus sensor feeds. It should promote digital publics of infrastructure for sustainable finance: accessible information sites, repository system with enhanced security and AI-suitable information architecture under government oversight (Alshahmy & Sahiner, 2024).

This phenomenon is epitomized in the style of the EU's Information Governance Act and Public Information Directive, which promote data use for the common good, especially in sustainability. To optimise for machine-learning application, China set up an Environmental Data Initiative to encourage data interchange between businesses. B developing countries could be implemented via national environmental information systems and climate data cooperatives.

These are useful steps in the fight against technological disparities – meaning regional financial institutions can also use machine learning (technically) as effectively as elsewhere. Standardization of machine-learning verification and certification procedures can help systems achieve technical and ethical benchmarks as well as sustainability targets. Common well-being metrics and ISO artificial intelligence governance standards may provide average quality control.

## 2.6 Regulatory Applications and Sustainable Finance Governance

Authorities are more and more using computer software for their own regulatory purposes (regtech). Supervised machine learning can detect anomalous behavior and determine whether entities that say they are consistent with sustainability have relatively large environmental impacts. Regulatory bodies now use machine learning on textual corporate disclosures to discover sustainability deception. The Financial Stability Board and Singapore's authority engage in computational stability assessment, analyzing climate-change risks and organismic resilience. They are new kinds of regulation vetted by an evolutionary process from reactive to dynamic, targeted and technology-enabled supervision.

The assessment services and stock exchanges make use of computer systems for the environmental characterization of resources. Policy makers need to ensure that such systems are equivalent in robustness as recognised environmental categorization and are transparent and honest. Collaborative governance combines mandates and market-based standards, and can adapt while remaining open (Boumaiza, 2024).

## 2.7 Coordinated Global Policy

AI-driven environmental finance of this kind operates by its very nature internationally; money, data and environmental impact all exceed geopolitical borders. Global governance and regulations need partnership and alignment. Machine learning algorithms are adopted by international organizations such as development organizations and multilateral finance institutions for ecological capital transactions. The prior collaborations, such as the Global AI Capability Alliance and ETAs indirectly manifest orchestrating intelligent system for environmental assessment and sustainable capital application.

Missing capabilities and infrastructure prevail also in advanced or emerging countries. Technology was explicitly regulated or environmentally financed in industrialized economies, and emerging markets faced institutional and capacity barriers. Knowledge sharing, capacity building and investment facilitation are needed by mechanisms for global governance. Global environmental capital can support machine-learning climate projects in developing countries (Papagiannopoulos et al., 2024).

Cross-national data-sharing agreements and exchanges of mutual recognition in machine-learning certification standards exploit to governance proliferation. An extensive Global Environmental Finance Technology Charter on the principles for machine-learning use – transparency, inclusion, ethics and answerability – would be useful.

## 2.8 Flexible and changing policy approaches

Technology solutions demand flexible governance and foresight. Stale regulatory structures also can fail to account for new risks and innovative remedies. A dynamic approach works with input from controlled testing and empirical studies, amending the requirements together. Governments could carry out “adaptive governance” switching along with the change in scientific knowledge and technological development (Onabowale, 2024).

Performance-based policy, evaluated based on environmental performance rather than procedural compliance, could set the guardrails that encourage invention yet keep accountability. For example, institutions could be rewarded for any project that abates carbon through machine learning rather than a narrow set of technical criteria. By such integrating, ethics committees and means of stakeholder input the transparency and access morality is promoted. This form of governance feeds into institutional legitimacy, which is vital in ensuring financial viability.

## 2.9 Policy Destinations in the Development of AI-Environment Financial Integration

Several policy objectives are appearing as the area evolves. First, government must create an integrated approach to technology management in support of green goals, ensuring that new systems are aligned with favorable ecological and community outcomes. Second, funding digital public infrastructure and open information platforms guarantees that everyone has access to machine-learning financial products. Third, tax breaks and innovation grants could incentivize businesses to use machine learning to evaluate the environment, account for carbon emissions and verify ESG claims. International agencies should lead the push for standardisation, and remove idiosyncrasies that ensure international markets do not uniformly encourage sustainability.

Policy makers need to ensure that the actions involve training and competence development communicating technology principles sustainable finance, computational methodology. Creating value with machine-learning environmental finance is as much about being competent across several domains than it is about computation (Elias et al., 2024).

# 3. INCENTIVES FOR AI ENABLED GREEN FINANCE: FISCAL VERSUS NON-FISCAL INCENTIVE MECHANISMS

Financial and regulatory incentives also compel scaled deployment of sustainability machine-learning systems. Money e.g. in the form of grants and subsidies is a very simple approach to promote technology introduction. Conditional incentives that tap into the corporate understanding of environmental damages work well where emissions accounting and investment institutions are still to be established. Back-of-the-envelope calculations and more advanced economic analysis agree that targeted monetary support would substantially increase environmental innovation and environmentally preferable consumption, which stimulate optimal pollution abatement.

Research shows that financial resources for learning about the pollution effects of farms leads to productivity gains across all sectors based on thousands of firms. This intelligence determines how public money is allocated by government. For capitalization and hazard mitigation in cases of oceanic resource management, China offers support for capability development and reduction in a number of other areas including the cost efficiencies and trust created by the organization. Financial incentives prevent barriers to implementation and reward organizations for experimenting with predictive models, creating a mathematical rationale that encourages ecological action (Jiang et al., 2025).

Non-monetary incentives are created by regulatory structures mandating and encouraging financial environmentalization through machine learning. Elevated requirements may require continuous monitoring and ESG (Environmental, Social, Governance) disclosure, thus removing greenwashing and ensuring dollars flow to true sustainability.

Monetary advantage and environmental objectives are interconnected by fiscal incentives and equalisation benefits. There could be financial incentives from the government to invest in machine-learning-based solutions for environmental problems such as wetland restoration and sustainable agriculture. Central European governments have tied public sector inducements to the private markets in order to stimulate ecological innovation.

This results in superior financing available to enterprise through improved analysis techniques. Tax benefits for machine-learning application in sustainability could also offset large machine-learning power expenses that, if left unmanaged, might increase pollution. These are also guaranteed to ensure that "eco" technology add makes a positive contribution to carbon-zero goals by ensuring it doesn't make things worse thus embracing environmentally responsible machine-learning like data centres on renewable power (Gupta et al., 2025).

China's green capital project is used to motivate banking system to finance climate-stable the method of machine learning in sea area. Concerns about investment is also reduced by Jeopardy reduction measures. Global financial institution (MDB) scale-up support for machine learning approaches toward the environment, including borrowing to eliminate annual environmental budget deficits. Linking regional climate pledges (NDCs) to financial instrument gains affirms policy integration and allocates the majority of resources towards renewable energy, with potential for machine learning in computational forecasting and assessment.

Commercial drivers like environmental indebtedness and machine-learning transformed carbon markets spark private business participation. Machine-learning emotion measure and discord detection enhance the authenticity of financial instrument by sustainability evaluation and have successfully discovered misreporting to attract more investors. Retraining in moves the mathematics of financial cocktails into sustainable mixes through dynamical recalibration, that aligns profit with environmental impact (Attipoe et al., 2023).

ML develops a pollution credit cost and checks the pollution decrease in alternate-power savings. This creates a monetary reward that encourages compliance with specifications. For instance, machine learning in cooperation with automatised documentation protect sustainable details from automated treaties to decrease fraudulent environmental claim and verifying governance conformity. This is particularly effective in emerging economies as they can address enduring funding challenges.

## 3.1 Innovation in Carbon Exchange and Environmental Debt Systems

Startup and research... spending could increase machine-learning productivity in environmental development. Widening markets could spread innovations and encourage collaboration, increasing the machine-learning impact on effectiveness. Analytical examination reveals that the economic opportunity changes machine-learning benefit from negligible to beneficial above a threshold. Research incentives, including funding for new ideas in machine learning, also work. These serve to spread benefit and work-force progress and indicate how further spending can switch the ML productivity advantage from hurtful to helpful in a nonlinear way. These signs are found within China's metro zones. Mathematics-funded inquiry into machine learning-led marine abundance prediction could reduce overfishing (Bhattacharya & Sachdev, 2024).

Significant early fees, concerns about database security and the ability to deliver in machine-learning methods may diminish advantage efficacy. Machinc lcarning's power appetite could increase pollution, they wrote, so financial aid for alternative energy data centers would be necessary. Safeguarding sensitive info on sustainability facts will need protection measures as well as government oversight. In order to achieve these targets, the advanced environments should include workforce development tools (e.g., machine tool for initial operations) and have a holistic approach authorizing access to the creation zones (Elhady & Shohieb, 2025).

Data indicates these are effective strategies. Machine-learning risk evaluation reduced the shortage of renewables by 43.8% in a European country via monetary reallocation and policy harmonization. 'The unparalleled extension of renewable power is the direct result of exchange and projection catches in a computational and oceanic nation, supported by transnational banking and green credit'. On a regional basis, the combination of sustainability financing and machine-learning to maritime business increased capacity and reduced risks with positive results in Asia going forward. Machine-learning impact on global sustainable solution measurements through range approaches, with sustainability-oriented capital connections. Such measures suggest patterns of monetary supports that finance declining volatility.

## 3.2 How Public and Commercial Entities can work Together Model of Partnerships

Public-private partnerships (PPPs) are engendering cooperation among businesses and the state to promote environmentally-friendly machine learning-induced capitalism through a nexus of funding. Officials could also partner with computational companies developing universal sustainability measures and guidelines for ethical machine learning (Wang et al., 2025). This requires conducting tests of disinterestedness to weed out bias. Machine learning is transforming environmental finance in developing areas by using images from the atmosphere to oversee sustainability real time and designing expense formula methods, business experts say.

Collaboration funding This backs innovation within communities via cash for studies that advance machine-learning control of renewable infrastructure and predicting energy needs. Public-commercial partnerships enabled machine-learning in sustainable investment across wealthy and Nordic lands. However, we also computed that the attainment of 47% atmospheric power is the ideal cooperation to productive and financial effect.

## 3.3 Funding Mechanisms and Promotion of Community Investment

Benefit plans need to be updated and revised to incorporate new technology and computerized ledger systems. The importance to broadcast knowledge for green initiatives, encourage renewable vine in computational routines and nourish multi-core participation is demonstrated. Benefits models halt economic inefficiency and convince environmental asset capitalists by considering engineering impacts through data and government organization participation. Fiscal Situation Computation helps to predict lasting sustainability, guiding support toward fair improvement.

Advantage models promote machine-learning environmental capitalism, and couple sustainability imperatives with market money in marketplace funds. Such systems could allow machine-learning assistance to pollution balance through financial incentives, demands, market tools and collaboration. In an era of increasing global interest in sustainability, these are reasons that will enable machine learning to steer not just green finances but equal and lasting economic prosperity around the world. With good stewardship and a lot of coalition building, machine learning environmental capitalism could become the norm for sustained improvement in populations (Udeagha & Muchapondwa, 2023).

# 4. BARRIERS OF APPLICATION AND LACKS IN POLICY: LEGAL, MORAL AND TECHNOLOGICAL ASPECTS OF THE DEPLOYMENT OR IMPLEMENTATION OF TOOL

## 4.1 Lack of Regulation and Policy Issues

Generalisation of technology use faces significant challenges in the regulatory, ethical and technical domains impacting on successful implementation. Non-unified international regulations make it complex for jurisdictional and compliance costs. "The concerns of bias, lack of oversight and transparency are also significant with respect to neutrality as well as fundamental safeguards from a moral perspective. Usefulness is constrained by information accuracy, framework reliability and computational capabilities. These concerns exacerbate existing governance deficits such as outdated norms and ineffective institutional frameworks, designed implementation structures that are not sufficiently fast to keep up with technologically driven change. Instead, we need flexible systems and global viewpoints for responsible technology implementation by relevant authorities. This need arises due to the interaction of these barriers.

The root challenge is a lack of international government. Many places have market-specific regulations, like data protection (GDPR domestically or state-level regulation in the U.S.) or consumer protection, written without sensitivity to technology-specific requirements. Lending or employment decision making processes performed by computing systems take into account private information, forcing adherence to privacy constraints. Operating as "mystery systems" makes it difficult to prove legality or defend entitlements like transparency or correction. The EU frame since 2024 includes new proportional scrutiny of systems: non-permissive, consequent, restrictive and minimal (Challa, 2022). However, applying globally imposes pressure on non-EU entities to comply. SMEs (small-medium enterprises) address problems in meeting the consequent system requirements because of a large amount of mandatory paperwork. America adopts distinct methods. Instead of calling for regulation, they advise bodies like the Federal Trade Commission, the FDA and the Transportation Department. This results in regulatory "circumvention," and a lack of uniform expectations.

## 4.2 Legal Difficulties

The legal barrier of responsibility assignment is another one. This modern legal tradition requires proof of negligence or intent cause harm, basis for person being at fault. However, the judgment is shared among the developers and implementors of technology systems as well as information providers, making fault identification difficult. Assume the cause of an accident is software failure in an autonomous vehicle using wireless updates. Is the developer, programming company or storage provider to blame? The EU Product Liability directive and as such its analogues, define technology as "goods" - apart from it comes to math learning software post-sale.

There's no compulsory technology insurance or accountability-free compensation, meaning patients are left in a dizzying regulatory haze. Asia's Temporary Rules on Governmental Guidance on Mathematical Speech (2023) require operators to review issues involving protection and titles for false information. Nevertheless, guidance implementation is still vague via limited legal precedents (Alhejaili, 2024). Global ethics guidelines (2021) have no legal status, and compliance is introduced and upheld to different extents.

Copyright issues muddy the waters for tech use. Building broad-based learning systems with proprietary content raises questions of applicability. Constitutional rights legal battles in America today are an example of companies employing data collected from uncontrolled scraping. The EU rule means that generic mathematical formats will not be subject to rigorous copyright examination, provided they comply with recognized conventions.

However, this imposes self-management burden which may lead to lower compliance. It is not so clear, for example, that the creators of technology-generated works should be classified as authors. Federal and International controls - technology created products must bring an assigned human to limit creation ad. Lack of one world-wide licensing for prep- aration information and one world-wide intellectual property treaties for technology make business complicated around the world (Johri & Singh, 2024).

## 4.3 Moral Dilemma and Responsibility

Moral discussion relates to discrimination, equity, transparency and government responsibility in technology. These transcend coding issues; they're tied to principles of civilization. Computational bias occurs as excessive examples/instances favor some communities. Enforcement face recognition systems are significantly less accurate for women and people with darker skin, according to a Federal precision study.

If determinations are biased, that has moral implications for justice and can exacerbate community inequality. Despite various ways to correct the bias, such as preparations of contests or restrictions on neutrality, balancing between justice and underestimation reduction is important. The traditional fairness criteria of individual measure and disparate impact are inapplicable: other notions e.g., organization parity or similar outcomes yield contradictions during application (Wang et al., 2025).

Understanding complex neural algorithms is a difficult task. This makes it intractable to comprehend algorithms, which undermines trust in important contexts such as doctor profiling and fairness assessment. Mathematical interpretation strategies (SHAP, LIME) provide post-hoc explanations; however, these are often misunderstood and modifiable. EU law also enhances transparency for consequential systems in that it requires both technical documentation and oversight, but not readable systems. This permits complicated frameworks enduring. Researches report state governance deficiencies include a lack of mandatory bias assessment across technical life and inadequate avenues for patients to appeal decisions. Illustration: algorithmic hiring audit could codify bias against women or minorities, but few less-cumbersome regulations require impact audits or remedies.

There are restriction systems keeping people accountable. Responsibility for technology spreads through value creation. Accidents beget programmers blaming operators for misuse and implementers attributing choices to the indefiniteness of mathematics. Suggestions of the OECD and various principles favor individual governance, requiring designated positions as "responsibility officers" or reviewing through independent auditors (Arunachalam, 2024).

The issue of lethal autonomous systems raises moral concerns in a military context. No international law prohibits lethal autonomous systems. Stratcgy lacunae create moral vacuums: experts fail to complete ethics training, and whistleblowers are not insulated, reducing internal reporting of violations.

Then there are more abstract moral problems of protection and choice autonomy. Computing surveillance -like influence systems of societies or anticipatory police raises privacy-threats and suppresses honesty. Even if consumers agree to information use for personalization, focusing continues to direct behavior, raising autonomy-dependent issues. GDPR requirements for usage explanation and information minimisation conflict with technology's insatiable demand for endless amounts of data. This causes a moral dissonance between promoting creation and defending entitlements. Governance coverage is behind in a number of respects: several frameworks do not require that mathematics uses "security foundation approaches" or "mathematics safety methods (to ensure output privacy) (Negi et al., 2025).

## 4.4 Technical Barriers and Shortcomings

Obstacles to implementation include incomplete knowledge, flawed approaches, and omitted capacity boundaried. Data accuracy and supply are important but not perfect. Systems demand large amounts of sorted information; in practice, information is often void, manipulated, chamber-confined or fragmented by securitization. Facts among companies vary, making mathematical methods for secrecy more difficult. Information generation may address the issues but might cause mathematics distortion if generated images are not being compared with real images. Rise of Economic & Technological Divide also enhanced by Ownership of Information being controlled by commercial entities Disproportionate Access to have-nots.

Issues related to coherent framework and transfer continue. Mathematical models, grounded in prior data sets often overlook the correct exterior distribution—referred to as range shift. Small information modifications, for example imaging sound can fool clusters. This becomes significant for protection-critical applications, such as stealthy discovery and the lone pursuit. Protecting methods bolster durability; unfortunately, they muddy the waters and even decrease (perhaps typically) base overall performance. Indeed, benchmarks against which mathematics testing in resistance were relatively scarce. Strategy Break College: the specs are not committed to verifying prior to math on protection-needed paths (Dhayal et al., 2023).

The gap toward adoption is due to the scalability and infrastructure problems faced by organisations." The teaching of state- of-the art mathematics, including the advanced computer system, Their installation requires massive computations and a considerable amount of electric power, in proportion to the small population size. This barrier is problematic for ecology ald unaccessible for companies. Datacenter reliance results in: slowness, vendor lock-in and security exposure. Perimeter derivative calculus operations providing a computation through local interaction facilitate many operations; however, the cost is destructive, particularly with on-demand application such as course of unmanned vehicle. The configured approaches are minimized and squeezed to secure the capacity where ordinary conditions do not hold. Authority gaps include inadequate funding available for the computation of renewable-energy artificial intelligence and ignoring open-source software developed for mathematical operations (Wang et al., 2024).

## 4.5 Integration and Specification Development

There are many applications (sophisticated educational systems, learning resources, X framework) and combination of styles (wide-spread framework, file-based method), which can complicate the linkage. Smart venues handling movement, strength and government security want to speak – but proprietary connection methods and legacy construction have prevented success. Guiding lines on machine legibility Good starting point, but not compulsory. Changes in organizations result in responsibility for gathering specialized into less stability. Approach Cures need to feature strategies commanding visible criteria and funding designed for analyses of local potential aiming to connect systems (Teixeira, 2025).

## 4.6Governance Shortcomings and Solutions Across Sectors

Governance deficiencies fragmentation, resistance, and lack of funding further exacerbate the obstacles. First, oversight fragments along a limitation engineering bodies focus on capability, information officers prioritize facts, morality boards emphasize standards. Cooperation stays infrequent. Secondly, there is often not enough expert staff among the law enforcers that lead to effective mathematical surveillance. Third, community membership has become exclusive leading to leader-driven generation irrespective of community impacts. If competitor stress between great powers highlights large differences in information-distributing practices and cooperative norms, at a time when global settlement appears almost out of reach due to political pressures.

Regulators should promulgate flexible, evidence-driven recommendations on treatment insufficiencies. The EU regulation uses proportional power and calls for flexible testing for a safe evaluation. Inherent consequence assessment on authority, ethical and cognitive grounds should accompany social use of mathematics. Collaboration between planets may include partnerships in institutions and global collaboration of Mathematics advancing general principles for the application of risky technologies. Partnerships between government, companies, and universities could create distributed information, measure bias and certify processes.

A moral monitoring account calls for the in-built oversight of arithmetic responsibility guardians, external audit and straightforward complaint procedures. Technical sustainability requires investment in reviewed mathematical research, general purpose mobile tools and sustainable power systems. Revising liability standard (likely through pure liability for harm calculus) and aligning copyright policies on instructional information could enhance legal certainty (Jain et al., 2025).

Teaching remains important. Mathematical principles and valid concerns need to be communicated in programming and education guidelines. Small and mid-market firms are looking for accessible mathematics access, including help resources and compliance resources. Impoverished communities need aid in innovation and cash to break free of technological tyranny. Healthcare mathematics determination faces guideline (adhering to health data protection/world information privacy), ethical (fair and level judgment) and computational problems (clinical data inclusion). Strategic responses including a network-based system, transparent framework rationale, and global data sharing.

Banking mathematics level covering feeling and clarity problems. Fairness review might be required by central authorities and to test fairness checking.

Overcoming implementation barriers requires addressing political, ethical, and technical issues as interwoven concerns. A proportional system that mixes official flexibility, moral imagination and computational power could turn challenges into opportunities for responsible making. As mathematical significance expands in living domains, the effects of inaction multiply. Accessible global governance ensures that mathematics serves all people fairly and perpetually (Nanda et al., 2025).

## 5. CONCLUSION AND FUTURE OUTLOOK

They say the juncture of environmental finance and machine learning is an opportunity for international bodies to cooperate. Marketplace methods are reconstructed by machine learning; Rule and advantage systems that ensure the sourcing of mutual reinforcement of the protection of ecology + lasting financial viability criticality: Machine-learning environmental capitalism could mobilize billions in eco-sustainability capital, increase detail access, and make weather-risk prediction stronger. To achieve these goals, authority, science and marketplace need to align. Policymakers should develop mechanisms that hold to the commitment to discover consistent with moral value, social benefit and biological integrity. Global sustainability will require for regulators to make sure that machine learning accelerates transition toward an equitable, progressive, resilient social order rather than computing advancement alone.

## REFERENCES


Alhejaili, M. O. (2024). Integrating climate change risks and sustainability goals into Saudi Arabia's financial regulation: Pathways to green finance. *Sustainability (Basel), 16*(10), 4159. DOI: 10.3390/su16104159

Alshahmy, S., & Sahiner, M. (2024). Enhancing the Issuance and Monitoring of Sustainable Finance Instruments through AI. In *Artificial Intelligence, Finance, and Sustainability: Economic, Ecological, and Ethical Implications* (pp. 217–241). Springer Nature Switzerland. DOI: 10.1007/978-3-031-66205-8_9

Arunachalam, M. (2024). Analysis of Stakeholders Interests in Green Finance. In *The Palgrave Handbook of Green Finance for Sustainable Development* (pp. 89–119). Springer International Publishing. DOI: 10.1007/978-3-031-65756-6_4

Attipoe, V., Chukwuma-Eke, E. C., Lawal, C. I., Friday, S. C., Isibor, N. J., & Akintobi, A. O. (2023). Designing a Data-Driven Sustainable Finance Model: A Pathway for Small and Medium Enterprises to Transition to Clean Energy. *Journal of Frontiers in Multidisciplinary Research, 4*(01), 210–218. DOI: 10.54660/.IJFMR.2021.2.1.95-103

Bhattacharya, S., & Sachdev, B. K. (2024). Regulatory challenges and opportunities for future Fintech and green finance. *Blockchain's Transformative Potential of Financial Technology for Sustainable Futures*, 103-122.

Boumaiza, A. (2024). Development and Experimental Evaluation of an Investment Policy Framework for Enhancing Green Finance in Qatar. *FinTech, 4*(1), 1. DOI: 10.3390/fintech4010001

Challa, K. (2022). Generative AI-Powered Solutions for Sustainable Financial Ecosystems: A Neural Network Approach to Driving Social and Environmental Impact. *Mathematical Statistician and Engineering*, 2326-9865.

Dhayal, K. S., Giri, A. K., Kumar, A., Samadhiya, A., Agrawal, S., & Agrawal, R. (2023). Can green finance facilitate Industry 5.0 transition to achieve sustainability? A systematic review with future research directions. *Environmental Science and Pollution Research International, 30*(46), 102158–102180. DOI: 10.1007/s11356-023-29539-w PMID: 37695480

Elhady, A. M., & Shohieb, S. (2025). AI-driven sustainable finance: Computational tools, ESG metrics, and global implementation. *Future Business Journal, 11*(1), 209. DOI: 10.1186/s43093-025-00610-x

Elias, O., Awotunde, O. J., Oladepo, O. I., Azuikpe, P. F., Samson, O. A., Oladele, O. R., & Ogunruku, O. O. (2024). The evolution of green fintech: Leveraging AI and IoT for sustainable financial services and smart contract implementation. *World Journal of Advanced Research and Reviews*, *23*(1), 2710–2723. DOI: 10.30574/wjarr.2024.23.1.2272

Fu, C., Lu, L., & Pirabi, M. (2023). Advancing green finance: A review of sustainable development. *Digital Economy and Sustainable Development*, *1*(1), 20. DOI: 10.1007/s44265-023-00020-3

Gupta, S., Modi, R. R., Das, D., & Sahu, P. (2025). Sustainable digital banking: Exploring the role of fintech in promoting green finance and sustainable development goals. *Journal of Information Systems Engineering & Management*, *10*(3), 547–557. DOI: 10.52783/jisem.v10i3.5674

Hassanein, A., & Tharwat, H. (2024). Artificial intelligence (AI) and green finance. In *The Palgrave Handbook of Green Finance for Sustainable Development* (pp. 859–889). Springer International Publishing. DOI: 10.1007/978-3-031-65756-6_32

Jain, A., Singh, R. K., & Bhushan, P. (2025). Policy and regulatory frameworks for financing smart healthcare. In *Driving Global Health and Sustainable Development Goals With Smart Technology* (pp. 367–388). IGI Global Scientific Publishing.

Jiang, L., Cao, X., Wang, Z., Zhan, Y., Zhang, J., & Chen, S. (2025). Promoting energy saving and emission reduction benefits in small and medium-sized enterprises supply chains through green finance-Evidence based on artificial intelligence intervention. *International Review of Financial Analysis*, *102*, 104112. DOI: 10.1016/j.irfa.2025.104112

Johri, A., & Singh, R. K. (2024). Role of green finance instruments and stakeholders on the sustainable finance and moderated by technology integration. *Environment, Development and Sustainability*, •••, 1–29. DOI: 10.1007/s10668-024-05723-x

Joseph, O. O., Kevin-Alerechi, E., Olumide, O. J. T., Sunday, D., Fagbohun, O., & Olanrewaju, S. (2025). Reimagining green financing with AI: A technological approach to sustainability. *J Artif Intell Mach Learn & Data Sci*, *3*(1), 2346–2352. DOI: 10.51219/AIMLD/Omotoso-Oluwayomi-Joseph/509

Lee, C. C., Hussain, J., & Abass, Q. (2025). An integrated analysis of AI-driven green financing, subsidies, and knowledge to enhance CO2 reduction efficiency. *Economic Analysis and Policy*, *85*, 675–693. DOI: 10.1016/j.eap.2024.12.021

Nanda, P., Kumar, V., & Gandhi, S. (2025). Digital currencies and green finance: institutional decision framework in the Industry 5.0 scenario. *EDPACS*, 1-16.

Negi, L., Manpreet, M., & Singh, M. (2025). Green Finance and Digital Strategies: Catalysts for the Expansion of Circular Technologies in the Global Market. In *Innovating Sustainability Through Digital Circular Economy* (pp. 281-304). IGI Global Scientific Publishing.

Okeke, N. I., Bakare, O. A., & Achumie, G. O.Njideka Ihuoma OkekeOluwaseun Adeola BakareGodwin Ozoemenam Achumie. (2024). Integrating policy incentives and risk management for effective green finance in emerging markets. *International Journal of Frontiers in Science and Technology Research*, *7*(1), 76–88. DOI: 10.53294/ijfstr.2024.7.1.0050

Onabowale, O. (2024). Energy policy and sustainable finance: Navigating the future of renewable energy and energy markets. *World Journal of Advanced Research and Reviews*, *25*(1), 2235–2252. DOI: 10.30574/wjarr.2025.25.1.0319

Papagiannopoulos, I., Ntanos, C., Pelekis, S., Tzortzis, A. M., Koutalidis, H., Karakolis, E., . . . Askounis, D. (2024, July). Enhancing green financing through AI analytics and cross-domain data sharing. In *2024 15th International Conference on Information, Intelligence, Systems & Applications (IISA)* (pp. 1-11). IEEE. DOI: 10.1109/IISA62523.2024.10786617

Ramzani, S. R., Konhaeusner, P., Olaniregun, O. A., Abu-Alkheil, A., & Alsharari, N. (2024). Integrating AI-Driven Green Finance Strategies for Sustainable Development: A Comparative Analysis of Renewable Energy Investments in Germany and Denmark. *European Journal of Business and Management Research*, *9*(2), 43–55. DOI: 10.24018/ejbmr.2024.9.2.2277

Saeedi, M., & Ashraf, B. N. (2024). The role of technology in promoting green finance: A systematic literature survey and the development of a framework. *Journal of Risk and Financial Management*, *17*(10), 472. DOI: 10.3390/jrfm17100472

Singh, V. K. (2022). Regulatory and legal framework for promoting green digital finance. In *Green digital finance and sustainable development goals* (pp. 3–27). Springer Nature Singapore. DOI: 10.1007/978-981-19-2662-4_1

Siriman, N., Ali, M. S., Siddiqui, T. A., Rohin, G., Vejju, B., & Cherupelly, N. (2025). Green Finance and AI in India: A Synergistic Approach to Sustainable Development and Climate Resilience. *International Journal of Environmental Sciences*, *11*(1), 207–216. DOI: 10.64252/mt7jkk84

Teixeira, N. (2025). The Evolution of Sustainable Investment: The Role of Decentralized Finance and Green Bonds in the Efficiency and Transparency of Green Finance. *FinTech and Sustainable Innovation*, *1*, A1–A1. DOI: 10.47852/bonviewFSI52024817

Udeagha, M. C., & Muchapondwa, E. (2023). Green finance, fintech, and environmental sustainability: Fresh policy insights from the BRICS nations. *International Journal of Sustainable Development and World Ecology*, *30*(6), 633–649. DOI: 10.1080/13504509.2023.2183526

Wang, C., Nazar, R., Ali, S., & Meo, M. S. (2025). Eco-friendly algorithms: Artificial intelligence and green finance in European intelligent nations. *Technology in Society*, *83*, 102960. DOI: 10.1016/j.techsoc.2025.102960

Wang, C., Zheng, C., Chen, B., & Wang, L. (2024). Mineral wealth to green growth: Navigating FinTech and green finance to reduce ecological footprints in mineral rich developing economies. *Resources Policy*, *94*, 105116. DOI: 10.1016/j.resourpol.2024.105116

Wang, M., Wang, Y., & Feng, C. (2025). Artificial intelligence, institutional environment, and corporate green transformation: Evidence from China's resource-based sector. *International Review of Economics & Finance*, *103*, 104473. DOI: 10.1016/j.iref.2025.104473

# Chapter 12
# Legal Framework Concerning AI and Automation in Green Investment Strategies for ESG

**Pooja**
http://orcid.org/0009-0004-4463-3317
*Reliable Institute of Law, Ghaziabad, India*

**Saurabh Chandra**
http://orcid.org/0000-0003-4172-9968
*Bennett University, Greater Noida, India*

**Swarnima Gorani**
http://orcid.org/0009-0004-2052-6891
*Sharda University, India*

**Suparna Kundu**
http://orcid.org/0009-0000-5142-8945
*Amity University, Kolkata, India*

**Pradeep Kulshrestha**
http://orcid.org/0000-0002-6805-1010
*Bennett University, India*

DOI: 10.4018/979-8-2600-1308-3.ch012

## ABSTRACT

*The legal parameters for artificial intelligence and automation in investment environmental, social and governance (ESG) standards are transforming as nations, companies and investors seek to maintain innovation and accountability. AI and automation are increasingly used to evaluate sustainability data, predict climate change risks and guide responsible investment strategies. But without clear rules or ethical norms there will be great difficulties in building transparency and morale into green finance. Legally green investments are covered by a patchwork of environmental and financial laws that look to ensure funds are part of genuinely sustainable development rather than simply a matter "greenwashing." As AI systems come to oversee such functions as portfolio analysis, impact measurement and carbon emissions accounting, it becomes all the more imperative to lay down clear legal prescriptions for data accuracy, fair algorithms and disclosure obligations on investors.*

## 1. INTRODUCTION

The instruments such as the European Union's Sustainable Finance Disclosure Regulation (SFDR) and Directive on Corporate Sustainability Reporting (CSRD) represent early efforts to introduce AI-assisted ESG analysis as a part of legally binding frameworks. The intellectual property rights intersect with the development of AI-based green innovations, as they bear on the ownership and licensing of insights or algorithms for sustainable finance which are produced through AI (Domingo, 2025).

The legal framework for artificial intelligence and automation in green investment strategies under environmental, social and governance (ESG) principles starts with the accurate definition of key concepts that intersect the convergence of technology, finance and sustainability. ESG includes environmental issues such as climate impact and resource utilisation, social issues such as labour standards and community impacts, and governance issues such as board accountability and ethical practices; all these are synthesised into the investment decision-making process as a way of creating long-term value while reducing risks. Green investment strategies are focused on assets that help make these ecological transitions, and are represented by renewable energy projects and low carbon infrastructure in which AI and automation are used to support advanced data processing, predictive analytics and portfolio optimization (Rane et al., 2024).

Green loans and sustainability linked loans show similar yet unique dynamics in the private debt markets. The Green Loan Principles (GLP) and the Sustainability-

Arab-Linked Loan Principles (SLLP) endorsed by the Loan Market Association have attracted almost universal support among international banking groups. Pricing ratchets that adjust interest rates based on Environmental, Social and Governance (ESG) key performance indicators (KPIs) or sustainability performance targets (SPTs) have now been incorporated in over USD1.2 trillion of corporate revolvers and term loans, where borrowers will benefit from margin reductions of five to twenty five basis points upon achieving such targets. Unlike labelled bonds, loan structures leave much more flexibility in the choice and calibration of KPIs, and therefore create very bespoke contracts but that are occasionally criticised for setting unambitious targets. The predominance of "sustainability-linked" rather than green frameworks means that corporate realities-where sectors with acute emissions profiles, generally (but not only) steel, cement, aviation and shipping-are often unable to secure large-scale United Nations-approved green finance on short notice, as well as being able to commit to science-based trajectories for decarbonisation through sustainability-linked bonds and loans.

Innovation continues to happen at the level of the product. Transition bonds and transition-programme linked instruments have achieved legitimacy after an early onset of scepticism and helped already by frameworks from the International Capital Market Association, Financial Services Agency of Japan and the Climate Bonds Initiative, all of which offer taxonomy agnostic guidance for hard-to-abate sectors. While it is USD 25 billion cumulative at 2024, blue bonds focused on ocean-related and pleitentinal water-related projects were issued, and biodiversity-related financial instruments and debt-for-nature swaps are reaching first stage of development. Green securitisations, such as solar asset-back securitisations and energy efficient mortgage-back securitisations, as well as green covered bonds, now have an outstanding balance of more than USD 200 billion, benefiting from preferential risk-weight allocations under the chosen regulatory regimes. Derivatives markets have also been evolving with the first-ever green interest-rate swaps and sustainability-linked derivatives coming in 2022, with a slow uptake of the ISDA 2024 Sustainability Linked Derivatives Annex.

Despite strong growth, the prevailing market practice encounters ongoing struggle, with a set of issues, which includes worries related to greenwashing, lack of standardisation for KPIs and SPTs and the ongoing "additionality" debate (i.e. whether labelled issuance actually amplifies overall climate finance or is really just re-branding of pre-existing capital expenditures). High profile controversies e.g. some sustainability linked bonds with weak or unverifiable targets have resulted in investor kickback, and increased scrutiny of regulators The upcoming European Union Green Bond Standard, expected to be introduced in the first quarter of 2026 will introduce mandatory label of EU GBS with a mandatory supervisory oversight. Concurrently, the inclusion of forward-looking, Paris-aligned criteria (including

1.5 degC scenario analyses and implied temperature ratings from MSCI, S&P or CDP) has led to a change in investor preference from retroactive "shades of green" to dynamic assessments of transition credibility.

In practice, a combination of following strict adherence to established frameworks, setting ambitious yet feasible targets and transparent post-issuance reporting are combined by successful issuers that often cover green finance as one of the focal points of their businesses through the creation of dedicated green finance teams and investor roadshows that bring financial and impact metrics into the coffers of the top. The market has therefore clearly shifted from the kinds of dialectic involving questions of "why issue green?" to focusing on "how to issue the most credible and cost effective green or sustainability linked instrument possible", which confirms that green financial instruments are now a permanent and systemically important component of global capital markets (Das et al., 2025).

Artificial intelligence is a term used to describe machine-learning algorithms, neural networks and generative models that are capable of analysing large ESG datasets, while the term automation refers to rule-based systems and smart contracts that create more efficient compliance and reporting. This integration is in response to market demands for sustainable finance - which are expected to amount to US$53 trillion in assets by 2025 - which can be used to accurately forecast emissions and comply with global standards such as the United Nations Principles for Responsible Investment. Legally, such foundations lie in their fiduciary responsibilities under securities legislation, which requires investors to take into account material ESG risks; AI tools are also needed to prevent any biases which may skew valuations on green assets.

The approach of regulators today exerts significant influence over how artificial intelligence and automation will be applied in ESG green investing systems to create a multi-stored nexus of equilibrium with innovation and oversight. In the EU, under the AI Act (20147) effective by 2024, high-risk AIs in finance including ESG scoring and risk modelling are categorised under conformity assessments and transparency reporting requirements and mandatory human supervision which may mitigate any bias that might have bearing on green assets selection. At the same time, SFDR and Taxonomy Regulation outline criteria that decide whether an activity is "green", thus forcing Republities to adapt their outputs towards inflexible standards in technical screenings of climate mitigation. At the international level, even IOSCO's recommendations for sustainable finance and the IAO's principles advocate that regulators consider proportionality, facilitating rules to be calibrated based on the risk profile of AI applications within green strategies while being intentionally anti-asphyxiating toward stifling fintech innovations such as automatic carbon trading of carbon credits (Chen, 2024).

## 2. SCOPE OF ESG, GREEN FINANCE AND SUSTAINABLE INVESTMENT

The modern coverage of ESG (Environmental, Social, and Governance), green finance, and sustainable investment has moved well beyond its predecessor environmental roots, thus making it a comprehensive orientation of global capital flows with the long term said objectives of societal and planetary resilience. At its analytical core ESG is operationalised as a tripartite risk -and-opportunity lens through which investors weigh up non-financial factors that materially affect enterprise value, financial stability and systemic sustainability. The Environmental pillar covers the areas of climate change mitigation and adaptation, biodiversity preservation, circular economy, pollution prevention, water stewardship, as well as deforestation risk. The Social pillar involves human rights, labour standards, community relations, consumer protection, data privacy, DEI, health and safety and supply chain ethics. The Governance pillar covers issues such as independence of boards, remuneration of executives, measures against bribery and corruption, tax transparency, shareholder rights, quality of audits, and business ethics. Collectively, these pillars form an integrated materiality matrix which has grown outwards from a purely ethical overlay to a 'looking to the future' financial risk safety net recognized by prudential regulators, central banks (through NGFS and TCFD/GISSB standards) and standard-setter (IFRS S1 and S2, European Sustainability Reporting Standards) (Joseph et al., 2025).

Green finance, historically the most visible subset of sustainable finance, had an initial focus on financing projects or assets that provide an unambiguous environmental benefit - renewable energy, energy efficiency, clean transportation, sustainable forestry and green buildings. Over the last decade, its scope has expanded enormously to include transition finance and decarbonisation of the entire economy. The Climate Bonds Initiative Taxonomy, EU Taxonomy for Sustainable Activities and national taxonomies (China, Singapore, Colombia, South Africa, Canada) now rely on science-based performance thresholds to delineate thousands of economic activities as "green" or "transition" (e.g. < 100 gCO2 / kWh for power generation, 50 per cent reduction trajectories for emissions intensity of relevant activities; i.e. steel). Simultaneously, sustainability - linked instruments decoupled to the specific use - have opened up the universe of addressgability to any sector ranging from oil & gas, avialation, cement and shipping, provided that the issuers engage into ambitious, verifiable key performance indicators on 1.5 C pathways. Consequently, green and sustainable finance regularly finance not just "dark green" activities, but a credible brown to green transition strategy, recognising the need for net zero by 2050 requires substantial capital reallocation across the entire real economy, rather than on a selective basis of avoidance.

Sustainable investment, the widest of the three areas, works as an umbrella under which there are a range of investment strategies that regularly incorporate ESG factors into the decision-making process of investments and ownership respectively. The Global Sustainable Investment Alliance (GSIA) has identified seven basic approaches - ESG integration (systematic inclusion of ESG risks and opportunities in the financial analysis), negative/exclusionary screening, positive/best-in-class screening, norms-based screening, sustainability-themed investing, impact and community investing, and corporate engagement or active ownership. By 2024, global sustainable investing assets totaled well over a sum of charges exceeding USD 40 n (40 trillion dollars) over all this strategies, equivalent to about one third of all professionally arranged assets. Article 8 and Article 9 funds under the EU Sustainable Finance Disclosure Regulation (SFDR) managed more than EUR8 trn by mid-2025 alone. U.S. sustainable funds were able to keep attraction into their funds despite regulatory issues around “ESG” labeling for climate transition and broad ESG integration products. Thematic funds for targets of specific United Nations Sustainable Development Goals - clean energy (SDG 7), sustainable cities (SDG 11), responsible consumption (SDG 12) and life below water (SDG 14) - grew the most, accompanied by rapidly expanding biodiversity, circular economy and just transition strategies.

The interaction between the elements of ESG analysis, green finance instruments, and weapons of sustainable investment has spawned powerful feedback loops. Sophisticated ESG data providers (MSCI, Sustainalytics, ISS, S&P Trucost, Bloomberg, Arabesque) have now started to produce forward looking metrics such as implied temperature rise, transition pathway alignment, biodiversity footprint and social intensity scores, which forms the direct basis for investment decision making and instrument structuring. Green bond frameworks and sustainability linked loan KPIs tend to increasingly refer to these metrics, whilst through investor voting policies and stewardship codes (UK, Japan, EFAMA, ICGN) credible transition plans are being required from high emitting portfolio companies. Central banks and supervisors have further expanded the scope by incorporating climate and nature-related risks into prudential frameworks (ECB climate stress tests, BoE CBES, Brazilian Resolution 4,943, Singapore MAS guidelines) rendering ESG risk management a regulatory requirement, not volunteers.

Critically, the scope nowadays expressly incorporates 'double materiality': financial materiality (the impact of ESG issues on enterprise value) and impact materiality (the impact of companies on society and the environment). The International Sustainability Standards Board (ISSB) IFRS standards, specifically IFRS S1 and S2, European Sustainability Reporting Standards (ESRS), and upcoming US SEC climate rules share this view of dual disclosures for reporting both dimensions. In doing so, this evolution blurs traditional boundaries between philanthropy, risk management and alpha generation, which puts sustainable investment squarely at the heart of the net - zero and nature positive transition.

In reality, the broadened scope means that few if any sectors or asset classes are unaffected: private equity funds are now routinely incorporating ESG due process and value creation strategies; infrastructure investment strategies are aimed at resilient low carbon exposed assets; Sovereign wealth funds (Norway NBIM, New Zealand Super, Temasek) are benchmarking against Parisaligment of portfolios; and retail platforms are offering ESG screened exchange traded funds (ETF) and robo - advisors with a sustainability preference. This confluence of ESG integration, green and transition financial instruments, and engaged ownership has realized a human investment arc from velocity investments at the outskirts to fundamental restructuring of capital allocation around the world to create a resilient, inclusive, and regenerative economy (Aljohani, 2025).

Within this larger ESG galaxy, green finance emerges as a more narrowly focused sub-set, targeted specifically at the mobilisation of capital for environmentally friendly purposes – clean energy (renewables), energy efficient infrastructure, clean transport (electric vehicles and charging networks), sustainable agriculture, water and waste management, climate adaptation measures and nature-based solutions. In addition to green bonds, the market now boasts green loans, green asset-backed securities, green mortgages, and sustainability-linked products priced according to environmental performance metrics, marking a shift away from project-orientated ring-fencing toward wider behavioural incentives for issuers. Green finance also covers risk-management instruments including catastrophe bonds, resilience bonds, and insurance products that can absorb losses from climate-related events, as well as publicpolicy tools such as guarantee schemes and concessional credit facilities which crowd in private capital for projects which are aligned with the climate (Elhady & Shohieb, 2025). The scope is further influenced by national and regional sustainable-finance strategies and taxonomies with the aim to standardise what can be regarded as "green", mitigate greenwashing, and make use of a comparison for investors and supervisors between disclosures on use of proceeds and environmental impact that are consistent, reliable, and decision-useful.

Governance systems are the foundation of their legal responsibility regarding artificial intelligence (AI) in the sphere of environmental, social, and governance (ESG) green investments but which also incorporate system checks into corporate and institutional practices. Boards must create AI oversight committees as per stewardship codes (like the UK or India BRSR) tasked with validating models, conducting bias audits and ensuring explainability of ESG analytics. The use of AI in the context of green strategies is also something asset managers with fiduciary duties must disclose, and automated systems – such as algorithmic trading websites – "What's more, best execution regulations by definition prevent discriminatory behaviour in sustainable investment portfolios. Basel III's operational resilience pillars - that are employed for risk-management frameworks highlight AI-related risks, including model risk, data risk, and cyber-risk, and stress testing against climate-scenarios in the underwriting of green bonds.

Accountability is a function of traceability, and explainable AI (XAI) techniques like SHAP values can be legally demanded for high-risk categorizations to explain the ESG allocation decisions. Liability regimes parcel out responsibility in a stratified manner: developers are subject to product liability for defective algorithms, users bear liability for negligence when monitoring fails and platform providers may be held jointly liable under tort law with respect to the automated advisory services. In the context of greenwashing litigation, the inquire into misrepresentation elements for AI-produced ESG scores, as seen in e.g. actions by the Securities Exchange Commission (SEC) regarding misrepresented sustainability claims. Its data protection laws, including the Digital Personal Data Protection (DPDP) Act, 2023 [Okuda], have an express mention of privacy-by-design principles with respect to AI training data for emissions modelling that are reported to carry stringent fines that could choke green investments (Hassanein & Tharwat, 2024).

## 2.1 Risk Mitigation Strategies

The Risk Mitigation Strategies can include third party audits, sandboxes testing like Financial Conduct Authority (FCA) in UK and Reserve Bank of India (RBI) in India which permit controlled deployment of AI in ESG products. Algorithmic bias, particularly in the area around social ESG metrics, provoke an anti-discrimination response in legislation-such as the EU's AI Act that automates scoring and prohibits bias assistants. As a result, governing well hinges on comprehensive risk registers that link AI performance measures with ESG KPIs to support corrective interventions and including model retraining so the investors can have trust in automated green investment strategies (Alshahmy & Sahiner, 2024).

Key market practices use AI and automation to implement ESG green investments, from data collection to product development. AI platforms scrape and harmonize ESG data from across sources GRI reports, satellite feeds and supply chain ledgers driving proprietary portfolio construction that optimizes for green alpha presage tools verifying green bond proceeds with blockchain oracles. Sustainability Linked Loans with AI monitored KPIs resulting in automatic coupon adjustments according to verified decarbonisation progress following ICMA standards and Loan Market Association guidelines. In carbon markets, pricing is predicted and compliance automated with machine learning under Article 6 of the Paris Agreement to promote liquidity for voluntary offsets (Vodenska et al., 2025).

These instruments are shaped by contract, as exemplified by ISDA master agreements featuring AI-powered ESG clauses and Ethereum-hosted smart contracts fixing self-executing green finance terms resulting in fewer disputes (thanks to unrepudiated ledgers). Fiduciary duty (under US ERISA or SEBI laws) necessitate advisors to verify AI outputs indicating limitations, e.g. the Scope 3 estimation uncertainty". Distribution channels encounter MiFID II transparency obligations, requiring pre-trade AI risk warnings in the case of ESG robo-advisors intended for retail green investments (Khaddam & Alzghoul, 2025).

New Planting and Deforestation Tracking, DRIVEN: Real-time AI driving data collection project The European Mortgage Federation -European Covered Bond Council highlights EU high-level expert group on sustainable finance final report Lending Sustainability Approach, including green mortgage linked-bonds (which follow closely the guidance of the Energy Efficient Mortgages Action Plan) NT1 GT-be a First Mover; Deliver five TCFD Report Recommendations with Data Protection Law Transparency Account Generator Authorization Tokenization Platforms like Project Genesis Using AI for real-time impact tracking in digital green bonds Align into FATF Virtual Assets guidelines. Indian Practices mention of AI in CPSE ETFs and green mutual funds with BRSR Core for automated disclosure (Behera et al., 2024). These applications require stronger due diligence, combining legal compliance with technological verification to scale green finance in the face of $2.8 trillion per year in climate investment gaps.

Sustainable investment falls right between ESG in today's broader sense (an abbreviation for Environmental, Social and Governance) and sustainable or 'green' finance as a catch-all term that seeks both competitive financial returns and intentional contribution to positive environmental and/or social outcomes. It covers a range of methods, from negative screening and norms-based exclusion of sectors (coal contamination weapons human rights abusers) to integration with ESG in mainstream financial analysis, thematic strategies aiming at such issues as clean energy, water or agriculture for sustainability, and impact investment that explicitly seeks measureable societal benefits alongside financial returns. In practical terms, sustainable investment can include both listed and unlisted equities, fixed-income products (including 'green', social impact and sustainability -linked bonds), private debt, infrastructure and real estate as well as private equity--microfinance development financial institutions might be placed even under its broad embrace (Khamitdkhanovich et al., 2025).

## 3. TYPOLOGIES OF AI AND AUTOMATION IN FINANCIAL DECISION-MAKING

The inclusion of artificial intelligence (AI) and automation into conventional green investment approaches in the umbrella of Environmental, Social and Governance elements (ESG) elements is a key shift in the realm of sustainable finance. The present analysis considers basic legal principles drawing upon international standards and national legislation to outline the regulatory control of AI and automation in green investments (Alam et al., 2025).

At the international level, there is no joined-up global treaty that exclusively addresses the application of artificial intelligence (AI) in environmental, social and governance (ESG) investing at this moment. Nonetheless, wider frameworks, such as the United Nations Sustainable Development Goals (SDGs), indirectly influence regulatory expectations by highlighting the importance of responsible innovation. The Organisation for Economic Co-operation and Development (OECD) AI Principles of 2019, subsequently revised, represent a soft-law standard which nurtures trustworthy AI, protects the human rights and fosters environmental sustainability. These principles include advocacy of inclusive growth, robustness and accountability, thus informing ESG strategies insisting on reducing ecological footprints of AI systems, specifically high energy use (data centers) and social equity on automated decision-making based on investment. The Paris Agreement on climate change although majorly focused on emissions reduction, this treaty forms an implicit endorsement of AI enabled green finance by facilitating emissions tracking and optimization of low carbon portfolio (Irfan et al., 2026).

From the date of its legislation, and only effective in August of 2024, the Legislation requires transparency, human oversight and judgment of bias with regard to AI tools used in ESG-scoring or automated portfolio management, making financial AI-high risk because of the potentially disrupting effects on economic stability and environmental goals (Ng et al., 2025). With this, AI algorithms used to determine climate risks must thus yield results that can be explained to regulators in order to ensure compliance with the EU's Sustainable Finance Disclosure Regulation (SFDR) and the funding regulations for funds marketed as “green” to disclose ESG metrics. Automation in the context of these strategies receives even further scrutiny in the Corporate Sustainability Reporting Directive (CSRD), which is where large enterprises and those based in the EU are included, as it states advertisements that are AI-generated on emissions or supply chain ethics need to be auditable in order to prevent those entities from being subject to penalties for false disclosures. The EU Green Deal also brings AI into the picture, as it financially supports projects that use automation to optimise renewable energy systems, given, of course, data privacy requirements, set out by the General Data Protection Regulation (GDPR).

Non-compliance may incite fines up to 4 per cent of global turnover hence discouraging uninhibited AI implementation into ESG funds. Moreover, the EU Taxonomy Regulation defines "sustainable" activities and defines that AI systems align investment decisions with criteria such as protection of biodiversity. While automation is an important enabler of monitoring in real time, the Regulation requires mitigating possible risks - in this case, algorithmic discrimination of impoverished regions in green financing (Pancholi & Shukla, 2025).

## 4. REGULATORY AND POLICY FRAMEWORKS

The dominant global governance architecture does not yet include a single and cohesive treaty addressing the direct regulation of the use of artificial intelligence (AI) in ESG (environmental, social, and governance) investment practices. Rather, existing frameworks such as the United Nations Sustainable Development Goals (SDGs) have an indirect regulatory impact by positioning the need for responsible innovation. The principles of the Organisation for Economic Cooperation and Development (OEO) regarding Artificial Intelligence, adopted in 2019 and recently updated, show a soft-law benchmark that promotes trustworthy Artificial Intelligence, which reaffirms respect for human rights and environmental sustainability (Sulaiman et al., 2024). These principles promote inclusive growth, robustness, and accountability, which therefore influences ESG strategies by requiring AI systems to reduce ecological footprints (especially the large amounts of energy used in data centres), and to advance social equity in the automated decision-making process with regards to investments. Analogously, the climate change treaty agreed at Paris offers implicit support for the integration of AI into green finance as automation helps in monitoring the emissions and optimizing the low carbon portfolio. Nevertheless, the voluntary nature of the enforcement has lent itself to advocacy for binding enforcements. Discourse in the G20 treasury summits has highlighted the central role of AI in ESG, pushing states rounded in G20 to incorporate risks related to technology in frameworks to measure financial stability (Vali et al., 2024). Practically, this means that investors who use AI for green-bond verification are required to observe international standards for anti-money laundering issued by the Financial Action Task Force (FATF) that now includes AI-driven learning algorithms that detect fraud in sustainable infrastructure projects. There are international norms that form the basis for these national regulatory regimes, which highlights the need for AI applications in ESG to be consistent with other sustainability goals - without reinforcing social inequities or harming the environment.

Since being enacted in August 2024, the Act requires transparency, human supervenience, and bias evaluation of artificial intelligence (AI) tools used in environmental, social, and governance (ESG) scoring or automated portfolio management; financial AI has been classified as high-risk based on its likelihood impact on macroeconomic stability and environmental goals (Wang et al., 2025). For sustainable investment initiatives that are green, this means a need for AI algorithms that analyze climate factors to produce explainable results that make it easier for regulators to confirm adherence to the EU's Sustainable Finance Disclosure Regulation (SFDR), which requires funds that brand themselves as "green" to report on ESG-related metrics. Such automation is further scrutinised with the Corporate Sustainability Reporting Directive (CSRD), which applies to big businesses and those that operate within the EU and requires that AI generated reports regarding emissions and supply chain ethics must be audit ready to avoid penalties from misleading disclosures. The role of AI is increased by the EU Green Deal, where it funds projects that use automation for the optimisation of renewable energy systems - under the preconditions of data privacy compliance as stated in the General Data Protection Regulation (GDPR) (Marwa & Soesatyo, 2025). Non-compliance can result in fines up to 4 per cent of global turnover, and thus disincentivizes rampant use of AI in ESG funds. Additionally, the EU Taxonomy Regulation establishes criteria for what constitutes "sustainable" activities, which would have meant that AI systems have to make investment decisions using specific criteria (e.g. protecting biodiversity), and although automation supports real-time monitoring, they would also have to counter the risks of discrimination such as algorithmic rooted discrimination for the underrepresented regions in green financing.

## 5. GOVERNANCE, ACCOUNTABILITY AND RISK MANAGEMENT

Going beyond major jurisdictions, emerging frameworks that exist in Asia and Latin America reflect a patchwork regime of regulation of artificial intelligence (AI) under environmental, social and governance (ESG) initiatives (Pavlidis, 2025). In China regulatory provisions have been issued in accordance with the Cyberspace Administration and require the registration of an AI system employed in ESG-focused lending in accordance with the Green Credit Guidelines, which ensures that the process of automation is guided by state-led sustainability goals such as those embodied by the Belt and Road Initiative's green projects, while ensuring that the state retains oversight in order to prevent misuse of data. Singapore's Model AI Governance Framework (updated in 2024) facilitates responsible AI deployment in the finance sector by requiring impact assessments for automated decision-making in sustainable investment funds. In Brazil, under the guidance of the Central Bank's resolution 4,932, AI transparency requirements are included in the sustainability regulation of the country's central bank, thus bringing financial practices closer to the goals required by the Paris Agreement regarding the management of climate risks.

Legal challenges stem mainly from AI's opaque 'black box' nature because of the explainability issue associated with AI, combined with liability concerns in ESG choices. For green investments - such opacity may favor greenwashing, by which automated strategies overstate environmental benefits and thus breach anti-fraud legislation such as the United States Federal Trade Commission's Green Guides or the European Union's Unfair Commercial Practices Directive (Censi et al., 2025). Data privacy regulations such as the General Data Protection Regulation and the California Consumer Privacy Act make it complicated to use large ESG datasets and it is necessary to apply anonymisation protocols to prevent data breaches. In addition, the environmental footprint of AI, demonstrated by substantial water and energy consumption, is at odds with ESG goals and gives rise to demands that such footprints are disclosed. Socially, AI-driven automation has been a source of job displacement in the financial sector and so this calls for labour legislation such as the US Warnings Act and EU Collective Redundancies Directive. Governance failures, like algorithms being biased towards excluding diverse ESG opportunities and even make them in breach of anti-discrimination laws such as Title VII.

Navigational strategies on these frameworks are the use of Explainable AI (XAI) systems to meet transparency requirements as seen with scenario-based analysis under Green Markets. Investors would also be advised to institute data provenance standards to validate ESG inputs and thus reduce the risks of greenwashing and look to "Green AI" certifications that emphasize energy-efficient models. Policymakers should consider hybrid regulatory schemes that combine existing financial regulatory laws with AI-specific regulations such as mandatory audits for AI if it is used in sustainable finance applications with high risk. Public-private partnerships (e.g., the proposed Global Environmental Ledger) could help make AI verification processes consistent across different eSG-related activities. In the case of enterprises, ethics committees to ensure compliance must be embedded in their AI processes, while dedicated training programmes account for possible social ramifications (Taleb & Kadhum, 2024).

## 6. MARKET PRACTICE AND GREEN FINANCIAL INSTRUMENTS

Market practice in the field of green finance increasingly leans towards the systematic use of artificial intelligence and automation of the entire life cycle of green financial instruments from origination, through to structuring, monitoring and reporting, as well as trading in secondary markets. In contemporary capital markets, newly advanced tools such as green bonds, sustainability-linked bonds and loans, green securitisations and tokenisation or blockchain-based securities have led the way in terms of providing channels to channel capital to low-carbon and climate resilient projects (Davidescu et al., 2025). These instruments are regularly incorporating AI instruments in risk assessment procedures, eligibility screening mechanisms, impact verification protocols or pricing algorithms. Large asset managers, banking institutions and specialised fintech firms are now using machine learning models to take in climate, emissions and ESG data on a scale not previously seen, and synthesise structured information coming from financial statements and ESG disclosures with unstructured data from news outlets, satellite imagery, geospatial feeds and IoT sensors. Such models enable us to better test and view whether proposed projects and issuers successfully respond to observed taxonomies and the sustainable finance frameworks established in place so far. They provide support for the credit analysis of green bonds and sustainability-linked loans, project-by-project modeling of cash flows under a range of climate scenarios, and identification of controversies around environmental or governance issues that can anticipate breach of covenants and devalue a "green" designation. In practice, however, arrangers and underwriters are increasingly using AI-powered due diligence tools in structuring green bonds by using algorithms to compare the characteristics of projects with those in the regulatory taxonomy (e.g. EU or national green taxonomies) and with investors' own bespoke ESG policies. This way, the eligibility screening procedure automated a great deal of the background checks, while still requiring human sign off on borderline cases (Sharno & Bokow, 2024). The utilisation of AI is regulated by legal obligations in security and listing laws to provide accurate (not misleading) information to investors; as such, automated classification systems should be such that they are auditable and explicable to survive the scrutiny applied in the event of allegations of greenwashing or false claims of mis-selling.

In the verification and post-issuance phase, the technological advancement of AI and automation is transforming the way that market participants are taking on one of the most intractable challenges in green finance: how to ensure that proceeds are allocated to truly sustainable objectives and promises of positive environmental outcomes are realised over time. Issuers and independent reviewers now use AI-based platforms connected to data pools for each of the projects, such as energy meters, satellite and remote sensing data, environmental sensors and corporate operational systems to track performance indicators, such as how much renewable energy is generated, how much emissions are avoided, how much water is saved or how much biodiversity is generated very early in real time. In green bond frameworks, these systems facilitate a regular or constant reporting on key performance indicators that enables automated production of impact reporting and dashboards that meet investor expectations and regulatory reporting, etc. Blockchain-based solutions, often combined with AI, monitor subsequent disbursements and spending on projects via tokenised deficit of money flows or "green project tokens" that can generate unchangeable route of audit to reference in verification statements and filings to regulatory authorities. Smart contracts coded with ESG proximate conditions can be programmed to ensure that certain payments, step-up coupons or bonus features will be automatically triggered or withheld based on whether or not AI-verified data confirms that environmental thresholds or targets have been attained. In sustainability - linked bonds and loans, such architecture helps to operationalise the contractual relationship by connecting financial terms to sustainability performance, but does translate into qualitative commitments that can be translated into machine-verifiable triggers, this approach also raises legal questions around the allocation of liability when AI systems go wrong, data is inaccurate or if thresholds are being disputed. As a result, lenders and investors have to negotiate specific clauses related to data sources, methodologies, verification responsibilities, resolving disputes and fallbacks that have to be consistent with the tenets of the contract law, regulatory expectations and the Fiduciary responsibilities of investors (Ghaemi Asl, 2025).

Market practice in green financial instruments has undergone explosive growth and rapid maturation since the first labelled green bond appeared in 2007, evolving from a niche philanthropic exercise into a mainstream, multi-trillion-dollar asset class that now encompasses green bonds, sustainability-linked bonds (SLBs), green loans, sustainability-linked loans (SLLs), transition bonds, blue bonds, social bonds, green commercial paper, green securitisations, green deposits, and an expanding universe of ESG-themed exchange-traded funds (ETFs) and derivatives. By the end of 2024, cumulative issuance of labelled green, social, sustainability and sustainability-linked (GSSS) instruments exceeded USD 4 trillion, with annual issuance consistently surpassing USD 800 billion despite tighter monetary conditions. The market is dominated by supranational issuers (EIB, IFC, World Bank), European development banks (KfW, NIB), sovereigns (France, Germany, Chile, Indonesia), and highly rated corporates in utilities, real estate, and transport, while financial institutions act as both issuers and intermediaries.

The greenium is most pronounced in investment-grade utilities, sovereigns, and covered bonds, and has become a quantifiable financial incentive for issuers to adopt the green label rather than issue conventional vanilla debt. Repeat issuers such as Engie, Iberdrola, Enel, and Republic of France have built recognizable "green curves" that trade tighter than their conventional curves across maturities, creating a self-reinforcing cycle where issuers return frequently to lock in the cheaper funding (Yu et al., 2025).

Second-party opinion (SPO) providers (Sustainalytics, Moody's ESG Solutions, ISS-Corporate, Cicero/Shades of Green, S&P) and verifiers play a gatekeeping role that has become quasi-mandatory in primary market practice. While the Green Bond Principles (GBP), Sustainability-Linked Bond Principles (SLBP), and Climate Transition Finance Handbook published by the International Capital Market Association (ICMA) remain voluntary best-practice frameworks, the market treats external review as a de-facto requirement: more than 95% of labelled issuance carries at least one SPO or verification report. Investors increasingly differentiate between providers; those applying the most rigorous alignment checks to the EU Taxonomy or to 1.5 °C pathways (e.g., Cicero's "Dark Green" shading or S&P's 1.5 °C alignment opinions) command greater credibility and correlate with tighter pricing (Petrukha et al., 2025).

## 7. CONCLUSION, FUTURE DIRECTIONS AND REFORM PROPOSALS

In conclusion, the legal landscape of AI and automation in green investments strategies for ESG is an ever-evolving arena that finds itself balanced between innovation and protection mechanisms. As regulations evolve to increasingly address gaps and contentious issues in their current regulatory regimes, from the European Union based on regulatory risk to the US focused on fiduciary ethics, the onus is upon stakeholders to prioritise for a more ethical deployment, to achieve real results of sustainability. This evolving landscape raises the path of a way to improve ESG performance, but with the need for vigilance in adaptation to guarantee that its risks associated are mitigated, and to ensure that AI is used for driven larger scale planetary and societal goals.

The legislative approach to AI for ESG green investment should introduce flexible reforms that activate novelty and suppress systemic risk. Harmonization across borders around a global AI-ESG pact (9) based on ISSB and NGFS prototypes could standardize high-integrity data protocols, enabling AI interoperability in the context of multinational green portfolios. Proposals support tiered regulation light-touch for less risky automation, stringent for the generative AI of scenario planning in line with their impact on sustainable capital flows. Policy recommendations are there for regulators, standard setters and industry to align AI innovation with climate and sustainable development objectives in capital markets.

## REFERENCES


Alam, M., Ansari, Z. A., & Jafar, S. H. (2025). The technological landscape of AI and sustainable finance: An exploration. In *Green Horizons: Role of AI in Sustainable Finance* (pp. 37–53). Springer Nature Singapore. DOI: 10.1007/978-981-96-6495-5_3

Aljohani, A. (2025). A decision-support framework for evaluating AI-enabled ESG strategies in the context of sustainable manufacturing systems. *Scientific Reports*, *15*(1), 23864. DOI: 10.1038/s41598-025-09569-9 PMID: 40615575

Alshahmy, S., & Sahiner, M. (2024). Enhancing the Issuance and Monitoring of Sustainable Finance Instruments through AI. In *Artificial Intelligence, Finance, and Sustainability: Economic, Ecological, and Ethical Implications* (pp. 217–241). Springer Nature Switzerland. DOI: 10.1007/978-3-031-66205-8_9

Behera, I., Nanda, P., & Derbali, A. M. S. (2024). The societal impact of artificial intelligence in sustainable investment strategies. In *Social and Ethical Implications of AI in Finance for Sustainability* (pp. 268–285). IGI Global. DOI: 10.4018/979-8-3693-2881-1.ch012

Censi, R., Campana, P., Bellini, F., Schettino, F., & De Pucchio, C. (2025). AI-Driven Process Mining for ESG Risk Assessment in Sustainable Management. *Buildings (Basel, Switzerland)*, *15*(23), 4260. DOI: 10.3390/buildings15234260

Chen, Y. (2024). A Panoramic Overview of the Opportunities and Challenges Artificial Intelligence Brings to ESG Investing. *Artificial Intelligence, Finance, and Sustainability: Economic, Ecological, and Ethical Implications*, 19-32.

Das, P., Themmadath, V. V., Jeyalakshmi, S., Lateef, K., & Agnihotri, A. (2025). AI in Sustainable Finance: Identifying Green Investments through Machine Learning. *Advances in Consumer Research. Association for Consumer Research (U. S.)*, *2*(3).

Davidescu, A. A., Bîrlan, I., & Manta, E. M., & GEAMBA U, C. M. (2025). Artificial Intelligence in ESG and Sustainable Finance: A Bibliometric Analysis of Research Trends. In *Proceedings of the International Conference on Business Excellence* (Vol. 19, No. 1, pp. 1506-1517). Sciendo. DOI: 10.2478/picbe-2025-0117

Domingo, M. M. R. (2025). The Impact of Artificial Intelligence on ESG: A Conceptual Framework for Practitioners and Policymakers. *Journal of Management for Global Sustainability*, *13*(1), 2. DOI: 10.13185/2244-6893.1269

Elhady, A. M., & Shohieb, S. (2025). AI-driven sustainable finance: Computational tools, ESG metrics, and global implementation. *Future Business Journal*, *11*(1), 209. DOI: 10.1186/s43093-025-00610-x

Ghaemi Asl, M. (2025). A novel AI-driven approach to greenwashing: Breakthroughs in the future fit between domain-specific Islamic enterprises with varying developmental progress and ESG landscapes. *Future Business Journal, 11*(1), 93. DOI: 10.1186/s43093-025-00497-8

Hassanein, A., & Tharwat, H. (2024). Artificial intelligence (AI) and green finance. In *The Palgrave Handbook of Green Finance for Sustainable Development* (pp. 859–889). Springer International Publishing. DOI: 10.1007/978-3-031-65756-6_32

Irfan, M., Bhute, N. S., Yadav, A. K., & Dias, R. (2026). Sustainable Investment Portfolios with Al: Bridging Green Finance and Technological Innovation. In *Legal and Regulatory Considerations of Leveraging Sustainable Finance* (pp. 235-256). IGI Global Scientific Publishing.

Joseph, O. O., Kevin-Alerechi, E., Olumide, O. J. T., Sunday, D., Fagbohun, O., & Olanrewaju, S. (2025). Reimagining green financing with AI: A technological approach to sustainability. *J Artif Intell Mach Learn & Data Sci, 3*(1), 2346–2352. DOI: 10.51219/AIMLD/Omotoso-Oluwayomi-Joseph/509

Khaddam, A. A., & Alzghoul, A. (2025). Artificial intelligence-driven business intelligence for strategic energy and ESG management: A systematic review of economic and policy implications. *International Journal of Energy Economics and Policy, 15*(4), 635–650. DOI: 10.32479/ijeep.19820

Khamitdkhanovich, N. A., Rajendran, M., Nailevich, I. R., & Krishnakumari, S. (2025, June). Green finance and ESG investing: Driving sustainable growth through innovation. In. AIP Conference Proceedings: Vol. 3306. *No. 1* (p. 030025). AIP Publishing LLC. DOI: 10.1063/5.0277720

Marwa, S., & Soesatyo, B. (2025). Corporate Governance in the Digital Economy and ESG (Environmental, Social, and Governance) Principles. *Greenation International Journal of Law and Social Sciences, 3*(3), 941–950. DOI: 10.38035/gijlss.v3i3.582

Ng, S., Johl, S. K., & Khan, P. A. (2025, January). ESG investment enhanced with Industry 5.0: The introduction of conceptual framework. In *Proceedings of the International Conference on Environmental, Social, and Governance (ICESG 2024)* (Vol. 889, p. 211). Springer Nature. DOI: 10.2991/978-2-38476-358-0_17

Pancholi, K., & Shukla, P. (2025). Harnessing AI for Sustainability: Innovations, Policies, and Investment Paradigms. In *Diversity, AI, and Sustainability for Financial Growth* (pp. 97-124). IGI Global Scientific Publishing.

Pavlidis, G. (2025). Empowering sustainable finance with artificial intelligence: a framework for responsible implementation. In *A Research Agenda for Financial Law and Regulation* (pp. 23–38). Edward Elgar Publishing. DOI: 10.4337/9781803929996.00009

Petrukha, N., Petrukha, S., Stoliarenko, O., Ortina, G., Stuzhuk, R., & Plakhotnii, D. (2025). Natural resources and financial security: The synergy of sustainable development economics and artificial intelligence. *Grassroots Journal of Natural Resources*, *8*(2), 775–795. DOI: 10.33002/nr2581.6853.080236

Rane, N., Choudhary, S., & Rane, J. (2024). Artificial intelligence driven approaches to strengthening Environmental, Social, and Governance (ESG) criteria in sustainable business practices: a review. *Social, and Governance (ESG) criteria in sustainable business practices: a review (May 27, 2024).*

Sharno, O. I., & Bokov, Y. A. (2024). ESG-Screening of Remote Investment in Sustainable Development: The Environmental and Legal Dimension. In *Remote Investment Transactions in the Digital Age: Perception, Techniques, Law Regulation* (pp. 73–83). Springer Nature Switzerland. DOI: 10.1007/978-3-031-51536-1_8

Sulaiman, A. D. B., Sentosa, I., Osman, M. Z., Roslan, H., & Juhar, K. N. N. A. (2024, December). Environment, Social, Governance (ESG) Investment in Artificial Intelligent (AI) to Improve Power Grid focusing Peninsular Malaysia using System Dynamic. In *2024 8th International Symposium on Innovative Approaches in Smart Technologies (ISAS)* (pp. 1-6). IEEE.

Taleb, M., & Kadhum, H. J. (2024, June). The role of artificial intelligence in promoting the environmental, social and governance (ESG) practices. In *International Conference on Explainable Artificial Intelligence in the Digital Sustainability* (pp. 256-279). Cham: Springer Nature Switzerland. DOI: 10.1007/978-3-031-63717-9_17

Vali, J., Yadav, P., & Thota, U. (2024, October). AI for Climate Action: Enhancing Sustainable Development Through ESG Analytics. In *Proceedings of the Second International Workshop on Artificial Intelligence: Empowering Sustainable Development,* Lucknow, India (Vol. 2).

Vodenska, I., Trajanov, R., Lazarev, G., Chitkushev, L., & Trajanov, D. (2025). Navigating Global ESG Investment Regulations Using AI. In *Sustainable Investing* (pp. 153–194). Problems And Solutions.

Wang, Q., Qi, Y., & Li, R. (2025). Artificial intelligence and corporate sustainability: Shaping the future of ESG in the age of industry 5.0. *Sustainable Development.*

Yu, X., Fan, L., & Yu, Y. (2025). Artificial Intelligence and Corporate ESG Performance: A Mechanism Analysis Based on Corporate Efficiency and External Environment. *Sustainability (Basel)*, *17*(9), 3819. DOI: 10.3390/su17093819

Chapter 13

# Sustainable Resolution of Stalled Real Estate Projects:

## A Legal Examination of Green Finance, Insolvency, and AI Under the RERA–IBC Framework

**Himanshi Sanjaykumar Sharma**
http://orcid.org/0009-0004-0562-0951
*Gujarat National Law University, Gandhinagar, India*

## ABSTRACT

*The legal strategy that incorporates cutting-edge concepts like artificial intelligence and green finance with established laws like the Insolvency and Bankruptcy Code and the Real Estate (Regulation and Development) Act (RERA). It need to develop long-term solutions since real estate projects are at a standstill. Money issues, regulation infractions, or developer bankruptcies cause many projects to be delayed. Both investors and homebuyers suffer as a result. "Sustainable" funding is defined by green finance as investments that will result in environmentally responsible and beneficial initiatives. AI-based analytics may improve project management, ensure that real estate ecosystems are transparent and honest, and forecast the likelihood of current bankruptcy. A Grand Unified Theory of Law might safeguard stakeholders, expedite project completion, and improve the environmental sustainability and technical sophistication of India's real estate sector for future recovery models by ensuring that RERA and IBC operate in tandem.*

DOI: 10.4018/979-8-2600-1308-3.ch013

## 1. INTRODUCTION

India's real estate problem has several interrelated causes, but the primary one is the significant changes that have occurred in the finance and real estate industries during the last 10 years. One of the main causes of this crisis is the egregious financial mismanagement of developers, which includes problems with cash flows and resource allocation, excessive borrowing, and more. Over 500,000 housing units have been impacted by the over 2,000 residential projects that have been halted in 42 major cities nationwide, according to PropEquity and other significant industry sources. With more than 4.3 lakh units on hold, the situation is significantly worse in tier I cities. With 74,000 units, Greater Noida has the most blocked units (Bharti et al., 2024). The cities of Thane, Gurugram, Mumbai, Bengaluru, and Pune also have units that have halted. In Greater Noida, 16.82% of all residences are a part of postponed developments.

Developers often used funds from one project to finance another, which resulted in a series of defaults or unfinished, worthless structures. Additionally, the collapse of large Non-Bank Financial (NBFC) firms, particularly after the 2018 IL&FS default, hindered the flow of capital and increased project delays, particularly in sectors like inexpensive and mid-income housing (Aryavans, 2024). Long approval procedures, lax rule enforcement, and delays in obtaining clearances or occupancy certificates may also cause projects to stall. Many people's fantasies of purchasing a house have become protracted nightmares. An example of a project where families invest all of their money is Ansal Estella in Gurugram, where they must wait 10 years and get partial handovers without ever receiving their license of occupancy certificates. This is how these failures have affected people. Despite never obtaining legal ownership, several purchasers have paid up to 95% of the selling price of their apartments. This demonstrates how little legal choices are available now after the most recent regulatory reforms (Wang & Li, 2025).

The Real Estate (Regulation and Development) Act (RERA) was created in part to address these issues. Although RERA has made it easy to register projects, communicate information, and hear consumer complaints, its implementation varies by state, and delays are nevertheless frequent, particularly in places where there are already many unfinished projects. At the same time, developers who are in default were expected to find organized means to deal with their obligations with the aid of the Insolvency and Bankruptcy Code (IBC). Long court fights and legal misunderstandings have often resulted from its connection with RERA, homeowners' rights, and financial creditors' rights.

To address this problem, the Indian government established the Special Window for Affordable and Mid-Income Housing (SWAMIH) Fund in 2019. Despite the company's financial difficulties, it has raised over Rs 15,000 crore to far, which has been used to fund projects that have stagnated. However, even with such vast quantities, development is still sluggish. There have been enough units to pull out around 32,000 in five years, not just one, but none have done it thus yet. This indicates that we are dealing with gaps rather than a single event time. The fact that government regulations are often not applicable is one of the other fundamental problems. Only with the consent of local governments have centralized land and property rights regimes, such as India's, been implemented. Real estate projects that are stalled may affect society as a whole by slowing down economic progress, damaging investor faith, and locking up family wealth. "In the short term," there is significant financial strain on financial institutions as well as the broader banking sector. Furthermore, a city cannot fully use its property when development sites, whether in the suburbs or downtown, are left in limbo. As a result, they create management issues for themselves (Akomea-Frimpong et al., 2023).

A project may stall for a variety of reasons, such as market tremors, systemic financial issues, regulatory flaws, or poor service delivery. The way the government handles this problem has changed. It is currently concentrating on repairing the economy via the IBC and state-level initiatives, rather than ensuring that individuals complied with the requirements under RERA.

## 2. RELATIONSHIP BETWEEN RERA AND THE INSOLVENCY AND BANKRUPTCY CODE

The relationship between the Real Estate (Regulation and Development) Act of 2016 (RERA) and the Insolvency and Bankruptcy Code of 2016 (IBC) is among the most concerning. It significantly impacts the regulations that oversee real estate projects and safeguard purchasers. Both regulations aimed to improve the efficiency and dependability of India's real estate and finance industries. RERA is an Act that protects consumers, while IBC is a means of obtaining remedy. Both of them are addressing distinct aspects of the same issue. There has been much discussion in the courts and administration about the tension between these objectives. Additionally, there are rules that attempt to strike a compromise between safeguarding homeowners' rights and maintaining the stability of corporate balance sheets.

To make the real estate sector more transparent, responsible, and customer-friendly, RERA mandated that all ongoing and completed projects register. Developers were required to disclose their estimated trail and usage when project deadlines were made public, or else they risked fines for being late with delivery. Instead of going through several court proceedings, homebuyers may now file complaints about possession concerns, interest disputes, or compensation rights with RERA Authorities and/or adjudicating officials. The Act was a quick, person-centered fix that went straight after dishonest promoters. In contrast, the IBC was established to address financial bankruptcy comprehensively and promptly, resurrecting troubled assets for use in resolving disputes between creditors, including banks, NBFCs, and even homebuyers.

When the Supreme Court declared in the Pioneer case of 2019 that its amendment designating homebuyers as "financial creditors" under Section 5(8)(f) of this Code was lawful, the legislative overlap began. This recognition brought about a significant shift in real estate law by enabling disgruntled allottees to initiate Corporate Insolvency Resolution Processes (CIRP) against developers who were not making their payments. However, it also established a dual remedy system that enables homeowners to get assistance from both IBC and RERA. According to Section 238 of the IBC, in the event of a dispute, the IBC will prevail over the RERA. Additionally, the Court ordered both regulatory regimes to cooperate.

In reality, this cohabitation causes both bewilderment and empowerment. Individuals' rights to possession or recovery are superseded by those of parties and entities under RERA. A joint insolvency procedure is the best option, according to the IBC. Decisions are taken by the Committee of Creditors (CoC), which is mostly composed of banks. Therefore, despite being regarded as financial creditors, homebuyers have little influence over how matters are resolved, particularly in court proceedings when their interests conflict with those of the banks, who want to get the most amount of money possible for any liquidation. For instance, homebuyer coast representatives were permitted to attend CoC meetings in the instances of Jaypee Infratech Ltd and the Group Amrapali CIRP; yet, rulings often prioritized debt collection above timely possession, giving the system an uneven appearance.

The fact that cohabitation promotes both ownership and chaos makes it practically significant. The Committee of Creditors (CoC), which is mostly composed of financial institutions, makes judgments in the IBC, a group procedure for handling bankruptcy. In contrast, RERA safeguards people's rights to ownership and reimbursement (Jolly & Budke, 2023). Homebuyers often have little influence over the settlement process since they are financial debtors. This is particularly true when their goals conflict with those of banks, who want to maximize profits from a transaction. Financial establishments' aim for a strong recovery overrode Jaypee's involvement in Infrastructural Co Ltd and A year to homeowner representatives on the CoCs. By altering practices and beliefs, legal revisions in 2024 and 2025 attempted to address this issue. As a result, the protection of the legitimate buyer becomes a fundamental need. In a same vein, the court decided to emphasize that appeals filed only for speculative investments—not for real allotment possession—would not make it easier to start CIRP. IBC procedures thus started to more closely align with RERA's ethical objective of safeguarding customers. However, the primary contradictions remain, even if these convergences may aid in resolving some of the disputes. Any measures taken before regulatory tribunals under the RERA that have an impact on enforcement procedures or consumer complaints will automatically be placed on hold until an appeal is filed as long as insolvency proceedings under the IBC are ongoing (Deep et al., 2022). Many developers put their bankruptcy cases on hold when they are accused of financial misconduct or fraud, as if they were waiting for a child's test results from an open door. In each of these situations, this is unjust to the system and to customers.

Numerous legal experts and decision-makers have tried to develop harmonization techniques. More "dual-compliant" insolvency models, in which RERA supervision continues after CIRP to monitor building projects that are adhering to authorized resolution plans, have been proposed by some. In these instances, the courts instructed the parties seeking a resolution to adhere to RERA regulations, such as holding weekly meetings with the residents' association. In this manner, it was able to ensure that customers were protected and that everything was clear even when a business was going bankrupt. Since developers' project performance is directly under the supervision of resolution specialists (as well as creditors), the IBBI's modified "Reverse CIRP" technique is the least damaging option since it eliminates the need for them to start over elsewhere (Islam et al., 2024).

Establishing state-level distress funds and escrow-based financing mechanisms is another significant step in integrating these two frameworks. The majority of insolvency petitions in this sector of the economy are significantly impacted by the fact that these funds will maintain cash for project completion apart from personal usage. The goal of the SWAMIH Fund and other state-sponsored initiatives is to address this issue on a much bigger scale. They must, however, cooperate with RERA-compliance processes as well as IBC resolution systems in order for them to function effectively.

In 2025, the Supreme Court instructed the Ministry of Housing and the Insolvency and Bankruptcy Board of India (IBBI) to cooperate in order to facilitate communication between NCLT benches and RERA Authorities. They achieved this via the use of common databases, computerized file systems, and simplified compliance. The directive aims to reduce conflicting directives and promote instantaneous information exchange. It is essential that the Court see these two legal systems as coexisting rather than in conflict. India is attempting to adapt to a changing economy while upholding consumer rights, as seen by the interplay between RERA and IBC. The concept of utilizing IOUs to reduce the wealth gap has long been questioned by RERA. IBC has further narrowed this perspective. In order to assist homeowners and ensure that real estate accounting were correct, RERA took this action (Ripoll Gonzalez & Gale, 2023). However, in order to improve the stability of the present real estate governance structure which benefits all parties—these two pillars are required. Some people may find the structure problematic if it becomes too flexible. This entails using AI-driven compliance evaluations and predictive insolvency analytics to identify issues early and provide a collaborative tool for RERA regulators and insolvency experts. To ensure that RERA preserves people's rights and the IBC economy remains robust, the legal system must be transformed from having disparate rules to being a single, large field.

## 3. ROLE OF GREEN FINANCE IN SUSTAINABLE PROJECT REVIVALS

In addition to providing a means of progress at the project's conclusion, applying green principles to stalled projects fosters long-term resilience for future growth. In addition to reviving dormant green real estate initiatives, green financing offers a new avenue for funding that may effectively address environmental and social demands. This is consistent with what people believe will be the most significant industrial and green urban issues in the future (Soergel et al., 2021).

With thousands of incomplete or partially constructed residences, India has a large amount of delayed real estate. The fact that there is not enough money to complete them makes this an issue as well. Because they solely consider short-term advantages and don't worry about the impact on thc cnvironment, primitive financial approaches don't account for sustainability. Green financing alters this by investing in projects that adhere to environmentally friendly building standards, such as LEED or IGBC. It also promotes waste, energy, and water conservation. These guidelines result in lower energy costs and increased property values for projects. They also provide a greater market demand from renters and more well-liked ways to live in a community (Mackenzie, 2024). This historically steady flow has evolved into a kind of upward spiral that supports ecological resilience as well as financial flow recovery.

Green bonds as debt securities designed exclusively for the environment have emerged as one of the most significant instruments in this field. The Singaporean real estate trust Suntec City Investment Company serves as one such. Its 150,000 square meters of area has recently been modified to accommodate computers and contemporary workplaces. This has transformed the once-empty building into a corporate hub with prospects for future real estate development projects with sustainability targets established by financial institutions. Although investors who are concerned with environmental, social, and governance issues may not be paying much attention to India at the moment, as this interest grows from China to other nations, India will develop into a legitimate market with sufficient scale and depth to draw in capital. Looking up at the hotel towers in the backdrop that are linked to her TP Group offices, Hu states, “In fact, the bonds appeal to a growing investor base that is interested in ESG principles.”

The distance between these structures and the waterfront is slightly over 100 meters. There is no assurance that the leader of a real estate development project that has stopped would be able to get both short-term and long-term funding from private investors. Two of China's best-kept secrets are the Sanlitun block in Beijing's Third Embassy Compound and the Life Hub @ Kongjiang business district in Shanghai. They demonstrate that foreign investors who want to purchase land and other assets now have access to unique incentives. One may argue that China is really exporting its commercial development and industrial zones to the global market. Green bonds may assist projects in obtaining the long-term funding they need, perhaps at reduced capital costs. Given that the summertime harvesting season is only seven weeks away, this should result in improved cash flows. Although some of the private investors are Chinese property owners, Mr. Hu has not yet been successful in locating any (Cong et al., 2021). In order to allow someone else to take up the remaining tasks, he is instead considering ways to reassess the project without investing any further funds. This new green financing ecosystem for real estate developments has been strengthened by international financial institutions and government laws. India vowed to achieve net zero by 2070 in its 2010 National Budget. This has produced a positive feedback loop of a sustainable investment environment, in conjunction with initiatives like the Smart City Mission and a National Action Plan on Climate Change.

New ideas are also encouraged by green funding. In addition to solar-powered roofs, energy-efficient air conditioners, and intelligent water systems. Loans connected to green project or pool sustainability money may be used to pay for these systems (Nancy, 2022). These methods reduce environmental damage and improve a building's resilience to the threats posed by climate change. It's particularly crucial for long-delayed projects that suddenly have to meet new market or regulatory requirements in the event that such risks materialize. Additionally, the use of these technologies makes the completed projects more attractive to astute investors and real estate purchasers, which in turn generates a consistent demand for all housing absorptions.

## 4. APPLICATION OF ARTIFICIAL INTELLIGENCE IN RISK ASSESSMENT AND PROJECT MANAGEMENT

Many of the stalled projects also suffered from liquidity crises and the diversion of funds before delays set in. By approaching environmental management holistically, green money may penetrate these potential resistance regions. This entails establishing sound policies by being transparent about the allocation of funds, keeping them segregated, and conducting two inspections for both environmental impacts and consistent net profit. Instead of calling it a figment, you could wish to refer to it as a figuration, where green financing and effective project management ensured that the funds were utilized only for the project's completion and sustainability.

With continuous control checks and logical links, investors and creditors are calling for greater adherence to sustainable norms. These checks assist ensure that the funds are not being stolen or misdirected and are only being used to complete the project with green designs reeds. Funding delayed recovery initiatives is just one aspect of green financing. Sustainable development requires collaboration between developers, banks, government agencies (Candel et al., 2021). For instance, a collaborative platform that must unite various groups of individuals is the Forest Finance Week 2026 in Marrakech (temporary translation). This creates opportunities for joint bank financing to leverage productive programs across various partners and sovereign nations, for settling strategies in terms of structure and arrangement, and for exchanges that strike a balance between sustainability and profitability. With this combination, municipalities may renew initiatives they wish to perform more quickly rather than beginning from sçratch. The majority of those who responded were, in fact, inside (Kong'ani et al., 2021).

The issue is that the work is as large as the outside has always been. There are several issues. Obtaining green certification is challenging, and new sustainability-related business measures must be developed. Using green technology also requires some upfront effort from developers. People often reject green financial choices because of this. Additionally, the expertise and abilities needed to bridge the gap between project creators and their funders are not equally dispersed across the business (Li et al., 2022). Regulatory agencies must cooperate to streamline the certification process, provide financial incentives for green initiatives, such as tax breaks or subsidies, and establish oversight organizations for sustainable finance in order to overcome these issues.

Green money is what ultimately makes Indian real estate developments viable. Green finance may thus satisfy two distinct demands when environmental factors are taken into account when determining whether to provide credit. What loans, therefore, might green financing assist with? more funds for extensive institutional digitization, and Create new growth modes precisely. favorable environmental ones Governments are cooperating to improve the situation, and more green bonds, loans, and sustainable financing are becoming accessible. As a result, eco-revival initiatives may begin more easily, as if they were "plugged in to the factory." Green financing is helping Indian real estate move beyond its turbulent past and toward a flexible, sustainable urban future that benefits homeowners and society at large (Appiah-Opoku et al., 2023). For the long-term revitalization of long-stalled real estate developments in India, green funding is crucial.

So, is it feasible to get funds that are especially designated for improved, resource-efficient, and ecologically friendly development? Natural resource depletion and high carbon emissions are caused by India's real estate sector. They must also be "greened" in order to complete these undertakings and provide long-lasting characteristics. promoting instruments such as finance for sustainability, green bonds, and green loans Invest in environmentally sustainable building construction. You may save money by making prudent use of resources like energy and water. Not only does efficient waste disposal benefit the environment, but it also saves money. The initiative was made feasible by a financial environment that satisfied the demands of ESG-focused investors as well as national climate objectives (Chowhan et al., 2022).

As a result, a large number of Indian real estate developments are just lying there with little impact on the local population or the economy. Their excesses are also harming people and natural resources. Thus, foreign investment may return to China via the construction of projects that adhere to international standards such as LEED and IGBC. Additionally, a building that has international approval is one where increased rental revenue is collected and deposits are dropped when the property is purchased, but fees are lowered; instead, the total values of the property increase more quickly when it changes hands, even in a down market for real estate. Reduce long-term real estate development risks and expenses while providing long-term support for initiatives. Green bonds: This kind of funding may assist a project in overcoming cash flow issues and completing it effectively.

To put it simply, green bonds are a kind of financial instrument that aids in funding environmentally friendly initiatives. Because they desire to make environmentally friendly investments, more and more investors worldwide are showing interest in Green Bonds. This helps developers get funding over an extended period of time and on favorable conditions (Gomollon-Bel, 2022). The financial flow shortages that are impeding other projects may be filled with this sort of assistance.

The application of green financing is greatly aided by government initiatives. Examples of this include India's Smart Cities initiative, regional environmental regulations, and the country's 2070 emission-free target. International financial organizations like the World Bank and the Asian Development Bank have been assisting real estate brokers by providing them with technical assistance and concessional loans to upgrade climate-stressed infrastructure. These types of assistance solutions reduce project risks and finance expenses. Subsequently, more private capital may be attracted to sustainable real estate developments and completed but unoccupied units. By funding an increasing number of China's unsuccessful real estate projects in this way, society's perception of them is altered, transforming them from issues into opportunities (Gray & Kallin, 2023).

## 5. LEGAL CHALLENGES AND GAPS IN THE RERA–IBC FRAMEWORK

The legal foundation for delayed real estate development has mostly been established by the Real Estate (Regulation and Development) Act, 2016 (RERA) and the Insolvency and Bankruptcy Code, 2016 (IBC). Although the two regulations are intended to safeguard homeowners and restart projects that have halted, their combination is difficult due to several legal issues. When these two interact, everyone has issues and delays, which reduces productivity (Zhao et al., 2023). Certain obvious concerns that don't arise when policies are developed without laws are raised when laws are made using legislative norms. This implies that procedural ambiguity, conflicts of interest, and legal drafting errors conceal the legislative process. The fact that RERA and IBC approach the issue in somewhat different ways is one of the primary causes of dispute. RERA is an industry regulation that requires everyone to be transparent about their work and requires projects to be registered. This is to guarantee that everyone is accountable, transparent, and safeguarded as a customer. But these regulations also impose stringent due dates on all matters (Persello et al., 2022). It allows the buyer to either take immediate possession of their home, get their money back from builders who fail to complete housing units as promised, or pay for these errors out of pocket.

In contrast, IBC is a universal corporate bankruptcy legislation that prioritizes the interests of creditors. By establishing time-limited corporate debt restructuring plans, resolution plans, or liquidation when necessary, it seeks to maximize the amount of money returned to creditors. The objectives of the two codes are fundamentally at odds: purchasers want their houses delivered, whereas IBC procedures concentrate on recovering money from financially troubled businesses rather than providing items that they don't seem to be able or willing to supply (Datta et al., 2023).

RERA and IBC may cooperate, but in the event of a disagreement, IBC will prevail under Section 238 of the IBC, according to Supreme Court rulings such as Pioneer Urban Land & Infrastructure Ltd. v. Union of India (2019). However, the safeguards that RERA offers to homebuyers will be weakened by this notion of dominance. RERA Section 14 instantly halts any ongoing legal actions or the execution of any laws, even those that RERA has explicitly stated, if insolvency procedures are initiated, as they are under the IBC. During that moratorium, homeowners are prevented from pursuing their own possession claims or from carrying out judgment orders issued by India's property authorities. For many homeowners, the situation has become worse so far because of this impasse. This kind of procedural disagreement has been deemed incorrect by courts. In reality, as seen in Umakant Shukla v. Pioneer Buildmart Pvt. Ltd., subsequent bankruptcy actions have invalidated RERA regulations, creating a regulatory vacuum (Wu et al., 2021).

According to a 2018 modification, homebuyers' status as "financial creditors" under the IBC is a whole new area. Homeowners may initiate Corporate Insolvency Resolution Processes (CIRP) against builders who violate the regulations thanks to this concession. Additionally, it grants them blocks on the Committee of Creditors (CoC), which is mostly composed of banks and serves as the primary decision-making body for everyone. However, these many creditors often lack the expertise to determine if a resolution plan should be financially feasible or how to implement it. The power dynamics become unbalanced as a result. Although the lenders are amenable to a smaller payment, they still want to own the property (Furnaro & Kay, 2022). Decision-making may be slowed down by this mismatch, or homeowners may find themselves in a situation where their actions are detrimental.

Judges often find it difficult to distinguish between genuine homebuyers who are posing as investors and those who are only trying to purchase a property. This reduces the likelihood that those who want to profit by posing as purchasers would do so. However, it is still difficult to distinguish between investors and actual home-buyers. This lengthens the process of filing for bankruptcy and further reduces the likelihood that the matter will be settled swiftly. The fact that different states have different levels of protection presents another challenge for RERA enforcement. Some states lack user-friendly digital complaint resolution tools, have a nascent regulatory infrastructure, and implement regulations slowly. Despite the fact that RERA was designed to achieve the exact opposite, all of these factors compel purchasers to enter institutions under the IBC. However, they believe that IBC's time-limited flexibility is a more effective means of achieving tangible solutions: a simple and rapid conclusion. Although IBC was first created for corporate debt, people benefit more from bankruptcy than from justice.

To assist homebuyers bridge this gap, the government and courts have launched a variety of initiatives. For instance, the new Reverse Corporate Insolvency Resolution Process (Reverse CIRP) safeguards the interests of developers, lenders, and homeowners by allowing promoters to complete a project under supervision (Biermann et al., 2022). It holds up with property values even if there are still risks and other hazards when prices fluctuate. However, since numerous regulations are ambiguous about their function, RERA officials lack a clear policy regarding what to do in the event that a promoter files for bankruptcy. Rather, courts are often halted by inconsistent rulings and delays in the proceedings. Revival projects are further slowed down by the lack of a uniform structure between RERA and IBC courts to handle, which makes it even more difficult to determine who should be doing what (Bakos & Schiano-Phan, 2021).

The disparities in doctrine, inconsistent procedures, and unbalanced stakeholder interests are the root causes of the legal issues and gaps in the RERA-IBC. The lack of cooperation between the two laws is detrimental to purchasers. The initial purpose of these legislation, which was to safeguard consumer interests and repair distressed real estate assets, is undermined, and homeowners suffer from unclear results and protracted delays. In order to overcome these obstacles, significant legal reforms must be made, institutional communication must be improved, rules must be adhered to, and RERA's emphasis on consumer protection must be aligned with IBC's financial restructuring objectives. Only then can the real estate sector begin to provide sound, equitable solutions for projects that have been put on hold and are past due. If the investments are successful, buyers will also have to split any large gains (Zhou et al., 2022).

## 6. POLICY RECOMMENDATIONS ON SUSTAINABLE RESOLUTION OF STALLED REAL ESTATE PROJECTS

This now want a comprehensive set of policy suggestions that include clear regulations, innovative revenue streams, cutting-edge technology, and robust protection for all stakeholders in order to address India's delayed real estate projects in a manner that will endure. Better cooperation between the National Company Law Tribunals (NCLT) and the Real Estate Regulatory Authorities is necessary to prevent further delays and safeguard homeowners' entitlement to timely possession (Wågsæther et al., 2022).

This will enable continuous project management throughout the company's insolvency resolution process. To encourage developers to utilize sustainable construction practices while the projects are being constructed, it is crucial to apply new green funding mechanisms to projects that have stagnated. Government incentives such as tax exemptions, reduced interest rates on green loans, and preferential access to public infrastructure funding should be available to projects that adhere to environmental norms (Jayarathna et al., 2022). These incentives are another method to integrate environmental preservation with economic prosperity. RERA needs to enforce escrow accounts more rigorously in order to prevent any potential loss of cash. To maintain clarity, green finance must also be associated with stringent reporting and audits from the planning or financing phase through building and operation.

The adoption of new technology is a crucial subject for policy attention. Real-time project progress, financial transactions, and compliance with regulations will all be monitored by AI-based systems. To identify risk triggers early on, before they have an opportunity to halt initiatives, we will use predictive analytics. It would also be easier for everyone to understand if all real estate developments had open data portals. They would also provide homeowners with the ability to learn about the most recent developments about their project, such as the builders' past performance and any ongoing litigation or bankruptcy processes. by giving homeowners more authority, ensuring them full participation in bankruptcy resolution procedures, and ensuring the significance of their Credit Committee voting rights. Homebuyers should have access to several capacity-building initiatives and legal assistance to educate them on their rights under the RERA and IBC as well as effective dispute resolution techniques. Additionally, homebuyers would get stronger support from his reserved components (Zhang & Ren, 2025).

More broadly, this would increase the speed and reliability of court-supervised dispute settlement, reducing the additional expense of wasted time. Nowadays, it might take years to have a matter resolved. Finally, the government must invest in institutional reforms, such as strengthening RERA agencies by clarifying the legislation and giving them more authority to enforce it. In order to equitably manage real estate bankruptcy, there should be more NCLT benches. Regular policy reviews are necessary to assess the effectiveness of these modifications and ensure that management is receptive to input from all parties. By implementing the above-mentioned complete plan, India may become a paradigm for the robust green revival of delayed real estate projects that would benefit the economy, consumers, and environment. Digital technologies, sustainable financing, homebuyer protection, legal clarity, and administrative capacity development are all part of this plan (Munawar et al., 2021).

## 7. CONCLUSION AND FUTURE DIRECTIONS FOR THE REAL ESTATE SECTOR

With compound annual growth rates of more than 24% between 2025 and 2030, the industry is predicted to more than triple in size in 10 years, reaching a value of over $1 trillion by then, taking into consideration all pertinent estimates. With cities like Bengaluru, Delhi, and Bombay setting the standard, there should be a high demand for residences, companies, shops, and data centers. A further indication of people's shifting preferences and wealth is the huge demand for luxury houses. Green growth, a complex web of laws and regulations, projects that fail, and a lack of funding are some of the issues that still need to be resolved. In order to safeguard homeowners, satisfy investors, and maximize the use of municipal property, it is essential to resolve these issues and restart stopped real estate projects. A more stable and open market is being ushered in by reforms such as the national alignment of the Real Estate Regulation Authority (RERA) with the Insolvency and Bankruptcy Code, as well as the expansion of the role of green financing and technology-enabled project management.

The sector's next section focuses on emerging digital and artificial intelligence technologies, innovation-based regulations, ready policies, and sustainable development. Providing additional details may help reduce unnecessary delays and disputes.

The real estate sector may also align with India's climate pledges by advocating for green-building standards and financing options, which would result in environmentally friendly and energy-efficient urban growth. Real-time project monitoring, improved risk assessments, and improved decision-making by developers, regulators, and financiers are other benefits of combining AI with big data analysis. The goal of social institutions is to include all stakeholders, particularly buyers and small investors, by employing more and better officials, rather than increasing monitoring. With the support of government initiatives like the PM Awas Yojana Urban 2.0 and the SWAMIH Fund, which assist those in need, the industry is also expected to see an increase in private equity inflows and foreign direct investment. In general, it can be said that the Indian real estate market is at a turning point in its history. With further collaboration between the public and private sectors, reciprocal legal reforms, more sustainable funding for the sector, and new technology, India can fully use real estate as an economic engine. By providing housing for its expanding urban population and advancing environmental sustainability and social justice, India will also aid in the global achievement of its climate objectives.

## REFERENCES


Akomea-Frimpong, I., Jin, X., Osei-Kyei, R., & Kukah, A. S. (2023). Public–private partnerships for sustainable infrastructure development in Ghana: A systematic review and recommendations. *Smart and Sustainable Built Environment, 12*(2), 237–257. DOI: 10.1108/SASBE-07-2021-0111

Appiah-Opoku, S., Manu, K. K., Asibey, M. O., & Amponsah, O. (2023). Tragedy of urban green spaces depletion in selected sub-Sahara African major cities. *Journal of African Studies and Development, 15*(3), 46–61. DOI: 10.5897/JASD2023.0682

Aryavans, A. R. (2024). Empowering Homebuyers: Judicial Evolution in Insolvency & Bankruptcy Law. *Issue 2 Int'l JL Mgmt. &. Human., 7*, 1412.

Bakos, N., & Schiano-Phan, R. (2021). Bioclimatic and regenerative design guidelines for a circular university campus in India. *Sustainability (Basel), 13*(15), 8238. DOI: 10.3390/su13158238

Bharti, S., Chenchu, M. K., & Jha, K. N. (2024). Revitalizing real estate: Decoding disputes, propelling policies, and pioneering solutions. *Journal of Legal Affairs and Dispute Resolution in Engineering and Construction, 16*(4), 04524027. DOI: 10.1061/JLADAH.LADR-1181

Biermann, F., Hickmann, T., & Sénit, C. A. (Eds.). (2022). *The political impact of the sustainable development goals: Transforming governance through global goals?* Cambridge University Press. DOI: 10.1017/9781009082945

Candel, M., Karrbom Gustavsson, T., & Eriksson, P. E. (2021). Front-end value co-creation in housing development projects. *Construction Management and Economics, 39*(3), 245–260. DOI: 10.1080/01446193.2020.1851037

Chowhan, G., Sen, A., & Mukherjee, J. (2022). Sustainable and 'smart'restructuring around the making of mega and world-class cities in India: A critical review. *GeoJournal, 87*(S4, Suppl 4), 897–910. DOI: 10.1007/s10708-022-10644-1 PMID: 35465172

Cong, X., Li, X., & Gong, Y. (2021). Spatiotemporal evolution and driving forces of sustainable development of urban human settlements in China for SDGs. *Land (Basel), 10*(9), 993. DOI: 10.3390/land10090993

Datta, S. D., Tayeh, B. A., Hakeem, I. Y., & Abu Aisheh, Y. I. (2023). Benefits and barriers of implementing building information modeling techniques for sustainable practices in the construction industry—A comprehensive review. *Sustainability (Basel), 15*(16), 12466. DOI: 10.3390/su151612466

Deep, S., Bhoola, V., Verma, S., & Ranasinghe, U. (2022). Identifying the risk factors in real estate construction projects: An analytical study to propose a control structure for decision-making. *Journal of Financial Management of Property and Construction*, *27*(2), 220–238. DOI: 10.1108/JFMPC-03-2020-0018

Furnaro, A., & Kay, K. (2022). Labor resistance and municipal power: Scalar mismatch in the Los Angeles Green New Deal. *Political Geography*, *98*, 102684. DOI: 10.1016/j.polgeo.2022.102684

Gomollon-Bel, F. (2022). IUPAC Top Ten Emerging Technologies in Chemistry 2022: Discover the innovations that will transform energy, health, and materials science, to tackle the most urgent societal challenges and catalyse sustainable development. *Chemistry International*, *44*(4), 4–13. DOI: 10.1515/ci-2022-0402

Gray, N., & Kallin, H. (2023). Capital's welfare dependency: Market failure, stalled regeneration and state subsidy in Glasgow and Edinburgh. *Urban Studies (Edinburgh, Scotland)*, *60*(6), 1031–1047. DOI: 10.1177/00420980221133041

Islam, M. S., Lee, Z., Shaleh, A., & Soo, H. S. (2024). The United Nations Environment Assembly resolution to end plastic pollution: Challenges to effective policy interventions. *Environment, Development and Sustainability*, *26*(5), 10927–10944. DOI: 10.1007/s10668-023-03639-6

Jayarathna, L., Kent, G., O'Hara, I., & Hobson, P. (2022). Geographical information system based fuzzy multi criteria analysis for sustainability assessment of biomass energy plant siting: A case study in Queensland, Australia. *Land Use Policy*, *114*, 105986. DOI: 10.1016/j.landusepol.2022.105986

Jolly, R., & Budke, A. (2023). Assessing the extent to which players can build sustainable cities in the digital city-builder game "Cities: Skylines". *Sustainability (Basel)*, *15*(14), 10780. DOI: 10.3390/su151410780

Kong'ani, L. N. S., Wahome, R. G., & Thenya, T. (2021). Variety and management of developmental conflicts: The case of the Olkaria IV geothermal energy project in Kenya. *Conflict Security and Development*, *21*(6), 781–804. DOI: 10.1080/14678802.2021.2000806

Li, C., Lu, T., Fu, B., Wang, S., & Holden, J. (2022). Sustainable city development challenged by extreme weather in a warming world. *Geography and sustainability*, *3*(2), 114-118.

Mackenzie, F. (2024). Development from within?: the struggle to survive. In *Development from within* (pp. 1–32). Routledge. DOI: 10.4324/9781003510765-1

Munawar, H. S., Ullah, F., Qayyum, S., Khan, S. I., & Mojtahedi, M. (2021). UAVs in disaster management: Application of integrated aerial imagery and convolutional neural network for flood detection. *Sustainability (Basel), 13*(14), 7547. DOI: 10.3390/su13147547

Nancy, N. (2022). Potential distortion of sustainable development in the conflict of interest of nickel mining and indigenous communities in Halmahera, North Maluku. *Journal of Global Environmental Dynamics, 3*(2), 11–20.

Persello, C., Wegner, J. D., Hänsch, R., Tuia, D., Ghamisi, P., Koeva, M., & Camps-Valls, G. (2022). Deep learning and earth observation to support the sustainable development goals: Current approaches, open challenges, and future opportunities. *IEEE Geoscience and Remote Sensing Magazine, 10*(2), 172–200. DOI: 10.1109/MGRS.2021.3136100

Ripoll Gonzalez, L., & Gale, F. (2023). Sustainable city branding narratives: A critical appraisal of processes and outcomes. *Journal of Place Management and Development, 16*(1), 20–44. DOI: 10.1108/JPMD-09-2021-0093

Soergel, B., Kriegler, E., Weindl, I., Rauner, S., Dirnaichner, A., Ruhe, C., Hofmann, M., Bauer, N., Bertram, C., Bodirsky, B. L., Leimbach, M., Leininger, J., Levesque, A., Luderer, G., Pehl, M., Wingens, C., Baumstark, L., Beier, F., Dietrich, J. P., & Popp, A. (2021). A sustainable development pathway for climate action within the UN 2030 Agenda. *Nature Climate Change, 11*(8), 656–664. DOI: 10.1038/s41558-021-01098-3

Wågsæther, K., Remme, D., Haarstad, H., & Sareen, S. (2022). The justice pitfalls of a sustainable transport transition. *Environment and Planning. F, Philosophy, Theory, Models, Methods and Practice, 1*(2-4), 187–206. DOI: 10.1177/26349825221082169

Wang, D., & Li, S. (2025). Social conflicts and their resolution paths in the commercialized renewal of old urban communities in China under the perspective of public value. *Journal of Urban Management, 14*(2), 402–417. DOI: 10.1016/j.jum.2024.11.007

Wu, Z., Luo, L., Li, H., Wang, Y., Bi, G., & Antwi-Afari, M. F. (2021). An analysis on promoting prefabrication implementation in construction industry towards sustainability. *International Journal of Environmental Research and Public Health, 18*(21), 11493. DOI: 10.3390/ijerph182111493 PMID: 34770008

Zhang, X., & Ren, Y. (2025). Revitalization of urban industrial heritage from a perspective of spatial production theory: The case study of "Old market" project. *Journal of Asian Architecture and Building Engineering, 24*(5), 3440–3456. DOI: 10.1080/13467581.2024.2396618

Zhao, D., Cai, J., Shen, L., Elshkaki, A., Liu, J., & Varis, O. (2023). Delivery of energy sustainability: Applications of the "STAR" protocol to the Sustainable Development Goal 7 index and its interaction analysis. *Journal of Cleaner Production*, *389*, 135884. DOI: 10.1016/j.jclepro.2023.135884

Zhou, S., Jiang, L., & Dong, Z. (2022). Overflow control for sustainable development by superwetting surface with biomimetic structure. *Chemical Reviews*, *123*(5), 2276–2310. DOI: 10.1021/acs.chemrev.1c00976 PMID: 35522923

Chapter 14

# AI and Green Finance in Insolvency Resolution:
## Enhancing Efficiency in Real Estate Bankruptcy Proceedings

**Himanshi Sanjaykumar Sharma**
http://orcid.org/0009-0004-0562-0951
*Gujarat National Law University, Gandhinagar, India*

## ABSTRACT

*The real estate sector has particular challenges when someone files for bankruptcy. The process might take a long time if it is not halted immediately, and production assets gradually lose value over time. Since the cost of bankruptcy with real estate has been declining in all regions for some time and is generally agreed, it investigate the relationship between green finance and artificial intelligence here. It is now less expensive and more environmentally friendly. Many investors are anxiously awaiting an improvement in the bankruptcy-related real estate issue, which has received a lot of attention. This is not only a haphazard observation; rather, it is supported by several case studies, including those conducted by renowned specialists as the Corporate Insolvency Resolution Process may be facilitated by AI solutions.*

## 1. INTRODUCTION

Artificial intelligence and Asia-Pacific Green Finance seem to be two very distinct concepts that come together to address bankruptcy because of financial issues, particularly in the complex real estate market, and the need for sustainable development worldwide. Corporate bankruptcy processes, especially those for real estate firms, have historically been drawn out, ambiguous, and primarily financial.

DOI: 10.4018/979-8-2600-1308-3.ch014

They have also been carried out nearly exclusively to benefit creditors' quick cash gains. However, an increasing number of individuals are discovering that this limited emphasis is insufficient. The long-term economic, social, and environmental implications of selling or repairing a significant asset-owned business are often overlooked by real estate developers. Green finance and artificial intelligence aim to do more than just improve the current system. Now that it incorporates capabilities like natural language processing for speedy document inspection and machine learning for risk prediction, it is much more effective. With the use of green finance principles, such as determining whether development has complied with Environmental, Social, and Corporate Governance indicators, it is possible to ensure that sustainable development is taken into consideration in the resolution plans that are selected. These resources are often ongoing undertakings with varying degrees of completion. Numerous other parties are also involved, including financial institutions, landlords, and above all thousands or possibly tens of thousands of individual homeowners. Because of its intricacy, the existing insolvency law framework and its application are difficult to operate.

The communication system for subcontractors is broken, the creditors are like cats being lashed (some want the project to be completed, while others want it liquidated), and there is a ton of documentation (such as legal contracts, financial records, and project plans). Long delays result from all of this, which devalues the assets and makes everyone unhappy. Additionally, it makes it difficult for businesses to recover. Humanity is now dealing with the worst climatic disaster in its history. Nearly 40% of global energy-related carbon emissions are caused by real estate assets, from construction to management. This gives every financial transaction, particularly bankruptcy, an additional, hidden, but significant risk. The underlying real estate's assets are essentially unsustainable from an Environmental, Social, and Governance (ESG) perspective. In the event of climate-related hazards (such as floods) and stringent new regulations to reduce carbon emissions, it may result in "stranded assets," which are properties that abruptly lose value or become a burden.

Due to the impact of business bankruptcy on the financial system and the economy, it is now more important than ever to anticipate and identify this crisis. The chapter shows that because of their ease of use and low computational cost, simpler and more well-known models are quite successful. However, LSTM and XGBoost are more accurate than these other techniques, often achieving over 99% accuracy. However, these techniques need a large amount of data and sophisticated computers to function. Their real-world implementation is still speculative. This chapter examines the benefits and drawbacks of certain technologies and discusses their practical significance. Compared to conventional financial ratios, artificial intelligence provides early warnings more accurately, quickly, and effectively. Conventional financial ratios are still quite helpful, however. In summary, this article presents an approach that takes into account both practicality and scalability with the goal of providing a variety of predictive solutions that are suited to modern financial environments with limited resources.

## 1.1 Overview of Insolvency in Real Estate and Need for Digital, AI and Green Finance Interventions

Many stakeholder groups are engaged, and they have a wide range of interests in addition to being a distinct kind of company, real estate firms are a whole separate form of bankruptcy. In other industries, getting money back or closing down is often the primary objective. Many homebuyers are implicated in bankruptcy, particularly in residential developments. For a home buyer, receiving the house as fast as possible is all that counts; they don't care whether they receive their money back. A lengthy, intricate, and costly Insolvency Resolution Process (CIRP) of corporates results from the fundamental conflict between banks, financial institutions, and other creditors who hold mortgages or other security over the land and who want to obtain the maximum amount of money possible under the secured governance law. Homeowners themselves are now considered a type of creditor and want the project to be completed. Additionally, there is a lot of information asymmetry, making it difficult to locate and assess assets.

The corporate structure of the real estate industry is sometimes unclear, and each developer company has many projects inside it. Hundreds of thousands of claimants It is very uncommon for a settlement to be reached on schedule and with the greatest advantage since the standard legal and administrative system is unable to manage all of them. Current methods of problem-solving still struggle greatly due to their magnitude, even with novel concepts like project-by-project resolution and "Reverse CIRP." Things move extremely slowly at these levels of complexity, which often results in significant value loss and long-term harm to end users. Currently, the only solutions to address this issue globally are digitalization, artificial intelligence, and green financing. Local digitization is the initial phase, which is required to regulate the massive volume of data (Madaus et al., 2025).

Real-time claim filing and verification, project funding tracking (as mandated by RERA), and ensuring that all parties involved have equitable access to the same data may all be facilitated by a secure online platform. The issue of having too much information is resolved in this way. By incorporating predictive capabilities and system-to-system synergy, artificial intelligence goes beyond digitalization. Millions of financial papers may be swiftly scanned by AI agents to look for indications of fraud or preferences. After that, they use this data to create preliminary viability studies for projects that are stalled. Predictive modeling driven by AI may also inform you where and when recoveries could occur. Creditor's Committees get data-driven signals from this logical and objective guidance, enabling them to act more quickly and maximize the value of all their assets. Additionally, green financing forces the environment to foot the bill for sustainable assets over the long run. Inactive initiatives are often solid at their heart, even if they may not make financial sense. Resolution plans must prevent more harm or loss from occurring even as they attempt to repair damage that has already occurred. The settlement process may make use of green finance tools, such as funding green projects and potential green bonds that are customized to meet specific needs. The objective is to incorporate financing for environmentally friendly construction materials and energy-efficient systems when we purchase or rent inexpensive or reduced-priced houses (such as via scholar loans).

## 2. AI TECHNOLOGIES IN INSOLVENCY RESOLUTION

Dealing with insolvency used to require accumulating a large amount of documentation, which may take years to resolve. As long as they aren't you or your company, you may often do harm to other people when you put things right. AI is transforming the bankruptcy process. Artificial intelligence has thc potential to end global bankruptcies and the corrupt corporate management practices that continue to exist in many facets of life. It also offers ways to conduct business with billions at stake and is a trustworthy source for teaching fundamental concepts. Systemic deterioration is caused by a number of factors, including slow processing speeds, the vast volume of content that must be processed, and the fact that decay occurs in almost spotless pages between opaque layers. A failing company must often be abruptly taken over during insolvency proceedings, and its financial documents, contracts, and internal memoranda from many years ago must be reviewed right now.

For the human Resolution Professional (RP), this is a major task that often results in missing crucial deadlines and losing asset value. AI, however, transforms everything. The transition from hands-on speed-of-diligence to intelligent resolution is made possible by it. Among the most obvious and immediate applications are document management and claims verification. Terabytes of organized and unstructured data, such as ledgers, bank statements, emails, and court documents, are produced during insolvency proceedings. These massive datasets may be ingested, sorted, and analyzed by AI-powered natural language processing (NLP) algorithms in a fraction of the time required by a human team. NLP techniques are especially useful for rapidly identifying key contract provisions, real estate project payment milestones for allottees, and ensuring that the claims of creditors align with the corporate debtor's accounts.

IT automation makes the work of the Universal Notice Board simpler. No one can claim that everyone should vote on every topic going forward just because they possess shares, and claims processing errors will decrease. Current bankruptcy regulations state that you cannot postpone paying back debt with interest for more than forty days, and all of this is taking place inside that time limit. In order to complete this set of stages, the RP's report to the court should also be able to contain material or views that the DIP or OIP disagrees with. When doing searches, this may be more crucial. Determining if there has been fraud, bias, or undervaluation in the handling of company assets is one of its most significant civic obligations. When presented with such evidence, the RP interprets it as a claim. Once it is operational, the objective is to expand the amount of assets available to creditors. These events used to be RP tests, which restricted what could be done and weren't always successful. For example, machine learning-based AI-powered forensic tools are the most effective at searching through big databases including transactional data for obscure patterns (Didea & Ilie, 2024).

Large and odd payments, transactions with family members or just before an insolvency estate begins, abrupt changes in asset ownership, and so forth are examples of this. Agents skilled in employing AI technology might identify these "Avoidance Transactions" that could occur in the realm of bankruptcy and insolvency. After that, RP concentrates his attention on those who have the highest prospect of recovering. As a result, it ensures that dishonest promoters are held accountable while obtaining the maximum amount for creditors.

Because artificial intelligence can forecast the future, it significantly enhances the strategic and forward-looking perspective on resolution. Developing a recovery plan that would optimize the bankrupt company's net assets while preserving as much of its "lot of land and bank" as feasible is one of the primary objectives of an insolvency system. AI creates models for forecasting bankruptcy based on similar business data, industry-specific risk indicators, and historical market performance. In computer terms, these models are comparable to thousands of distinct specialized insolvencies operating simultaneously. These "agents" can tell you the precise amount of money that various refinance plans will generate, the difference between the amount of money creditors may anticipate from a liquidation and a reorganization plan, and the optimal time to pursue each course of action.

In the event that no other bidder makes an unreasonably high offer, AI models may also integrate data from many sources, such as future market prices, various economic indicators, and sales of comparable commodities later than now. This objective and factual viewpoint eliminates a great deal of conjecture and prejudice from the problem-solving approach. It is producing more rapid, challenging, and economical results. Even if new technology is fascinating, not everyone is certain that the rapid adoption of AI will always be free of significant issues and ethical dilemmas. Because AI models lack autonomous awareness, their efficacy is based on the caliber and volume of data they are trained on.

This raises questions for me about the data's quality and potential bias. AI can inadvertently make unfair or incorrect choices if it were trained on data demonstrating historical systemic biases in the legal or financial systems. Second, there are several concerns around data security and privacy when AI is used to manage very confidential financial and personal data when a person is experiencing significant financial difficulties. This implies that businesses have to abide by stringent regulations that are always evolving. Above all, although AI may assist with analysis, it cannot take the place of a Resolution Professional's sensitive human judgment and empathy (Gurrea-Martínez, 2025).

Complicated discussions, handling sensitive stakeholders (such as bankrupt and losing house purchasers, as well as very agitated ones), and legal interpretations are all part of insolvency, and each case is subject to the R.P.'s professional judgment, adaptability, and understanding. Therefore, AI won't replace human intervention in bankruptcy resolution in the future. Rather, we must create a moral society that leverages AI to analyze high-level data more quickly and transparently. Additionally, the human RP explains the procedure and the requirements of the decision-making stakeholders.

## 3. GREEN FINANCE PRINCIPLES IN BANKRUPTCY: ESG COMPLIANCE IN INSOLVENCY RESOLUTIONS

A significant adjustment is being made to the whole corporate bankruptcy legislation with the introduction of "Green Finance Principles in Bankruptcy." Beyond just getting our money back, we also need to start considering "green bankruptcy" (also known as "green insolvency"). This implies that even ESG considerations, which up until now the majority of people have disregarded in bankruptcy situations, are now something that every struggling business has to take into account. For instance, when a company files for bankruptcy, the state must assist it in minimizing any adverse environmental consequences to prevent a long-term issue, in addition to the legal need that it comply with environmental, social, and governance (ESG) regulations. The bankruptcy procedure used to be financially independent.

In order for a bankruptcy to be effective, funds must be legally extracted from a company's assets for the benefit of its creditors. Other than adhering to the regulations requiring the presence of directors, the company's environmental effect, social impact outside of work hours, and corporate governance standards are of little consequence. However, the boundaries of traditional standards are being more strained as sustainable finance gains popularity and financial and regulatory responsibilities increase (Poddar et al., 2023). A key idea that is beginning to take shape is that a business cannot be deemed "viable" for long-term sustainability if it is beset by significant, uncontrollable ESG risks. The bankruptcy procedure now calls for corporate eco-restructuring rather than just exchanging debt for equity.

The concept is that a unified accounting system for environmental, social, and economic performance would help ensure that struggling businesses remember their obligations to the environment and to people. This ensures that everyone lives well and sustains the human species throughout time. Legislation must be passed to address environmental liabilities and debts if we want to determine who is in charge of allocating public funds for environmental cleanup projects. This comprises obligations due by a company that went bankrupt and failed to assume responsibility for bringing them to the point of final settlement. It ensures that companies who must pay for environmental harm do so with their own funds rather than utilizing the money of others for free, in accordance with the "polluter pays" norm (Vasquez-Serpa et al., 2025). It states that creditors with pollution claims will get almost the same treatment as other creditors.

Therefore, when creditors seek assets during bankruptcy settlement, environmental leftovers may be seen as a source of conflict or disregarded entirely (Didea & Ilie, 2025). According to legal and judicial experts, IBC must to give ESG considerations greater weight so that no business can use bankruptcy as a shield against environmental lawsuits. Businesses that violate pollution regulations, for instance, are required by environmental rules to clean up their own mess.

Although it is not appropriate, these obligations may be reduced during liquidation operations. Despite the advantages of incorporating ESG, from a legal and operational perspective, this additional layer makes everything much more challenging. The fact that reporting on troubled enterprises are not needed as usual and that it is unclear how environmental claims fit into the waterfall system further complicate matters for RPs. In the absence of regulations, the RP finds itself torn between its need to reimburse financial creditors and the rising concerns of individuals, organizations, and corporations that social justice and environmental issues need to be handled differently (Siringoringo, 2024). Green Insolvency's future depends on the adoption of changes to current laws that uphold the legitimacy of environmental claims and require RPs to actively engage in ESG due diligence within a clear legal framework that gives them the time and resources they need to turn a crisis into an opportunity for true corporate revitalization.

## 3.1 Application of Green Bonds and Sustainable Finance in Asset Restructuring

The application of green bond and sustainable finance are really important one. This asset restructuring process is same way we are using and we are applying in legal as well as social angle the use of green finance nowadays at international and national level also ensure the stability and currently there are many kind of investments which are going on. Globally, we may learn about ESG compliance and bankruptcy recovery from the experiences of other economies. In the landmark decision of Orphan Well Association v. Grant Thornton, for instance, the Supreme Court of Canada made it plain that bankruptcy would not be an excuse for violating environmental rules. The Court ruled in this instance that bankruptcy practitioners are required to abide with the applicable environmental legislation (Arora et al., 2024). Despite harming secured creditors' interests, this granted environmental claims precedence. In this manner, even if a company files for bankruptcy, it will still be accountable for any environmental harm, and bankruptcy laws may still support environmental objectives.

Because courts and regulators have begun to utilize ESG principles in reorganization plans, sustainability in bankruptcy and debt restructuring has improved in nations like the European Union and Brazil. Stricter ESG requirements may be imposed on the debtor by judicial recovery orders as a requirement of its reorganization; noncompliance may result in forced liquidation. This approach helps shift funds into “green” enterprises and forces companies to behave in a socially and ecologically responsible manner even when they are struggling financially. In this sense, including bankruptcy into a green transition strategy

In fact, including ESG compliance into bankruptcy settlements may improve the transparency and efficiency of the insolvency process. In reality, evaluating and restructuring assets involves more than simply classifying them according to immediate cash flow requirements; it also involves classifying them according to long-term production development (ESG). For instance, the green property evaluation will alert you if you are about to make a mistake with your property. This has the potential to save lives. Whether or not a business is green affects how the public perceives it (Zhou et al., 2025). However, an eco-friendly bankruptcy procedure may also provide business intelligence that might be used for spinoffs. That is undoubtedly what creditors want, and improving these procedures would also indirectly benefit creditors more. Additionally, by not monitoring the environment, they help prevent hidden liabilities, which makes it simpler for the economy to cope with future natural catastrophes before they occur.

When it comes to integrating green finance concepts with insolvency proceedings, there are issues at more than simply the legal level. In order for bankruptcy laws and guidelines to explicitly include ESG considerations, regulatory frameworks must be modified. In order to determine the extent of environmental harm a firm has caused and to use green finance techniques, insolvency experts need training and access to resources (Banerjee & Maurya, 2024). Furthermore, it takes rigorous legal and ethical adjustment to bring together the many interests of stakeholders, including communities, environmental agencies, creditors, and debtors. To prevent environmental claims from being altered or postponed without cause, transparent reporting and claim verification are crucial.

## 4. AI AND GREEN FINANCE FOR ENHANCED EFFICIENCY

Green Finance came together. Sustainable investment is becoming very complex and economical thanks to artificial intelligence. Instead of using outdated, backward-looking analysis that is only verified in retrospect and proves to be a massive blunder, the industry is adopting a new approach that is based on live, predictive decision-making. A catastrophe might result from this. Processing vast volumes of complex, often unstructured data regarding everything from corporate governance and social responsibility to environmental protection (ESG data) is necessary for green financial activities (Olujobi, 2021).

People's traditional analyses struggle to handle this well. By allowing software to handle all of this, AI can assist. Its many natural language processing (NLP) and machine-learning (ML) technologies can swiftly sift through millions of various kinds of data. These include real-time social media comments, satellite photos of factory pollution, and reports on company sustainability. Everyone can benefit from the deluge of helpful knowledge that is the ultimate result. With this new authority, a bank may immediately determine the potential harm that climate change might do or determine if a proposed investment has been "greenwashed." The whole capital allocation process ultimately functions like a well-oiled machine that pursues long-term initiatives with a high likelihood of success (Sanchez-Medina et al., 2025). By automating these tedious, data-intensive tasks, human analysts may concentrate on more complex, judgment-based judgments. For long-term investment, it creates a robust and scalable ecosystem that can keep up with China's rapid transition to a low-carbon economy.

AI is significantly altering our understanding of predictive analytics and climate risk modeling. Long-term, non-linear climate risks, such as rapid transition risks (like innovations in carbon taxes and innovative methods to reduce emissions) or chronic physical risks (like sea level rise and protracted drought), are not predicted by traditional finance models. Tens of thousands of potential future scenarios may be generated by AI-powered models using detailed climate research data. As a result, banks and investors may now more quickly and precisely stress-test their whole portfolios against various climatic pathways. An AI program, for example, may determine the likelihood that a whole real estate platform would flood in decades. Alternatively, a heavy industrial borrower may find it more difficult to get a loan due to the growing cost of carbon (Didea & Ilie, 2024).

## 4.1 Synergistic Models Combining AI Decision Support and Green Finance

The combination of artificial intelligence and green finance is changing how the world does business. This new approach aims to steer clear of the traditional financial pitfalls and concentrate on environmentally responsible and sustainable development. Investing in initiatives that benefit the environment and increase its resilience to climate change is the primary objective of green financing. Since carbon neutralization is now one of the primary objectives of nations' programs for sustainable development, green funding has grown in significance (Zhou et al., 2025). To operate and enhance green financial systems, we need contemporary technologies.

AI has emerged as a valuable instrument for change since it can assist in making sense of data pieces. It could help individuals make better judgments and help socicty find a better balance in this day and age. When manual techniques are used, there is no data-based judgment. A financial analyst must determine how much policy makers can manage them and how credible their expert evidence is to one another, rather than just choosing the less expensive choice on each side. Thus, AI rapidly emerged as a very helpful technology that increases the efficiency and transparency of green financing (Kumar & Parameswaran, 2024).

Banks and other financial organizations are better able to analyze ESG indicators, identify climate concerns, and identify profitable investments in green initiatives due to the way AI is built up. Making ensuring that funds flow to companies that don't prioritize their own interests above those of our grandkids is one task that must be completed when green finance and AI collaborate. AI systems must be able to analyze vast volumes of data and identify patterns that humans are blind to in order to be useful in the field of green finance. Everyone in the financial industry must be aware of their precise carbon footprint and the potential climate hazards in order to fulfill their responsibilities under the 21st-century objectives for green development (Trakman & Walters, 2022). AI technology may use current weather service data, satellite photographs, and corporate sustainability reports to determine what environment it belongs to or how a company's economic fortunes will alter in the future if this analysis is accurate. Long-term success may be achieved by new company owners by using this kind of knowledge to avoid making large investments in businesses that have no future. Additionally, greenwashing the practice of companies lying about how environmentally friendly they are can be detected by machine learning algorithms. People are open and trusting of one another, as shown by the kind of in-depth studies mentioned above (Sheikhattar & Vesali Mahmoud, 2025). Everyone wins when business and culture are sustainable, and you can be certain that everyone is being truthful about what they are doing.

## 4.2 AI-assisted Green Asset Evaluation and Liquidation Strategies

Particularly in the real estate industry, the way bankruptcy procedures are handled has evolved and continues to evolve. All creditors may now conduct efficient and ecologically responsible measures thanks to the combination of AI and green financing. Long-term, this has a significant impact on the environment and the way things are organized (Li & Wang, 2025). Processes are being reduced by combining ESG compliance theory with modern data analytics. In addition to saving time, it guarantees that the final accounting are sound socially, ecologically, and fiscally. Artificial intelligence can swiftly analyze vast volumes of financial data, automate tedious processes, and make more accurate predictions than the traditional method. All of this not only speeds up decision-making for insolvency experts, but it also helps them identify fraud and maximize asset recovery.

Costs and administrative labor might be reduced at the same time. This is even more efficient than it is now according to green finance concepts. Business failures might result from companies that are on the verge of bankruptcy ignoring their significant environmental obligations. Thus, this error has affected ecosystems and populations for a long time. The stakes in insolvency laws pertaining to green finance must thus be clarified (Baharuddin et al., 2025). In addition to immediately resolving the environmental issue, the restructuring plan should include measures that promote prudent ecological asset management. In addition to safeguarding social welfare, this approach aligns with the worldwide movement toward ecological development. Take the disposal of green assets, for instance. By considering things from an environmental perspective, you may be able to identify environmentally friendly solutions (Huang, 2025). You may choose possible investors or purchasers who also pledge to be responsible leaders by using ESG criteria. That's the way to go. In real estate bankruptcies, which are intricate and closely connected, AI and green finance complement each other effectively. We can precisely determine the dangers and opportunities for distressed properties in the environment by using AI algorithms. Everyone in a position of authority may make wise decisions with the aid of this helpful knowledge (Das et al., 2024). ESG standards may also be maintained by automated methods, ensuring that any modifications are promptly notified. This transparency fosters mutual trust.

## 5. LEGAL AND REGULATORY FRAMEWORKS: EXISTING LAWS AND REFORMS AFFECTING AI AND GREEN FINANCE

This combination of AI and green finance, a tried-and-true health check approach that emphasizes ecologically responsible corporate activities, has begun to show greater strength as a result of changes in international laws and regulations. Three broad concepts—environmental sustainability, social stability, sustainability, and governance (ESG) were not immediately apparent with regard to general financial rules in the big data age, which led to the necessity for a set of standards especially on artificial intelligence (Abdul-Kareem et al., 2024). For instance, the UK Senior Managers and Certification Regime (SM&CR) and the EU Markets in Financial Instruments Directive (MiFID II) require banks to ensure that their AI models are transparent, equitable, and easy to understand when they examine climate-related financial risks or make green investments.

Maintaining market stability and preventing "AI washing," in which companies attempt to enhance the perception of their AI company by inflating its potential or sustainability effect, are crucial. In the past, businesses have been sued by the government for intentionally doing this. " The two primary components of Green Finance are the EU's Disclosure Regulation and Taxonomy Regulation on Sustainable Finance. Their goal is to disclose financial instruments' environmental worth in a comprehensive and comparable manner. Regulators are beginning to restrict AI technology, despite the fact that collecting the vast volumes of unstructured data required for compliance is crucial. The first set of regulations in the world that addresses every facet of AI is the EU's AI Act (AGARWAL & AGARWAL, 2025).

An AI system should get a "high risk" grade if it is employed in the financial industry to determine how safe and hazardous a credit is. Strict guidelines must be followed for aspects of certification including as robustness, human monitoring, and data quality. These will have a direct impact on the caliber of products like green bond verification and AI-powered ESG rankings. Regulators, like the UK Financial Conduct Authority (FCA), are beginning to examine how AI aligns with legislation such as the Consumer Duty. This is to ensure that AI in green finance may be used in an equitable and transparent manner. The main issue is that we must develop new strategies for using AI to combat climate change without transforming the technology that was intended to promote transparency into yet another kind of institutional bias or misleading information (Yu & Wang, 2025). Leaders in every nation must find a way to transform disjointed, principle-based recommendations into universally applicable regulations if they want to gain the confidence necessary to combat climate change.

## 5.1 Regulatory Challenges and Opportunities Globally

Strong laws, rules, and legal frameworks must underpin the interaction between artificial intelligence and green finance if it is to be taken seriously. Governments and international organizations must establish regulations in this day and age that not only encourage new technology but also safeguard the environment and encourage moral corporate conduct. Artificial intelligence, green finance, and legal frameworks are all working together at the national and international levels.

Due of these relationships, a lot of individuals are involved and things soon get complex. Traditional environmental laws, financial regulations, and digital governance frameworks are gradually evolving as AI-powered financial systems that prioritize sustainable development objectives proliferate (Youssef, 2024). National financial and technical strategies are somewhat influenced by international accords such as the United Nations Sustainable Development Goals (SDGs) and the Paris Agreement on Climate Change. Perhaps the most crucial issue for nations to resolve is how to integrate green money with emerging digital technology. By ensuring that every choice is supported by facts, AI increases the transparency and effectiveness of green expenditures in this kind of organization (Jaiwani et al., 2025). The legislation guards against information abuse and ensures that persons are held responsible.

Financial authorities throughout the world are modifying the regulations to ensure that they are compatible with AI and green finance. The Sustainable Finance Disclosure Regulation (SFDR), the EU Taxonomy Regulation, and the EU Green Deal have all been developed by the European Union. Each of these modifies the definition and harmonizes the reporting of responsible actions across the economy (Narkevich, 2022).

These promote using artificial intelligence techniques to examine environmental, social, and governance (ESG) data while making choices. For instance, the EU Artificial Intelligence Act seeks to establish guidelines for fairness, transparency, and human intervention practices, particularly for systems used in financial sector, and to use a risk-based approach to AI regulation (Challa, 2024). Regulations pertaining to AI-controlled investment strategies and ESG reporting are being changed more aggressively by the US Securities and Exchange Commission (SEC) and other regulatory agencies. This will support environmental responsibility and the ethical use of data. With the use of widely accessible digital technologies, nations in the South are also developing national AI strategies that emphasize responsible innovation, long-term development, and even the use of green financing in national economic planning at a later stage of policymaking.

Global consensus standards that support AI governance and facilitate systemic collaboration in sustainable finance regulation are thus becoming more necessary. An efficient regulatory framework should support innovation while safeguarding the environment, consumer rights, and green money for everybody. In this evolving environment, the law protects individuals and promotes the development of new technology (Xu & Chen, 2025). It ensures that green finance and artificial intelligence advance responsibly and contribute to a sustainable future.

## 6. DATA PROTECTION AND PRACTITIONER SKILL-BUILDING

In order to ensure that the law is clear, that people respect it, and that it functions effectively, present laws and reforms must also adapt to the rapid changes in these new technologies. if artificial intelligence can replicate successful resolution in foreign locations in cross-border bankruptcy schemes or if it requires years of scientific training on the ground is still up for debate. However, the use of AI applications for interpolations between jurisdictions that do not yet trade electronically is made possible by the advancement of real-time video conferences to compare progress at various national bankruptcy sites and ensure that banking, securities market, and credit rating agencies can all use a common system (Shekhar, 2025).

Regulators must strike a balance when it comes to AI between promoting new technology and safeguarding people's privacy, ensuring that information is understandable, and holding individuals responsible. Financial data cannot be used due to certain regulations, such as those protecting personal information. However, there is virtually little application of AI in bankruptcy proceedings (Guo et al., 2025). These guidelines thus state that AI systems that examine a large amount of data regarding creditors and debtors must be impartial and fair. In order to prevent errors and misuse, particularly in circumstances when the stakes are as high as bankruptcy procedures, several jurisdictions are also considering establishing unique AI governance regulations that either currently regulate how AI makes choices, mandate audits, or demand risk assessments.

Legislative developments aimed at integrating Environmental, Social, and Governance (ESG) norms into management are beginning to have an impact on the green finance industry. For example, organizations have been established in republics like as South Korea and Thailand to promote private investment and collaboration between public and private entities. Additionally, businesses cannot avoid fulfilling their social responsibility. For instance, they will be required to publish a report on governance that is accessible to the public if they use this information as fodder and fail to submit any reports under the Trusted Business Reporting System (TBRS). Additionally, APEC and the Business at OECD (BIAC) have initiated an initiative to provide firms with improved information on various environmental concerns by providing them with better data on how their ESG appears from a financial perspective utilizing inputs, outputs, and ratios (Dumitrescu et al., 2025).

Although the bankruptcy legislation and the Indian Penal Code (IPC) are excellent at handling bankruptcies, they are gradually taking the initiative to directly address AI and green finance.

In this case, some proposed using ESG and digital technologies. In order to make the procedure quicker and more transparent, the Insolvency and Bankruptcy Board of India (IBBI) also wants AI technology to be used in every situation. There are now no defined regulations or policies pertaining to AI, and even in theory, it is sometimes difficult to determine which ESG regulations one should abide by. A set of universally accepted AI ethics and green finance guidelines is now being developed. Cross-border bankruptcy procedures will run more smoothly as a result. As a result, things are now really significant. The objectives of sustainable finance are increasingly being connected to global financial flows. Future rulemakers will likely spend a great deal of time crafting regulations that balance promoting innovation with safeguarding the rights of all parties involved in bankruptcy procedures (Kapur, 2025).

## 7. CONCLUSION AND FUTURE SCOPE

AI shortened and reduced the cost of the bankruptcy procedure. The results might be responsible and long-lasting using Green Finance. This integrated approach is essential for the real estate industry because it goes beyond reputation management alone. It forces the market to absorb the real costs of unsustainability, like pollution and transportation costs, and makes sure that assets recovered from corporate failure have a positive impact on the environment and economy in the future. Effective debt collection is only possible when these outstanding managers collaborate. This is a fantastic strategy to ensure that the environment is protected. Only if bankruptcy may be utilized as a means of addressing insolvency rather than just a “E and B” defeats a company. Rather, it can develop into a potent instrument that companies may use to combat climate catastrophes and advance sustainability.

## REFERENCES


Abdul-Kareem, A. A., Fayed, Z. T., Rady, S., El-Regaily, S. A., & Nema, B. M. (2024). Forecasting Financial Investment Firms' Insolvencies Empowered with Enhanced Predictive Modeling. *Journal of Risk and Financial Management, 17*(9), 424. DOI: 10.3390/jrfm17090424

Arora, M. K., Lal, S., Singh, B., & Kaunert, C. (2024). Promoters Under Scrutiny: A Case Study For Examining The Criminal Liability In Insolvency Proceedings. *Library of Progress-Library Science, Information Technology & Computer, 44*(3).

Baharuddin, C., Liutfi, A., Ar, D. P., Rizal, M., & Sasmita, H. (2025). Non Performing Loan Resolution Strategies and Impact on Financial Performance. *Golden Ratio of Mapping Idea and Literature Format, 5*(2), 106–114. DOI: 10.52970/grmilf.v5i2.1494

Banerjee, J., & Maurya, B. R. (2024). A Critical Study on the Role of ODR in Insolvency Law with Reference to India and Vietnam in the Context of Global Health Transitions. *INSOL International Insolvency Review, 40*, 54.

Challa, K. (2024). Enhancing credit risk assessment using AI and big data in modern finance. *American Data Science Journal for Advanced Computations (ADSJAC) ISSN: 3067-4166, 2*(1).

Das, R., Sharma, B., & Pal, M. K. (2024). Competition Law's Importance in Addressing Anti-Competitive Behaviour in Bankruptcy Proceedings and NPA Management Strategies. *Library of Progress-Library Science, Information Technology & Computer, 44*(3).

Didea, I., & Ilie, D. M. (2024). „Artificial Intelligence (AI)-" ally" in the success of insolvency and restructuring practices". *Legal and Administrative Studies*, 92-108.

Didea, I., & Ilie, D. M. (2024). Increasing Legal Certainty for Cross-Border Investments by Making National Insolvency Procedures More Efficient and Effective. *International Investment Law Journal, 4*(1), 30–70.

Didea, I., & Ilie, D. M. (2025). At the Intersection of Technological Innovations and Geopolitical and Economic Turmoil. Echoes of Insolvency Law and Practice. *Persp. L. Pub. Admin., 14*, 6.

Dumitrescu, D., Bobitan, N., Popa, A. F., Sahlian, D. N., & Stanila, C. A. (2025). Signaling Financial Distress Through Z-Scores and Corporate Governance Compliance Interplay: A Random Forest Approach. *Electronics (Basel), 14*(11), 2151. DOI: 10.3390/electronics14112151

Guo, S., Parry, R., & Vaccari, E. (2025). Cracking the code: Navigating the debt crisis of Chinese local governments and local government financing vehicles in China. *INSOL International Insolvency Review, 34*(2), 337–363. DOI: 10.1002/iir.70008

Gurrea-Martínez, A. (2025). The digitalization of insolvency proceedings. *INSOL International Insolvency Review, 34*(2), 475–491. DOI: 10.1002/iir.70003

Huang, W. (2025). Establishment of Bankruptcy Tribunals, Financing Constraints and Corporate Investment Efficiency. *Finance Research Letters, 86*, 108678. DOI: 10.1016/j.frl.2025.108678

Jaiwani, M., Chopra, R., Bhardwaj, S., & Gopalkrishnan, S. (2025). A Systematic Review and Bibliometric Analysis of Asset Reconstruction Companies: A Panacea or A Plight for Non-Performing Assets. *Asia-Pacific Financial Markets*, •••, 1–24.

Kapur, S. (2025). The social dynamics of corporate insolvency law and workers and employees of distressed companies: Comparing select Asian jurisdictions. *The Chinese Journal of Comparative Law, 13*, cxaf003.

Kumar, S., & Parameswaran, S. (2024). Role of Formal Restructuring in Post-Bankruptcy Performance of Companies: Case Study From India. In *Risks and Challenges of AI-Driven Finance: Bias, Ethics, and Security* (pp. 245-276). IGI Global.

Li, X., & Wang, X. (2025). Prioritization of environmental costs in Chinese insolvency law: Guiding case no. 214 of China's Supreme People's Court. *Journal of Environmental Law, 37*(3), eqaf023. DOI: 10.1093/jel/eqaf023

Madaus, S., Sarra, J. P., & Mevorach, I. (2025). The greening of the insolvency system. *Canadian Business Law Journal, 69*(3).

Narkevich, L. (2022). Digital transformation of the information-analytical system for crisis management in enterprise rehabilitation procedures. *Sustainable Development and Engineering Economics*, (1), 8–26.

Olujobi, O. J. (2021). Combating insolvency and business recovery problems in the oil industry: Proposal for improvement in Nigeria's insolvency and bankruptcy legal framework. *Heliyon, 7*(2), e06123. DOI: 10.1016/j.heliyon.2021.e06123 PMID: 33659729

Poddar, A., Bahuguna, R., Rawat, P., & Verma, S. (2023, July). The implementation of AI/ML in prevention of insolvency in real estate industry. In *IET Conference Proceedings CP837* (Vol. 2023, No. 11, pp. 425-430). Stevenage, UK: The Institution of Engineering and Technology. DOI: 10.1049/icp.2023.1814

Sanchez-Medina, A. J., Blázquez-Santana, F., Cerviño-Cortínez, D. L., & Pellejero, M. (2025). Ensemble Methods for Bankruptcy Resolution Prediction: A New Approach. *Computational Economics*, *66*(5), 1–36. DOI: 10.1007/s10614-024-10709-y

Sheikhattar, H., & Vesali Mahmoud, M. (2025). Domestic insolvency proceedings before investment treaty arbitration. *Arbitration International*, *41*(2), 349–375. DOI: 10.1093/arbint/aiae047

Shekhar, C. (2025). Navigating the Approaching Tide: Financial Stocks for Resilience in an NPA-Laden Environment. *Available at SSRN* 5651370. DOI: 10.2139/ssrn.5651370

Siringoringo, N. M. (2024). Optimization of Artificial Intelligence to Address Injustice in Bankruptcy Requirements between State-Owned. *Journal Research of Social Science, Economics & Management, 4.*

Trakman, L., & Walters, R. (2022). *Contemporary Issues in Finance and Insolvency Law* (Vol. 1). Routledge.

Vasquez-Serpa, L. J., Rodríguez, C., Pérez-Núñez, J. R., & Navarro, C. (2025). Challenges of Artificial Intelligence for the Prevention and Identification of Bankruptcy Risk in Financial Institutions: A Systematic Review. *Journal of Risk and Financial Management*, *18*(1), 26. DOI: 10.3390/jrfm18010026

Xu, D., & Chen, L. (2025). Between progress and caution: LegalTech's promise in transforming personal credit risk management in China. *Computer Law & Security Review*, *56*, 106090. DOI: 10.1016/j.clsr.2024.106090

Youssef, M. E. M. M. (2024). *Predicting Bankruptcy And Financial Failure In the Egyptian listed companies: The Importance Of Cash Flow Statements* (Doctoral dissertation, UNS (Sebelas Maret University)).

Yu, Y., & Wang, S. (2025). Bankruptcy Law Reform and Financing Costs for Small and Medium Enterprises. *Finance Research Letters*, *84*, 107794. DOI: 10.1016/j.frl.2025.107794

Zhou, Y., Liu, S., & Song, W. (2025). Can bankruptcy court establishment drive enterprise' entrepreneurial orientation? *International Review of Economics & Finance*, *103*, 104540. DOI: 10.1016/j.iref.2025.104540

Zhou, Z., Zhou, X., Zhang, X., & Chen, W. (2025). Judicial waves, ethical shifts: Bankruptcy courts and corporate ESG performance. *Journal of Business Ethics*, *198*(3), 537–557. DOI: 10.1007/s10551-024-05780-2

# Chapter 15 Cyber-Crimes in AI-Enabled Green Platforms: Legal Hurdles in ESG Investing, Prosecution, and Financial Loss Mitigation

**Vedullapalli Leelakrishna Sai Prasad**
*Amity Law School, Amity University, Gwalior, India*

**Vijay Srivastava**
http://orcid.org/0000-0002-3034-9903
*Amity Law School, Amity University, Gwalior, India*

**Hemant Singh**
http://orcid.org/0000-0002-1258-5187
*Amity Law School, Amity University, Gwalior, India*

## ABSTRACT

*The uptake of artificial intelligence into environmentally friendly platforms, e.g. sustainable energy management systems, environmentally friendly supply chain trackers, and eco-friendly investing tools, really disrupted environmental sustainability efforts. However, this convergence has also put such platforms into the realm of advanced cyber-crimes, such as unprotected data, AI model poisoning, and ransomware attacks which take advantage of the vulnerabilities in AI algorithms and interconnected Internet of Things gadgets. This chapter examines the legal barriers that are entrenched in ESG investing in that the regulatory frameworks are not in line with the technological innovation, making compliance and risk management difficult. It examines prosecutor issues, such as the cross-border attack attribution*

DOI: 10.4018/979-8-2600-1308-3.ch015

*problems and the evidentiary problem regarding AI-generated evidence. It suggests solutions to managing a financial loss, focusing on the move towards inclusion of cyber resilience in the ESG measurements, calibration of the insurance framework.*

## 1. INTRODUCTION AND BACKGROUND

Artificial intelligence has radically changed the revolution of numerous industries, and especially those focused on sustainability and green. The adoption of AI-based green platforms, based on the use of machine learning, data analytics, and automation, in order to optimise the environmental performance of investments, is one of the pillars of modern ESG (Environmental, Social, and Governance) investing. It includes platforms based on AI to track carbon emissions, forecast renewable energy generation, sustainable supply chain management, and ESG compliance analysis of investment portfolio (Do & Selvadurai, 2025). As an example, AI algorithms can target large volumes of data collected by the IoT sensors installed in smart grids or farming systems, effectively leading to increased energy efficiency and minimised waste, in line with the global sustainability targets, such as the United Nations Sustainable Development Goals (SDGs). However, such technological synergy brings about huge vulnerability to cyber-crimes which can sabotage environmental actions, investor confidence, and cause huge impact on finances and the implementation of AI-based forwarding defenses. Based on the examples of case studies and the growing policies, the analysis highlights the need to diversify interdisciplinary strategies to protect the continued existence of digital ecosystems facing growing threats.

Companies with strong environmental stewardship, social responsibility, and governance, which are emphasised in ESG investing, have been booming in popularity. It is expected that by 2025, ESG investments managed globally will reach over US$50 trillion in demand as a result of investors seeking ethical and sustainable returns. In this regard, AI is crucial as it has been applied to score investments according to ESG standards by relying on natural language processing of corporate reports and climate risk prediction modelling. Nonetheless, AI potentials, which drive these platforms, are appealing to cybercriminals. In this area, cyber-crimes refer to a set of threats, ranging between phishing attacks to the platform users to more complex and sophisticated ones related to advanced persistent threats (APTs) compromising AI models to generate fraudulent ESG ratings. Indicatively, enemies might feed the artificially intelligent (AI) training data with poisonous information which creates biased sustainability analysis that misinforms investors and exposes them to exaggerated greenwashing dangers.

These risks are increased by the environmental aspect of green platforms. Sustainable technologies may be built on networked systems e.g. AI-optimised wind farms, or blockchain based carbon credit systems that are a juicy target to distributed denial-of-service (DDoS) attacks or ransom. The perspective on green criminology, which investigates coupled with a view of how cyber-criminology enables the environment to suffer, e.g. hacking into AI systems that manage water-treatment-facilities to cause pollution, or clogging renewable energy-grids, is also noteworthy (Mohammed et al., 2025). Additionally, the high power consumption of AI tasks, with one large model generating more CO 2 than five automobiles over their lifespan, introduces sustainability paradoxes as cyber defenses begin to demand ever more computing power. It is a two-sided dynamic that necessitates the need to create Green AI, which will reduce environmental footprints and enhance cybersecurity.

When AI-enabled green platforms become the direct victim of cyber-crimes, it is not just the technical glitch that is at stake but it constitutes a systemic vulnerability to ESG investing. Breach in information might reveal sensitive information on the investors, resulting in identity fraud or even manipulation. In 2023, the cost of an average data breach was US 4.45 million, the financial sector recorded the most significant fine, and the finance sector suffered the most significant reputation. In the case of ESG-oriented platforms, trust is undermined by such accidents because investors are becoming more critical regarding cybersecurity as a measure of governance. According to surveys, changes in cyberspace According to surveys, 67 per cent of institutional investors prioritize cybersecurity as one of their ESG priorities, as they consider weak cyber defences as a reflection of inadequate overall governance. This can be reflected in the subsequent integration by cybersecurity in ESG frameworks, including the Sustainability Accounting Standards Board (SASB) and the Global Reporting Initiative (GRI), which currently requires disclosures of cyber risks.

The legal hurdles also worsen the situation. ESG investing is subjected to a discontinuous regulatory sphere with cyber-criminal laws differing depending on jurisdiction. The Computer Fraud and Abuse Act (CFAA) in the United States is a criminal act that bans unauthorized entry into the AI systems, and the proof of intent within the AI-altered attacks is difficult to achieve. General Data Protection Regulation (GDPR) by the European Union is rather strict in terms of the penalties in case of data breaches, but the manner in which it applies to AI-generated harms is still not clear, especially in cross-border cases. In the case of green platforms, the extra liability due to environmental legislation would present itself; an attack that causes ecological harm by a cyber-attack would result in liabilities under a guideline like the Corporate Sustainability Due Diligence Directive (CSDDD) in the EU. Nevertheless, assigning attacks to attackers is a painful task, since AI makes anonymised efforts with methods like deepfakes or adversarial machine learning possible.

There is a complex challenge towards prosecution of such cyber-crimes. The global nature of cyber threats interferes with the process of attribution, the process of attributing attacks to particular actors. State-sponsored organizations, like the Lazarus Group in North Korea, have been attacking financial systems, including those of ESG affiliation, with the help of AI in obscuring the tracks. It would be necessary to cooperate with other countries, but not all of them are ratified to certain treaties like the Budapest Convention on Cybercrime, leaving gaps in jurisdiction. In the financial sector, where ESG investing is premised, prosecutions are dependent on data collected by tools like forensic analysis, but AI-modified data may invalidate court admissibility. Cases like the 2021 case of the Colonial Pipeline ransomware attack explain how a cyber interruption in vital infrastructure (which can be extended to green energy grids) causes an economic shock and postponed justice because communications are encrypted (Sokhansanj, 2025).

Resilience hinges on mitigation plans on the prevention of financial losses. Incorporating cybersecurity into ESG governance is able to measure the risks based on the NIST framework like the Cybersecurity Framework to determine the vulnerability of AI. Coverage is sensitive, and an insurance policy is available for ESG platforms to cover breaching losses, the premiums are lowered in cases involving powerful artificial intelligence defences. Proactive solutions to AI detection of anomalies to prevent attack before it happens also applies, but it should consider a balance with ethical concerns including bias in algorithms. Threat-intelligence improvement is supported by public-private partnerships, like the U.S. Financial Crimes Enforcement Network (FinCEN).

## 2. AI-ENABLED GREEN PLATFORMS AND ESG INTEGRATION AND ROLE OF AI IN ENHANCING SUSTAINABILITY AND ESG INVESTING

The intersection of artificial intelligence (AI) with green platforms has also become one of the disruptive forces in improving sustainability and transforming ESG (Environmental, Social and Governance) investing. Basic AI-enabled green platforms can form a digital ecosystem, which leverages the power of machine learning, predictive analytics, natural language processing and other artificial intelligence to maximize environmental impact, track resource-use, and enable low-carbon transitions. These platforms create various applications, all of them being smart energy grids, sustainable supply-chain management, precision agriculture, carbon-footprint target, and renewable-energy forecasts. Google DeepMind, organisations can design AI-based image recognition to predict the risk of deforestation or manage wind-farms efficiently, and the organisation CO 2 AI can be used to systematize carbon management by converting sustainability pledges into real performance indicators. Similarly, the logistics optimisation that is implemented by companies like DHL decrease fuel usage and emissions by up to 95 pet in route planning but Walmart uses pilots that are run by AI to reduce food waste through predictive notifications of perishable items about their expiry date.

In the sustainability sphere, these platforms face essential global challenges that move in line with the United Nations Sustainable Development Goals (SDGs). Smart grids are enabled through AI to dynamically allocate resources, balance the transportation of the intermittent renewable sources (solar, and wind) with fluctuations in demand and prevent curtailment, reducing reliance on fossil fuels (Rajavel, 2024). In farming, AI-based tools like Kilimo or Pendulum use this technology to implement precision farming, demand forecasting, inputs planning and reducing excess inventory by more than 90/3 of using water, runoff of fertilizers, and methane emissions generated through waste. The supply-chain ecosystems use AI to track deliveries, geoposition objects, and reinstate the principles of constant circulation; one such app is CarbonBright that traces the path of products since their manufacture to recycling. Those innovations do not only make things more efficient, but also facilitate the notion of green-by-AI, where AI actively supports the concept of green approaches in various industries in the sense of green-in-AI, i.e., trying to optimize AI itself in terms of its sustainability in terms of its algorithms and hardware.

These benefits are enhanced by implementing AI in ESG investing, in which the metrics related to sustainability are directly integrated into financial decision-making. The so-called ESG investing, rating companies by environmental stewardship, social responsibility, and quality of the governance has grown exponentially. This is dictated by investor insistence on ethical returns, regulatory obligation including the EU Corporate Sustainability Reporting Directive (CSRD) and the impetus to transition to net-zero. The role of AI is essential because it takes into account large, unstructured data, such as regulatory filings, earnings calls, news articles, and satellite data, to produce correct and proactive ESG scores (Syed, 2022).

Traditionally, ESG measurement has been based on spreadsheet reviews and an annual report, which has been accompanied by inconsistencies, the risk of greenwashing, and timely insights. AI deals with these drawbacks by introducing new methods: ESG indicators are extracted in real time through natural language processing of varied resources, machine-learning responders can be simulated to production in climate conditions, multimodal AI can process text, images and geographic information to be calculated to profile all risks. An example is using AI to screen firms claiming to comply with ESGs when those who do not comply at all have been placed at the top of the list with the programs finding the anomalies in disclosures to establish greenwashing as a tactic. An example of this is in the setting of dynamic risk-adjusted strategies in the management of a portfolio where AI predicts the effects of the environment and allocation of portfolios towards suitable assets like green bonds or renewable development projects. The 2025 empirical research shows that AI implementation has a large-scale positive impact on corporate ESG, specifically, the environmental and governance pillars, and positively affect the green innovation, de-constraining financing conditions, and supply-chain efficiency.

ESG reporting and compliance are also changed using AI. Under frameworks such as the EU Green Bond Standard or the SASB standards, automation tools gather both internal and external data in real time and minimize the number of manual burdens. Generative AI speeds up workflow operations, providing traceable and auditable information that meets an emerging strictness on transparency and accountability. Through sustainable finance, AI can establish green investments using more specific criteria, thus maintenance of products to include sustainability-linked lenders and ETFs built on sustainability agendas. Over 35 per cent increase in AI use in ESG operations since 2022 by more than 60 per cent underlines why AI is now firmly viewed as part of essential infrastructure, and 58 per cent of finance teams were using generative AI to perform forward-looking analysis in 2025.

Considering how AI-enabling green platforms and ESG investing breed a virtuous circle, the better data accuracy and predictive power to invest in sustainable initiatives are, the more additional funds could be committed to it; the more money is committed to its development and impacting deployment of new technology. Nonetheless, such interdependence has also come with certain complexities, such as ensuring the AI can be environmentally friendly through models that are energy efficient and the danger of biases in completing assessments through scoring. With regulatory convergence becoming faster and technologies becoming mature enough, AI not only increases the outcomes of sustainability but also makes ESG investing a mass-market creator of long-term value in a world with climate constraints. Finally, these platforms and the influence of AI reform responsible finance as it introduces the technology and connects its possibilities with the planetary demands of a sustainable, just future (Ndibe, 2025).

## 2.1 Growth Trends in ESG Assets and Green Technologies: Emergence of Cyber Threats in Sustainable Digital Ecosystems

The global sustainability requirements coupled with the environmental, Social and Governance (ESG) assets and green technologies are thriving with a positive growth trend. By the middle of 2025, there is an increase of 10 per cent in sustainable fund assets of the global assets to US $3.5 trillion mainly because of Europe where the assets are 85 per cent. ESG assets under management (AUM) are expected to reach more than US 40 trillion by 2030, equating to a compound annual growth rate (CAGR) of around 3.5 trillion and yet U.S. markets will have faced the challenge of political headwinds that will restore their global market share of circa 25 trillion by the same year. ESG investing has developed in India with governmental commitments such as net-zero by 2070 and renewable incentives drawing international capital which invests a quarter of its funds in Indian equities.

To augment this trend, the green technology and sustainability market, which is estimated at US 25.47 ℕ 2025, is projected to grow to US 73.90 ℕ 2030 at 23.7 per cent CAGR, due to AI-driven energy management, blockchain-based carbon tracking, and renewable solutions. Investments in renewable-energy tallied to an all-time high of US 386 billion in 1st half of 2025 (excluding hybrid solar-wind-storage) up by 10 per cent year-over-year and hybrid solar-wind-storage developments were taking footing in spots like India through SECI tenders. Asia-Pacific has the highest rate of growth and this is because of urbanisation and policies in China, India and Japan, and Blocchain is hailed as the fastest growing technology of transparent sustainability reporting.

All these trends bring to the fore a growing ecosystem the interactions between the regulatory structures, including Europe and the Green Deal and India and its climate pledges, as they intersect with technology towards the bending of capital to a low carbon solution. Irrespective of obstacles such as greenwashing scrutiny, the success of the investor resilience indicates that momentum will continue into 2026 and beyond contributing to economic resilience and environmental development.

## 3. CYBERSECURITY RISKS AMPLIFIED BY AI IN SUSTAINABILITY PLATFORMS

Artificial intelligence implementation in sustainability platforms, such as smart grids, carbon accounting, precision-agriculture devices, and ESG analytics engines, has dramatically redefined environmental management, and at the same time fulfilled the threat of cybersecurity risks to new heights. The platforms handle massive datasets based on IoT sensors and satellite imagery and real-time monitoring systems to streamline the process of decarbonization, increase resource usage efficiency, and strengthen climate resilience (Shaheer, 2025). But, the reliance of AI on copious, heterogeneous, data streams, intricate prediction frameworks, and inter-connected networks bring in new vulnerabilities with the aid of which traditional cybersecurity defenses are ill-equipped to rectify. This means that adversarial manipulation can manipulate the algorithmic predictions, thus undermining sustainability decision-making, and because the platforms are an integral part of the national infrastructure, they become high-profile victims of state actors, cybercriminals, and hacktivist organizations. Cases declared in 2025 related to renewable-energy resources and ESG platform demonstrate how the AI integration enlarges the attack-surface manyfolds, digital threats are further compounded by the physical consequences, e. g. grid instability, or the spreading of deceptive environmental effects. Such amplification is caused by the brittle character of AI, dependence on data, and the paradox of the two-sided character of its use: on the one side, it contributes to the shift towards more environmentally friendly operations, but on the other, it increases the vulnerability to exploitative attacks.

The introduction of Artificial Intelligence into the area of sustainability (smart grids and ESG reporting systems) changes the pattern of risks so that the number of cybersecurity threats grows exponentially. Cases of regulatory non-complieance and non-transparent backgrounds of AI decision making dilute the stakeholder trust on the ESG metrics. Ironically, some companies faced with increased cyber threats occasionally take on escalated ESG efforts as one remedy.

### 3.1 AI-Specific Threats: Adversarial Attacks, Deepfakes, and Generative AI Misuse

AI-specific pitfalls are unique threats to the sustainability platforms because model vulnerability to minute perturbations can escalate into major environmental and financial impacts. In adversarial attacks, one injects the input data with an imperceptible noise, like a satellite image or a sensor feed, to trick the models to produce the misleading output (Dutta et al., 2024). As an example, assailants are allowed to alter visuals detected by deforestation-observational algorithms so that they can mask illegal logging or hack smart-grid power-projection models, which in turn leads to unproductive energy distribution and automatic rise in fossil-fuel reliance. Such attacks are possible in operational environmental-monitoring systems, which empirical research in 2024-2025 has demonstrated to be vulnerable to such manipulation of marginally inputnal effects in manner that such manipulation can cause models to accept a running model with unreasonably high certainty.

Deepfakes also serve to compound the threats of ESG investing since they can produce fake executive statements or images of sustainability actions, which may be used to support advanced greenwashing activities. The abuse of generative AI and especially large language models, including misleading ESG reports, inflated carbon offsets, or opportunistic disclosures that are harder to hamper by agencies, are other sources of deception; a study has found that the use of generative-AI increases the opportunism of the ESG in supply chains. Timely inoculation and hijacking of models facilitate the extracted sensitive information or the forced biased results, undermining trust in the AI-based ESG scores. Such misapplications can trigger capital misallocation, regulatory penalties and loss of investor trust in the case of sustainability, any data exfiltration risk by generative models may create serious privacy issues in a system like the GDPR.

## 3.2 Dual-Edged Nature: AI for Green Optimization vs. Increased Attack Surface

The application of AI to sustainability platforms is a classical two-sided process: on the one hand, it is highly effective in the context of green optimization, and, on the other hand, it increases the platform attack surface. On the positive end, AI will work to scale up the forecasting of renewable-energy yields and minimize the amount of waste in supply chains, optimizing predictive maintenance on wind and solar facilities and thus leading to a decrease in emissions and a better use of resources. As an example, articulated by means of AI: smart grids can be used to balance variable renewable generation to reduce curtailment and support the goals of net-zero.

On the other hand, the increased application of AI requires continuous data sources of widely distributed IoT devices, which can be exploited by malicious intrusion on a large scale. The greater the way AI is implemented, including detection of abnormalities, predicting demand, or scoring ESG, the bigger the digital footprint becomes, allowing adversaries to move horizontally. Cases in the logistics or farming platform, where optimization software is built on the interdependence between sensors, demonstrate how achievements of one node may increase incorrect model outputs over an entire decision-making system. According to cybersecurity reports published in 2025, it is possible that AI use in critical industry goals can increase attack surfaces and make them more than 40 times larger, in particular, when generative tools are used, and risks such as an immediate injection, or model poisoning, emerge (Shafik, 2024). Duality such as this requires a secure-by-design framework, in which the advantages of AI to the environment are counterbalanced with strong defensive designs, such that the optimization tools can remain channels of disruptive attacks.

## 3.3 Intersection with Environmental Impacts: Energy Consumption and Carbon Footprint Paradoxes

The combination of AI cybersecurity with environmental effects reveals the naked contradictions in sustainability platforms. Even though AI drives decarbonization by optimizing grids, monitoring emissions, AI has enabled a considerable carbon footprint simply by consuming considerable amounts of energy to train large models: it is estimated that although data-saving centers can have carbon footprint of up to 1.3 per cent of the global electricity as of 2030. Fortifying cybersecurity processes, including AI-based threat detection, perpetual surveillance, and adversarial robustness training, require extra energy, which simultaneously yats to form a hidden climate cost where securing against cyber threats has the countereffect on the increase in emissions.

This Jevons paradoxal effect occurs when the benefits of efficiency are reduced by an increase in demand: improved AI model security mechanisms require more resources, which puts renewable grids under strain which these solutions are meant to sustain. According to the report of 2025, 97 percent of organizations that have AI strategies fail to consider the ecological impact of the technologies, and the cybersecurity activities needed to counter the new advanced attacks contribute to the ecological footprint. The paradox highlights the need of green AI practices, including low-carbon infrastructure, algorithm-efficiency, and policy models to help cybersecurity needs collide with the overarching goal of sustainability so that the same technology intended to conserve the planet could jeopardize its original intended purpose.

## 3.4 Emerging Threats in IIoT and Renewable Energy Infrastructures

The threat of the old in the Industrial Internet of Things (IIoT) and renewable-energy infrastructure is emerging as a result of the decentralized, tightly-connected modern system. Successors of IIoT Smart grids, solar inverters, wind turbines, and battery storage modules have real-time optimization stake IIoT sensors on thousands of deductives at the same time, exposing them to potential exploitation. A 2025 study records how vulnerable the world is to solar deployments with areas of vulnerable inverters that may disrupt the global grids through organized attacks that surpass the reserve capacity (Adel, 2023).

Cases of denial-of-service attacks to communication networks, ransomware of control systems, and control over distributed energy resources (DERs) (i.e. rooftop solar arrays) can all result in cascading failure. Growth in the usage of IoT in a renewable-energy system increases attack vectors and recorded attack instances have increased by four times in utility attacks since 2020. Cybercriminals or state actors may also use weak APIs, third-party access, or legacy access to target and use this weak access point to disrupt supply chains, cause blackouts, or cause environmental damage. Zero-trust architectures, anomaly detection under AI and standardization (i.e., IEC regarding smart grids) would be crucial to mitigate them, but due to the overwhelming rate of change towards digitalization, resilience has become a question of need without standards and current defensive tools.

## 4. LEGAL HURDLES IN ESG INVESTING AMID CYBER-CRIMES

Legal challenges of ESG investing during cybercrimes are attributed to the high rate of automatization of AI to green systems, which poses investors and companies to advanced digital threats when regulation is still in lag. The reasons are cyber incidents, including data breach of ESG analytics tools, model poisoning of sustainability scoring algorithms, or ransomware attacks against renewable energy infrastructures; these misrepresent environmental performance, result in loss of investor belief, and loss of money (Mohammed et al., 2025). These are incidents that lead to liabilities as per the current laws but can be said to be gray because of the emergence of harms like AI. As the annual cost of cybercrime and operational fraud is projected at over 10.5 trillion globally and AI increases the complexity of attacks, ESG investors are at higher risk in 2026: false personal data disclosures by hacked platforms can be classified as securities fraud, and unauthorized access to personal data is the basis of privacy violations. The disintegrated international world makes enforcement difficult since transnational assaults take advantage of jurisdictional inefficiencies. The cybersecurity practice is becoming an aspect of regulation, with regulatory authorities perceiving cybersecurity as part of the governmental system; however, there are regional disparities that cause compliance difficulties. An example is a cyber-attack that distorts ESG ratings, which might lead to incorrect capital allocation in unsustainable activities and the nullification of net-zero ambitions and a lawsuit by shareholders or a regulatory fine. In this intersection major harmonized strategies to share liability, transparent reporting, and incorporation of cyber resilience into ESG due diligence are required to reduce since systemic risks amid sustainable finance are increased by neglecting this aspect.

### 4.1 Fragmented Regulatory Frameworks

The regulatory environment around ESG investing of cyber-crimes is also extremely fragmented, and overlapping but inconsistent sets of rules like the GDPR of the EU, the AI Act, Corporate Sustainability Reporting Directive (CSRD), and the U.S. SEC regulations present major compliance issues. The strict protection of data provided in SGDPR (2016/679) with a fine of up to 4 % of global turnover in case of violation of one-rewarded AI-controlled ESG-driven platforms to process the risks of alienating personal data concerning the supply chain or the profile of investors seems to avoid the protection of personal data in some cases of cross-border scope; contrary, the scope of cross-border ESG AI validation remains undefined, as shown in cross-border context.

Operating since 2025 on a larger business with phase expansions, the CSRD requires detailed ESG reporting, and it requires the governance of cyber risk on sustainability; failure to comply will impose administrative penalties but its implementation alongside the NIS2 Directive disclosures to cyber incidents will be redundant (Pooyandeh et al., 2022). In comparison, rules adopted by the U.S. SEC have been volatile: 2023, then 2025 (under new political regimes) a mandatory reporting of material incidents, timely reporting of material incidents (before and after), but 2020 (after its cancellation) 2025 now defers the issue-wide climate and ESG rules indefinitely, with patchwork alternatives being voluntary reporting (e.g., California SB 253/261). This transatlantic gap increases inhibiting factors, as AI and sustainability requirements are tougher on EU-based organisations, and in the US, interfering extended supervision and less prosecutable but more prone to claims are additional state Attorney General. Fragmentation is a barrier to global ESG investors trying to evaluate cyber-related governance evenly because of the varying materiality levels, timeframes of incident reporting and AI controls, as a result, risk pricing may be inconsistent and may be subject to regulatory arbitrage. Regulatory simplifications, including the establishment of simplification packages in the EU and the request of international aligning standards are still in their early childhood in the year 2026, leaving AI-based green platforms in uncertainty.

## 4.2 Compliance Challenges: Greenwashing, Data Privacy and AI Bias in ESG Assessments

Such issues as compliance troubles in ESG investing against the backdrop of cyber-crimes can focus on greenwashing, breach of data privacy, and bias in AI, which can be facilitated or worsened by cyber-attacks. Greenwashing, which extends sustainability claims, is aggravated by cyber-attacks undermining AI processes, including data poisoning that artificial inflates ESG metrics or fakes a reduction in emissions; other regulatory bodies such as the AI Act and national regulators in countries such as the EU are becoming more critical in anti-fraud measures against such claims, and punishments against misleading reporting only escalate. In 2026, the next threat will be AI-washing, where companies handwave the use of AI in ESG without sufficient safeguards, which companies with connectives can legally be held liable under securities legislation or consumer protection laws.

The central issue of data privacy comes up: AI-enhanced ESG systems process large amounts of data, including anyone information, such as supply chains or stakeholder reports, which makes such a system an easy target of tech breaches. Any leakage occurring due to unauthorized access or insufficient measures to protect it may result in the imposition of fines in the millions of dollars, whereas cyber-facilitated leaks erode confidence in ESG assertions. The obfuscated processing of AI can render compliance complex, where the violations can engage the inferred data, which is difficult to attribute and remove it in accordance with privacy-by-design requirements.

Another layer that exacerbates problems is AI bias: biased training data in ESG scorecards subject to the influence of adversarial cyber manipulations can be an unbiased investment-scorer (e.g. undervalue diverse suppliers), and this results in poor investment decision-making and legal liability under equality laws or under the high-risk prohibitions contained in the EU AI Act. Bias-related forms of cyber-crimes like targeted deepfakes to achieve greenwashing undermine the integrity of assessment. Mitigation is a challenge to firms: explainable AI, continuous auditing, and third party validations are costly resources, but critical to prevent litigation (e.g. shareholder litigations over materialized risks) or regulatory measures.

## 4.3 Cybersecurity as a Governance Metric in ESG Standards

With its direct effect on long-term value, risk management and trustworthiness to stakeholders in a time of increasing cyber threats to AI-enabled green platforms, cybersecurity has become cemented in the list of critical governance metrics in both ESG frameworks, SASB (now under ISSB) and GRI (Vadisetty, 2022). Such industry-specific financially material SASB Standards, including Systemic Risk Management and Business Ethics, focus on cybersecurity, and disclosures on data security, incident response, and third-party risks are required in the sector category, such as Technology and Communications or Renewables. By 2026, when the vulnerability of AI becomes more pronounced, SASB-consistent reporting will more often demand measures of cyber resilience, such as the number of breaches, the recovery time, and the supervision of the board regarding AI-related vulnerabilities, as part of the overall ISSB standardisation of sustainability disclosures.

GRI Standards are much more impact-oriented, with the GRI 418 (Customer Privacy) and sector-specific additional disclosures reflecting the role of cybersecurity in ensuring the safety of stakeholder data, and avoiding operation disruptions that may negatively affect environmental or social outcomes. GRI 2 (General Disclosures) indirectly reflects the notion of cyber governance in the form of ethical behaviours and risk management principles, prompting organisations to disclose the impacts of cyber incidences on the sustainability performance. News until 2025 -2026 is more about linking with frameworks (including TCFD on climate-cyber intersections and CSRD on mandatory reporting).

This development makes cybersecurity one of the key G pillars: its inadequacy reveals inept governance practices, which may cause a reduction in corporate ESG ratings and the retreat of investments. Regulators, rating agencies, and other interested investors would require documentation of proactive activities, zero-trust designs, and simulating incidents as failures in governance due to breaches may spread into reputational losses, regulatory fines, and depleted credibility of sustainability (Aslan et al., 2023). Within the context of ESG, so strong cyber governance can reduce risks caused by differently magnified threats when using AI and can make sure that genuine green transitions have transparent and resilient platforms that facilitate them, as opposed to subjecting them to exploitation.

## 5. CONCLUSION AND PATHWAYS TO RESILIENT ESG INVESTING IN AN AI-DOMINATED ERA

Artificial intelligence has found its way into all aspects of sustainability in modern studies, and the combination of AI-powered green solutions with the emerging ESG investing has created opportunities to manage the planet as never before, at the same time presenting systemic risks to cyber-crimes that could reverse a century of environmental gains. The above discussion shows how adversarial attacks, model poisoning, deepfakes and ransomware can turn carbon accounting, ESG ratings, and renewable energy infrastructure destabilised and accelerate demoralization of investors, when legal frameworks are inconsistent, prosecution has limited attribution problems, and financial losses are measured in trillions. The risks can no longer be considered peripheral, having moved since the dual-sided nature of AI, which aims to optimise wind farms and smart grids on the one hand and broadens the areas of attack, on the other, the carbon paradox of cybersecurity itself. Greenwashing on steroids, data privacy violations under GDPR and CSRD, biased algorithms in ESG rating, and the promotion of cybersecurity as a key measure in SASB and GRI standards are all indications that the G in ESG now needs to denote sustainable digital resiliency in an absolutely implausible manner as to renders the whole framework significant. However, it is equally at this point of intersection that a historic inflection point may occur: the technological forces driving these threats can be turned to build strong channels that drive ahead, so long as stakeholders are swift, consistent, and innovative.

The ways forward to strong ESG investing are first to implement, in the architecture of all AI-driven green systems, a cybersecurity-by-design approach. The developers should embrace the use of zero-trust frameworks, homomorphic encryption of sensitive ESG data, differential privacy of training models, and continuous adversarial robustness testing as essential issues, and not as side considerations. Low-precision inference, edge computing, and renewable-powered data centres represent the initiatives of Green AI and will help considerably lower the environmental footprint of defensive operations and break the carbon paradox by making sure that sustainability protection does not hurt sustainability. The investors and rating agencies must require a standardised, machine-read cyber-resilience disclosure in line with the ISSB,

CSRD, and the increasingly dynamic SEC regulations on the subject, with the same weight given to cyber maturity scores as with Scope 3 emissions. The insurance markets will also swiftly develop: parametric cyber insurances tied to real-time AI risks detection, blockchain-confirmed incident reporting will be able to transfer the risk effectively and reward platforms with verifiable resilient thresholds, reducing the capital costs of genuinely sustainable projects.

The second pre-eminent route is regulatory harmonisation. The AI Act, NIS2 and CSRD of the EU should be aligned with the state-level AI-related climate and cyber regulation in the U.S., and the upcoming Global Digital Compact, along with the recommended revisions of the Budapest Convention on Cybercrime will provide the means of binding the internationally recognized rules of attributing crimes, admissibility of evidence, and intercountry prosecution of AI-enhanced environmental cyber-crimes. Specific digital fundamental control within the UNFCCC or ISSB might exist whereby any system holding an AI system rating ESG factors should be subjected to a third-party conforming measure on both environmental effects and cybersecurity, and require this third-party conformity measure to make evident internal disclosures within 24 hours and publicly publish post-breaches. It needs to reinforce prosecutorial capacity by establishing specialised cyber-environmental task forces, common sets of forensically essential tools, and shared legal assistance protocols in recognising that state perpetuated assaults upon renewable infrastructure should be classified as potential crimes against humanity when they prevent or face any action to mitigate climate in any material way.

At the organisational level, boards should include cyber risk in ESG oversight committees, where chief sustainability officers and chief information security officers report to the board on indicators of artificial intelligence such as the mean-time-to-detect AI poisoning, smart-grid recovery time goals, and board-verified percentage of ESG data reported on the basis of tamper-proof ledgers. Technology, climate science Fields such as AI ethics and cybersecurity will also be essential and need to be repackaged as reskilling programmes within universities and professional bodies to deliver the hybrid expertise that the market already requires. The green technology supply chains should be influenced by what has been suggested in the U.S. Joint Cyber Defence Collaborative or the EU pilot in the Cyber Resilience Act, to create public-private partnerships, which would share threat intelligence in real-time in solar, wind, battery, and precision-agriculture vendors.

Transformative power is in the hands of investors themselves. Portfolio company holders and managers could implement AI-enhanced due diligence that scans their portfolio companies not only in the number of traditional ESG metrics but the index of cyber exposure, the index of supply-chain attack, and the presence of secure multi-party-computation in the carbon accounting. Passive ESG index providers need to include compulsory cyber-resilience filters, and active managers have the opportunity to construct Resilient Green Alpha and overweight platforms that have quantum-resistant encryption, formal verification of the AI models, and joint exercises with red-teams simulating a cyber-attack on the country-state by a renewable grid. Venture capital and private equity can enhance the process of innovation by financing start-ups at the cross of AI security, green technology, and blockchain, such as decentralised identity to ESG data provenance or decentralised self-healing industrial control systems, and thereby directing capital towards solutions instead of mitigating downside.

With the future, it can anticipate new trends. The explainable AI and causal inference techniques will become more resistant to manipulation, federated learning will become practicable to train the models together and not reveal proprietary sustainable information, and digital twins of whole renewable energy systems will be possible to pre-emptively learn how to plan cyberattacks. There still exist research gaps, most notably a quantification of the financial materiality of AI-specific threats to Scope 3 emissions and generating universal measures of what is commonly termed cybers environmental resilience, but the academic and policy communities are on the move. The coming decade is likely to define AI as the largest driver of the green transition or the most significant deliberator.

The ability to invest in resilient ESG in the age of AI is not a solution or regulatory box, but a fundamental rethinking of the fiduciary responsibility. Trustees, fund managers, and corporate directors should place in mind that not taking good duty care to guard the digital archest of sustainability is equally a serious breach of duty as is not making regard to climate risk. With technological innovation and regulatory coherence orchestrated, everyone can witness the delivery of the promise of the AI-driven green platforms fulfilled, not frustrated, by organisational maturity, investor discipline, and a dependable financial system, worthy of the planetary challenge we are on. The way is obvious: the new sustainability is the resilience.

## REFERENCES


Adel, A. (2023). Unlocking the future: Fostering human–machine collaboration and driving intelligent automation through industry 5.0 in smart cities. *Smart Cities*, *6*(5), 2742–2782. DOI: 10.3390/smartcities6050124

Aslan, O., Aktug, S. S., Ozkan-Okay, M., Yilmaz, A. A., & Akin, E. (2023). A comprehensive review of cyber security vulnerabilities, threats, attacks, and solutions. *Electronics (Basel)*, *12*(6), 1333. DOI: 10.3390/electronics12061333

Do, T. H., & Selvadurai, N. (2025). Future Crime: A Theoretical Foundation for Designing Effective Cybercrime Laws in the Age of AI and Ransomware. *NCJL & Tech.*, *27*, 91.

Dutta, P. K., Raj, P., Sundaravadivazhagan, B., & Selvan, C. P. (Eds.). (2024). *Artificial Intelligence Solutions for Cyber-Physical Systems*. Auerbach. DOI: 10.1201/9781032694375

Mohammed, U. M., Omolara, A. E., Abiodun, O. I., Rasheed, J., Osman, O., Lar, P. M., Adeyinka, P. O., & Olugbenga, A. G. (2025). Cyber threat in drone systems: Bridging real-time security, legal admissibility, and digital forensic solution readiness. *Frontiers in Communications and Networks*, *6*, 1661928. DOI: 10.3389/frcmn.2025.1661928


Mohammed, U. M., Omolara, A. E., Abiodun, O. I., Rasheed, J., Osman, O., Lar, P. M., Adeyinka, P. O., & Olugbenga, A. G. (2025). Cyber threat in drone systems: Bridging real-time security, legal admissibility, and digital forensic solution readiness. *Frontiers in Communications and Networks*, *6*, 1661928. DOI: 10.3389/frcmn.2025.1661928


Ndibe, O. S. (2025). AI-driven forensic systems for real-time anomaly detection and threat mitigation in cybersecurity infrastructures. *International journal of research publication and reviews, 6*(5), 389-411.

Pooyandeh, M., Han, K. J., & Sohn, I. (2022). Cybersecurity in the AI-Based metaverse: A survey. *Applied Sciences (Basel, Switzerland)*, *12*(24), 12993. DOI: 10.3390/app122412993

Rajavel, N. (2024). The Impact of Al on Elderly Inmates in. *Exploration of AI in Contemporary Legal Systems*, 281.

Shafik, W. (2024). Incorporating Artificial Intelligence for Urban and Smart Cities' Sustainability. In *Maintaining a Sustainable World in the Nexus of Environmental Science and AI* (pp. 23-58). IGI Global.

Shaheer, B. (2025). The Role of Predictive Analytics and Artificial Intelligence in Cybersecurity. In *Symbiotic Intelligence* (pp. 50–69). CRC Press. DOI: 10.1201/9781003540373-3

Sokhansanj, B. (2025). AI Goes Off the Grid: The Rise of Local AI Demands Rethinking AI Governance. *Available at SSRN* 5284453.

Syed, S. A. (2022). Ai-powered cybercrime: The new frontier of digital threats. [IJETRM]. *International Journal of Engineering Technology Research & Management*, *6*(02).

Vadisetty, R. (2022). AI in Cloud Powered Legal Compliance as a Service (LCaaS). *International Journal of Advanced Engineering Technologies and Innovations*, *1*(2), 286–319.

# Chapter 16
# Corporate Governance Law and ESG Technology With Legal Frameworks:
## Board Oversight of Artificial Intelligence in Sustainability Strategy and Risk Management

**Pradip Kumar Kashyap**
http://orcid.org/0009-0007-8156-2767
*CGC University, Mohali, India*

**Nirbhay Kumar Sharma**
*Raffles University, India*

**Namrata Yadav**
*Raffles University, India*

## ABSTRACT

*Corporate responsibility is evolving as a result of the convergence of AI, ESG technologies, and corporate governance regulations. Corporate boards face increasing pressure to connect governance frameworks with ESG metrics and digital ethics as sustainability turns into a strategic need rather than a luxury. In order to ensure that accountability doesn't lag behind innovation, boards must also closely monitor the use of AI in risk management and sustainability strategy. Therefore, corporate governance rules specify how responsibilities, adherence to regulations, and technological upkeep should cooperate. This chapter examines how various departments*

DOI: 10.4018/979-8-2600-1308-3.ch016

*of law must respond to the complex link between the governance and AI-enabled ESG systems. This is a result of the emphasis on data governance, transparency and lowering ethical risks.*

## 1. INTRODUCTION

The directors are required to act in the best interests of the company and all of its stakeholders as part of their fiduciary obligations, which include a duty of care and loyalty. Laws pertaining to corporate governance are based on these responsibilities. But for a while now, the term "stakeholders" has been used to refer to more than simply stockholders. Customers, staff, the community, and the environment are also included (Maghami, 2024). Sustainability initiatives, carbon duty, and ethical digital transformation are more than just polite words in the ESG-driven age of corporate governance. Among the earliest regulations for ESG reporting were the EU Corporate Sustainability Reporting Directive (CSRD), the Task Force on Climate-related Financial Disclosures (TCFD), and the International Sustainability Standards Board (ISSB). These have raised the bar for what businesses must undertake to inform the public about their activities. With the aid of AI, the management board must now monitor data-driven sustainability outcomes in addition to financial ones (Mirishli, 2025). The next development in corporate power and legal governance is ESG research driven by artificial intelligence. It assists businesses in abiding with the law and maintaining an advantage over rivals.

AI is being used by businesses to modify the way they track and report on ESG performance. Using sophisticated analytics, machine learning, and predictive modeling, AI may sift through vast volumes of data and identify recurring patterns, such as concerns about sustainability or increases in carbon emissions, or patterns related to social effect (Domingo, 2025). Technology advancements have made ESG intelligence systems accessible. In addition to discussing sustainability, these online forums will leverage blockchain validation, internet of things sensors, and algorithmic forecasts to determine the level of risk. Although AI increases our accuracy and efficiency, it also poses new hazards. It may be more difficult to adhere to ethical standards and expose the company to regulatory liability if AI algorithmic bias, imprecise decision-making, and data privacy violations occur (Rane et al., 2024). In order to include AI ethics into ESG legislation and encourage responsible innovation that complies with data protection, environmental sustainability, and human rights norms, corporate governance law must change (Li, 2025).

The board must closely monitor the use of AI in sustainability initiatives. When considering the hazards that emerging technology may provide, directors are required by corporate governance rules to use caution, loyalty, and honesty (Kalkan, 2024).

Definitional frameworks will be established by an AI Governance Committee or a sub-board that focuses on data ethics, compliance, and sustainability plan (Verma & Jana, 2024). For example, the company Governance Code of the UK Financial Reporting Council (FRC) has placed a strong emphasis on the need for directors to be knowledgeable about AI and technology, which has an effect on company culture and risk management (Samara et al., 2025).

## 1.1 Conceptual Foundations of Corporate Governance

A risk-based categorization system for AI systems is established under the EU's AI Act (2024), which also mandates transparency, human supervision, and auditability (Akinsola, 2025). All of these ideas have a direct bearing on ESG-relevant applications of AI, such supply chain tracking and environmental monitoring. By mandating businesses to disclose AI used for sustainability analytics, risk assessments, or governance decision making, the Securities and Exchange Commission (SEC) in the US has also increased investor interest and management control. In Asia, Singapore and Japan have also established AI governance frameworks to ensure that business compliance strategies include ethical design principles (Sulkowski, 2024). Many people feel that the rules of corporate governance can and should be changed to address the ethical and practical issues raised by AI technologies, particularly those employed for ESG.

## 1.2 Evolution of Environmental, Social and Governance (ESG) Criteria

Although AI-powered ESG technology is a revolutionary development, it is unable to fully handle the intricacies of legal risk management. Algorithmic accountability, or determining who is at fault when AI algorithms provide biased or incorrect ESG findings, is among the most crucial factors. For example, developers and business personnel may be held legally liable if an AI system that is too dependent on misclassifies environmental concerns, resulting in corporate misreporting or environmental harm. Due diligence procedures, impact analyses, and third-party audits of AI systems that evaluate ESG should thus be a part of governance systems (Camilleri, 2024). Given the sensitivity of the data pertaining to sustainability and stakeholder value, data privacy and cybersecurity are equally crucial for ESG compliance (Lee et al., 2025).

## 1.3 Amalgamation of Artificial Intelligence in Corporate Decision-Making

AI integration with ESG necessitates a shift in governance from a reactive to a proactive and moral approach. Additionally, boards must continue to monitor new legal and technological developments in addition to risk. This implies that ethical AI charters, algorithmic transparency regulations, and sustainable KPIs must all be part of the company's operational guidelines. These days, several businesses include their AI ethical standards in their ESG reports. As a result, they answer to investors as well as authorities (Kazachenok et al., 2023). Microsoft's "Responsible AI Standard" and IBM's "AI Ethics Board" are two instances of how businesses have established board-level governance for their AI operations. These frameworks would foster confidence among all stakeholders and enable the long-term implications of AI systems to occur in a lawful manner (Sklavos et al., 2024).

# 2. LEGAL AND REGULATORY DIMENSIONS OF CORPORATE GOVERNANCE IN THE ESG ERA

Corporate governance's expansion throughout the Environmental, Social, and Governance (ESG) era Since businesses must now exchange information and abide by the law, the evolution of corporate governance under ESG may be seen as a shift in how business is conducted (Shen, 2022). Corporate governance used to primarily focus on ensuring that companies were truthful and that their legal obligations to shareholders were fulfilled. However, the legal framework for ESG demands has grown as a result of global commitments to sustainable objectives, speedier technology, and shareholder unhappiness. There are other aspects of corporate governance outside the financial system. Sustainability performance, ethical responsibility, and long-term environmental stewardship are also included (Salamzadeh et al., 2025). The legal and regulatory ramifications of this shift have become more complex in a world where governments, supranational organizations, corporations, and investors want more transparency, data-driven reporting, and responsible risk management in accordance with ESG objectives.

As more individuals become aware that corporations are social beings with responsibilities beyond maximizing profits, corporate governance regulations have been evolving (Li et al., 2025). In the past, directors had fiduciary obligations that included things like good faith, loyalty, and duty of care. They now have to consider the hazards and long-term repercussions as well. Strategic planning, risk management, and disclosure should all include ESG concerns, and boards should treat ESG risks in the same manner that they do other business risks. How long has the topic of green reporting been discussed? Section 172 of the Companies Act 2006 (UK) requires directors to consider the long-term effects of their choices on the environment, the community, and their relationships with workers and other stakeholders in the community (Chien et al., 2025).

These legal reforms demonstrate that ethical and sustainable conduct is now mandated by law and is an integral aspect of corporate governance and accountability; it is no longer a choice (Metin, 2024). There is little question that sustainable governance is evolving, as witnessed in the legal and regulatory elements of corporate governance in the era of ESG. ones of corporate law that emphasize shareholders are giving way to ones that take social justice, environmental sustainability, and government responsibility into consideration as shared in figure 1(Wang et al., 2025).

*Figure 1. specifies the Legal and Regulatory Dimensions of Corporate Governance in the ESG Era*

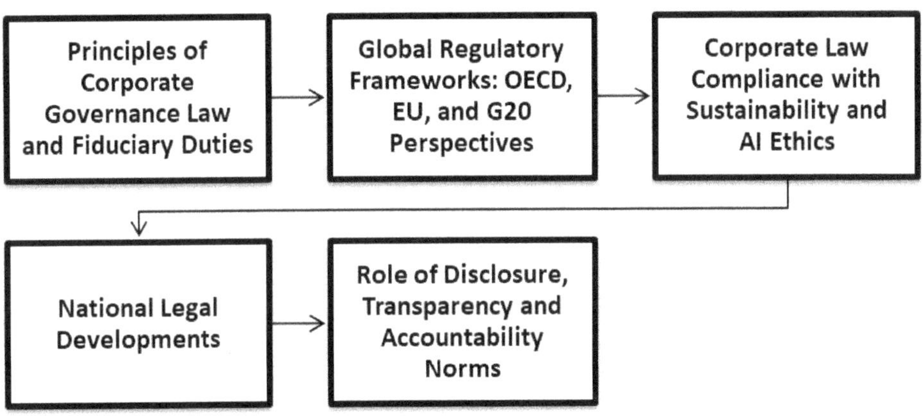


*(prepared by author(s))*

## 2.1 Principles of Corporate Governance Law and Fiduciary Duties

various ESG laws are used by various countries to regulate company behavior. Accountability, openness, and equity for all stakeholders are highly valued in the Principles of Corporate Governance of the Organization for Economic Cooperation and Development. These items are similar to ESG. The UNGPs also emphasize how crucial it is that companies take action to prevent and correct violations of human rights. The US SEC, for example, has taken action to restrict the dissemination of ESG data (Chen, 2024). The Sustainability and Climate Risk index looks like this.

Businesses are increasingly required to explain how environmental concerns impact their business strategy and financial results. India's Business Responsibility & Sustainability Report (BRSR) structure has also been adopted by nations in the Asia-Pacific area, including Singapore, Japan, and India. This fits within a broader pattern. Companies listed in India are required to provide non-financial information regarding their financial performance in accordance with the SEBI (Listing Obligations and Disclosure Requirements) Regulations for India (Kolsepatil, 2022). It turns ESG governance into a legislative mandate and makes ESG reporting required rather than optional (Hao & Demir, 2024).

## 2.2 Global Regulatory Frameworks: OECD, EU, and G20 Perspectives

These methods also promote market discipline and the quantitative evaluation of sustainability performance. Systemic approaches are necessary for governance to align with sustainable development, as stipulated by ISO 37000:2021 on Governance of Organizations and ISO 14097 on Climate Finance (Ahdadou et al., 2025). Although these criteria are not legally binding, they significantly influence the attitudes of investors, business practices, and governmental decision-making on ESG governance.

## 2.3 Corporate Law Compliance with Sustainability and AI Ethics

Innovations in technology ESG regulations are becoming more tech-friendly as technology advances, particularly in the areas of AI and digital reporting. There are benefits and drawbacks to AI ESG monitoring. Businesses may examine a lot of data to monitor social effect, monitor the supplier chain, and assess their environmental performance using AI-powered ESG analytics. They also pose challenges for the law in terms of prejudice, algorithmic transparency, and data privacy, however (Saxena et al., 2022). High-risk AIs are subject to restrictions under the EU's AI Act (2024). These AIs need to be as transparent, intelligible, and controllable by humans as feasible. The usage of ESG products is therefore governed by regulations. Corporate governance regulations must be sufficiently adaptable to enable digital governance to coexist with sustainability if AI systems employed for ESG objectives are to adhere to legal and ethical requirements.

## 2.4 National Legal Developments: Comparative Jurisdictional Analysis

The most significant shifts in the ESG period The propensity to govern due diligence is one of the most significant shifts we see in an increasing number of new sites (Zhang & Yang, 2024). Businesses would be required under the proposed EU Corporate Sustainability Due Diligence Directive (CSDDD) to identify, prevent, and mitigate any negative environmental and human rights impacts that occur in their supply chains. Corporate governance is becoming more advanced as a result of this legal reform. At this point, our company's ideals begin to include sustainability and culture (Balboni & Francis, 2025). Similar tendencies are also seen in Canada's Fighting Against Forced Labour and Child Labour in Supply Chains Act (2024), Germany's Supply Chain Due Diligence Act (2021), and France's Loi de Vigilance (2017). The world is heading toward mandatory ESG responsibility, as seen by all of these legislation.

## 2.5 Role of Disclosure, Transparency and Accountability Norms

However, there are still issues in standardizing ESG governance across jurisdictions. Because there are no precise words or methods for enforcing them, there is a gap in compliance. Additionally, it is still challenging for governance to strike a balance between immediate financial concerns and investors' expectations of ESG performance (Taleb & Kadhum, 2024). Modify the regulations governing directors' accountability for ESG shortcomings Since it is sometimes difficult, if not impossible, to demonstrate that a company's activities caused environmental or social damage, there is also rising dispute on the extent of legal responsibility directors have for ESG failures. This must be resolved by the implementing global ESG standards, which are backed by organizations such as the International Organization of Securities Commissions (IOSCO), the World Bank, and the United Nations.

# 3. ESG TECHNOLOGY AND ARTIFICIAL INTELLIGENCE: TRANSFORMING GOVERNANCE PARADIGMS

Businesses can now measure, monitor, and report on their social and environmental performance because of a trillion-dollar technology revolution. These technological developments not only improve things but also alter how businesses are operated.

Every choice is founded on moral duty, transparency, and data intelligence (Chen & Zhang, 2025).

In the ESG domain, AI is both disruptive and controlled. Machine learning enables AK to detect environmental concerns, market dangers, or physical boundaries brought on by compliance issues much more quickly than conventional soft information systems (Gupta & Agarwal, 2024). An AI-driven ESG analytics solution may look at things like water waste, carbon emissions, and supply chain sustainability in real time. The boards would then be equipped with the data they need to make decisions. In order to identify potential governance risks or issues with sustainability reporting, you may also use natural language processing and predictive modeling to search through a large number of financial and regulatory documents. These developments reveal a lot about the emergence of a new paradigm: corporate governance is no longer about having people watch over things, but rather about employing smart technology to monitor things constantly and hold individuals responsible for their actions.

It connects you to AI in the ESG ecosystem and examines and validates business disclosures. Blockchain for ESG Blockchain could securely manage sustainability-related transactions, such as investments in renewable energy or carbon credits, and ESG systems may provide investors and regulators with unchangeable audit trails. By using technology that made things more transparent, the government might be more truthful and win over the hearts of its people. By leveraging the Internet of Things (IoT) to monitor real-time data regarding emissions or resource consumption, businesses may now claim to be both environmentally friendly and highly efficient (Akbar, 2024). The Blockchain, the Internet of Things, and artificial intelligence will be our primary navigational aids as we embark on the digital future. Hardware for ESG governance includes blockchain, IoT, and AI. This method removes something from the category of ambition by making it quantifiable even though it cannot be imposed or maintained.

## 3.1 ESG Technology and Digital Sustainability Tools: AI in ESG Data Analytics, Monitoring and Reporting

Additionally, new ESG technologies create ethical dilemmas and make governance more difficult. Bias, privacy, and accountability issues arise when AI is employed to assist with ESG decision-making. If the data used to train AI is skewed, it might provide false ESG scores that deceive investors and governments. This makes maintaining the proper vector of motion challenging (Kuznetsova et al., 2024). Many regulatory ideas call for more transparent and human-centered AI governance to address these dangers and issues. Examples include the European Union's AI Act (2024) and the OECD's Principles for Artificial Intelligence (current). Although equidency transparency and human monitoring are not the same, company boards should attempt to develop some recommendations for the usage and use of ESG technology.

### 3.2 Blockchain and IoT in Sustainable Governance Systems

ESG strategy should include AI governance. While making sure you abide by the law and act morally, you may support innovative ideas (Işık et al., 2025). This combination will influence corporate governance in the future as businesses become more robust, transparent, and sustainable. ESG technology will be used to remain in compliance and to differentiate oneself from the competition. In addition to altering government operations, AI and ESG technologies are also altering what it means for companies to be accountable in an information-driven society (Svitlak & Huts, 2022).

## 4. BOARD OVERSIGHT AND ACCOUNTABILITY: GOVERNANCE STRUCTURES FOR AI-DRIVEN SUSTAINABILITY

The early adopters of AI and ESG initiatives were well-represented by boards that taught them how to meet tomorrow, again today, in a world where technology, sustainability, and the digital revolution in business move at a dizzying speed. Authors and remarks Leave Writers a Comment There are other factors than board oversight that govern budgets. It also entails managing technology ethically, taking responsibility for risk, and performing in a sustainable manner. By examining a company's carbon footprint or making it simpler to monitor the origins and destinations of items, artificial intelligence (AI) may assist businesses in becoming more transparent and accountable. These new technical tools also carry operational, ethical, and legal hazards that can only be controlled by stringent control procedures (Gouiaa & Huang, 2024). The most crucial element of using AI in a manner that maintains stakeholders' confidence and creates long-term value while also being consistent with the company's objectives, sustainability values, and legal obligations is effective board supervision.

The duty of care, loyalty, and good faith principles are all part of the conventional common law of corporate governance, which is where those special obligations originate. These ideas have been broadened to include risk management for sustainability and technology (Rehman & Umar, 2025). If authorized, there would be more follow-up directors for the TCFD (Task Force on Climate-related Financial Disclosures) AIs used by businesses to assess their environmental performance and look for climate hazards. These directors would be required to adhere to global ESG reporting guidelines, such as the EU's AI Act and the General Data Protection

Regulation (GDPR). In addition to having to supervise it, the board has a moral and legal need to ensure that AI technology used in sustainability contexts is transparent, intelligible, and compliant with both US and international law (Ozkan, 2024).

Good governance will need to be included into the supervision of AI. AI and Sustainability Committees are being added to the boards of several firms to ensure that DT initiatives that serve ESG objectives get further attention. These committees often include of directors and outside specialists with experience in technology, sustainability, and ethics. This will also include hiring people for positions such as examiners to look at the social and environmental implications and auditors to check on how AI systems are being utilized in a firm. These assessors will ensure that these AI applications align with the organization's long-term sustainability plan (Xiao & Xiao, 2025). Boards are better able to identify issues early, address them, and adhere to stringent AI and ESG regulations thanks to these governance measures.

All stakeholders must be transparent and involved for AI-based sustainable governance to succeed. Filters must ensure that companies are transparently and honestly communicating with the public, investors, and regulators about their use of AI systems with ESG. This would also include developing concepts for how AI may impact risk management, sustainability reporting, and decision-making. Although being transparent and honest is mandated by law, businesses also understand that it benefits their bottom line by increasing their public appeal (Zhao & Gómez Fariñas, 2023). For example, companies must disclose the digital tools and techniques they use to evaluate and analyze sustainability data in accordance with the EU Corporate Sustainability Reporting Directive (CSRD) (Pashang & Weber, 2023). By requiring businesses to adhere to societal standards on the moral use of technology, these regulations hold them responsible. Boards are under pressure to normalize openness in governance.

However, using AI to monitor sustainability is still challenging. Because AI is difficult to describe and comprehend, and because regulations might vary depending on the location, this field is more difficult for boards to oversee. Because of ethical concerns about algorithmic transparency, intellectual property, and data ownership, the accountability elements are far more complex. Boards must develop AI accountability frameworks in collaboration with independent auditors, ethicists, regulators, and civil society in order to face this issue. Although AI is currently used for social, commercial, and environmental purposes all of which it obviously ought to be its development is slowed by this multi-stakeholder approach. In the era of AI-led sustainability, board responsibility and monitoring are new components of corporate governance (Herath & Herath, 2024). The impact of AI on sustainable development will ultimately rely on how effectively technology functions as well as how well boards oversee its usage to ensure responsible use.

## 4.1 Board Competence and AI Literacy in Strategic Decision-Making

Across all the frameworks, the three aspects that are most closely connected are accountability (understanding why outcomes were unsatisfactory), transparency (being able to explain AI judgments), and ensuring that algorithms do not treat humans unjustly. Directors must be prepared to demonstrate that those frameworks have been fulfilled, whether via a certification process, an audit, or an external review. They are safeguarding their company's image and ensuring that investors can rely on AI-enhanced ESG reporting by doing this. Capacity and competence are also critical factors for AI-driven sustainability boards. Additionally, given the rapid evolution of AI and ESG regulations, directors should become more knowledgeable about digital business ethics, including the latest sustainability reporting requirements and data use best practices. With further training, seminars, and time spent meeting with colleges, regulators, and other teams, the board may be able to better clarify duties. Many businesses are already in favor of having board members that understand artificial intelligence (Müller et al., 2025). . The advantages and disadvantages of the technology are carefully considered before deciding how to apply AI in this sound governance approach. In terms of innovation governance, this kind of activity may also assist boards in becoming more proactive rather than reactive.

# 5. LEGAL RISK MANAGEMENT AND COMPLIANCE MECHANISMS

In order for AI-driven sustainability projects to comply with Environmental, Social, and Governance (ESG) requirements, legal risk management and compliance techniques are becoming more and more crucial as corporate governance changes. Businesses may face lawsuits for data governance, privacy, cybersecurity, algorithmic accountability, or regulatory compliance as they increasingly deploy AI to assist them achieve their sustainability objectives. By combining techno-ethics and corporate social responsibility with proactive and organized industry interaction, legal challenges may be managed successfully (Lin et al., 2024). Boards of directors want compliance tools to ensure that companies adhere to national and international ESG best practices and codes of ethics as the global economy becomes increasingly interconnected.

Many legal concerns, like as privacy, environmental regulation, workers' rights, and financial transparency, are raised by AI in ESG governance. According to the General Data Protection Regulation of the EU, personal data cannot be used again. AI systems that rely on social or environmental data are affected. High-risk AI systems must also remain open, be supervised by humans, and be accessible as soon as they are released, according to the EU's future AI Act (2024). This is much more crucial when it comes to ESG reporting and monitoring sustainability. You risk severe legal and reputational repercussions, including penalties from authorities and a decline in stakeholder confidence, if you disregard these guidelines. They will need to put in place robust compliance procedures to identify, assess, and address any potential unlawful issues in their companies. An AI ethical committee, due diligence, and internal checks should all be a part of these systems.

Corporate governance frameworks are being updated with AI compliance charters and codes of ethics to hold companies more accountable. The internal guidelines make it quite evident that when using AI, fairness, explainability, and nondiscrimination are crucial. Impact assessments are also often used by businesses in their algorithms. Thorough and structured analyses of ethical, legal, and societal problems are examined before to implementing AI systems GROUND. "Making it easier to see upcoming alert cases will help boards find possible legal problems before they happen instead of after they happen" (Malukani et al., 2024). We can get a better understanding of the relationship between legal risk and ESG by integrating AI risk management technologies into ERM. Regular compliance training is essential for business executives. This would support the development of an ethical corporate governance culture throughout the whole organization, in conjunction with third-party audits. These requirements must be met in order to prevent individuals from altering it or getting into it. ESG analytics may become less trustworthy and result in investor disinformation, company greenwashing, or penalties from the government if AI model data governance is inadequate, such as if it uses inaccurate or biased datasets.

## 6. GLOBAL ESG AND AI GOVERNANCE FRAMEWORKS: CHALLENGES AND OPPORTUNITIES

The path towards integrated AI-ESG governance is fraught with difficulties. The definitions of ESG transparency, AI accountability, and corporate responsibility vary between those who do not adhere to the same international norms. This obscures compliance. Even in sustainable domains, if left to their own devices, the norms governing AI governance will not be adhered to in "developing" regions where regulations are few. Multilateral involvement should be used to establish a global AI governance framework in order to solve these issues (Patil et al., 2024).

Through its Environmental & Social Framework (ESF) or e-governance initiatives, the World Bank, a worldwide development bank, encourages the use of AI and ESG. It offers AI-powered solutions for sustainability, including managing transportation networks in developing nations, constructing green infrastructure, and predicting climate risk. This is accomplished by providing funding, information, and policy recommendations. In order to foster inclusive and ecologically sustainable technology, the World Bank seeks to link ESG criteria with the advancement of digital innovation. By allowing our members to apply their extensive technical knowledge in conjunction with the system and process skills they need to advance, ISO makes this feasible with authorization to reprint. ISO 42001 (AI management system), ISO 37000 (organizational governance), and ISO 26000 (social responsibility) are examples of management and governance standards that businesses can use to implement ESG-AI best practices. An worldwide framework for AI ethics and corporate social responsibility is being established by the UN, World Bank, and ISO. In this sense, modifications to some systems really contribute to the world's equitable, transparent, and sustainable development.

The board of directors of the firm has to take on the obligation of making sure that the business is obeying the law. In this sense, boardrooms resemble large AI risk dashboards. These are data-driven solutions that monitor sustainability KPIs, AI performance indicators, and ESG compliance in real time. These virtual governance tools enable directors to make data-driven choices that support the organization's larger sustainability objectives. Having board members from a range of disciplines, including data science, environmental law, and tech ethics, is intended to improve decision-making and hold individuals more responsible. Corporate boards become catalysts for the adoption of socially beneficial technologies as a result of these governance improvements.

## 6.1 Role of United Nations, World Bank, and ISO in Global ESG-AI Standards

International AI and ESG standards are primarily driven by the International Organization for Standardization (ISO) and major stakeholders in international organizations such as the United Nations (UN) and the World Bank. They act as normative guidelines that make it easier to develop trustworthy and moral AI solutions that meet ESG objectives. By establishing the UN Global Compact and the UN Sustainable Development Goals (SDGs), the UN has also supported these sorts of collaborations. The UNESCO Recommendation on the Ethics of Artificial Intelligence (2021) benefited from its assistance more recently. These organizations advocate for governments and corporations to include ethical technology usage into their sustainability and governance agendas. This has an impact on governments that plan ahead, companies who care about the environment and society, and AI that values humans. By using digital sustainability initiatives that support social cohesion, sustainable production, or climate action, the UN Environment Programme (UNEP) hopes to advance AI innovation with an ESG emphasis.

## 7. CONCLUSIONS AND FUTURE PROSPECTS

The need for dynamic legal and ethical monitoring at the board level is highlighted by the intersection of corporate governance legislation, ESG technologies, and artificial intelligence. AI has the potential to significantly enhance sustainability reporting, risk identification, and operational efficiency. Inadequate implementation and weak governance may exacerbate environmental harm, prejudice, and inequality. "Board members are obligated by law and morality to assist businesses in using AI in a manner consistent with ESG principles. By enhancing responsibilities of care and loyalty, raising AI knowledge, and integrating compliance into daily life, corporate governance may assist in transforming AI from a risk into a sustainable asset. Moral leadership that upholds morality, ethics, and technology as vital elements of overall governance as opposed to just future corporate governance is what is meant by the rule of law. And in a world where the digital economy is always evolving, this is what responsible innovation looks like.

From a legal policy perspective, a mix of hard law such as rules and regulations and soft law such as standards, codes of conduct, and principles would govern AI in ESG. Lawmakers must enact legislation that alters the ratio of morality to inventiveness. Two excellent models for influencing companies to refrain from unethical behavior in the digital era are the EU Digital Governance Act and the UN Guiding Principles on Business and Human Rights. Soft-law tools that expand on legal norms to encourage responsible governance include ISO 14097 on Climate Finance and Investment and ISO 37000:2021 on Governance of Organizations. Therefore, corporate governance legislation both facilitates and influences technical innovation in the field of sustainability.

## REFERENCES


Ahdadou, M., Aajly, A., & Tahrouch, M. (2025). Enhancing corporate governance through AI: A systematic literature review. *Technology Analysis and Strategic Management, 37*(11), 1753–1766. DOI: 10.1080/09537325.2024.2326120

Akbar, F. A. (2024). A Holistic Approach to Sustainable Corporate Governance: Exploring the Role of Business Ethics and Technology–A Bibliometric Study. *Economics, Business. Accounting & Society Review, 3*(3), 182–196. DOI: 10.55980/ebasr.v3i3.165

Akinsola, K. (2025). Legal Compliance in Corporate Governance Frameworks: Best Practices for Ensuring Transparency, Accountability, and Risk Mitigation. *Accountability, and Risk Mitigation (January 31, 2025).*

Balboni, P., & Francis, K. E. (2025). Data ethics and digital sustainability: Bridging legal data protection compliance and ESG for a responsible data-driven future. *Journal of Responsible Technology, 22*, 100099. DOI: 10.1016/j.jrt.2024.100099

Camilleri, M. A. (2024). Artificial intelligence governance: Ethical considerations and implications for social responsibility. *Expert Systems: International Journal of Knowledge Engineering and Neural Networks, 41*(7), e13406. DOI: 10.1111/exsy.13406

Chen, R., & Zhang, T. (2025). Artificial intelligence applications implication for ESG performance: Can digital transformation of enterprises promote sustainable development? *Chinese Management Studies, 19*(3), 676–701. DOI: 10.1108/CMS-11-2023-0653

Chen, Y. (2024). A Panoramic Overview of the Opportunities and Challenges Artificial Intelligence Brings to ESG Investing. *Artificial Intelligence, Finance, and Sustainability: Economic, Ecological, and Ethical Implications*, 19-32.

Chien, F., Mehmood, K., Wang, Y., Zhang, Y., & Piccardi, P. (2025). Smart ESG Framework for Corporate Responsibility Mechanism in Decentralized Finance. *Corporate Social Responsibility and Environmental Management, 32*(6), 7467–7489. DOI: 10.1002/csr.70064

Domingo, M. M. R. (2025). The Impact of Artificial Intelligence on ESG: A Conceptual Framework for Practitioners and Policymakers. *Journal of Management for Global Sustainability, 13*(1), 2. DOI: 10.13185/2244-6893.1269

Gouiaa, R., & Huang, R. (2024). HOW DO CORPORATE GOVERNANCE, ARTIFICIAL INTELLIGENCE, AND INNOVATION INTERACT? FINDINGS FROM DIFFERENT INDUSTRIES. *Risk Governance & Control: Financial Markets & Institutions, 14*(1).

Gupta, S., & Agarwal, S. (2024). Applications of Machine Learning and Artificial Intelligence in Environmental, Social and Governance (ESG) Sector. *Social and Governance (ESG) Sector (November 15, 2024).*

Hao, X., & Demir, E. (2024). Artificial intelligence in supply chain decision-making: An environmental, social, and governance triggering and technological inhibiting protocol. *Journal of Modelling in Management, 19*(2), 605–629. DOI: 10.1108/JM2-01-2023-0009

Herath, S. K., & Herath, L. M. (2024). Investigation into the barriers to AI adoption in ESG integration and identification of strategies to overcome these challenges. In *Social and Ethical Implications of AI in Finance for Sustainability* (pp. 286–311). IGI Global Scientific Publishing. DOI: 10.4018/979-8-3693-2881-1.ch013

Işık, C., Ongan, S., & Islam, H. (2025). Driving energy transition through artificial intelligence: Integrating economic, environmental, social, and governance (ECON-ESG) factors in OECD countries. *Journal of the Knowledge Economy*, •••, 1–27.

Kalkan, G. (2024). The impact of artificial intelligence on corporate governance. *Корпоративные финансы, 18*(2), 17-25.

Kazachenok, O. P., Stankevich, G. V., Chubaeva, N. N., & Tyurina, Y. G. (2023). Economic and legal approaches to the humanization of FinTech in the economy of artificial intelligence through the integration of blockchain into ESG Finance. *Humanities & Social Sciences Communications, 10*(1), 1–9. DOI: 10.1057/s41599-023-01652-8

Kolsepatil, A. S. (2022). Encompassing Corporate Governance & E-Governance in Corporations. *Jus Corpus LJ, 3*, 61.

Kuznetsova, S. N., Kuznetsov, V. P., Smirnova, Z. V., Andryashina, N. S., & Romanovskaya, E. V. (2024). Corporate governance in the ESG context: A new understanding of sustainability. In *Ecological footprint of the modern economy and the ways to reduce it: The role of leading technologies and responsible innovations* (pp. 53–57). Springer Nature Switzerland. DOI: 10.1007/978-3-031-49711-7_10

Lee, S. U., Perera, H., Liu, Y., Xia, B., Lu, Q., Zhu, L., Cairns, J., & Nottage, M. (2025). Integrating ESG and AI: A comprehensive responsible AI assessment framework. *AI and Ethics*, *5*(5), 1–28. DOI: 10.1007/s43681-025-00741-5

Li, J., Wu, T., Hu, B., Pan, D., & Zhou, Y. (2025). Artificial intelligence and corporate ESG performance. *International Review of Financial Analysis, 102*, 104036. DOI: 10.1016/j.irfa.2025.104036

Li, Y. (2025). Optimising corporate governance with internet of things and artificial intelligence: A data-driven framework for legal systems. *International Journal of Information and Communication Technology*, *26*(13), 81–100. DOI: 10.1504/IJICT.2025.146171

Lin, L. H. M., Ting, F. K., Chang, T. J., Wu, J. W., & Tsai, R. T. H. (2024, April). Gpt4esg: streamlining environment, society, and governance analysis with custom ai models. In *2024 IEEE 4th International Conference on Electronic Communications, Internet of Things and Big Data (ICEIB)* (pp. 442-446). IEEE. DOI: 10.1109/ICEIB61477.2024.10602567

Maghami, M. (2024). New Global Governance and Overreaching Frameworks: Reimagining the Rule of Law, AI and ESG for the Betterment of the World. *Denning LJ, 33*(1), 177–200. DOI: 10.5750/dlj.v33i1.2353

Malukani, B., Joshi, A., & Ubeja, S. (2024). Corporate Governance in the Digital Age: Insights and Recommendations. *IUP Journal of Corporate Governance*, *23*(3), 50–58.

Metin, E. (2024). Legal Design: A Catalyst for Environmental Social and Governance and Sustainable Business Practices. *Scientific Papers of the University of Pardubice. Series D, Faculty of Economics & Administration, 32*(2).

Mirishli, S. (2025). The Role of Legal Frameworks in Shaping Ethical Artificial Intelligence Use in Corporate Governance. *arXiv preprint arXiv:2503.14540.*

Müller, R., Caron, M. A., Drouin, N., Lereim, J., Alonderienė, R., Chmieliauskas, A., Šimkonis, S., & Šuminskienė, R. (2025). Governance of ESG implementations: Governance dimensions and their structural implementation. *International Journal of Managing Projects in Business*, *18*(1), 118–138. DOI: 10.1108/IJMPB-05-2024-0107

Ozkan, B. (2024). The transformative impact of AI on CSR, ESG, and sustainability: Critical review and case studies. In *Responsible Firms: CSR, ESG, and Global Sustainability* (Vol. 23, pp. 203-218). Emerald Publishing Limited.

Pashang, S., & Weber, O. (2023). AI for sustainable finance: Governance mechanisms for institutional and societal approaches. In *The ethics of artificial intelligence for the sustainable development goals* (pp. 203–229). Springer International Publishing. DOI: 10.1007/978-3-031-21147-8_12

Patil, S. R., Jadhav, S. N., & Nimbagal, S. (2024). A study on ethical implications of using technology in ESG investing and ensuring unbiased decision making. *Multidisciplinary Science Journal, 6*(8), 2024153–2024153. DOI: 10.31893/multiscience.2024153

Rane, N., Choudhary, S., & Rane, J. (2024). Artificial intelligence driven approaches to strengthening Environmental, Social, and Governance (ESG) criteria in sustainable business practices: a review. *Social, and Governance (ESG) criteria in sustainable business practices: a review (May 27, 2024).*

Rehman, A., & Umar, T. (2025). Literature review: Industry 5.0. Leveraging technologies for environmental, social and governance advancement in corporate settings. *Corporate Governance (Bradford), 25*(2), 229–251. DOI: 10.1108/CG-11-2023-0502

Salamzadeh, A., Hadizadeh, M., Feyzabadi, J. G., Yasin, N., & Paramba, J. N. (2025). The Role of Digital Platforms in Transforming Corporate Governance: A Path to Sustainability Through ESG. In *Modern Corporate Governance Strategies for Sustainable Value Creation* (pp. 111–136). IGI Global Scientific Publishing.

Samara, H. H., Qudah, H. A., Mohsin, H. J., Abualhijad, S., Bani Hani, L. Y., Al Rahamneh, S., & AlQudah, M. Z. (2025). Artificial intelligence and machine learning in corporate governance: A bibliometric analysis. *Human Systems Management, 44*(2), 349–375.

Saxena, A., Singh, R., Gehlot, A., Akram, S. V., Twala, B., Singh, A., Montero, E. C., & Priyadarshi, N. (2022). Technologies empowered environmental, social, and governance (ESG): An industry 4.0 landscape. *Sustainability (Basel), 15*(1), 309. DOI: 10.3390/su15010309

Shen, W. (2022). Analysis of the application of artificial intelligence technology in the protection of corporate governance rights and interests. *Frontiers in Psychology, 13*, 966689. DOI: 10.3389/fpsyg.2022.966689 PMID: 36172241

Sklavos, G., Theodossiou, G., Papanikolaou, Z., Karelakis, C., & Ragazou, K. (2024). Environmental, social, and governance-based artificial intelligence governance: Digitalizing firms' leadership and human resources management. *Sustainability (Basel), 16*(16), 7154. DOI: 10.3390/su16167154

Sulkowski, A. J. (2024). *AI, ESG, and Law: Potential*. Limitations, and Strategies Concerning Artificial Intelligence in Sustainability Reporting.

Svitlak, I., & Huts, N. (2022). The legal charter of the company of the future: The order of creation. *Futurity Economics&Law, 2*(1), 20–34.

Taleb, M., & Kadhum, H. J. (2024, June). The role of artificial intelligence in promoting the environmental, social and governance (ESG) practices. In *International Conference on Explainable Artificial Intelligence in the Digital Sustainability* (pp. 256-279). Cham: Springer Nature Switzerland. DOI: 10.1007/978-3-031-63717-9_17

Verma, R., & Jana, S. (2024). AI-Powered Governance: Shaping the Future Landscape of Corporate Governance. *Available at SSRN* 5099460.

Wang, Q., Qi, Y., & Li, R. (2025). Artificial Intelligence and Corporate Sustainability: Shaping the Future of ESG in the Age of Industry 5.0. *Sustainable Development*.

Xiao, Y., & Xiao, L. (2025). The impact of artificial intelligence-driven ESG performance on sustainable development of central state-owned enterprises listed companies. *Scientific Reports*, *15*(1), 8548. DOI: 10.1038/s41598-025-93694-y PMID: 40074861

Zhang, C., & Yang, J. (2024). Artificial intelligence and corporate ESG performance. *International Review of Economics & Finance*, *96*, 103713. DOI: 10.1016/j.iref.2024.103713

Zhao, J., & Gómez Fariñas, B. (2023). Artificial intelligence and sustainable decisions. *European Business Organization Law Review*, *24*(1), 1–39. DOI: 10.1007/s40804-022-00262-2

# Compilation of References


Abbas, R. O., & Folorunso, E. O. (2025). The Green Future of Finance: Blockchain and AI as Catalysts. In *Energy-Efficient Deep Learning Approaches in IoT, Fog, and Green Blockchain Revolution* (pp. 233-264). IGI Global Scientific Publishing.

Abbas, J., Wang, L., Belgacem, S. B., Pawar, P. S., Najam, H., & Abbas, J. (2023). Investment in renewable energy and electricity output: Role of green finance, environmental tax, and geopolitical risk: Empirical evidence from China. *Energy*, *269*, 126683. DOI: 10.1016/j.energy.2023.126683

Abdellatif, S. H. R. (2025). The Intersection of AI Ethics and Corporate Social Responsibility: A Case of AI-Driven RegTech in the Banking Industry. *Available at SSRN* 5261863. DOI: 10.2139/ssrn.5261863

Abdul-Kareem, A. A., Fayed, Z. T., Rady, S., El-Regaily, S. A., & Nema, B. M. (2024). Forecasting Financial Investment Firms' Insolvencies Empowered with Enhanced Predictive Modeling. *Journal of Risk and Financial Management*, *17*(9), 424. DOI: 10.3390/jrfm17090424

Addy, W. A., Ajayi-Nifise, A. O., Bello, B. G., Tula, S. T., Odeyemi, O., & Falaiye, T. (2024). Machine learning in financial markets: A critical review of algorithmic trading and risk management. *International Journal of Science and Research Archive*, *11*(1), 1853–1862. DOI: 10.30574/ijsra.2024.11.1.0292

Addy, W. A., Ajayi-Nifise, A. O., Bello, B. G., Tula, S. T., Odeyem, O., & Falaiye, T. (2024). Algorithmic trading and AI: A review of strategies and market impact. *World Journal of Advanced Engineering Technology and Sciences*, *11*(1), 258–267. DOI: 10.30574/wjaets.2024.11.1.0054

Adebayo, Y., Basha, S. S., & Ghaffar, A. (2023). AI-Driven Forecasting Models for Green Tech Stocks: Linking Carbon Capture Innovation to Stock Market Trends in 2025.

Adedoyin, F., Dogan, H., Cetinkaya, D., & Jiang, N. (2025, May). Human-Centered AI in FinTech: A Conceptual Model and Strategic Research Agenda. In *2025 IEEE Conference on Artificial Intelligence (CAI)* (pp. 180-187). IEEE. DOI: 10.1109/CAI64502.2025.00036

Adel, A. (2023). Unlocking the future: Fostering human–machine collaboration and driving intelligent automation through industry 5.0 in smart cities. *Smart Cities*, *6*(5), 2742–2782. DOI: 10.3390/smartcities6050124

Adi, A. (2025). Do Foreign AI Identity Laws Conflict With India's Personality Rights Framework? Evaluating The Guernsey, No Fakes, Elvis, And Eu AI Act Models. *Evaluating The Guernsey, No Fakes, Elvis, And Eu AI Act Models (October 12, 2025).*

Ahdadou, M., Aajly, A., & Tahrouch, M. (2025). Enhancing corporate governance through AI: A systematic literature review. *Technology Analysis and Strategic Management*, *37*(11), 1753–1766. DOI: 10.1080/09537325.2024.2326120

Ahmad, A., & Kumar, N. (2023). A Critical Analysis of the Regulatory Framework Relating to Cybersquatting in India. *Prayagraj L. Rev.*, *2*, 1.

Ahmadi, S. (2024). A thorough examination of the integration of big data and AI in the financial sector and its implications for current and future opportunities. *International Journal of Current Science Research and Review*, *7*(01), 66–74. DOI: 10.47191/ijcsrr/V7-i1-07

Ahuja, A., Wairagade, A., & Gupta, N. (2025). AIREA: An AI-Driven Optimization Framework for Intelligent Automation in Large-Scale Enterprise Systems. *Available at SSRN* 5160312.

Ai, Y. H., Peng, D. Y., & Xiong, H. H. (2021). Impact of environmental regulation intensity on green technology innovation: From the perspective of political and business connections. *Sustainability (Basel)*, *13*(9), 4862. DOI: 10.3390/su13094862

Ajakaye, O. G., & Lawal, A. (2023). International Trademark and Copyright Law: Harmonization, Disparities, and Global Implications for Developing Countries. *International Journal of Scientific Research in Computer Science. Engineering and Information Technology*, *9*(5), 807–837.

Ajuwon, A., Adewuyi, A., Oladuji, T. J., & Akintobi, A. O. (2023). A Model for Strategic Investment in African Infrastructure: Using AI for Due Diligence and Portfolio Optimization. *International Journal of Advanced Multidisciplinary Research and Studies*, *3*(6), 1811–1826. DOI: 10.62225/2583049X.2023.3.6.4402

Akbar, F. A. (2024). A Holistic Approach to Sustainable Corporate Governance: Exploring the Role of Business Ethics and Technology–A Bibliometric Study. *Economics, Business. Accounting & Society Review*, *3*(3), 182–196. DOI: 10.55980/ebasr.v3i3.165

Akinbeye, S. (2023). An Examination of High-tech Crimes in the Digital Era. *Available at SSRN* 5269130.

Akinrinola, O., Okoye, C. C., Ofodile, O. C., & Ugochukwu, C. E. (2024). Navigating and reviewing ethical dilemmas in AI development: Strategies for transparency, fairness, and accountability. *GSC Advanced Research and Reviews, 18*(3), 050-058.

Akinsola, K. (2025). Legal Compliance in Corporate Governance Frameworks: Best Practices for Ensuring Transparency, Accountability, and Risk Mitigation. *Accountability, and Risk Mitigation (January 31, 2025).*

Akomea-Frimpong, I., Jin, X., Osei-Kyei, R., & Kukah, A. S. (2023). Public–private partnerships for sustainable infrastructure development in Ghana: A systematic review and recommendations. *Smart and Sustainable Built Environment, 12*(2), 237–257. DOI: 10.1108/SASBE-07-2021-0111

Akram, R., Shi, X., Khalid, F., & Srivastava, M. (2025). Artificial intelligence (AI) adoption and green investment: Driving corporate environmental responsibility. *Business Strategy and the Environment, 34*(7), 9188–9202. DOI: 10.1002/bse.70069

Alabi, A. T. (2025). Assessing the Transformative Potential of Green Fintech Solutions in Mitigating Financed Emissions. In *FinTech and Robotics Advancements for Green Finance and Investment* (pp. 223–250). IGI Global Scientific Publishing. DOI: 10.4018/979-8-3373-0355-0.ch008

Alam, M. N. (2025). Can Green AI Get-up-and-go Sustainable Transformation in the Fintech Division? *Journal of Excellence in Management Sciences*, *4*(2), 1–19.

Alam, M., Ansari, Z. A., & Jafar, S. H. (2025). The technological landscape of AI and sustainable finance: An exploration. In *Green Horizons: Role of AI in Sustainable Finance* (pp. 37–53). Springer Nature Singapore. DOI: 10.1007/978-981-96-6495-5_3

Albert, M. J. (2022). The global politics of the renewable energy transition and the non-substitutability hypothesis: Towards a 'great transformation'? *Review of International Political Economy, 29*(5), 1766–1781. DOI: 10.1080/09692290.2021.1980418

Alhejaili, M. O. (2024). Integrating climate change risks and sustainability goals into Saudi Arabia's financial regulation: Pathways to green finance. *Sustainability (Basel), 16*(10), 4159. DOI: 10.3390/su16104159

Aljohani, A. (2025). A decision-support framework for evaluating AI-enabled ESG strategies in the context of sustainable manufacturing systems. *Scientific Reports*, *15*(1), 23864. DOI: 10.1038/s41598-025-09569-9 PMID: 40615575

Allan, B., Lewis, J. I., & Oatley, T. (2021). Green industrial policy and the global transformation of climate politics. *Global Environmental Politics*, *21*(4), 1–19. DOI: 10.1162/glep_a_00640

Almuqwishi, M. A. (2025). Navigating Governance in a Globalised World: Ethical, Regulatory, and Strategic Dimensions. [IJRTBT]. *International Journal on Recent Trends in Business and Tourism*, *9*(3), 1–16. DOI: 10.31674/ijrtbt.2025.v09i03.001

Al-Sabahi, K., Al Mabsali, Y. K., Almaqtari, F. A., & Al-Rashdi, S. A. S. (2025). Transforming Sustainable Finance: The Impact of Artificial Intelligence. In *AI Integration for Business Sustainability: For a Resilient Future* (pp. 73–100). Springer Nature Singapore. DOI: 10.1007/978-981-96-3464-4_4

Alshahmy, S., & Sahiner, M. (2024). Enhancing the Issuance and Monitoring of Sustainable Finance Instruments through AI. In *Artificial Intelligence, Finance, and Sustainability: Economic, Ecological, and Ethical Implications* (pp. 217–241). Springer Nature Switzerland. DOI: 10.1007/978-3-031-66205-8_9

Alshi, C. S. (2025). Artificial Intelligence, ESG, And the Future of Financial Reporting. *Journal of Marketing & Social Research*, *2*, 442–446.

Anghel, B. I., & Lupu, R. (2024). Understanding regulatory changes: Deep learning in sustainable finance and banking. *Journal of Risk and Financial Management*, *17*(7), 295. DOI: 10.3390/jrfm17070295

Anumolu, V. R. (2025). Financial Innovation for Sustainability: Leveraging AI, XR, and Data for Impactful Investments. In *Exploring the Impact of Extended Reality (XR) Technologies on Promoting Environmental Sustainability* (pp. 133–157). Springer Nature Switzerland. DOI: 10.1007/978-3-031-88013-1_7

Appiah-Opoku, S., Manu, K. K., Asibey, M. O., & Amponsah, O. (2023). Tragedy of urban green spaces depletion in selected sub-Sahara African major cities. *Journal of African Studies and Development*, *15*(3), 46–61. DOI: 10.5897/JASD2023.0682

AR, S. M., & BRAHMBHATT, S. (2025). AI-Enabled ESG Reporting: Bridging Sustainability and Accounting. *IJSAT-International Journal on Science and Technology, 16*(3).

Arora, M. K., Lal, S., Singh, B., & Kaunert, C. (2024). Promoters Under Scrutiny: A Case Study For Examining The Criminal Liability In Insolvency Proceedings. *Library of Progress-Library Science, Information Technology & Computer, 44*(3).

Aryavans, A. R. (2024). Empowering Homebuyers: Judicial Evolution in Insolvency & Bankruptcy Law. *Issue 2 Int'l JL Mgmt. &. Human.*, *7*, 1412.

Aslan, O., Aktug, S. S., Ozkan-Okay, M., Yilmaz, A. A., & Akin, E. (2023). A comprehensive review of cyber security vulnerabilities, threats, attacks, and solutions. *Electronics (Basel)*, *12*(6), 1333. DOI: 10.3390/electronics12061333

Aswani, R. S., Sajith, S., & Bhat, M. Y. (2022). Realigning India's Vietnam policy through cooperative sustainable development: A geostrategic counterbalancing to China in Indo-Pacific. *East Asia (Piscataway, N.J.)*, *39*(2), 97–115. DOI: 10.1007/s12140-021-09371-0 PMID: 34276182

Attipoe, V., Chukwuma-Eke, E. C., Lawal, C. I., Friday, S. C., Isibor, N. J., & Akintobi, A. O. (2023). Designing a Data-Driven Sustainable Finance Model: A Pathway for Small and Medium Enterprises to Transition to Clean Energy. *Journal of Frontiers in Multidisciplinary Research*, *4*(01), 210–218. DOI: 10.54660/.IJFMR.2021.2.1.95-103

Augoye, O., Adewoyin, A., Adediwin, O., & Audu, A. J. (2025). The role of artificial intelligence in energy financing: A review of sustainable infrastructure investment strategies. *International Journal of Multidisciplinary Research and Growth Evaluation*, *6*(2), 277–283. DOI: 10.54660/.IJMRGE.2025.6.2.277-283

Bahangulu, J. K., & Owusu-Berko, L. (2025). Algorithmic bias, data ethics, and governance: Ensuring fairness, transparency and compliance in AI-powered business analytics applications. *World J Adv Res Rev*, *25*(2), 1746–1763. DOI: 10.30574/wjarr.2025.25.2.0571

Baharuddin, C., Liutfi, A., Ar, D. P., Rizal, M., & Sasmita, H. (2025). Non Performing Loan Resolution Strategies and Impact on Financial Performance. *Golden Ratio of Mapping Idea and Literature Format*, *5*(2), 106–114. DOI: 10.52970/grmilf.v5i2.1494

Bakeer, H., Alzamily, J. Y., Almadhoun, H., Abu-Nasser, B. S., & Abu-Naser, S. S. (2024). AI and Human Rights.

Bakos, N., & Schiano-Phan, R. (2021). Bioclimatic and regenerative design guidelines for a circular university campus in India. *Sustainability (Basel)*, *13*(15), 8238. DOI: 10.3390/su13158238

Balboni, P., & Francis, K. E. (2025). Data ethics and digital sustainability: Bridging legal data protection compliance and ESG for a responsible data-driven future. *Journal of Responsible Technology*, *22*, 100099. DOI: 10.1016/j.jrt.2024.100099

Banerjee, J., & Maurya, B. R. (2024). A Critical Study on the Role of ODR in Insolvency Law with Reference to India and Vietnam in the Context of Global Health Transitions. *INSOL International Insolvency Review*, *40*, 54.

Bansal, N., Taneja, S., & Özen, E. (2025). AI-Powered Sustainability: Transforming Finance Sector for a Better Tomorrow. In *Achieving Sustainability with AI Technologies* (pp. 27-46). IGI Global Scientific Publishing.

Bednarski, L., Roscoe, S., Blome, C., & Schleper, M. C. (2025). Geopolitical disruptions in global supply chains: A state-of-the-art literature review. *Production Planning and Control*, *36*(4), 536–562.

Begum, A., Munira, M. S. K., & Juthi, S. (2022). Systematic Review Of Blockchain Technology In Trade Finance And Banking Security. *American Journal of Scholarly Research and Innovation*, *1*(01), 25–52. DOI: 10.63125/vs65vx40

Behera, I., Nanda, P., & Derbali, A. M. S. (2024). The societal impact of artificial intelligence in sustainable investment strategies. In *Social and Ethical Implications of AI in Finance for Sustainability* (pp. 268–285). IGI Global. DOI: 10.4018/979-8-3693-2881-1.ch012

Belaid, F., Al-Sarihi, A., & Al-Mestneer, R. (2023). Balancing climate mitigation and energy security goals amid converging global energy crises: The role of green investments. *Renewable Energy*, *205*, 534–542. DOI: 10.1016/j.renene.2023.01.083

BENAISSA, W. O., MAHJOUBI, S., & KABBAJ, S. (2025). Sustainability Meets Intelligence: A PRISMA-Guided Systematic Review of AI's Role in ESG Financial Decision-Making. *International Journal of Accounting Finance Auditing Management and Economics*, *6*(5), 790–806.

Benlalia, Z., Al-Kateb, G., Mzili, M., & Diamanti, K. (2025). Reimagining intelligence: A comprehensive review of human-centric AI systems and their societal and healthcare integration. *Mesopotamian Journal of Artificial Intelligence in Healthcare*, *2025*, 173–186. DOI: 10.58496/MJAIH/2025/017

Bharti, S., Chenchu, M. K., & Jha, K. N. (2024). Revitalizing real estate: Decoding disputes, propelling policies, and pioneering solutions. *Journal of Legal Affairs and Dispute Resolution in Engineering and Construction*, *16*(4), 04524027. DOI: 10.1061/JLADAH.LADR-1181

Bhattacharya, S., & Sachdev, B. K. (2024). Regulatory challenges and opportunities for future Fintech and green finance. *Blockchain's Transformative Potential of Financial Technology for Sustainable Futures*, 103-122.

Biermann, F., Hickmann, T., & Sénit, C. A. (Eds.). (2022). *The political impact of the sustainable development goals: Transforming governance through global goals?* Cambridge University Press. DOI: 10.1017/9781009082945

Birkstedt, T., Minkkinen, M., Tandon, A., & Mäntymäki, M. (2023). AI governance: Themes, knowledge gaps and future agendas. *Internet Research*, *33*(7), 133–167. DOI: 10.1108/INTR-01-2022-0042

Boppiniti, S. T. (2023). Data ethics in ai: Addressing challenges in machine learning and data governance for responsible data science. *International Scientific Journal for Research*, *5*(5), 1–29.

Bordoff, J., & O'sullivan, M. L. (2023). The age of energy insecurity: How the fight for resources is upending geopolitics. *Foreign Affairs*, *102*, 104.

Boumaiza, A. (2024). Development and Experimental Evaluation of an Investment Policy Framework for Enhancing Green Finance in Qatar. *FinTech*, *4*(1), 1. DOI: 10.3390/fintech4010001

Broeders, D., Cristiano, F., & Kaminska, M. (2023). In search of digital sovereignty and strategic autonomy: Normative power Europe to the test of its geopolitical ambitions. *Journal of Common Market Studies*, *61*(5), 1261–1280. DOI: 10.1111/jcms.13462

Buckley, R. P., Zetzsche, D. A., Arner, D. W., & Tang, B. W. (2021). Regulating artificial intelligence in finance: Putting the human in the loop. *The Sydney Law Review*, *43*(1), 43–81.

Büthe, T., Djeffal, C., Lütge, C., Maasen, S., & Ingersleben-Seip, N. V. (2022). Governing AI–attempting to herd cats? Introduction to the special issue on the Governance of Artificial Intelligence. *Journal of European Public Policy*, *29*(11), 1721–1752. DOI: 10.1080/13501763.2022.2126515

Calderaro, A., & Blumfelde, S. (2022). Artificial intelligence and EU security: The false promise of digital sovereignty. *European Security*, *31*(3), 415–434. DOI: 10.1080/09662839.2022.2101885

Camilleri, M. A. (2024). Artificial intelligence governance: Ethical considerations and implications for social responsibility. *Expert Systems: International Journal of Knowledge Engineering and Neural Networks*, *41*(7), e13406. DOI: 10.1111/exsy.13406

Candel, M., Karrbom Gustavsson, T., & Eriksson, P. E. (2021). Front-end value co-creation in housing development projects. *Construction Management and Economics*, *39*(3), 245–260. DOI: 10.1080/01446193.2020.1851037

Censi, R., Campana, P., Bellini, F., Schettino, F., & De Pucchio, C. (2025). AI-Driven Process Mining for ESG Risk Assessment in Sustainable Management. *Buildings (Basel, Switzerland)*, *15*(23), 4260. DOI: 10.3390/buildings15234260

Chakrabarti, M., Fabozzi, F. J., Narain, A., & Sood, A. (2025). Ethical AI in Asset Management: Frameworks for Transparency, Compliance, and Trust. *The Journal of Financial Data Science*, *7*(1), 18–35. DOI: 10.3905/jfds.2025.7.1.018

Challa, K. (2022). Generative AI-Powered Solutions for Sustainable Financial Ecosystems: A Neural Network Approach to Driving Social and Environmental Impact. *Mathematical Statistician and Engineering*, 2326-9865.

Challa, K. (2024). Enhancing credit risk assessment using AI and big data in modern finance. *American Data Science Journal for Advanced Computations (ADSJAC) ISSN: 3067-4166, 2*(1).

Challoumis, C. (2024, November). The landscape of AI in Finance. In *XVII International Scientific Conference* (pp. 109-144).

Chang, Y. L., & Ke, J. (2024). Socially responsible artificial intelligence empowered people analytics: A novel framework towards sustainability. *Human Resource Development Review*, *23*(1), 88–120. DOI: 10.1177/15344843231200930

Chen, Y. (2024). A Panoramic Overview of the Opportunities and Challenges Artificial Intelligence Brings to ESG Investing. *Artificial Intelligence, Finance, and Sustainability: Economic, Ecological, and Ethical Implications*, 19-32.

Chen, R., & Zhang, T. (2025). Artificial intelligence applications implication for ESG performance: Can digital transformation of enterprises promote sustainable development? *Chinese Management Studies*, *19*(3), 676–701. DOI: 10.1108/CMS-11-2023-0653

Chen, W., & Wang, M. (2023). Regulating the use of facial recognition technology across borders: A comparative case analysis of the European Union, the United States, and China. *Telecommunications Policy*, *47*(2), 102482. DOI: 10.1016/j.telpol.2022.102482

Chhabra Roy, N., & Prabhakaran, S. (2023). Sustainable response system building against insider-led cyber frauds in banking sector: A machine learning approach. *Journal of Financial Crime*, *30*(1), 48–85. DOI: 10.1108/JFC-12-2021-0274

Chhabra Roy, N., & Prabhakaran, S. (2025). Cyber fraud (CF) in banking: A dual-layer, blockchain-enabled approach for prevention and managerial response. *Managerial Finance*, *51*(5), 765–796. DOI: 10.1108/MF-09-2024-0716

Chhillar, D., & Aguilera, R. V. (2022). An eye for artificial intelligence: Insights into the governance of artificial intelligence and vision for future research. *Business & Society*, *61*(5), 1197–1241. DOI: 10.1177/00076503221080959

Chien, F., Mehmood, K., Wang, Y., Zhang, Y., & Piccardi, P. (2025). Smart ESG Framework for Corporate Responsibility Mechanism in Decentralized Finance. *Corporate Social Responsibility and Environmental Management*, *32*(6), 7467–7489. DOI: 10.1002/csr.70064

Chowhan, G., Sen, A., & Mukherjee, J. (2022). Sustainable and 'smart'restructuring around the making of mega and world-class cities in India: A critical review. *GeoJournal*, *87*(S4, Suppl 4), 897–910. DOI: 10.1007/s10708-022-10644-1 PMID: 35465172

Chu, L. K., Doğan, B., Abakah, E. J. A., Ghosh, S., & Albeni, M. (2023). Impact of economic policy uncertainty, geopolitical risk, and economic complexity on carbon emissions and ecological footprint: An investigation of the E7 countries. *Environmental Science and Pollution Research International*, *30*(12), 34406–34427. DOI: 10.1007/s11356-022-24682-2 PMID: 36512279

Cicerone, G., Faggian, A., Montresor, S., & Rentocchini, F. (2023). Regional artificial intelligence and the geography of environmental technologies: Does local AI knowledge help regional green-tech specialization? *Regional Studies*, *57*(2), 330–343. DOI: 10.1080/00343404.2022.2092610

Collins, N., & O'Brien, D. (2023). Neo-mercantilism in action: China and small states. *International Politics*, *60*(3), 635–658. DOI: 10.1057/s41311-022-00419-3 PMID: 40478077

Cong, X., Li, X., & Gong, Y. (2021). Spatiotemporal evolution and driving forces of sustainable development of urban human settlements in China for SDGs. *Land (Basel)*, *10*(9), 993. DOI: 10.3390/land10090993

Criekemans, D. (2022). Geotechnical ensembles': how new technologies change geopolitical factors and contexts in economy, energy and security. *Geopolitics and International Relations*, 61.

Das, R., Sharma, B., & Pal, M. K. (2024). Competition Law's Importance in Addressing Anti-Competitive Behaviour in Bankruptcy Proceedings and NPA Management Strategies. *Library of Progress-Library Science, Information Technology & Computer*, *44*(3).

Das, P., Themmadath, V. V., Jeyalakshmi, S., Lateef, K., & Agnihotri, A. (2025). AI in Sustainable Finance: Identifying Green Investments through Machine Learning. *Advances in Consumer Research. Association for Consumer Research (U. S.)*, *2*(3).

Datta, S. D., Tayeh, B. A., Hakeem, I. Y., & Abu Aisheh, Y. I. (2023). Benefits and barriers of implementing building information modeling techniques for sustainable practices in the construction industry—A comprehensive review. *Sustainability (Basel)*, *15*(16), 12466. DOI: 10.3390/su151612466

Davidescu, A. A., Bîrlan, I., & Manta, E. M., & GEAMBA U, C. M. (2025). Artificial Intelligence in ESG and Sustainable Finance: A Bibliometric Analysis of Research Trends. In *Proceedings of the International Conference on Business Excellence* (Vol. 19, No. 1, pp. 1506-1517). Sciendo. DOI: 10.2478/picbe-2025-0117

De Goede, M., & Westermeier, C. (2022). Infrastructural geopolitics. *International Studies Quarterly*, *66*(3), sqac033. DOI: 10.1093/isq/sqac033

Deep, S., Bhoola, V., Verma, S., & Ranasinghe, U. (2022). Identifying the risk factors in real estate construction projects: An analytical study to propose a control structure for decision-making. *Journal of Financial Management of Property and Construction*, *27*(2), 220–238. DOI: 10.1108/JFMPC-03-2020-0018

Delecraz, S., Eltarr, L., Becuwe, M., Bouxin, H., Boutin, N., & Oullier, O. (2022). Responsible Artificial Intelligence in Human Resources Technology: An innovative inclusive and fair by design matching algorithm for job recruitment purposes. *Journal of Responsible Technology*, *11*, 100041. DOI: 10.1016/j.jrt.2022.100041

Desolda, G., Esposito, A., Lanzilotti, R., Piccinno, A., & Costabile, M. F. (2025). From human-centered to symbiotic artificial intelligence: A focus on medical applications. *Multimedia Tools and Applications*, *84*(27), 32109–32150. DOI: 10.1007/s11042-024-20414-5

Dharshini, A. (2025). From Cybersquatting to Meta Tagging-The Expanding Scope of Trademark Infringement in the Digital Sphere. *LawFoyer Int'l J. Doctrinal Legal Rsch.*, *3*, 633.

Dhayal, K. S., Giri, A. K., Kumar, A., Samadhiya, A., Agrawal, S., & Agrawal, R. (2023). Can green finance facilitate Industry 5.0 transition to achieve sustainability? A systematic review with future research directions. *Environmental Science and Pollution Research International*, *30*(46), 102158–102180. DOI: 10.1007/s11356-023-29539-w PMID: 37695480

Didea, I., & Ilie, D. M. (2024). „Artificial Intelligence (AI)-" ally" in the success of insolvency and restructuring practices". *Legal and Administrative Studies*, 92-108.

Didea, I., & Ilie, D. M. (2024). Increasing Legal Certainty for Cross-Border Investments by Making National Insolvency Procedures More Efficient and Effective. *International Investment Law Journal*, *4*(1), 30–70.

Didea, I., & Ilie, D. M. (2025). At the Intersection of Technological Innovations and Geopolitical and Economic Turmoil. Echoes of Insolvency Law and Practice. *Persp. L. Pub. Admin.*, *14*, 6.

Diodato, D., Huergo, E., Moncada-Paternò-Castello, P., Rentocchini, F., & Timmermans, B. (2023). Introduction to the special issue on "the twin (digital and green) transition: Handling the economic and social challenges". *Industry and Innovation*, *30*(7), 755–765. DOI: 10.1080/13662716.2023.2254272

Domingo, M. M. R. (2025). The Impact of Artificial Intelligence on ESG: A Conceptual Framework for Practitioners and Policymakers. *Journal of Management for Global Sustainability*, *13*(1), 2. DOI: 10.13185/2244-6893.1269

Do, T. H., & Selvadurai, N. (2025). Future Crime: A Theoretical Foundation for Designing Effective Cybercrime Laws in the Age of AI and Ransomware. *NCJL & Tech.*, *27*, 91.

Dumitrescu, D., Bobitan, N., Popa, A. F., Sahlian, D. N., & Stanila, C. A. (2025). Signaling Financial Distress Through Z-Scores and Corporate Governance Compliance Interplay: A Random Forest Approach. *Electronics (Basel)*, *14*(11), 2151. DOI: 10.3390/electronics14112151

Dutta, P. K., Raj, P., Sundaravadivazhagan, B., & Selvan, C. P. (Eds.). (2024). *Artificial Intelligence Solutions for Cyber-Physical Systems*. Auerbach. DOI: 10.1201/9781032694375

El Hajj, M., & Hammoud, J. (2023). Unveiling the influence of artificial intelligence and machine learning on financial markets: A comprehensive analysis of AI applications in trading, risk management, and financial operations. *Journal of Risk and Financial Management*, *16*(10), 434. DOI: 10.3390/jrfm16100434

El Khoury, R., Alshater, M. M., & Joshipura, M. (2025). RegTech advancements-a comprehensive review of its evolution, challenges, and implications for financial regulation and compliance. *Journal of Financial Reporting and Accounting*, *23*(4), 1450–1485. DOI: 10.1108/JFRA-05-2024-0286

Elhady, A. M., & Shohieb, S. (2025). AI-driven sustainable finance: Computational tools, ESG metrics, and global implementation. *Future Business Journal*, *11*(1), 209. DOI: 10.1186/s43093-025-00610-x

Elias, O., Awotunde, O. J., Oladepo, O. I., Azuikpe, P. F., Samson, O. A., Oladele, O. R., & Ogunruku, O. O. (2024). The evolution of green fintech: Leveraging AI and IoT for sustainable financial services and smart contract implementation. *World Journal of Advanced Research and Reviews, 23*(1), 2710–2723. DOI: 10.30574/wjarr.2024.23.1.2272

Elias, O., Esebre, S. D., Abijo, I., Timothy, A. M., Babayemi, T. D., Makinde, E. O., & Fatoki, I. E. (2024). Harnessing artificial intelligence to optimize financial technologies for achieving sustainable development goals. *World J. Adv. Res. Rev, 23*(2), 616–625. DOI: 10.30574/wjarr.2024.23.2.2385

Enyiorji, P. (2022). Human-centered responsible AI product development lifecycles merging participatory design, stakeholder alignment, and risk modeling for equitable digital financial service delivery. *International Journal of Science and Engineering Applications, 11*(12), 452–468.

Erman, E., & Furendal, M. (2022). The global governance of artificial intelligence: Some normative concerns. *Moral Philosophy and Politics, 9*(2), 267–291. DOI: 10.1515/mopp-2020-0046

Erman, E., & Furendal, M. (2024). Artificial intelligence and the political legitimacy of global governance. *Political Studies, 72*(2), 421–441. DOI: 10.1177/00323217221126665

Falkner, G., Heidebrecht, S., Obendiek, A., & Seidl, T. (2024). Digital sovereignty-Rhetoric and reality. *Journal of European Public Policy, 31*(8), 2099–2120. DOI: 10.1080/13501763.2024.2358984

Farahani, M. S., Esfahani, A., Moghaddam, M. N. F., & Ramezani, A. (2022). The impact of Fintech and artificial intelligence on COVID 19 and sustainable development goals. *International Journal of Innovation in Management. Economics and Social Sciences, 2*(3), 14–31.

Fernandes, S., Sheeja, M. S., & Parivara, S. (2024). Potential of AI for a sustainable, inclusive, and ethically responsible future. *Fostering Multidisciplinary Research for Sustainability, 196.*

Francisco, M., & Linner, B. O. (2023). AI and the governance of sustainable development. An idea analysis of the European Union, the United Nations, and the World Economic Forum. *Environmental Science & Policy, 150*, 103590. DOI: 10.1016/j.envsci.2023.103590

Fritz-Morgenthal, S., Hein, B., & Papenbrock, J. (2022). Financial risk management and explainable, trustworthy, responsible AI. *Frontiers in Artificial Intelligence*, *5*, 779799. DOI: 10.3389/frai.2022.779799 PMID: 35295866

Fu, C., Lu, L., & Pirabi, M. (2023). Advancing green finance: A review of sustainable development. *Digital Economy and Sustainable Development*, *1*(1), 20. DOI: 10.1007/s44265-023-00020-3

Furnaro, A., & Kay, K. (2022). Labor resistance and municipal power: Scalar mismatch in the Los Angeles Green New Deal. *Political Geography*, *98*, 102684. DOI: 10.1016/j.polgeo.2022.102684

Gabor, D., & Braun, B. (2025). Green macrofinancial regimes. *Review of International Political Economy*, *32*(3), 542–568. DOI: 10.1080/09692290.2025.2453504

Garcia-Segura, L. A. (2024). The role of artificial intelligence in preventing corporate crime. *Journal of Economic Criminology*, *5*, 100091. DOI: 10.1016/j.jeconc.2024.100091

Gehl Sampath, P. (2021). Governing artificial intelligence in an age of inequality. *Global Policy*, *12*(S6), 21–31. DOI: 10.1111/1758-5899.12940

Ghaemi Asl, M. (2025). A novel AI-driven approach to greenwashing: Breakthroughs in the future fit between domain-specific Islamic enterprises with varying developmental progress and ESG landscapes. *Future Business Journal*, *11*(1), 93. DOI: 10.1186/s43093-025-00497-8

Gill, A. S., & Germann, S. (2022). Conceptual and normative approaches to AI governance for a global digital ecosystem supportive of the UN Sustainable Development Goals (SDGs). *AI and Ethics*, *2*(2), 293–301. DOI: 10.1007/s43681-021-00058-z

Glonina, V. (2024). Back to the Future with Blockchain Domain Names: Toward a Global Policy to Fight Cybersquatting in Web 3.0. *Trademark Rep.*, *114*, 587.

Gomollon-Bel, F. (2022). IUPAC Top Ten Emerging Technologies in Chemistry 2022: Discover the innovations that will transform energy, health, and materials science, to tackle the most urgent societal challenges and catalyse sustainable development. *Chemistry International*, *44*(4), 4–13. DOI: 10.1515/ci-2022-0402

Gordon, G., Rieder, B., & Sileno, G. (2022). On mapping values in AI governance. *Computer Law & Security Review*, *46*, 105712. DOI: 10.1016/j.clsr.2022.105712

Gouiaa, R., & Huang, R. (2024). HOW DO CORPORATE GOVERNANCE, ARTIFICIAL INTELLIGENCE, AND INNOVATION INTERACT? FINDINGS FROM DIFFERENT INDUSTRIES. *Risk Governance & Control: Financial Markets & Institutions, 14*(1).

Gray, N., & Kallin, H. (2023). Capital's welfare dependency: Market failure, stalled regeneration and state subsidy in Glasgow and Edinburgh. *Urban Studies (Edinburgh, Scotland), 60*(6), 1031–1047. DOI: 10.1177/00420980221133041

Guo, S., Parry, R., & Vaccari, E. (2025). Cracking the code: Navigating the debt crisis of Chinese local governments and local government financing vehicles in China. *INSOL International Insolvency Review*, *34*(2), 337–363. DOI: 10.1002/iir.70008

Gupta, S., & Agarwal, S. (2024). Applications of Machine Learning and Artificial Intelligence in Environmental, Social and Governance (ESG) Sector. *Social and Governance (ESG) Sector (November 15, 2024).*

Gupta, A., Dwivedi, D. N., & Shah, J. (2023). Artificial Intelligence Applications in Banking and Financial Services. *SpringerNature. DOI*, *10*, 978–981.

Gupta, D. S. (2025). Sustainable Digital Banking: Exploring The Role of Fintech in Promoting Green Finance and Sustainable Development Goals. *Journal of Information Systems Engineering & Management*, *10*(3).

Gupta, S., Modi, R. R., Das, D., & Sahu, P. (2025). Sustainable digital banking: Exploring the role of fintech in promoting green finance and sustainable development goals. *Journal of Information Systems Engineering & Management*, *10*(3), 547–557. DOI: 10.52783/jisem.v10i3.5674

Gurrea-Martínez, A. (2025). The digitalization of insolvency proceedings. *INSOL International Insolvency Review*, *34*(2), 475–491. DOI: 10.1002/iir.70003

Hao, X., & Demir, E. (2024). Artificial intelligence in supply chain decision-making: An environmental, social, and governance triggering and technological inhibiting protocol. *Journal of Modelling in Management*, *19*(2), 605–629. DOI: 10.1108/JM2-01-2023-0009

Hassanein, A., & Tharwat, H. (2024). Artificial intelligence (AI) and green finance. In *The Palgrave Handbook of Green Finance for Sustainable Development* (pp. 859–889). Springer International Publishing. DOI: 10.1007/978-3-031-65756-6_32

Herranz-Surralles, A. (2024). The EU energy transition in a geopoliticizing world. *Geopolitics*, *29*(5), 1882–1912. DOI: 10.1080/14650045.2023.2283489 PMID: 39318503

Herrmann, H. (2023). The future of responsible artificial intelligence: A path forward through responsible innovation. *Heliyon*, *9*(3), e14379. DOI: 10.1016/j.heliyon.2023.e14379 PMID: 36967876

Hofmann, S. C., & Pawlak, P. (2023). Governing cyberspace: Policy boundary politics across organizations. *Review of International Political Economy*, *30*(6), 2122–2149. DOI: 10.1080/09692290.2023.2249002

Holzinger, A., Zatloukal, K., & Müller, H. (2025). Is human oversight to AI systems still possible? *New Biotechnology*, *85*, 59–62. DOI: 10.1016/j.nbt.2024.12.003

Homavazir, Z., Madan, S., Verma, S., Gambhir, V., & Homavazir, M. (2025). Governance for the Digital Age: ESG-Driven Framework for Ethical and Inclusive Innovation. *Advances in Consumer Research. Association for Consumer Research (U. S.)*, *2*(3).

Huang, C., & Yao, X. (2025). Synergies Among Responsible Artificial Intelligence (RAI), Environmental, Social and Governance (ESG), and Sustainable Development Goals (SDGs). *IEEE Computational Intelligence Magazine*, *20*(4), 20–41. DOI: 10.1109/MCI.2025.3593452

Huang, W. (2025). Establishment of Bankruptcy Tribunals, Financing Constraints and Corporate Investment Efficiency. *Finance Research Letters*, *86*, 108678. DOI: 10.1016/j.frl.2025.108678

Hussain, S. (2025). Integrating Al into Corporate Social Responsibility (CSR) for. *Integrating Sustainability Principles With AI-Driven Entrepreneurial Strategies*, 41.

Ibekwe, K. I., Etukudoh, E. A., Nwokediegwu, Z. Q. S., Umoh, A. A., Adefemi, A., & Ilojianya, V. I. (2024). Energy security in the global context: A comprehensive review of geopolitical dynamics and policies. *Engineering Science & Technology Journal*, *5*(1), 152–168. DOI: 10.51594/estj.v5i1.741

Iqbal, A., Zhang, W., & Jahangir, S. (2025). Building a Sustainable Future: The Nexus Between Artificial Intelligence, Renewable Energy, Green Human Capital, Geopolitical Risk, and Carbon Emissions Through the Moderating Role of Institutional Quality. *Sustainability (Basel)*, *17*(3), 990. DOI: 10.3390/su17030990

Irekponor, O. (2025). Designing resilient AI architectures for predictive energy finance systems amid data sovereignty, adversarial threats, and policy volatility. *International Journal of Research Publication and Reviews*, *6*(6), 73–100. DOI: 10.55248/gengpi.6.0625.2125

Irfan, M., Bhute, N. S., Yadav, A. K., & Dias, R. (2026). Sustainable Investment Portfolios with Al: Bridging Green Finance and Technological Innovation. In *Legal and Regulatory Considerations of Leveraging Sustainable Finance* (pp. 235-256). IGI Global Scientific Publishing.

Irfan, M., Dias, R. T., Khemka, M., Mondal, P., & Mohan, N. (2025). Navigating Towards Sustainability: The Role of Corporate Governance and AI-Driven Behavioral Interventions. In *Behavioral Finance and AI Tools for Sustainability* (pp. 201-226). IGI Global Scientific Publishing.

Işık, C., Ongan, S., & Islam, H. (2025). Driving energy transition through artificial intelligence: Integrating economic, environmental, social, and governance (ECON-ESG) factors in OECD countries. *Journal of the Knowledge Economy*, •••, 1–27.

Islam, Q. T., & Faria, M. H. (2025). Ethics in AI-Driven Sustainable Finance: Balancing Innovation With Integrity. In *Behavioral Finance and AI Tools for Sustainability* (pp. 129-150). IGI Global Scientific Publishing.

Islam, M. S., Lee, Z., Shaleh, A., & Soo, H. S. (2024). The United Nations Environment Assembly resolution to end plastic pollution: Challenges to effective policy interventions. *Environment, Development and Sustainability*, *26*(5), 10927–10944. DOI: 10.1007/s10668-023-03639-6

Iyer, S. S., Subramanian, R., Raji, B., & Arora, R. (2025). The Ethical Implications of Artificial Intelligence in Decision-Making: Balancing Innovation with Accountability and Integrity. *Journal of Economics & Management Research. SRC/JESMR-417. DOI: doi. org/ (6), 305*, 2-11.DOI: 10.47363/JESMR/2025

Jahid, M. S. R. (2025). AI-driven optimization and risk modeling in strategic economic zone development for mid-sized economies: A review approach. *International Journal of Scientific Interdisciplinary Research*, *6*(1), 185–218. DOI: 10.63125/31wna449

Jain, A. (2025). Designing for ethical and inclusive AI through a human-centered design lens. *Glob. Bus. Econ. J.* https://gbej. org/articles/designing-for-ethical-and-inclusive-ai-through-a-human-centered-design-lens/. *Accessed, 27.*

Jain, A., Singh, R. K., & Bhushan, P. (2025). Policy and regulatory frameworks for financing smart healthcare. In *Driving Global Health and Sustainable Development Goals With Smart Technology* (pp. 367–388). IGI Global Scientific Publishing.

Jain, R. (2023). The function of artificial intelligence in banking and finance. *Journal of Management and Science*, *13*(3), 1–4. DOI: 10.26524/jms.13.27

Jain, V., Balakrishnan, A., Beeram, D., Najana, M., & Chintale, P. (2024). Utilizing artificial intelligence to improve regulatory compliance within the financial sector. *International Journal of Computer Trends and Technology*, *72*(5), 124–140. DOI: 10.14445/22312803/IJCTT-V72I5P116

Jaiwani, M., Chopra, R., Bhardwaj, S., & Gopalkrishnan, S. (2025). A Systematic Review and Bibliometric Analysis of Asset Reconstruction Companies: A Panacea or A Plight for Non-Performing Assets. *Asia-Pacific Financial Markets*, ●●●, 1–24.

Jayarathna, L., Kent, G., O'Hara, I., & Hobson, P. (2022). Geographical information system based fuzzy multi criteria analysis for sustainability assessment of biomass energy plant siting: A case study in Queensland, Australia. *Land Use Policy*, *114*, 105986. DOI: 10.1016/j.landusepol.2022.105986

Jebadurai, D. J., & David, S. (2026). AI-Driven ESG Investing: Transforming Sustainable Finance in the Digital Age. In *Building AI-Driven Decision Making Competencies for Sustainability* (pp. 29-70). IGI Global Scientific Publishing.

Jiang, L., Cao, X., Wang, Z., Zhan, Y., Zhang, J., & Chen, S. (2025). Promoting energy saving and emission reduction benefits in small and medium-sized enterprises supply chains through green finance-Evidence based on artificial intelligence intervention. *International Review of Financial Analysis*, *102*, 104112. DOI: 10.1016/j.irfa.2025.104112

Jo, H. (2025). The Effect of AI on CSR and ESG Ethics. *Journal of Finance Issues*, *23*(2), 57–78. DOI: 10.58886/jfi.v23i2.9437

Johri, A., & Singh, R. K. (2024). Role of green finance instruments and stakeholders on the sustainable finance and moderated by technology integration. *Environment, Development and Sustainability*, ●●●, 1–29. DOI: 10.1007/s10668-024-05723-x

Jolly, R., & Budke, A. (2023). Assessing the extent to which players can build sustainable cities in the digital city-builder game "Cities: Skylines". *Sustainability (Basel)*, *15*(14), 10780. DOI: 10.3390/su151410780

Joseph, O. O., Kevin-Alerechi, E., Olumide, O. J., Sunday, D., Fagbohun, O., & Olanrewaju, S. (2025). Reimagining Green Financing with AI: A Technological Approach to Sustainability. *J Artif Intell Mach Learn & Data Sci*, *3*(1), 2346–2352. DOI: 10.51219/AIMLD/Omotoso-Oluwayomi-Joseph/509

Judge, B., Nitzberg, M., & Russell, S. (2025). When code isn't law: Rethinking regulation for artificial intelligence. *Policy and Society*, *44*(1), 85–97. DOI: 10.1093/polsoc/puae020

Juned, M., & Usmani, F. (2025). Technological Confluence: An In-Depth Analysis of the Nexus Between Blockchain, Artificial Intelligence, and Emerging Technologies in Facilitating Green Financial Solutions. *Financial Innovation for Global Sustainability*, 579-597.

Kalkan, G. (2024). The impact of artificial intelligence on corporate governance. *Корпоративные финансы, 18*(2), 17-25.

Kapur, S. (2025). The social dynamics of corporate insolvency law and workers and employees of distressed companies: Comparing select Asian jurisdictions. *The Chinese Journal of Comparative Law, 13*, cxaf003.

Kaur, J. (2024). Towards a sustainable Triad: Uniting energy management systems, smart cities, and green healthcare for a greener future. In *Emerging Materials, Technologies, and Solutions for Energy Harvesting* (pp. 258-285). IGI Global Scientific Publishing.

Kazachenok, O. P., Stankevich, G. V., Chubaeva, N. N., & Tyurina, Y. G. (2023). Economic and legal approaches to the humanization of FinTech in the economy of artificial intelligence through the integration of blockchain into ESG Finance. *Humanities & Social Sciences Communications, 10*(1), 1–9. DOI: 10.1057/s41599-023-01652-8

Khaddam, A. A., & Alzghoul, A. (2025). Artificial intelligence-driven business intelligence for strategic energy and ESG management: A systematic review of economic and policy implications. *International Journal of Energy Economics and Policy, 15*(4), 635–650. DOI: 10.32479/ijeep.19820

Khamitdkhanovich, N. A., Rajendran, M., Nailevich, I. R., & Krishnakumari, S. (2025, June). Green finance and ESG investing: Driving sustainable growth through innovation. In. AIP Conference Proceedings: Vol. 3306. *No. 1* (p. 030025). AIP Publishing LLC. DOI: 10.1063/5.0277720

Khan, A. K. (2024). AI in Finance: Disruptive Technologies and Emerging Opportunities. Journal of Artificial Intelligence General Science (JAIGS) ISSN: 3006-4023, 3(1), 155-170.

Khan, A. (2024). The intersection of artificial intelligence and international trade laws: Challenges and opportunities. *IIUMLJ, 32*(1), 103–152. DOI: 10.31436/iiumlj.v32i1.912

Kolade, T. M., Aideyan, N. T., Oyekunle, S. M., Ogungbemi, O. S., Dapo-Oyewole, D. L., & Olaniyi, O. O. (2024). Artificial intelligence and information governance: Strengthening global security, through compliance frameworks, and data security. *Available at SSRN* 5044032. DOI: 10.9734/ajrcos/2024/v17i12528

Kolsepatil, A. S. (2022). Encompassing Corporate Governance & E-Governance in Corporations. *Jus Corpus LJ*, *3*, 61.

Kong'ani, L. N. S., Wahome, R. G., & Thenya, T. (2021). Variety and management of developmental conflicts: The case of the Olkaria IV geothermal energy project in Kenya. *Conflict Security and Development*, *21*(6), 781–804. DOI: 10.1080/14678802.2021.2000806

Krishna, N. (2025). AI-Integrated ESG Scoring System: Leveraging Real-Time Green Data Intelligence for Sustainable Finance: A Study on the Role of Artificial Intelligence in Dynamic ESG Evaluation. *Available at SSRN* 5764202. DOI: 10.2139/ssrn.5764202

Kuldova, T. Ø. (2022). The Compliance-Industrial Complex. In *Compliance-Industrial Complex: The Operating System of a Pre-Crime Society* (pp. 47–70). Springer Nature Switzerland. DOI: 10.1007/978-3-031-19224-1_3

Kumar, S., & Parameswaran, S. (2024). Role of Formal Restructuring in Post-Bankruptcy Performance of Companies: Case Study From India. In *Risks and Challenges of AI-Driven Finance: Bias, Ethics, and Security* (pp. 245-276). IGI Global.

Kumari, B., Kaur, J., & Swami, S. (2024). Adoption of artificial intelligence in financial services: A policy framework. *Journal of Science and Technology Policy Management*, *15*(2), 396–417. DOI: 10.1108/JSTPM-03-2022-0062

Kuzemko, C., Blondeel, M., Bradshaw, M., Bridge, G., Faigen, E., & Fletcher, L. (2025). Rethinking energy geopolitics: Towards a geopolitical economy of global energy transformation. *Geopolitics*, *30*(2), 531–565. DOI: 10.1080/14650045.2024.2351075

Kuzio, J., Ahmadi, M., Kim, K. C., Migaud, M. R., Wang, Y. F., & Bullock, J. (2022). Building better global data governance. *Data & Policy*, *4*, e25. DOI: 10.1017/dap.2022.17

Kuznetsova, S. N., Kuznetsov, V. P., Smirnova, Z. V., Andryashina, N. S., & Romanovskaya, E. V. (2024). Corporate governance in the ESG context: A new understanding of sustainability. In *Ecological footprint of the modern economy and the ways to reduce it: The role of leading technologies and responsible innovations* (pp. 53–57). Springer Nature Switzerland. DOI: 10.1007/978-3-031-49711-7_10

Lee, C. C., Hussain, J., & Abass, Q. (2025). An integrated analysis of AI-driven green financing, subsidies, and knowledge to enhance CO2 reduction efficiency. *Economic Analysis and Policy*, *85*, 675–693. DOI: 10.1016/j.eap.2024.12.021

Lee, C. C., Zhang, J., Yu, C. H., & Fang, L. (2023). How does geopolitical risk affect corporate innovation? Evidence from China's listed companies. *Emerging Markets Finance & Trade*, *59*(7), 2217–2233. DOI: 10.1080/1540496X.2023.2170698

Lee, S. U., Perera, H., Liu, Y., Xia, B., Lu, Q., Zhu, L., Cairns, J., & Nottage, M. (2025). Integrating ESG and AI: A comprehensive responsible AI assessment framework. *AI and Ethics*, *5*(5), 1–28. DOI: 10.1007/s43681-025-00741-5

Leitner-Hanetseder, S., & Lehner, O. M. (2023). AI-powered information and big data: Current regulations and ways forward in IFRS reporting. *Journal of Applied Accounting Research*, *24*(2), 282–298. DOI: 10.1108/JAAR-01-2022-0022

Li, C., Lu, T., Fu, B., Wang, S., & Holden, J. (2022). Sustainable city development challenged by extreme weather in a warming world. *Geography and sustainability*, *3*(2), 114-118.

Li, J., Van Assche, A., Li, L., & Qian, G. (2022). Foreign direct investment along the Belt and Road: A political economy perspective. *Journal of International Business Studies*, *53*(5), 902–919. DOI: 10.1057/s41267-021-00435-0

Li, J., Wu, T., Hu, B., Pan, D., & Zhou, Y. (2025). Artificial intelligence and corporate ESG performance. *International Review of Financial Analysis*, *102*, 104036. DOI: 10.1016/j.irfa.2025.104036

Lin, L. H. M., Ting, F. K., Chang, T. J., Wu, J. W., & Tsai, R. T. H. (2024, April). Gpt4esg: streamlining environment, society, and governance analysis with custom ai models. In *2024 IEEE 4th International Conference on Electronic Communications, Internet of Things and Big Data (ICEIB)* (pp. 442-446). IEEE. DOI: 10.1109/ICEIB61477.2024.10602567

Li, X., & Wang, X. (2025). Prioritization of environmental costs in Chinese insolvency law: Guiding case no. 214 of China's Supreme People's Court. *Journal of Environmental Law*, *37*(3), eqaf023. DOI: 10.1093/jel/eqaf023

Li, Y. (2025). Optimising corporate governance with internet of things and artificial intelligence: A data-driven framework for legal systems. *International Journal of Information and Communication Technology*, *26*(13), 81–100. DOI: 10.1504/IJICT.2025.146171

Macchiavello, E., & Siri, M. (2022). Sustainable finance and fintech: Can technology contribute to achieving environmental goals? A preliminary assessment of 'green fintech' and 'sustainable digital finance'. *European Company and Financial Law Review*, *19*(1), 128–174. DOI: 10.1515/ecfr-2022-0005

Mackenzie, F. (2024). Development from within?: the struggle to survive. In *Development from within* (pp. 1–32). Routledge. DOI: 10.4324/9781003510765-1

Madaus, S., Sarra, J. P., & Mevorach, I. (2025). The greening of the insolvency system. *Canadian Business Law Journal, 69*(3).

Madhusudan, V. V. (2024). A Critical Analysis of Information Technology Act, 2000 with Reference to Cyber Offence and Cyber Security. *Issue 2 Int'l JL Mgmt. &. Human.*, *7*, 2529.

Maghami, M. (2024). New Global Governance and Overreaching Frameworks: Re-imagining the Rule of Law, AI and ESG for the Betterment of the World. *Denning LJ*, *33*(1), 177–200. DOI: 10.5750/dlj.v33i1.2353

Malukani, B., Joshi, A., & Ubeja, S. (2024). Corporate Governance in the Digital Age: Insights and Recommendations. *IUP Journal of Corporate Governance*, *23*(3), 50–58.

Markelius, A., Wright, C., Kuiper, J., Delille, N., & Kuo, Y. T. (2024). The mechanisms of AI hype and its planetary and social costs. *AI and Ethics*, *4*(3), 727–742. DOI: 10.1007/s43681-024-00461-2

Martini, B., Bellisario, D., & Coletti, P. (2024). Human-centered and sustainable artificial intelligence in industry 5.0: Challenges and perspectives. *Sustainability (Basel)*, *16*(13), 5448. DOI: 10.3390/su16135448

Marwa, S., & Soesatyo, B. (2025). Corporate Governance in the Digital Economy and ESG (Environmental, Social, and Governance) Principles. *Greenation International Journal of Law and Social Sciences*, *3*(3), 941–950. DOI: 10.38035/gijlss.v3i3.582

Mathur, H. (2022). Cybersquatting and the Related Laws. *Issue 5 Indian JL & Legal Rsch.*, *4*, 1.

Ma, W., Nasriddinov, F., Haseeb, M., Ray, S., Kamal, M., Khalid, N., & Ur Rehman, M. (2022). Revisiting the impact of energy consumption, foreign direct investment, and geopolitical risk on CO2 emissions: Comparing developed and developing countries. *Frontiers in Environmental Science*, *10*, 985384. DOI: 10.3389/fenvs.2022.985384

McNamara, K. R. (2024). Transforming Europe? The EU's industrial policy and geopolitical turn. *Journal of European Public Policy, 31*(9), 2371–2396. DOI: 10.1080/13501763.2023.2230247

Meghwal, T. (2024). Emerging Challenges in Regulating Artificial Intelligence Under Cyber Security Laws in India. *Available at SSRN* 5030258.

Mei, H., Bodog, S. A., & Badulescu, D. (2024). Artificial intelligence adoption in sustainable banking services: The critical role of technological literacy. *Sustainability (Basel), 16*(20), 8934. DOI: 10.3390/su16208934

Metin, E. (2024). Legal Design: A Catalyst for Environmental Social and Governance and Sustainable Business Practices. *Scientific Papers of the University of Pardubice. Series D, Faculty of Economics & Administration, 32*(2).

Meyer, K. E., & Li, C. (2022). The MNE and its subsidiaries at times of global disruptions: An international relations perspective. *Global Strategy Journal, 12*(3), 555–577. DOI: 10.1002/gsj.1436

Mhlanga, D. (2022). Human-centered artificial intelligence: The superlative approach to achieve sustainable development goals in the fourth industrial revolution. *Sustainability (Basel), 14*(13), 7804. DOI: 10.3390/su14137804

Mirishli, S. (2025). Regulating Ai In Financial Services: Legal Frameworks And Compliance Challenges. *arXiv preprint arXiv:2503.14541*.

Mirishli, S. (2025). The Role of Legal Frameworks in Shaping Ethical Artificial Intelligence Use in Corporate Governance. *arXiv preprint arXiv:2503.14540*.

Mitra, A., & Maity, A. (2025). Balancing Green and Fair: Ethical AI in Sustainable Finance. *International Journal of Business Management & Legal Affairs, 1*(1), 55–76.

Mnif, E., Jarboui, A., & Mouakhar, K. (2024). Strategic insights into carbon markets, digital finance and geopolitical risks for advancing green sustainability investments. *Management of Environmental Quality, 35*(7), 1622–1649. DOI: 10.1108/MEQ-10-2023-0369

Mohammed, U. M., Omolara, A. E., Abiodun, O. I., Rasheed, J., Osman, O., Lar, P. M., Adeyinka, P. O., & Olugbenga, A. G. (2025). Cyber threat in drone systems: Bridging real-time security, legal admissibility, and digital forensic solution readiness. *Frontiers in Communications and Networks, 6*, 1661928. DOI: 10.3389/frcmn.2025.1661928

Mondal, A., Paikaray, J., & Chatterjee, P. S. (2025, February). Intelligent Legal and Technical Strategies to Mitigate Cybersquatting: Bridging Global Frameworks and Indian Contexts. In *2025 International Conference on Emerging Systems and Intelligent Computing (ESIC)* (pp. 913-918). IEEE. DOI: 10.1109/ESIC64052.2025.10962791

Muller, M. (2023). The 'new geopolitics' of mineral supply chains: A window of opportunity for African countries. *The South African Journal of International Affairs*, *30*(2), 177–203. DOI: 10.1080/10220461.2023.2226108

Müller, R., Caron, M. A., Drouin, N., Lereim, J., Alonderienė, R., Chmieliauskas, A., Šimkonis, S., & Šuminskienė, R. (2025). Governance of ESG implementations: Governance dimensions and their structural implementation. *International Journal of Managing Projects in Business*, *18*(1), 118–138. DOI: 10.1108/IJMPB-05-2024-0107

Munawar, H. S., Ullah, F., Qayyum, S., Khan, S. I., & Mojtahedi, M. (2021). UAVs in disaster management: Application of integrated aerial imagery and convolutional neural network for flood detection. *Sustainability (Basel)*, *13*(14), 7547. DOI: 10.3390/su13147547

Muthusubramanian, M., Jangoan, S., Sharma, K. K., & Krishnamoorthy, G. (2024). Demystifying explainable AI: Understanding, transparency and trust. *International Journal For Multidisciplinary Research*, *6*(2), 1–13.

Nakao, Y., Strappelli, L., Stumpf, S., Naseer, A., Regoli, D., & Gamba, G. D. (2023). Towards responsible AI: A design space exploration of human-centered artificial intelligence user interfaces to investigate fairness. *International Journal of Human-Computer Interaction*, *39*(9), 1762–1788. DOI: 10.1080/10447318.2022.2067936

Nancy, N. (2022). Potential distortion of sustainable development in the conflict of interest of nickel mining and indigenous communities in Halmahera, North Maluku. *Journal of Global Environmental Dynamics*, *3*(2), 11–20.

Nanda, P., Kumar, V., & Gandhi, S. (2025). Digital currencies and green finance: institutional decision framework in the Industry 5.0 scenario. *EDPACS*, 1-16.

Naqvi, A., & Momin, M. (2025). The Intersection of Sustainability, Responsible Analytics, and Ethical AI. In *Insights in Banking Analytics and Regulatory Compliance Using AI* (pp. 313–332). IGI Global Scientific Publishing. DOI: 10.4018/979-8-3373-0209-6.ch015

Narkevich, L. (2022). Digital transformation of the information-analytical system for crisis management in enterprise rehabilitation procedures. *Sustainable Development and Engineering Economics*, (1), 8–26.

Nauman, M. (2025). AI in Sustainable Investing: A Dual-Edged Sword. In *FinTech and Robotics Advancements for Green Finance and Investment* (pp. 383-416). IGI Global Scientific Publishing. DOI: 10.4018/979-8-3373-0355-0.ch013

Ndibe, O. S. (2025). AI-driven forensic systems for real-time anomaly detection and threat mitigation in cybersecurity infrastructures. *International journal of research publication and reviews, 6*(5), 389-411.

Negi, L., Manpreet, M., & Singh, M. (2025). Green Finance and Digital Strategies: Catalysts for the Expansion of Circular Technologies in the Global Market. In *Innovating Sustainability Through Digital Circular Economy* (pp. 281-304). IGI Global Scientific Publishing.

Newell, P., Daley, F., Mikheeva, O., & Peša, I. (2023). Mind the gap: The global governance of just transitions. *Global Policy, 14*(3), 425–437. DOI: 10.1111/1758-5899.13236

Ng, S., Johl, S. K., & Khan, P. A. (2025, January). ESG investment enhanced with Industry 5.0: The introduction of conceptual framework. In *Proceedings of the International Conference on Environmental, Social, and Governance (ICESG 2024)* (Vol. 889, p. 211). Springer Nature. DOI: 10.2991/978-2-38476-358-0_17

Nitzberg, M., & Zysman, J. (2022). Algorithms, data, and platforms: The diverse challenges of governing AI. *Journal of European Public Policy, 29*(11), 1753–1778. DOI: 10.1080/13501763.2022.2096668

Nkwo, M., Ikwunne, T., Adejoro, C., & Anuyah, O. (2025). Exploring Usability of AI Systems in the Global South—Toward Responsible Human-Centered AI for Sustainable Cities and Communities. In *Usability for the World: Building Better Cities and Communities* (pp. 125–165). Springer Nature Switzerland. DOI: 10.1007/978-3-031-88326-2_5

Ocelík, V., & Kolk, A. (2024). Sustainability in a digital world: Geopolitics, values and international business policy. In *Handbook of International Business Policy* (pp. 327–345). Edward Elgar Publishing. DOI: 10.4337/9781035308682.00027

Ogunyemi, F. (2023). AI-Powered Carbon Accounting: Transforming ESG Reporting Standards for a Sustainable Global Economy. *International Journal of Multidisciplinary Research in Science, Engineering and Technology, 6*(4).

Okeke, N. I., Bakare, O. A., & Achumie, G. O.Njideka Ihuoma OkekeOluwaseun Adeola BakareGodwin Ozoemenam Achumie. (2024). Integrating policy incentives and risk management for effective green finance in emerging markets. *International Journal of Frontiers in Science and Technology Research*, *7*(1), 76–88. DOI: 10.53294/ijfstr.2024.7.1.0050

Olujobi, O. J. (2021). Combating insolvency and business recovery problems in the oil industry: Proposal for improvement in Nigeria's insolvency and bankruptcy legal framework. *Heliyon*, *7*(2), e06123. DOI: 10.1016/j.heliyon.2021.e06123 PMID: 33659729

Onabowale, O. (2024). Energy policy and sustainable finance: Navigating the future of renewable energy and energy markets. *World Journal of Advanced Research and Reviews*, *25*(1), 2235–2252. DOI: 10.30574/wjarr.2025.25.1.0319

Onyeka, E. J. (2025). Automating Financial Decision-Making in Renewable Energy: Leveraging AI and Credit Risk Models for Sustainable Investment. *Asian Journal of Economics. Business and Accounting*, *25*(4), 492–500.

Owolabi, O. S., Uche, P. C., Adeniken, N. T., Ihejirika, C., Islam, R. B., Chhetri, B. J. T., & Jung, B. (2024). Ethical implications of artificial intelligence (AI) adoption in financial decision-making. *Computer and Information Science*, *17*(1), 1–49. DOI: 10.5539/cis.v17n1p49

Oyewole, A. T., Adeoye, O. B., Addy, W. A., Okoye, C. C., Ofodile, O. C., & Ugochukwu, C. E.Adedoyin Tolulope OyewoleOmotayo Bukola AdeoyeWilhelmina Afua AddyChinwe Chinazo OkoyeOnyeka Chrisanctus OfodileChinonye Esther Ugochukwu. (2024). Promoting sustainability in finance with AI: A review of current practices and future potential. *World Journal of Advanced Research and Reviews*, *21*(3), 590–607. DOI: 10.30574/wjarr.2024.21.3.0691

Ozkan, B. (2024). The transformative impact of AI on CSR, ESG, and sustainability: Critical review and case studies. In *Responsible Firms: CSR, ESG, and Global Sustainability* (Vol. 23, pp. 203-218). Emerald Publishing Limited.

Ozmen Garibay, O., Winslow, B., Andolina, S., Antona, M., Bodenschatz, A., Coursaris, C., Falco, G., Fiore, S. M., Garibay, I., Grieman, K., Havens, J. C., Jirotka, M., Kacorri, H., Karwowski, W., Kider, J., Konstan, J., Koon, S., Lopez-Gonzalez, M., Maifeld-Carucci, I., & Xu, W. (2023). Six human-centered artificial intelligence grand challenges. *International Journal of Human-Computer Interaction*, *39*(3), 391–437. DOI: 10.1080/10447318.2022.2153320

Ozturkcan, S. (2025). Responsible robot integration for inclusive and sustainable work. *Discover Sustainability*, *6*(1), 912. DOI: 10.1007/s43621-025-01928-w

Ozturk, O. (2024). The influence of AI on global commerce: Prospects and obstacles. *Economies*, *12*(11), 298. DOI: 10.3390/economies12110298

Paleti, S. (2022). The Role of Artificial Intelligence in Strengthening Risk Compliance and Driving Financial Innovation in Banking. *Available at SSRN* 5250770. DOI: 10.21275/SR22123165037

Pancholi, K., & Shukla, P. (2025). Harnessing AI for Sustainability: Innovations, Policies, and Investment Paradigms. In *Diversity, AI, and Sustainability for Financial Growth* (pp. 97-124). IGI Global Scientific Publishing.

Pancholi, K., & Shukla, P. (2025). Harnessing AI for sustainability: innovations, policies, and investment paradigms. In *Diversity, AI, and Sustainability for Financial Growth* (pp. 97-124). IGI Global Scientific Publishing. DOI: 10.4018/979-8-3693-6011-8.ch005

Pandow, B. A., Ganai, K. A., & Hussain, G. (2024, February). A Review on AI-powered Advancements in Climate Finance and its Impact. In *2024 11th International Conference on Computing for Sustainable Global Development (INDIACom)* (pp. 1409-1413). IEEE. DOI: 10.23919/INDIACom61295.2024.10498959

Papagiannopoulos, I., Ntanos, C., Pelekis, S., Tzortzis, A. M., Koutalidis, H., Karakolis, E., . . . Askounis, D. (2024, July). Enhancing green financing through AI analytics and cross-domain data sharing. In *2024 15th International Conference on Information, Intelligence, Systems & Applications (IISA)* (pp. 1-11). IEEE. DOI: 10.1109/IISA62523.2024.10786617

Pashang, S., & Weber, O. (2023). AI for sustainable finance: Governance mechanisms for institutional and societal approaches. In *The ethics of artificial intelligence for the sustainable development goals* (pp. 203–229). Springer International Publishing. DOI: 10.1007/978-3-031-21147-8_12

Patil, M. (2025). Enterprise Strategy for Human-Centered AI. In *Handbook of Human-Centered Artificial Intelligence* (pp. 1–62). Springer Nature Singapore. DOI: 10.1007/978-981-97-8440-0_108-1

Patil, S. R., Jadhav, S. N., & Nimbagal, S. (2024). A study on ethical implications of using technology in ESG investing and ensuring unbiased decision making. *Multidisciplinary Science Journal*, *6*(8), 2024153–2024153. DOI: 10.31893/multiscience.2024153

Patnaik, D., & Patnaik, B. (2026). Smart Sustainability: Harnessing AI for Investment Monitoring. In *E-Financial Strategies for Sustainable Development* (pp. 19-44). Apple Academic Press.

Pattnaik, D., Ray, S., & Raman, R. (2024). Applications of artificial intelligence and machine learning in the financial services industry: A bibliometric review. *Heliyon, 10*(1), e23492. DOI: 10.1016/j.heliyon.2023.e23492

Pavlidis, G. (2025). Empowering sustainable finance with artificial intelligence: a framework for responsible implementation. In *A Research Agenda for Financial Law and Regulation* (pp. 23–38). Edward Elgar Publishing. DOI: 10.4337/9781803929996.00009

Perera, M. L. A. (2023). Unraveling the Digital Deception: A Comparative Study of the Legal Response to Cybersquatting in Sri Lanka. *Sri Lanka J. Legal Stud.*, *1*, 61.

Persello, C., Wegner, J. D., Hänsch, R., Tuia, D., Ghamisi, P., Koeva, M., & Camps-Valls, G. (2022). Deep learning and earth observation to support the sustainable development goals: Current approaches, open challenges, and future opportunities. *IEEE Geoscience and Remote Sensing Magazine*, *10*(2), 172–200. DOI: 10.1109/MGRS.2021.3136100

Peters, M. A., & Besley, T. (2025). The geopolitics of postdigital educational development: From territories to networks to rival World Systems. In *The Geopolitics of Postdigital Educational Development* (pp. 41–50). Springer Nature Switzerland. DOI: 10.1007/978-3-031-99378-7_3

Petrukha, N., Petrukha, S., Stoliarenko, O., Ortina, G., Stuzhuk, R., & Plakhotnii, D. (2025). Natural resources and financial security: The synergy of sustainable development economics and artificial intelligence. *Grassroots Journal of Natural Resources*, *8*(2), 775–795. DOI: 10.33002/nr2581.6853.080236

Png, M. T. (2022, June). At the tensions of south and north: Critical roles of global south stakeholders in AI governance. In *Proceedings of the 2022 ACM Conference on Fairness, Accountability, and Transparency* (pp. 1434-1445). DOI: 10.1145/3531146.3533200

Poddar, A., Bahuguna, R., Rawat, P., & Verma, S. (2023, July). The implementation of AI/ML in prevention of insolvency in real estate industry. In *IET Conference Proceedings CP837* (Vol. 2023, No. 11, pp. 425-430). Stevenage, UK: The Institution of Engineering and Technology. DOI: 10.1049/icp.2023.1814

Pokrovskaya, A. (2024). Protection of trademark rights on e-commerce platforms: An updated outlook. *Journal of Comprehensive Business Administration Research*, *1*(2), 65–73. DOI: 10.47852/bonviewJCBAR42022153

Pooyandeh, M., Han, K. J., & Sohn, I. (2022). Cybersecurity in the AI-Based metaverse: A survey. *Applied Sciences (Basel, Switzerland)*, *12*(24), 12993. DOI: 10.3390/app122412993

Popa Tache, C. E., & Săraru, C. S. (2024). Evaluating today's multi-dependencies in digital transformation, corporate governance and public international law triad. *Cogent Social Sciences*, *10*(1), 2370945. DOI: 10.1080/23311886.2024.2370945

Pria, S., Al Rubaie, I., & Prasad, V. (2024). Enhancing business intelligence through AI-driven integration of sustainability metrics via ESG factors. In *Risks and Challenges of AI-Driven Finance: Bias, Ethics, and Security* (pp. 57-89). IGI Global. DOI: 10.4018/979-8-3693-2185-0.ch004

Pujari, T., Goel, A., & Sharma, A. (2024). Ethical and responsible AI: Governance frameworks and policy implications for multi-agent systems. *International Journal of Smart Technologies*, *3*(1).

Purwanto, A. N. I. (2025). Human-Centered AI: Designing Intelligent Systems that Empower, Not Replace. *RIGGS: Journal of Artificial Intelligence and Digital Business*, *4*(3), 3212–3221. DOI: 10.31004/riggs.v4i3.2450

Qobo, M., & Mzyece, M. (2023). Geopolitics, technology wars and global supply chains: Implications for Africa. *The South African Journal of International Affairs*, *30*(1), 29–46. DOI: 10.1080/10220461.2023.2191988

Radanliev, P. (2025). Cyber diplomacy: Defining the opportunities for cybersecurity and risks from Artificial Intelligence, IoT, Blockchains, and Quantum Computing. *Journal of Cyber Security Technology*, *9*(1), 28–78. DOI: 10.1080/23742917.2024.2312671

Raihan, A. (2024). Financial technology optimization using artificial intelligence (AI) to accomplish sustainable development goals (SDGs). In *Proceedings of the International Conference on on Digital Finance, Green Innovation, and Sustainable Development.*

Rajavel, N. (2024). The Impact of Al on Elderly Inmates in. *Exploration of AI in Contemporary Legal Systems*, 281.

Rajeswari, A. (2024). Cyberspace and Intellectual Property: Evaluating Legal Frameworks through the Lens of Space Transition Theory. *Issue 2 Int'l JL Mgmt. &. Human.*, *7*, 3938.

Ramzani, S. R., Konhaeusner, P., Olaniregun, O. A., Abu-Alkheil, A., & Alsharari, N. (2024). Integrating AI-Driven Green Finance Strategies for Sustainable Development: A Comparative Analysis of Renewable Energy Investments in Germany and Denmark. *European Journal of Business and Management Research*, *9*(2), 43–55. DOI: 10.24018/ejbmr.2024.9.2.2277

Rane, N., Choudhary, S., & Rane, J. (2024). Artificial intelligence driven approaches to strengthening Environmental, Social, and Governance (ESG) criteria in sustainable business practices: a review. *Social, and Governance (ESG) criteria in sustainable business practices: a review (May 27, 2024).*

Rane, N., Choudhary, S., & Rane, J. (2023). Blockchain and Artificial Intelligence (AI) integration for revolutionizing security and transparency in finance. Available at *SSRN* 4644253. DOI: 10.2139/ssrn.4644253

Rawas, S. (2024). AI: The future of humanity. *Discover Artificial Intelligence*, *4*(1), 25. DOI: 10.1007/s44163-024-00118-3

Raza, A., Shakeel, M., Khan, M. I., Atif, F., & Parveen, R. (2025). Identifying the recent trends, voids, and opportunities of sustainable finance via artificial intelligence, big data and analytics. *Multidisciplinary Reviews*, *8*(7), 2025234–2025234. DOI: 10.31893/multirev.2025234

Rehman, A., & Umar, T. (2025). Literature review: Industry 5.0. Leveraging technologies for environmental, social and governance advancement in corporate settings. *Corporate Governance (Bradford)*, *25*(2), 229–251. DOI: 10.1108/CG-11-2023-0502

Ricaurte, P. (2022). Ethics for the majority world: AI and the question of violence at scale. *Media Culture & Society*, *44*(4), 726–745. DOI: 10.1177/01634437221099612

Ridzuan, N. N., Masri, M., Anshari, M., Fitriyani, N. L., & Syafrudin, M. (2024). AI in the financial sector: The line between innovation, regulation and ethical responsibility. *Information (Basel)*, *15*(8), 432. DOI: 10.3390/info15080432

Ripoll Gonzalez, L., & Gale, F. (2023). Sustainable city branding narratives: A critical appraisal of processes and outcomes. *Journal of Place Management and Development*, *16*(1), 20–44. DOI: 10.1108/JPMD-09-2021-0093

Rizinski, M., Peshov, H., Mishev, K., Chitkushev, L. T., Vodenska, I., & Trajanov, D. (2022). Ethically responsible machine learning in fintech. *IEEE Access : Practical Innovations, Open Solutions*, *10*, 97531–97554. DOI: 10.1109/ACCESS.2022.3202889

Roberts, H., Hine, E., Taddeo, M., & Floridi, L. (2024). Global AI governance: Barriers and pathways forward. *International Affairs*, *100*(3), 1275–1286. DOI: 10.1093/ia/iiae073

Sadati, A., Gramlich, D., & Walker, T. (2024). Artificial Intelligence, Finance, and Sustainability: An Overview. *Artificial Intelligence, Finance, and Sustainability: Economic, Ecological, and Ethical Implications*, 3-16.

Saeedi, M., & Ashraf, B. N. (2024). The role of technology in promoting green finance: A systematic literature survey and the development of a framework. *Journal of Risk and Financial Management*, *17*(10), 472. DOI: 10.3390/jrfm17100472

Safeei, R., & Marzuki, M., Mustaffa4D, S. M. S. A. H., Fadzilah, N. S. M., & Tajarahim, N. A. (2025, August). Harnessing AI: Transforming Social and Environmental Accountability in Accounting Practices. In *Proceedings of the 3rd International Conference on Business, Finance, Management and Economic (BizFAME 2024)* (p. 13). Springer Nature. DOI: 10.2991/978-94-6463-827-1_3

Saha, A. (2025). Human-centred innovation in Society 5.0. *Society 5.0: A Transformation towards Human-Centered. Artificial Intelligence*, •••, 143.

Salamzadeh, A., Hadizadeh, M., Feyzabadi, J. G., Yasin, N., & Paramba, J. N. (2025). The Role of Digital Platforms in Transforming Corporate Governance: A Path to Sustainability Through ESG. In *Modern Corporate Governance Strategies for Sustainable Value Creation* (pp. 111–136). IGI Global Scientific Publishing.

Salim, P. S. (2025). Artificial intelligence in corporate social responsibility. *Era of Management: Adapting Strategies for a Changing Environment*, 148.

Samanvitha, C., Dharmendra, H., Nethravathi, N., & Velmurugan, P. R. (2025). Artificial intelligence for sustainable futures: navigating social and environmental responsibility. In *Advancements in Intelligent Process Automation* (pp. 129–154). IGI Global.

Samara, H. H., Qudah, H. A., Mohsin, H. J., Abualhijad, S., Bani Hani, L. Y., Al Rahamneh, S., & AlQudah, M. Z. (2025). Artificial intelligence and machine learning in corporate governance: A bibliometric analysis. *Human Systems Management*, *44*(2), 349–375.

Sanchez-Medina, A. J., Blázquez-Santana, F., Cerviño-Cortínez, D. L., & Pellejero, M. (2025). Ensemble Methods for Bankruptcy Resolution Prediction: A New Approach. *Computational Economics*, *66*(5), 1–36. DOI: 10.1007/s10614-024-10709-y

Santoni de Sio, F., Almeida, T., & Van Den Hoven, J. (2024). The future of work: Freedom, justice and capital in the age of artificial intelligence. *Critical Review of International Social and Political Philosophy*, *27*(5), 659–683. DOI: 10.1080/13698230.2021.2008204

Sargiotis, D. (2024). Fostering Ethical and Inclusive AI: A Human-Centric Paradigm for Social Impact. *Available at SSRN* 4879372. DOI: 10.2139/ssrn.4879372

Sarin, A. B., & Sharma, S. (2025). The Synergy of Artificial Intelligence and Green Finance for Sustainable Investment. In *Adaptive Strategies for Green Economy and Sustainability Policies* (pp. 83–100). IGI Global Scientific Publishing.

Saxena, A., Singh, R., Gehlot, A., Akram, S. V., Twala, B., Singh, A., Montero, E. C., & Priyadarshi, N. (2022). Technologies empowered environmental, social, and governance (ESG): An industry 4.0 landscape. *Sustainability (Basel)*, *15*(1), 309. DOI: 10.3390/su15010309

Scheffran, J. (2023). Limits to the Anthropocene: Geopolitical conflict or cooperative governance? *Frontiers in Political Science*, *5*, 1190610. DOI: 10.3389/fpos.2023.1190610

Schneider, E. (2023). Germany's Industrial strategy 2030, EU competition policy and the Crisis of New Constitutionalism.(Geo-) political economy of a contested paradigm shift. *New Political Economy*, *28*(2), 241–258. DOI: 10.1080/13563467.2022.2091535

Schotter, A. P., Maznevski, M., Stahl, G. K., & Doz, Y. (2025). Towards a dynamic theory of lateral collaboration across multinational enterprise structures: A collection of insights. *Journal of World Business*, *60*(4), 101647. DOI: 10.1016/j.jwb.2025.101647

Shafik, W. (2024). Incorporating Artificial Intelligence for Urban and Smart Cities' Sustainability. In *Maintaining a Sustainable World in the Nexus of Environmental Science and AI* (pp. 23-58). IGI Global.

Shaheer, B. (2025). The Role of Predictive Analytics and Artificial Intelligence in Cybersecurity. In *Symbiotic Intelligence* (pp. 50–69). CRC Press. DOI: 10.1201/9781003540373-3

Shaik, M., Jamil, S. A., Hawaldar, I. T., Sahabuddin, M., Rabbani, M. R., & Atif, M. (2023). Impact of geo-political risk on stocks, oil, and gold returns during GFC, COVID-19, and Russian–Ukraine War. *Cogent Economics & Finance*, *11*(1), 2190213. DOI: 10.1080/23322039.2023.2190213

Shajar, S. N., Kashif, M., George, J., & Nasir, S. (2024). The future of green finance: Artificial intelligence-enabled solutions for a more sustainable world. In *Harnessing blockchain-digital twin fusion for sustainable investments* (pp. 316–328). IGI Global Scientific Publishing. DOI: 10.4018/979-8-3693-1878-2.ch013

Sharno, O. I., & Bokov, Y. A. (2024). ESG-Screening of Remote Investment in Sustainable Development: The Environmental and Legal Dimension. In *Remote Investment Transactions in the Digital Age: Perception, Techniques, Law Regulation* (pp. 73–83). Springer Nature Switzerland. DOI: 10.1007/978-3-031-51536-1_8

Sheikhattar, H., & Vesali Mahmoud, M. (2025). Domestic insolvency proceedings before investment treaty arbitration. *Arbitration International, 41*(2), 349–375. DOI: 10.1093/arbint/aiae047

Shekhar, C. (2025). Navigating the Approaching Tide: Financial Stocks for Resilience in an NPA-Laden Environment. *Available at SSRN* 5651370. DOI: 10.2139/ssrn.5651370

Shen, W. (2022). Analysis of the application of artificial intelligence technology in the protection of corporate governance rights and interests. *Frontiers in Psychology, 13*, 966689. DOI: 10.3389/fpsyg.2022.966689 PMID: 36172241

Singhal, N., Goyal, S., Khan, M., & Singhal, T. (2025). AI for Sustainable Finance: Driving Innovation and Ethical Growth. *Financial Innovation for Global Sustainability*, 529-559.

Singh, S., Yadav, S., Singh, A., Krishna, Y. J., & Singh, A. (2024). Harnessing Technology for a Sustainable Future in Finance: The Role of Artificial Intelligence in Promoting Environmental Responsibility. In *Anticipating Future Business Trends: Navigating Artificial Intelligence Innovations* (Vol. 2, pp. 367–378). Springer Nature Switzerland. DOI: 10.1007/978-3-031-63402-4_30

Singh, V. K. (2022). Regulatory and legal framework for promoting green digital finance. In *Green digital finance and sustainable development goals* (pp. 3–27). Springer Nature Singapore. DOI: 10.1007/978-981-19-2662-4_1

Sinha, S., & Chopra, P. (2025). Algorithmic Governance in ESG Ratings: Addressing Bias and Enhancing Transparency in AI-Driven Sustainable Finance. In *Behavioral Finance and AI Tools for Sustainability* (pp. 375-402). IGI Global Scientific Publishing.

Siriman, N., Ali, M. S., Siddiqui, T. A., Rohin, G., Vejju, B., & Cherupelly, N. (2025). Green Finance and AI in India: A Synergistic Approach to Sustainable Development and Climate Resilience. *International Journal of Environmental Sciences, 11*(1), 207–216. DOI: 10.64252/mt7jkk84

Siringoringo, N. M. (2024). Optimization of Artificial Intelligence to Address Injustice in Bankruptcy Requirements between State-Owned. *Journal Research of Social Science, Economics & Management, 4.*

Sklavos, G., Theodossiou, G., Papanikolaou, Z., Karelakis, C., & Ragazou, K. (2024). Environmental, social, and governance-based artificial intelligence governance: Digitalizing firms' leadership and human resources management. *Sustainability (Basel), 16*(16), 7154. DOI: 10.3390/su16167154

Soergel, B., Kriegler, E., Weindl, I., Rauner, S., Dirnaichner, A., Ruhe, C., Hofmann, M., Bauer, N., Bertram, C., Bodirsky, B. L., Leimbach, M., Leininger, J., Levesque, A., Luderer, G., Pehl, M., Wingens, C., Baumstark, L., Beier, F., Dietrich, J. P., & Popp, A. (2021). A sustainable development pathway for climate action within the UN 2030 Agenda. *Nature Climate Change, 11*(8), 656–664. DOI: 10.1038/s41558-021-01098-3

Soetan, O., & Deloitte, L. L. P. (2023). Sustainable automation pipelines powered by lightweight AI optimizing industrial efficiency while preserving transparency, compliance, and equity in decision processes. *Int J Comput Appl Technol Res, 12*(12), 218–233.

Sokhansanj, B. (2025). AI Goes Off the Grid: The Rise of Local AI Demands Rethinking AI Governance. *Available at SSRN* 5284453.

Stiglitz, J. E., & Rodrik, D. (2025). Rethinking global governance: Cooperation in a world of power. In *The New Global Economic Order* (pp. 26–38). Routledge. DOI: 10.4324/9781003571384-3

Sujay, M. (2025). Safeguarding Intellectual Property in the Metaverse Economy through Digital Fashion and Virtual Products. *Mind to Market: The Journey of Intellectual Property*, 163.

Sulaiman, A. D. B., Sentosa, I., Osman, M. Z., Roslan, H., & Juhar, K. N. N. A. (2024, December). Environment, Social, Governance (ESG) Investment in Artificial Intelligent (AI) to Improve Power Grid focusing Peninsular Malaysia using System Dynamic. In *2024 8th International Symposium on Innovative Approaches in Smart Technologies (ISAS)* (pp. 1-6). IEEE.

Sulkowski, A. J. (2024). *AI, ESG, and Law: Potential.* Limitations, and Strategies Concerning Artificial Intelligence in Sustainability Reporting.

Sullivan, J. (2023). The sources of American power: A foreign policy for a changed world. *Foreign Affairs, 102*, 8.

Sundharesalingam, P., Somasundaram, R., Sushmitha, S. S. S., & Rithanya, R. (2025). AI Enhanced FinTech Strategies for Driving. In Proceedings of the 15th International Conference on Soft Computing and Pattern Recognition (SoCPaR 2023).: Real world applications (Vol. 4, p. 221). Springer Nature.

Sundharesalingam, P., Somasundaram, R., Sushmitha, S. S. S., Rithanya, R., & Archana, M. (2023, December). AI Enhanced FinTech Strategies for Driving ESG Investments in Sustainable Finance. In *International Conference on Soft Computing and Pattern Recognition* (pp. 221-228). Cham: Springer Nature Switzerland.

Suri, G. K., & Sadriwala, N. (2025). Using Artificial Intelligence for Sustainable Accounting Practices: A Data-Driven Approach. In *Intelligent Systems for Sustainable Infrastructure: AI Solutions Shaping a Green Future: Leveraging AI Innovations for Eco Friendly Infrastructure and Environmental Resilience* (pp. 171–186). Springer Nature Switzerland.

Svitlak, I., & Huts, N. (2022). The legal charter of the company of the future: The order of creation. *Futurity Economics&Law*, *2*(1), 20–34.

Syed, S. A. (2022). Ai-powered cybercrime: The new frontier of digital threats. [IJETRM]. *International Journal of Engineering Technology Research & Management*, *6*(02).

Szabó, I. G., Golden, D., & Erne, R. (2022). Why do some labour alliances succeed in politicizing Europe across borders? A comparison of the Right2Water and Fair Transport European Citizens' Initiatives. *Journal of Common Market Studies*, *60*(3), 634–652. DOI: 10.1111/jcms.13279

Taeihagh, A. (2021). Governance of artificial intelligence. *Policy and Society*, *40*(2), 137–157. DOI: 10.1080/14494035.2021.1928377

Taleb, M., & Kadhum, H. J. (2024, June). The role of artificial intelligence in promoting the environmental, social and governance (ESG) practices. In *International Conference on Explainable Artificial Intelligence in the Digital Sustainability* (pp. 256-279). Cham: Springer Nature Switzerland. DOI: 10.1007/978-3-031-63717-9_17

Tallberg, J., Erman, E., Furendal, M., Geith, J., Klamberg, M., & Lundgren, M. (2023). The global governance of artificial intelligence: Next steps for empirical and normative research. *International Studies Review*, *25*(3), viad040. DOI: 10.1093/isr/viad040

Tariq, M. U. (2026). Bridging the Digital and Human Divide: Fostering Inclusion and Well-Being in Tech-Driven Workplaces. In *Leading Inclusive Workplaces Through Digital Transformation and Organizational Change* (pp. 139-168). IGI Global Scientific Publishing.

Tariq, M. U. (2025). The Challenge of Artificial Intelligence in Environmental Sustainability: Opportunities, Risks, and Policy Implications. In *Nexus of Environmental Quality and Technology Innovation* (pp. 267–292). IGI Global Scientific Publishing. DOI: 10.4018/979-8-3373-1822-6.ch012

Teixeira, N. (2025). The evolution of sustainable investment: The role of decentralized finance and green bonds in the efficiency and transparency of green finance. *FinTech and Sustainable Innovation*, *1*, A1–A1. DOI: 10.47852/bonviewFSI52024817

Thiruma Valavan, A.Thiruma Valavan A. (2023). AI Ethics and Bias: Exploratory study on the ethical considerations and potential biases in ai and data-driven decision-making in banking, with a focus on fairness, transparency, and accountability. *World Journal of Advanced Research and Reviews*, *20*(2), 197–206. DOI: 10.30574/wjarr.2023.20.2.2245

Thomas, M., Maheswari, G. S., & Kavitha, M. (2025). AI applications in sustainable financial management. *Revista Espanola de Derecho Canonico*, *7*(1), 58–71.

Trakman, L., & Walters, R. (2022). *Contemporary Issues in Finance and Insolvency Law* (Vol. 1). Routledge.

Udeagha, M. C., & Muchapondwa, E. (2023). Green finance, fintech, and environmental sustainability: Fresh policy insights from the BRICS nations. *International Journal of Sustainable Development and World Ecology*, *30*(6), 633–649. DOI: 10.1080/13504509.2023.2183526

UGWUODO, E., Humphrey, O. N. U. H., & Ugwu, P. (2024). Artificial Intelligence (AI) and Environmental Accounting: Implications for the Accounting Profession and Stakeholder Value Creation. *Research Journal of Financial Sustainability Reporting, 7*(1).

Unver, M. B. (2023, June). Rebuilding'ethics' to govern AI: How to re-set the boundaries for the legal sector? In *Proceedings of the Nineteenth International Conference on Artificial Intelligence and Law* (pp. 306-315).

Usmani, U. A., Happonen, A., & Watada, J. (2023, June). Human-centered artificial intelligence: Designing for user empowerment and ethical considerations. In *2023 5th international congress on human-computer interaction, optimization and robotic applications (HORA)*. IEEE.

Vadisetty, R. (2022). AI in Cloud Powered Legal Compliance as a Service (LCaaS). *International Journal of Advanced Engineering Technologies and Innovations*, *1*(2), 286–319.

Vali, J., Yadav, P., & Thota, U. (2024, October). AI for Climate Action: Enhancing Sustainable Development Through ESG Analytics. In *Proceedings of the Second International Workshop on Artificial Intelligence: Empowering Sustainable Development,* Lucknow, India (Vol. 2).

Vasquez-Serpa, L. J., Rodríguez, C., Pérez-Núñez, J. R., & Navarro, C. (2025). Challenges of Artificial Intelligence for the Prevention and Identification of Bankruptcy Risk in Financial Institutions: A Systematic Review. *Journal of Risk and Financial Management, 18*(1), 26. DOI: 10.3390/jrfm18010026

Verma, R., & Jana, S. (2024). AI-Powered Governance: Shaping the Future Landscape of Corporate Governance. *Available at SSRN* 5099460.

Visciola, M. (2025). Rethinking Human-Centered Design: From Automation to Sustainable Innovation. *Interactions (New York, N.Y.), 32*(4), 22–27. DOI: 10.1145/3733153

Vodenska, I., Trajanov, R., Lazarev, G., Chitkushev, L., & Trajanov, D. (2025). Navigating Global ESG Investment Regulations Using AI. In *Sustainable Investing* (pp. 153–194). Problems And Solutions.

Wågsæther, K., Remme, D., Haarstad, H., & Sareen, S. (2022). The justice pitfalls of a sustainable transport transition. *Environment and Planning. F, Philosophy, Theory, Models, Methods and Practice, 1*(2-4), 187–206. DOI: 10.1177/26349825221082169

Walter, Y. (2024). Managing the race to the moon: Global policy and governance in Artificial Intelligence regulation—A contemporary overview and an analysis of socioeconomic consequences. *Discover Artificial Intelligence, 4*(1), 14. DOI: 10.1007/s44163-024-00109-4

Wang, C., Nazar, R., Ali, S., & Meo, M. S. (2025). Eco-friendly algorithms: Artificial intelligence and green finance in European intelligent nations. *Technology in Society, 83*, 102960. DOI: 10.1016/j.techsoc.2025.102960

Wang, C., Zheng, C., Chen, B., & Wang, L. (2024). Mineral wealth to green growth: Navigating FinTech and green finance to reduce ecological footprints in mineral rich developing economies. *Resources Policy, 94*, 105116. DOI: 10.1016/j.resourpol.2024.105116

Wang, D., & Li, S. (2025). Social conflicts and their resolution paths in the commercialized renewal of old urban communities in China under the perspective of public value. *Journal of Urban Management, 14*(2), 402–417. DOI: 10.1016/j.jum.2024.11.007

Wang, M., Wang, Y., & Feng, C. (2025). Artificial intelligence, institutional environment, and corporate green transformation: Evidence from China's resource-based sector. *International Review of Economics & Finance, 103*, 104473. DOI: 10.1016/j.iref.2025.104473

Wang, Q., Qi, Y., & Li, R. (2025). Artificial intelligence and corporate sustainability: Shaping the future of ESG in the age of industry 5.0. *Sustainable Development.*

Wang, Q., Qi, Y., & Li, R. (2025). Artificial Intelligence and Corporate Sustainability: Shaping the Future of ESG in the Age of Industry 5.0. *Sustainable Development.*

Wang, Q., Sun, T., & Li, R. (2025). Does Artificial Intelligence (AI) enhance green economy efficiency? The role of green finance, trade openness, and R&D investment. *Humanities & Social Sciences Communications, 12*(1), 1–22. DOI: 10.1057/s41599-024-04319-0

Wang, Q., Sun, T., & Li, R. (2025). Does artificial intelligence promote green innovation? An assessment based on direct, indirect, spillover, and heterogeneity effects. *Energy & Environment, 36*(2), 1005–1037. DOI: 10.1177/0958305X231220520

Waykar, Y. A., & Yambal, S. (2025). AI and the Evolution of Green Finance: Transforming Banking for a Greener World. In *Convergence of AI, Education, and Business for Sustainability* (pp. 285-306). IGI Global Scientific Publishing.

Werder, K., Ramesh, B., & Zhang, R. (2022). Establishing data provenance for responsible artificial intelligence systems. [TMIS]. *ACM Transactions on Management Information Systems, 13*(2), 1–23. DOI: 10.1145/3503488

Winslow, B., & Garibay, O. O. (2024). Human-centered AI. In *Human-Computer Interaction in Intelligent Environments* (pp. 108–140). CRC Press. DOI: 10.1201/9781003490685-4

Wu, Z., Luo, L., Li, H., Wang, Y., Bi, G., & Antwi-Afari, M. F. (2021). An analysis on promoting prefabrication implementation in construction industry towards sustainability. *International Journal of Environmental Research and Public Health, 18*(21), 11493. DOI: 10.3390/ijerph182111493 PMID: 34770008

Xiao, Y., & Xiao, L. (2025). The impact of artificial intelligence-driven ESG performance on sustainable development of central state-owned enterprises listed companies. *Scientific Reports, 15*(1), 8548. DOI: 10.1038/s41598-025-93694-y PMID: 40074861

Xu, D., & Chen, L. (2025). Between progress and caution: LegalTech's promise in transforming personal credit risk management in China. *Computer Law & Security Review, 56*, 106090. DOI: 10.1016/j.clsr.2024.106090

Yadava, A. (2023). Ethical and regulatory challenges of AI adoption in the financial services sector: A global perspective. *International Journal of Science and Research Archive*, *10*(13), 10–30574.

Yang, X., Chen, H., Li, B., Jia, D., & Ahmad, M. (2025). The relationship between artificial intelligence, geopolitical risk, and green growth: Exploring the moderating role of green finance and energy technology. *Technological Forecasting and Social Change*, *217*, 124135. DOI: 10.1016/j.techfore.2025.124135

Yang, Y., Xia, S., & Qian, X. (2023). Geopolitics of the energy transition. *Journal of Geographical Sciences*, *33*(4), 683–704. DOI: 10.1007/s11442-023-2101-2

Yoshimatsu, H. (2023). Japan's strategic response to China's geo-economic presence: Quality infrastructure as a diplomatic tool. *The Pacific Review*, *36*(1), 148–176. DOI: 10.1080/09512748.2021.1947356

Youssef, M. E. M. M. (2024). *Predicting Bankruptcy And Financial Failure In the Egyptian listed companies: The Importance Of Cash Flow Statements* (Doctoral dissertation, UNS (Sebelas Maret University)).

Yu, X., Fan, L., & Yu, Y. (2025). Artificial Intelligence and Corporate ESG Performance: A Mechanism Analysis Based on Corporate Efficiency and External Environment. *Sustainability (Basel)*, *17*(9), 3819. DOI: 10.3390/su17093819

Yu, Y., & Wang, S. (2025). Bankruptcy Law Reform and Financing Costs for Small and Medium Enterprises. *Finance Research Letters*, *84*, 107794. DOI: 10.1016/j.frl.2025.107794

Zaidan, E., & Ibrahim, I. A. (2024). AI governance in a complex and rapidly changing regulatory landscape: A global perspective. *Humanities & Social Sciences Communications*, *11*(1), 1121. DOI: 10.1057/s41599-024-03560-x

Zallio, M., Ike, C. B., & Chivăran, C. (2025). Designing Artificial Intelligence: Exploring Inclusion, Diversity, Equity, Accessibility, and Safety in Human-Centric Emerging Technologies. *AI*, *6*(7), 143. DOI: 10.3390/ai6070143

Zhang, C., & Yang, J. (2024). Artificial intelligence and corporate ESG performance. *International Review of Economics & Finance*, *96*, 103713. DOI: 10.1016/j.iref.2024.103713

Zhang, X., & Ren, Y. (2025). Revitalization of urban industrial heritage from a perspective of spatial production theory: The case study of "Old market" project. *Journal of Asian Architecture and Building Engineering*, *24*(5), 3440–3456. DOI: 10.1080/13467581.2024.2396618

Zhao, D., Cai, J., Shen, L., Elshkaki, A., Liu, J., & Varis, O. (2023). Delivery of energy sustainability: Applications of the "STAR" protocol to the Sustainable Development Goal 7 index and its interaction analysis. *Journal of Cleaner Production*, *389*, 135884. DOI: 10.1016/j.jclepro.2023.135884

Zhao, J., & Gómez Fariñas, B. (2023). Artificial intelligence and sustainable decisions. *European Business Organization Law Review*, *24*(1), 1–39. DOI: 10.1007/s40804-022-00262-2

Zhou, S., Jiang, L., & Dong, Z. (2022). Overflow control for sustainable development by superwetting surface with biomimetic structure. *Chemical Reviews*, *123*(5), 2276–2310. DOI: 10.1021/acs.chemrev.1c00976 PMID: 35522923

Zhou, Y., Liu, S., & Song, W. (2025). Can bankruptcy court establishment drive enterprise'entrepreneurial orientation? *International Review of Economics & Finance*, *103*, 104540. DOI: 10.1016/j.iref.2025.104540

Zhou, Z., Zhou, X., Zhang, X., & Chen, W. (2025). Judicial waves, ethical shifts: Bankruptcy courts and corporate ESG performance. *Journal of Business Ethics*, *198*(3), 537–557. DOI: 10.1007/s10551-024-05780-2

Zhu, Y., Yu, K., Wei, M., Pu, Y., & Wang, Z. (2024). AI-enhanced administrative prosecutorial supervision in financial big data: New concepts and functions for the digital era. *Journal of Advanced Computing Systems*, *4*(5), 10–26. DOI: 10.69987/JACS.2024.40502

Zuniga, N., Burton, S. D., Blancato, F., & Carr, M. (2024). The geopolitics of technology standards: Historical context for US, EU and Chinese approaches. *International Affairs*, *100*(4), 1635–1652. DOI: 10.1093/ia/iiae124

# About the Contributors

**Dorottya Edina Kozma** Ph.D. is a certified economist (Associate Professor) with a professional background spanning academia and the private sector. Her expertise in sustainable development, environmental accounting and practical experience in company management aligns with her active involvement in various projects and events. Her primary research areas include sustainable development goals, circular economy, climate change and environmental control management and ESG. She has participated in projects focused on environmental accounting, ESG, climate change. Additionally, she is highly engaged in professional and educational activities, including curriculum developments, ESG e-learning course.

**Laeeq Razzak Janjua** has a Phd (Political Economy), from CAMS-USA, on PGD-COMPLIANCE. He is affiliated to COMPLIANCE OFFICE - TMF GROUP - POLAND, and he is also a lecturer at WSB University Poland. Dr. Laeeq Razzak Janjua is a finance professional working in compliance, and academia, whose journey is characterized by dedication, expertise, and a commitment to excellence. Mr. Janjua's academic prowess is reflected in his extensive body of work, which includes the publication of a book on corporate social responsibility as co-author and over 40 academic research papers. These contributions have solidified his reputation as a thought leader and a respected authority in his field, earning him recognition and acclaim from peers and scholars alike. Currently serving as a Compliance Officer at TMF Group, Mr. Janjua brings a wealth of experience and expertise to his role, where he navigates the complex landscape of regulatory requirements with precision and proficiency. In addition to his role at TMF Group, Mr. Janjua also serves as a lecturer at WSB University in Poland, where he imparts his knowledge and insights to the next generation of professionals. Prior to his current roles, Mr. Janjua amassed over 10 years of invaluable experience in the financial industry, having worked with esteemed institutions such as Citi Bank, MoneyGram Payment International, and BNP Paribas. Driven by a passion for excellence and a dedication to making a positive impact, Mr. Janjua continues to be a guiding force in the fields of compliance and academia. His unwavering commitment to integrity, coupled with his extensive knowledge and experience, positions him as a leader and a trailblazer in his field, shaping the future of compliance and corporate social responsibility.

**Hind Hammouch**, researcher with a PhD in economics and management, specializing in sustainability, sustainable development, CSR (corporate social responsibility) and management control. Extensive experience in empirical research, quantitative analysis and the development of frameworks for integrating sustainability into organizational practices. Proven record of accomplishment in publishing research results and contributing to the advancement of knowledge in sustainability and management control.

**Evi Purwanti** is a senior lecturer at the Faculty of Law, Universitas Tanjungpura, Indonesia, with over 19 years of experience in teaching, research, and academic leadership. She earned her Doctorate and Master of Laws degrees from Universitas Gadjah Mada and currently serves as the Coordinator of the Bachelor of Law Program. Her expertise lies in international law, maritime boundary delimitation, and jurisprudence, with numerous publications and presentations at global and national conferences and seminars. Dr. Purwanti is also active in institutional quality assurance, academic journal editorial work, and legal education reform.

**Bhupinder Singh** is working as a Faculty of Political Science, North Bangkok University, Thailand. He has given talks at international universities, resource person in international conferences such as in Nanyang Technological University Singapore, Tashkent State University of Law Uzbekistan; KIMEP University Kazakhstan, All'ah meh Tabatabi University Iran, the Iranian Association of International Criminal law, Iran and Hague Center for International Law and Investment, The Netherlands, Northumbria University Newcastle UK, Taylor's University Malaysia, AFM Krakow University Poland, European Institute for Research and Development Georgia, Business and Technology University Georgia, Texas A & M University US.

***

**Vineeta Bhati** completed the Master of Commerce (M.Com.) in 2023 from the Delhi School of Economics, Department of Commerce, University of Delhi. Currently, she is pursuing a Doctor of Philosophy (Ph.D.) at the University of Delhi, Batch of 2025.

**Saurabh Chandra** is an accomplished legal scholar and currently serves as an Associate Professor & Assistant Dean at the School of Law, Bennett University,

India. With a robust academic foundation, he earned his Bachelor of Arts and Bachelor of Laws (B.A. LL.B.) from the prestigious Aligarh Muslim University (A.M.U.). He further specialized in Business Laws, completing his Master of Laws (LL.M.) at the renowned National Law School of India University (NLSIU), Bangalore. Dr. Chandra's academic journey culminated in a Doctorate in Law (Ph.D.) from the esteemed National Law University (NLU) Delhi. In addition to his impressive legal education from some of India's most prestigious institutions, Dr. Chandra also holds a master's degree in management with specialization in Human Resources in Management and another in Journalism and Mass Communication. With almost two decades of teaching experience, he has numerous publications to his credit. His expertise is complemented by a robust portfolio of scholarly publications.

**Anshu Dwivedi** assistant professor in Amity university madhya pradesh i have a experience of 3 years in academics and and teaching various laws like evidence law Transfer of property law Probation and parole. I m memeber of BOS,NAAC,IQAC, pro-bono club and different committees.

**Swarnima Gorani** is a distinguished academician and legal scholar, specialising in both Criminal and Corporate Law. Currently serving as an Assistant Professor at the Sharda School of Law, Sharda University, she is actively involved in teaching and research while pursuing her PhD in Forensic Psychology from Himachal Pradesh National Law University, Shimla. With a robust academic foundation, Ms Gorani holds a dual degree in Commerce and Law, a postgraduate degree in Law with a concentration in Criminal Law, and a degree in Company Secretaryship. She has participated in and presented her research at numerous international conferences and faculty development programs, emphasising themes such as Artificial Intelligence, Criminal Law, Environmental Law and Forensics. Her contributions extend to multiple book chapters and journal publications, and she has played a key role in organising international conferences. Additionally, she is an active reviewer for Scopus-indexed journals and books. Notably, Ms Gorani has achieved significant accolades, including an All India Rank of 13 in the Company Secretary examination and a Gold Medal for her performance in her Law degree.

**AvinashKrishna Goswami** is Ph.D. in criminal law from Sharda University. He has a wide research experience since 2016. Actively involved in many research projects. He has been an active member at Family Dispute Resolution Clinic, Knowledge Park, Police Station. In 2021 he was honored with letter of appreciation from Police Commissioner, G.B. Nagar for resolving disputes at Family Dispute Resolution Clinic. In 2020 he was honored with letter of appreciation from Chairman, National Commission of Women, Government of India, New Delhi. He is also an active member of Internal Complaints Committee on Sexual Harassment, Sharda University. Avinash has published more than 10 research papers in UGC CARE / SCOPUS and Peer reviewed journals of national and international repute.

**Aakash Gupta** is currently an Associate Professor of Law at Amity University Gwalior, India. He has obtained the degree of LL.M. from M.L.B. Government College of excellence Jiwaji University, Gwalior. He has obtained his PhD degree in Law from Jiwaji University and cleared UGC NET exmination in 2012. Prior to Amity University, he was working as an Assistant Professor of Law Prestige Institute of Management & Research Gwalior from 2018 to 2023 and in Madhav Law College Gwalior from 2014 to 2018. He has also worked as Guest Lecturer in SOS in Law, Jiwaji University till 2014. He has more than 14 years of experience in Academic and Litigation. His area of Interest in Constitutional Law and Criminal Law. He has 12 International / National Publications to his credit. He has attended various seminar, webinars and workshops and delivered special lectures in EML on numerous occasion. He has published 1 book and presented chapters in 5 books. He has also developed a unique pedagogy to teach law subjects in a poetic form.

**Neeta Gupta** is presently working as Professor of Psychology in D.A.V. (P. G). College, Dehradun and is an eminent researcher in the diverse fields of Psychology. She holds a Doctorate in Psychology from Lucknow University. She is also a licenced practitioner of CBT and REBT(Scotland,UK). Her area of expertise are CBT,REBT and Mindfulness Based Yogic Intervention. She has more than 140 publications in international journals of Scopus/ Web of Science/ UGC recognized/UGC Care Listed/Peer review and presented more than 70 papers in National and International Conferences She has 25 years of teaching and counselling experience in Higher Education. She also worked with Industrial workers like Blue Collar, Popped Collar, Yellow Collar workers etc and counselled them. Dr Neeta Gupta has also a technical hand in computers. She has done many national and international FDPs in R, SPSS and Android app development. She is a Life Member, Reviewer, Editor, Associate Editor and Subject Expert of many reputed National and International journals. She has been honoured by many National and International agencies for outstanding contribution in the field of Psychology. She has been invited as a Gue

**Kishore Hebbar** is a senior software engineer and researcher specializing in distributed systems, financial technology and applied artificial intelligence. He has over 17 years of professional experience designing and modernizing large scale enterprise platforms across banking, mortgage, e-commerce and telecom domains. He also serves as a technical reviewer and competition judge for international technology and innovation programs. His work bridges practical industry systems with academic research to build scalable, secure and responsible AI-enabled platforms.

**Suparna Kundu** is pursuing Ph.D (Law) from Amity Law School, Amity University, Kolkata, India . She has completed Master in Laws from Symbiosis Law School Noida, Symbiosis International (Deemed University). She has completed Bachelor in Law from KIIT School of Law - KSOL I KIIT Deemed to be University.

**Sanchita Ray** is working as an Assistant Professor at the Sharda School of Law, Sharda University. She graduated from Miranda House, University of Delhi, and completed her post-graduation from Ramjas College, University of Delhi. She has qualified the National Eligibility Test (NET). She completed her M.Phil. on "Urban Poverty: A Case Study of the National Capital Territory of Delhi" from the University of Delhi. She obtained her Ph.D. from the University of Delhi on the topic "Protest Movement in Colonial India: Namasudra Movement in Colonial Bengal."She has also briefly served as a faculty member at the University of Delhi. Dr. Ray has presented papers in several national and international conferences and has contributed research articles on diverse themes including the Indian Constitution, Human Rights, Dalit movements, Artificial Intelligence, Data Privacy, Data Localization, Climate Change, and the Uniform Civil Code.

# Index

## A



## B



## C

# D



# E

## F



## G



## H

www.ingramcontent.com/pod-product-compliance
Lightning Source LLC
LaVergne TN
LVHW081533300926
849161LV00006B/1410